BUS

8/22/03

Civil Litigation
for the New Millennium

**NOTICE: If any part of these contents
is lost or damaged, the Patron will be
charged for the total cost of all items.**

_____ Disk	_____ Video
_____ Cassette	__/__ CD
__/__ Text	_____ Other

CIRCULATING WITH THE LISTED PROBLEM(S):

CD missing   11-27-06

Civil Litigation for the New Millennium

A Guide for Paralegals

Barbara Kautz, CLA

Stacey A. Rowcliffe

ASPEN PUBLISHERS

NEW YORK

1 2 3 4 5 6 7 8 9 0

ISBN 0-7355-2789-X

Summary of Contents

Contents

Preface

The demand for paralegals is growing. The Bureau of Labor Statistics reports that the demand for paralegals is expected to grow 36 percent or more through 2008, ranking it among the fastest growing professions in the United States. Paralegals are used more and more as cost-cutting measures. Most everywhere you look paralegal positions and paralegal salaries are on the rise. However, most employers of paralegals are looking for a minimum of technological experience to include word processing and document management programs when hiring a paralegal. Those paralegals who can demonstrate a working knowledge of some of the more complicated systems and databases that make up the current trends in the legal industry will have an edge in the market. Paralegals can take advantage of the current technological boom by capitalizing on opportunities to learn about the technology being introduced in today's courtrooms.

Today the progressive and successful paralegals, and the attorneys who rely on them, will partner with technology to reach an ever-changing and modern audience, securing victory for their clients. A technology-ready courtroom is a logical extension of the modern technology-based law firm. The size and scope of today's complex litigation have fostered an ever-expanding demand for efficient document and file handling strategies and devices. Whatever the topic, whatever the case, the sheer volume of documentation, coupled with the logistics of handling a file effectively and efficiently, is making life without technology a practical impossibility for trial lawyers, their paralegals, and the legal community in general. The new millennium has dawned. We must accept that life in the legal field has changed drastically and be willing to experiment with modern technology in creative ways. It behooves every paralegal to get online with technology for economic reasons, marketability, trial management, client service, and efficient management of workloads.

Luckily, techo-savvy entrepreneurs have responded to the challenge, creating organizational databases and programming designed for the overburdened legal offices. Thus far the educational community has fallen short in the area of technology use. Although there is a plethora of legal texts available to paralegal students, none of them adequately discuss technology; nor do they effectively integrate legal theory with practical application in using such technology. We have encountered numerous paralegals, some fresh from school, others who have been practicing for years, who do not realize the potential of the technological tools that have become a professional necessity. Thus, the idea for this book was born.

The primary purpose of this textbook is to provide paralegal students with the skills necessary to perform the duties required in the working environment. This text is focused on providing a solid link between legal theories and practical application. Each chapter is formatted in a similar fashion with chapter objectives, text, ethics, conclusion and the use of technology. Key terms from the text are outlined as well as key technology terms.

To effectively link legal theory with practical application, the text provides legal theories and subsequently requires the students to work through exercises within the student study guide.

The student study guide is based on an actual civil lawsuit. Professors will have on CD-ROM the scanned documents pertaining to this lawsuit. The most effective way to learn how to draft legal documents, perform investigative tasks, and utilize technology is to perform the tasks and then be critiqued on the work done by the attorney you are doing the work for. The instructor will act as your attorney.

It is our sincere hope that after review of the textbook and completion of the student study guide, paralegal students will enter the work force fully capable of performing the duties required of them. When the attorney asks them to draft written discovery for a case, newly hired paralegals will be able to confidently and fully perform the task. When faced with technological questions or needs, recently graduated paralegals will be experienced and ready.

The text provides a detailed discussion of the required legal theories necessary to complete the student study guide's real case scenario. The real case scenario provides the facts of the matter dealt with. From those facts students will work with actual filed pleadings, documents, exhibits, and investigations to build their skills and become familiar with the technology necessary to become professionals.

Because this textbook is to be marketed and sold nationally within the United States, the U.S. Code, Federal Rules of Civil Procedure, and Federal Rules of Evidence have been used throughout. References to state statutes and rules are omitted since they effectively limit the topic of discussion to a specific state. Paralegal students will need to check state statutes and rules if they are working on lawsuits filed within a particular state.

To all students reading this book, enjoy your journey as a paralegal student.

Barbara Kautz
Stacey A. Rowcliffe

September 2002

Acknowledgments

Barbara Kautz

I would like to thank my husband, David Kautz, for his love, encouragement, support, and understanding. I appreciate all you do, especially your patience. You never complained. You are truly my best friend, and I love you very much. I also want to thank my children, Tara, Paul, and David. Even though you have grown and gone your own ways, you remain close to my heart, are an integral part of my life, and support and encourage me in all I do.

I also want to thank my best friend, Pat Vaile, for her encouragement and support. Thank you for always being there for me, for listening, caring, and providing your input on this project. Your support meant so much and kept me going. I value your opinions and thoughts.

Last but not least I would like to thank two women who have been mentors and role models for me throughout my career. First, to Supreme Court Justice Patricia O'Brien Cotter, thank you for believing in me and for your trust and confidence. You are a special person, an excellent attorney, and a good friend. Also, thanks to the Honorable Carolyn Ostby, Federal Magistrate, who exemplifies grace, wisdom, acceptance, and understanding. Your example taught me never to compromise and to always uphold the highest standards. You both truly represent the best of the legal profession and are excellent role models for all women in the legal field.

Stacey A. Rowcliffe

I would like to thank my husband, Mike Rowcliffe, along with my daughter Brittney and my son Ryan. You were so understanding when I couldn't get to things around the house because I was working on the book. This textbook was a very rewarding and demanding undertaking that I could not have completed without the love, support, and selfless sacrifices of my family. Thank you so much for supporting my need to contribute something to the paralegal profession. I want you to know that the success of this textbook would mean nothing to me without your love and support.

I would also like to thank Bruce A. Fredrickson, an attorney at the Crowley Law Firm, who has been a wonderful boss, mentor, and friend. Thank you, Bruce, for your support of this endeavor and your continued support of my thoughts and opinions regarding litigated cases. I consider myself lucky to know you both as a coworker and friend.

Finally, I would like to thank my first boss, Ronald K. Mullin, who took a chance and hired a girl from Montana with very little legal experience. Your confidence in my abilities and patience during the learning process enabled me to become the paralegal I am today.

Both authors would also like to thank the following businesses and individuals who assisted in the completion of this text.

- Thank you Litigation Abstract in Missoula, Montana, and Seattle, Washington, for labeling, scanning, creating image links, and generating digital files for the case documents used in the student study guide. Your work allowed us to provide case information in an efficient and effective manner.
- Thank you to Summation, InData, and CaseSoft for agreeing to provide instructional licenses to the paralegal instructors. This will afford paralegal students the opportunity to gain experience using litigation specific software before they enter the work force and increase their marketability as paralegals.
- Thank you to the Honorable Richard F. Cebull for allowing us to photograph the courtroom technology available in Montana. Recognition should be given to the Honorable Donald W. Molloy, an advocate of technology in the courtroom and one of the individuals responsible for technology integration and use throughout the federal court in the state of Montana. Recognition should also go to Cecil Chandler, who assists in the integration and maintenance of this technology within the federal court in Billings, Montana. This courtroom is a wonderful example of the federal courts throughout Montana. Montana should be proud to have so many technology-enhanced courtrooms. Technology truly does reduce trial time and increase jury understanding, and we are lucky to have these tools available.
- We would like to thank Jack Veth from the law firm of Speiser Kraise for providing us with the materials used throughout the student study guide. These case materials will provide instructors and students with the much needed information to practically apply what they have learned in this text, creating a solid link between legal theory and practical application. Thank you so much for your assistance.
- Finally, thank you to Greg Krehel, owner and founder of CaseSoft software, for your encouragement and the excellent product you developed for the legal field.

Civil Litigation
for the New Millennium

chapter 1

Setting the Stage

chapter objectives

In this chapter, we will discuss

- How paralegals can exhibit a professional image
- The seven habits of highly professional paralegals
- The key attributes of today's successful paralegal
- Tips on how to remain current
- An overview of the technological skills that will help you succeed in today's workforce

For the practicing paralegal, it is necessary to prepare a certain mindset—a mindset that should carry through everything a paralegal does. When reading the sections that follow, especially the section on image and professionalism, think about how you project yourself and what impression you leave with those you meet.

A. IMAGE AND PROFESSIONALISM

Paralegals have worried about their image for decades and paralegals continue to worry about their image today. There is much to worry about, because paralegals can take a beating—from employers who don't know how to utilize them, and from the public who doesn't even know who or what they are. Today this problem of image is even more important because paralegals are at the forefront of the legal profession; they are becoming more readily accepted, recognized, and available.

Image is of utmost importance and the only way to improve the image of paralegals is to improve their level of professionalism. Given all the paralegals in America today, it is clear that improving the professionalism of each and every one of them would take a major-league effort. The good news, however, is that most paralegals are already highly professional, and new paralegals are aware of the importance of image as they commence their careers. Still, we can each do better tomorrow, no matter how well we have done today.

The importance of image of paralegals starts when an individual makes the commitment to that career. Paralegal educators need to instill in each and every student the desire to be a professional of the highest caliber by supporting the student and assisting him or her in striving for the highest goals. Paralegal students need to support each other in the same way.

An excellent way to start this process of support and self-assessment is to examine the attributes of paralegals who are successful in their personal and professional lives. In these individuals we see a specific mindset. It is important to appreciate the power of this mindset in improving our own lives, image, and professionalism. The word *mindset* is rooted in the strong belief that people can learn to adopt more successful and empowering strategies for dealing with new challenges, difficult situations, and stress. Mindsets are a choice and therefore can be changed; they do not have to be dominated, for example, by fixed, rigid, or outdated ideas that force us to repeat the same ineffective behaviors day after day. Mindsets that include an attitude of "I can't" can be reformed to read "I can," no matter what the challenge or new learning situation is. Mindsets can be modified, and we don't need to be afraid of something new or different when we view it as just that—new or different.

What is part of this mindset necessary for a successful paralegal? For a minute, let's examine the foundation or core as it were of a "professional" paralegal. That professionalism embodies challenge, commitment, and control.

Challenge is based on the belief that change is a constant in one's life. Successful people tend to see change as a challenge to confront and master rather than as stress to avoid. They do not deny problems, but instead appreciate that change is an opportunity for self-reflection and growth.

Commitment can be described as being involved in rather than alienated from various aspects of one's life. When commitment is present, individuals have a sense of purpose and meaning for why they are doing what they are doing. When we have a purpose, when we are guided by a vision, when we never lose sight of why we are doing what we are doing, an energy and passion are triggered that give meaning to our lives and lessen the impact of stress. This commitment spills over into our professional careers and gives meaning, energy, and passion to our everyday work lives.

Control is the feeling of ownership. When individuals possess this personal control they believe that they are active participants in plotting the course of their own destinies, of solving problems and making decisions about their own lives, of wasting little time worrying about things that are beyond their influence. Even when their actions do not lead to success, they still feel a sense of accomplishment in knowing that they did not passively sit back, and, in addition, they are likely to adopt the view that they can learn from what went wrong. In other words, they learn from their mistakes and take the initiative to find out what went wrong or why something was not successful. They do not feel sorry for themselves, and they take responsibility for their actions.

B. WHAT IS PROFESSIONALISM?

Let's examine professionalism. It does, of course, encompass honesty, integrity, and good character. But professionalism is more. Professionalism means to be imbued with a sense that paralegals are important participants in the pursuit of justice and in the legal field. It is a sense of pride, of contributing and being a part of a team. Professional paralegals advance the profession, others, and themselves.

What attributes help in this area? The following are the seven habits of highly professional paralegals (with apologies to Stephen Covey). If every paralegal exercised these seven habits, and learned them in school, the image of the profession would be enhanced and we would all be better off. Of greater consequence, however, would be the positive impact on paralegals', own lives and the legal arena. Professional paralegals have these seven characteristics:

1. Communicators
2. Competent
3. Committed
4. Thoughtful; use good judgment
5. Responsible
6. Community-minded
7. Honest

1. Communication

Professional paralegals communicate—with each other, with their employers, with clients. Paralegals who talk to each other get the job done—whether it is setting depositions, networking, mentoring, or getting ready for trial. Paralegals who don't talk to each other invariably suffer and perhaps eventually turn to alternative occupations. Paralegals who use communication effectively do the following twelve things.

1. Learn to ask questions.
2. Learn to be assertive, but not aggressive, abusive, or abrasive.
3. Learn not to judge.
4. Learn to greet people, shake hands, and maintain eye contact.
5. Learn to be kind and courteous to everyone.
6. Learn civility.
7. Learn to speak quietly.
8. Learn to listen.
9. Learn to adopt a good attitude, which is of utmost importance and more important than your aptitude.
10. Learn mutual respect.
11. Learn not to interrupt others.
12. Smile.

Communication plays a crucial role in making the justice system work, as well as making working relationships effective. Highly professional paralegals know that.

2. Competence

Professional paralegals are competent. They stay abreast of the law, they seek continuing education, they commit to educating their peers and sharing information. It is in the area of competence that we especially need the help of paralegals, because today the law is so vast and complex that attorneys cannot keep up with everything. Since they depend on the competence of a paralegal, be sure to be right, be sure to be current, and be sure to understand your role as a paralegal.

3. Commitment

Professional paralegals are committed to their career. This component of professionalism requires a drive to further the profession in every aspect of our society. Being a part of any profession is a full-time, lifetime commitment. We need justice and fairness in all parts of our lives, not just in the courtroom or workplace, but in the home, on the playgrounds, in every human endeavor. You can't turn it on and then turn it off. When you are committed to your career you are an advocate for the position you hold. You don't complain, malign, or denigrate. If problems arise, you find solutions. You think positively and act positively at all times.

4. Good Judgment

Professional paralegals exercise good judgment. Good judgment encompasses many things, but is basically defined as doing the right thing. An apt description of good judgment is very difficult to provide, and every individual has his or her own. Develop yours. Keep it simple, but know what it is—always.

Everything that a paralegal does contributes to the impression that the court and attorneys have of the paralegal: whether the paralegal can be trusted and relied upon or whether the paralegal's work has to be taken with considerable skepticism. The most effective paralegal is one who appears to be fair and credible, confident, and above pettiness and grasping for unwarranted advantage.

A perfect definition of good judgment may be difficult to articulate, but we know it when we see it. Just like we know bad judgment when we see it.

5. Responsibility

Professional paralegals also accept responsibility. Everyone makes mistakes. We are not perfect by a long shot. We cannot expect to say and do the right thing 100 percent of the time. So what does that mean? It means that, when we make a mistake, we own up to it. Worst of all is the lame excuse, one that is obviously fabricated. It insults our collective intelligence, and it is the quickest way to ruin a reputation. The professional paralegal accepts responsibility and apologizes when he or she makes a mistake. Do the smart thing. Stand up and accept responsibility.

6. Community-Mindedness

Professional paralegals know that community is important and is to be nurtured. We are members of a community, with overreaching goals or purposes that give our lives meaning, as one people bound together in a common fate, with a common way of life, and hence a common concern for our mutual fulfillment. We are concerned, or we ought to be concerned, with one another's souls—with one another's virtues and excellences and happiness. Paralegals are such a community.

7. Honesty

Professional paralegals must be people of honesty, integrity, and good character. Although everyone in our society should be honest and good, these traits are critical for paralegals. It is important for each of us to reflect upon the various roles and responsibilities we assume in our personal and professional lives and to appreciate the values upon which these responsibilities rest. The more we keep in mind such questions as "why do we do what we do?," "what are our values?," "what do we wish to accomplish?," "what do we hope to leave as our legacy—to our children, our family, our colleagues?," the more easily we can bring purpose and passion to our lives and replace everyday stresses with an air of excitement and enthusiasm. We are then viewed as professionals.

C. TIPS ON REMAINING CURRENT

The best advice that can be passed on to prospective paralegal students is to stay current—on developments in the field and on their respective state and federal rules, regulations and statutes. Take the time on a yearly basis to read the complete Rules of Civil Procedure for both federal and state courts. Read them from Rule 1 through Rule 86. Become familiar with the forms at the end of the rules.

Subscribe to publications that are specific to the profession such as *Legal Assistant Today* or other magazines. Read, and then read some more. Pay particular attention to articles, newsletters, and publications printed in your field of work.

Paralegals should join a professional organization, whether national or local. Such organizations are great places to meet other paralegals, to network, and to share information. Organizations provide a sense of community and sharing. But remember that you will only get out of any organization what you put into it. Don't just take a passive stance with your membership. Become involved, become a proactive member who gives as much as you get.

Even after graduation, continue to educate yourself and continue to learn. Don't think that just because you graduated you now know everything. You need to keep an open mind and understand that you can learn something new on a daily basis. Take computer courses, technology courses, or attend technology showcases. Technology, a dynamic ever-changing area, continues to be an essential part of every law firm and corporate legal department. Because technology has become such an integral part of the practice of law, identifying, learning, and using the best tools for the job is essential. Using products effectively can help you leverage your resources and help you focus on what is really important to you and your firm—providing legal services to your client.

One of the most effective ways to build or enhance a reputation in any profession, but especially the legal profession, is through the written word. For years, colleges and universities have insisted on the "publish or perish" doctrine. Although legal firms usually don't encourage paralegals to write, they are certainly impressed when an employee takes the initiative to write and publish an article. Prospective employers are especially impressed when they review a resume to see published articles listed. It is not necessary to be a professional writer to submit an article for publication, just a competent one who has done the required homework. Volunteer to write an article for your local or state association newsletter. Not only will the article get you noticed, it will get your name out to members of the legal community. Another advantage to writing is that it will enable you to stay current on the topic of your choice. The research and preparation necessary to prepare an interesting, thorough article will force you to read and research.

PRACTICE TIP

Treat everyone with respect and dignity. Be aware of your personal appearance. You will be evaluated as a person at every opportunity not only by the clients you come in contact with and the attorneys you work for, but the public in general. Only you can control how you look, how you behave, how you speak, and how you act.

ETHICS

Paralegals must maintain high ethical standards, the same as attorneys. To do that requires that the paralegal be aware of and familiar with the ethical standards set by the American Bar Association (ABA), National Association of Legal Assistants (NALA), and National Federation of Paralegal Associations (NFPA), as well as local and state associations. If an ethical dilemma presents itself, speak with your supervising attorney, speak with other paralegal professionals, or present the question to ethics committees of the local, state, or national bar associations and paralegal associations. Being educated on ethical rules is the best way to stay armed against possible hazards. Ignorance is no excuse. Chances are that your particular situation has been encountered by someone else in the field. They therefore have had the chance to develop a solution. Don't try to reinvent the wheel; instead take advantage of the experience gained by practicing paralegals.

Since trial advocacy is adversarial in nature, it is important for the paralegal to understand his or her role in the process of litigation. Whether working for the plaintiff or the defendant, the paralegal influences the flow of litigation. How the paralegal exerts that influence is entirely up to him or her. However, it is most important that the paralegal always be mindful that to be adversarial does not mean to be unethical. The entire field of litigation is guided not only by technical rules of application, but by ethical dimensions, competency, integrity, and the highest forms of professional demeanor. Successful paralegals know this and adhere to high ethical standards at all times. One mistake, bad judgment call, or indiscretion can follow a paralegal his or her entire career or, for that matter, end a career. Always be aware of how you are being perceived and what impression you are leaving with the people you work for, work with, and work against.

CONCLUSION

Keeping an open mind, displaying a willingness to learn, and keeping an eye out for where you can be most helpful are all key attributes of the paralegal of today. No one person can know everything. Don't make the mistake of trying to take on too much. Learn the basics and learn them well. Then take initiative and take extra courses. Use the Internet, network with other paralegals, and take the time to explore some options available. Most employers will be very pleased with the paralegal who is willing to take some of his or her nonwork time to gain further training or expertise in an area used by the law firm.

Knowing what is out there can help in planning career moves while an overall willingness to learn may be the key to getting and keeping a good job. Most important however, is the need to develop your own style, which should include the highest ethical standards and professional demeanor. Honesty and integrity should always shine through your work product and through your working relationships. Determine to be the best paralegal you can be not only through knowledge and skill, but through commitment and community as well.

The best of luck in your education and pursuit of this rewarding career! Now let's commence our study.

USING TECHNOLOGY IN THE LAW OFFICE

At a minimum, paralegals today must have a certain set of skills—knowledge of word processing and document management programs and probably something extra in the way of technological experience and expertise. Those paralegals who can demonstrate a working knowledge of some of the more complicated systems, databases, and presentation systems that make up the current trends in the legal industry will certainly have an edge over other paralegals. Thus, paralegals today must by necessity be aware of what the legal industry is using for software and must have a good basic knowledge of what that software does, how to run it, and how to use it effectively in their jobs. Microsoft Word and Corel WordPerfect are the leading word processing software programs used in the legal field today. Microsoft Windows 95 and Microsoft Windows 98 are used by 72.7 percent of those polled in the *Legal Assistant Today's 2001* Legal Technology Survey, and Microsoft Windows NT and Microsoft Windows 2000 make up an additional 24.6 percent.

The student paralegal should commit to taking a Microsoft Office course that includes not only word processing and spreadsheet applications, but also covers Microsoft PowerPoint. No longer is on-the-job training the way to go, or even an option. Employers are looking for those paralegals who exhibit current knowledge in these areas and who already possess the knowledge necessary to work effectively and efficiently.

Once basic skills are mastered, the paralegal can consider specializing. Before the decision is made into which area to specialize in, though, the paralegal should do some homework. What applications are used in the law firms or legal areas the paralegal is interested in? What is the norm for the industry in a specific area? How would you go about finding out this information? The easiest way is simply to talk to practicing paralegals in the area. Cold calls can be effective, but the best way to get to know other paralegals is to join local professional associations. Get to know the people attending the meetings and talk with them. Develop a rapport. Most people love giving advice and are almost always willing to share information about their chosen career when approached by an interested party.

Employers today often expect the prospective paralegal employee to have a working knowledge of database programs. Knowing specific brands of database software is not as important as understanding concepts, aspects, and principles of those programs. For example, it is extremely important to understand the difference between a full-text system and a summary database. A full-text system contains the complete text of depositions in transcripts while a summary, or document management, database contains a summary of the documents that support a case. Paralegals should know how to annotate transcripts in full-text systems with notes; how to scan, load, organize, and retrieve documents; and how to do quick searches for names and information in a database. Also, the paralegal should possess a basic knowledge of input, indexing, coding conventions, and identification of duplicate entries.

The legal profession today uses such database programs as Microsoft Access and Coral Paradox, as well as Summation and Concordance. Summation has both a full-text system and a summary database already set up by the manufacturer. Document imaging and coding for databases, with its ability to transform a room full of boxes into three or four CD-ROMs, is the way the legal industry is heading. Knowing how to create an image of a document and load it into a database, then being able to search for it using varying criteria is important. Knowledge in this area can be the difference between landing that job or sending out more resumes.

Training can be, and usually is, obtained in-house, such as when an employer brings in an outside vendor to train its employees. Oftentimes, paralegals are sent to specific training schools conducted by specific vendors. There are also courses offered at local colleges and universities which provide the paralegal with a working knowledge of the basics of database design, maintenance, and data input.

A working knowledge of calendaring and docketing systems using databases and other software also plays a big role in advancing paralegal careers. Calendaring databases with tickler systems alert paralegals to deadlines and key dates during a discovery process by pulling the case up regularly. Outlook is one example of software commonly used as a calendaring and tickler system by legal professionals today.

Courtrooms across the nation are seeing an explosion of technology, steadily changing the way evidence is presented and the expectations for some paralegals. Many in the legal profession are citing the use of technology to control documents in the courtroom as the newest and biggest trend. Paralegals can benefit by capitalizing on opportunities to learn about the technology taking hold in today's courtrooms. Many courtroom presentation programs now involve the bar coding of evidence and the scanning of documents so they can be brought up as images on a screen during trial. Videotaped depositions and exhibits can be displayed simultaneously with imaged documents and related text using on-screen annotation tools and zoom capabilities. CD-ROMs, scripts, and macros control digitized images that can become flashy special effects in any presentation of evidence to a jury.

The responsibility of knowing how to use and run trial presentation software often falls on the paralegal. As more law firms incorporate this type of software into their litigation procedures, paralegals must be prepared to master technology that changes and expands quickly. Normally attorneys only want to know what a specific program can do; they want the paralegal to actually perform the work and run the program.

Knowing how to conduct research on the Internet is another valuable skill possessed by the technologically savvy paralegal of today. The challenge for a paralegal is to learn how to find specifics quickly and to distinguish between good and bad information. Knowing how to weed through a lot of garbage to effectively gather a small amount of specific information is a valuable skill. What is the best way to get familiar with the Internet? Probably the best way is to simply use it. Get familiar with what the Internet offers. Reading articles and books published on the subject certainly help, but there is no quick or easy way to gain the confidence and knowledge gleaned from taking the time to explore.

Start by becoming familiar with the different search engines and resources available on the Internet. Some of this information will be covered in this book. You will certainly take other courses that use other aspects of the Internet such as Lexis-Nexis or Westlaw to conduct traditional legal research as you continue in your education. The paralegal should become familiar with constructing search queries and locating and identifying expert witnesses through the use of the Internet. Know the description of location markers such as *.org, .com, .gov,* and *.edu,* and how they relate to the type of information on the site. Look at the Internet for Web sites and online courses that teach basic research skills.

chapter 2

Litigation, Client Contact, Interviewing, and General Legal Theory

chapter objectives

In this chapter, we will discuss

- An introduction to the process of litigation
- The role and responsibilities of the paralegal as part of the litigation team
- An overview of the interview process
- What takes place during the initial investigation
- How to check for conflicts
- How to use a calendaring or tickling system to keep track of deadlines
- How to create a client database
- Use of e-mail to communicate with clients

A. INTRODUCTION TO THE PROCESS OF LITIGATION

Litigation is the use of the legal process to settle disputes between people. **Litigation** is defined as a dispute in a court of law for purposes of enforcing a right or requesting a remedy. The litigation process is necessary to maintain a civilized society. It establishes an orderly way for people to argue their differences. Our legal system allows for disputes to be presented to an impartial person or persons for resolution. The litigants understand that a resolution will be determined by someone other than themselves. Do not assume, however, that all, or even most, disputes become the subject of litigation. Litigation is an expensive process in terms of money, time, aggravation, and uncertainty of outcome. Therefore, most civil disputes are resolved through settlement conferences, arbitration, or mediation, thus allowing the parties themselves to conclude the matter. Approximately 10 percent of the cases that come in the door of a law firm go to trial; the rest are settled prior to a decision in the courts.

The litigation process in U.S. courts is referred to as an adversarial system because it relies on the litigants to present their dispute before a neutral fact finder. According to American legal tradition, inherited from the English common law, the clash of adversaries before the court is most likely to allow the jury or the judge to determine the truth of the matters presented and to resolve the dispute at hand. In some other legal systems, judges or other court officials assist the parties to find relevant evidence or obtain testimony from witnesses. In the United States, however, the work of collecting, preparing, and presenting evidence to the court is accomplished by the litigants, their attorneys, and the paralegals working for those attorneys.

A paralegal should not only possess a general knowledge of the law and the litigation process, but also a thorough understanding of the court systems and how they work. Furthermore, those paralegals should possess a complete familiarity with the rules of procedure from the forum in which they operate. The paralegal needs to become intimately familiar with all courts within the immediate area of employment—from state courts (including city and county) to federal courts. Of course, this knowledge should also include an understanding of the various appellate court systems in the particular jurisdiction in which the paralegal works.

This knowledge and understanding of the law and the various court systems comes from taking the time to devote oneself to learning. The information contained in this book will equip the serious paralegal student to become a viable team member from the very first day of employment.

PRACTICE TIP

Be sure you understand your role as the paralegal on the litigation team. If you are unclear as to your role, duties, or responsibilities, ask questions. The only time you will look foolish is when you push forward, thinking you understand, and you perform inadequately or, worse, the wrong function. Never hesitate to ask the attorney to reiterate or explain more fully what is expected with an assignment.

B. CLIENT CONTACT

1. Creation of the Litigation Team—Defining Responsibilities and the Role of the Paralegal

The time to create the litigation team and define the appropriate responsibilities of the individuals involved is prior to the arrival of the client. Each person should be aware of his or her role in the process, how he or she will fulfill that role, and how that role impacts the remainder of the team members.

There are many people involved in the legal process of litigation—attorneys, paralegals, secretaries, clerks, associates. Each and every one of these individuals is a vital part of the litigation team. Each and every one of them needs to know his or her role in this process and needs to know how to interact with, support, and enhance the other members of the team. Paralegals are an especially vital link in this chain. Successful paralegals possess varied personal and professional characteristics (see Chapter 1's discussion on professionalism and image). Every paralegal possesses unique personality traits, educational levels, experience levels, geographic residency, general knowledge, and legal specialization. However, all good paralegals possess excellent organizational skills and communication skills.

Furthermore, successful paralegals display confidence, are competent and prepared, show initiative, display a willingness to learn, respect the competence of others, are problem-solvers, provide solutions to every dilemma, appreciate the value of timing, act like professionals, and are willing to help others. Obviously, these are characteristics found in all successful professionals, but they are particularly important to the paralegal. Why? Because the paralegal is the backbone of the litigation team. He or she is responsible for all aspects of the case and acts as an overall manager.

What, then, is a paralegal's role? It is threefold:

1. Communication (through client contact)
2. Organization (through record keeping)
3. Details (through keeping the case on track)

Let's look at some of those areas. As a paralegal, you are in invaluable aid to the attorney for maintaining relations with clients. Many attorneys feel that client contact is the most important job the paralegal does.

Cases may be won or lost because not enough information was obtained, there was no investigation, a document could not be found, or because the trial team did not have adequate time to prepare for a case. Conscientious and detailed attention to the tasks assigned will yield rewards and avoid embarrassment for the trial attorney and therefore make you a more valued member of the team.

2. Initial Client Interview

An **interview** is defined as a process of questioning someone to obtain facts and information. Little seems to have been written concerning the initial client interview. This seems quite curious in that the initial interview and the perception gleaned by the client of that interview is of primary importance. Certainly, the decision a client makes to accept an attorney as an advocate or to reject that attorney and seek other counsel can be reached at the initial contact phase. The initial interview is what lays the foundation for rapport and a certain level of trust, qualities that enable the litigation team to work well with the client. This in turn allows the case or litigation to go smoothly. However, always be mindful that another tenor can be set by this process that will make doing your job as the legal assistant so much more difficult.

Usually the paralegal will attend the initial client interview between the client and the attorney. This is important for two reasons. First, the paralegal starts to build a rapport with that client and provides the client with an easily accessible conduit through which to pass information to the attorney. Second, the paralegal becomes familiar with the case from the beginning and can assist the attorney from the start. No paralegal can do a good job if not allowed to be intimately familiar with the facts of the case. A paralegal needs to be part of the litigation team—an integral part. However, that may require, and usually does require, initiative on the part of the paralegal.

It is important to remember the role of the attorney which is to give legal advice. The paralegal is there as the fact gatherer and facilitator. What information the paralegal needs to obtain at this stage will obviously be dictated by the type of case. These roles should be discussed with the attorney prior to the initial interview.

The paralegal needs to focus on his or her role, and must be aware of what is to be accomplished in the interview. Not only does the paralegal need to give exhaustive thought on the type of interview to be conducted, he or she must be cognizant of the type of information to be gathered. How does the paralegal determine the type of interview as well as the type of information to be obtained? First, the paralegal probably will know what the client is coming in for during the initial interview. Second, a meeting with the supervising attorney to discuss the interview will be most helpful. During this meeting the paralegal can also discuss the type of information the attorney wishes to be obtained and get insight as to the type of information the attorney feels is helpful. As time goes on and the paralegal becomes more and more experienced, he or she will instinctively know what information is necessary for each type of case.

Checklists can be most helpful to the new paralegal, but caution must be used when utilizing them. There are pros and cons to checklists. Mainly, checklists allow you to remember all necessary information. Therefore, you can get all the facts at the initial interview in order to commence the action. There is nothing more unsettling to a client than to have a paralegal call three or four times to obtain necessary facts. Unfortunately, this type of unorganized approach can make the client question his or her decision to hire that particular firm.

As the case progresses, additional information will be necessary, which can be obtained at a later date. Personalize the checklist that you use so that the questions are flexible and particularized for the respective client. Think through the case—the particular facts and the situation—and use common sense. Remember you are not only looking for facts, but for sufficient detail of those facts to follow up with verification and pursuit of any leads identified through the discussion. Verification of fact details is accomplished through the use of other evidence used to support the client's contentions or assertions. The process of verifying details does not indicate that your client has lied to you; it simply means that you are looking at the facts from all angles. You are doing your job in preparing the best case when you assist your client and your attorney by going through this process.

A paralegal must remember to ask the five "Ws"—who, what, when, where, why—as well as the all important "how"—how do you know that? It is necessary to get specific details about time, place, witnesses, liability, damages, documentation, records, evidence, and all parties involved. You need to get information on the client's background, client objectives, and client needs.

Take a moment to consider how you would develop a checklist for an interview. What areas should you be concerned with? How about the following?

- Setting
- Purpose
- Focus
- Style of questions
- Facts needed
- Identification of role
- Putting client at ease

Organize your information. Develop a plan by which to handle your information. Think about developing a chronology as you go. Handling your information in an orderly way becomes important when you consider that cases typically take months to years and that you will probably handle numerous cases all at one time. It is not unusual for paralegals in smaller firms to be assigned and be responsible for 50 to 100 open and active cases simultaneously. The difficulty of keeping facts and details straight is evident. Think of complex litigation in which you may find you have hundreds of clients. Without a plan and organization, it would be impossible to keep relevant and pertinent information straight. The time to have that plan and organization in place is at the outset.

When the client arrives, all parties should introduce themselves, and the paralegal should be very clear about his or her title. Make sure the client understands that you are not an attorney. The easiest way to ensure the client remembers who you are and what your role is is to provide your business card. Some clients will understand that a paralegal cannot give legal advice, but some clients will not know that. Remember you will meet with people who have experience with the legal system and you will meet with clients who are having their first experiences. Whoever your client is, be sure to explain your role.

Keep in mind that the typical client will not know his or her rights and obligations. They will have been given advice from everyone—from friends and family to strangers. Law offices can be very intimidating. Therefore, the wise paralegal puts the client at ease right from the start. How can that best be accomplished? Perhaps by a smile, a handshake, an offer of a cup of coffee.

Consider your client before the interview date and time is set. Is it best to interview them at the law office? At their home? Is it best to meet them at a public place? For example, if your client is infirm, elderly, or disabled, he or she might be more at ease at home. If your client (or witness) is a child, it might be best to meet and interview him or her at a child-friendly location such as McDonald's.

The key to any good interview, especially the important initial interview, is preparation. Use a checklist to prepare yourself, to gather your information during the interview, and to keep the case on track. Figure 2.1 is an example of a preparatory checklist for an initial client interview.

✦ INITIAL CLIENT INTERVIEW CHECKLIST—PREPARATORY

❑   What is the purpose of the interview?
❑   What is my role in the interview?
❑   Conducting the interview
     ❑   Location—office, client's home, hospital, client's work
     ❑   Privacy and confidentiality—is the interview area private and confidential?
     ❑   Comfort—is the room too hot, too cold, furniture comfortable?
     ❑   Arrangement of room—where to place chairs, whether to sit next to client, across the desk from client
     ❑   Making client comfortable—offer coffee
     ❑   Time allotment—is there enough time allotted to conduct interview and gather all necessary information?
     ❑   Professionalism—demeanor and dress

Figure 2.1. Preparatory Checklist—Initial Client Interview

Figure 2.2 is an example of an initial client interview checklist for a personal injury claim.

✦ INITIAL CLIENT INTERVIEW CHECKLIST

Name:
Address:
Phone:
Problem presented:
Resolution requested:
Dates and times of accident:
Location of accident:
Parties involved:
Witnesses:
Documentation:

Figure 2.2. Initial Client Interview Checklist

There are numerous other things to think about. Consider what facts you need to obtain for the type of case presented; what type of questions need to be asked; what necessary forms or authorizations need to be prepared; what the client wants; and, at the conclusion, whether you have stated clearly to the client what you will do, what the office will do, and what the client is to do.

PRACTICE TIP

Plan ahead. Prepare for your initial client interview at least a day or two before the client walks in the door. Think through what you need, what you need to ask, what information you need to get started, and what paperwork you will need to have handy. Preparation eliminates those embarrassing moments when you have to excuse yourself from the room to get an answer to a question or to locate a needed release. Appear professional and that is the way you will be perceived.

Always make sure to check with your attorney on what role you should play with initial client contact. Oftentimes the attorney will sit in on the interview and the paralegal will assist him.

Remember: Treat everyone with respect and dignity, no matter who they are or what their legal problems are. Don't judge.

---

3. Summary of Initial Client Interview

Chose your location wisely. Ideally, the room should be private, controllable, free from distractions, and comfortably furnished. Conference rooms are the ideal situation in which to initially meet with a client, but the lawyer's office can also be used. If the lawyer's office is used instruct the receptionist to hold all calls while the interview is taking place. Also, make sure that all files and loose papers are neatly put away and to prevent a client from seeing confidential information concerning another client.

First impressions are extremely important. The appearance of the paralegal leaves a very distinct and lasting impression on the client. Carefully think about the impression you want to leave. Clients expect professionalism. Conservative dress, simple jewelry, and good grooming are all part of the package of the paralegal professional. Business suits are always a good bet.

Prepare for the interview ahead of time. Make sure you have all necessary paperwork ready for the client to sign. If the client comes in with a personal injury you would want to have medical releases and authorizations to obtain police reports prepared in advance. Every area of the law has its own forms for authorizations and releases of information. Each form allows the law firm to obtain privileged information necessary to prepare the case and evaluate any claims or allegations.

Preparing for the interview also means meeting with your supervising attorney to obtain his or her preliminary instructions. When at all possible, review any applicable statutes and case law. **Statutes** are a written enactments of a legislative body—federal, state, city, or county. **Case law** is law developed through cases that have been adjudicated. Not only will this refresh your memory, but it will define the legal issues and elements of proof required of a particular case.

Determine the appropriate checklist. Again, every case is different and every area of the law requires certain specific information. If you are at all unsure about what information is necessary, discuss it first with the attorney. Do not be afraid to ask questions. It is much better to ask a question than to pretend you know and be way off base.

Use a notepad to record any comments made and to record your own impressions. Never allow the taking of notes to interrupt the interview or make the client uncomfortable. As soon as the interview is concluded, the paralegal should dictate a memorandum while the interview is fresh. At that time the paralegal can also note any gaps in the information obtained and prepare a deficiency memo regarding that information. (Deficiency memos will be discussed further in later chapters.)

Greet the client warmly and request if you can get them anything such as coffee or a soft drink. Ideally the lawyer should introduce himself or herself and the paralegal. Prior to the arrival of the client, it should be decided who is the primary interviewer. Usually that will be the attorney until the paralegal has had enough experience and develops enough skill in that area. Frame your questions, carefully and use various types of questions, such as the following:

Open-ended questions.   Inquiries asked in a format requiring more than a yes or
  no answer
Closed questions.   Inquires asked in a format requiring only a yes or no response
Leading questions.   Inquiries asked in a format prompting a specific response

---

PRACTICE TIP

Prepare your questions carefully and ahead of time. Although prepared questions can inhibit spontaneity, you will not forget to get that crucial piece of information. If you are unsure of how a question sounds, read it out loud to yourself. You will be amazed at how different a written question sounds when read aloud.

Also, remember to let the client talk. Sometimes some of the best information is obtained from when a client provides a lengthy narrative of the problem. However, you should control the situation and not get too far from the subject matter. Try to adapt your questioning style to the client's style. Paraphrase what you heard the client say to minimize the possibility of any misunderstanding. Make sure your questions are always simple and clear. Encourage the client to supply as many details as possible. Questions need to be framed in terms of who, what, when, where, why, and how. Always ask how they know a particular fact. Did someone tell them? Did they see it with their own eyes? Get them to provide as much detail as possible about every fact discussed.

Ask the client about witnesses and carefully check every lead during the investigation process. Verify the facts given. Identify pertinent documents and ask the client what documents they have in their possession. Always keep documents supplied by the client separate from other documents and always identify the source of a document.

Practice active listening. Show concern and caring. You can sympathize with the client, but never empathize. **Empathy** can be defined as being aware or sensitive to the feelings, thoughts, and experiences of another, without having the feelings, thoughts, and experiences fully expressed. For example, if a your clients are a couple relating the incidents, thoughts, feelings, and experiences that occurred when their child ran out in front of a car and was killed right before their eyes, it would be impossible for you to understand or know what they were going through.

Never be judgmental and try not to make statements such as "what Mr. Smith did was very wrong." See if what is being said makes sense. Think.

Often you will receive conflicting or contradictory information from a client. See if the client can help you sort it out. If not, during your investigation, see if you can corroborate the statement made. **Investigation** is defined as the process of obtaining and observing facts and other information through questioning, observing, and tracking needed information. A client's perception of a situation can be colored by emotions, fear, previous experiences, health conditions, eyesight, or any number of preconceived notions. It is your job to help them sort it out through the process of verification.

When the interview is concluded, provide the client with your business card identifying yourself as a paralegal, review what they should expect, what they need to do, and when they will hear from you again.

PRACTICE TIP

Always, whenever practical, prepare your client interview summary immediately after the interview. That way the information will be fresh in your mind and if you forgot to write something down, you may simply remember it. If you wait a week or two to prepare the summary, that immediate recall and recollection of what was said will have faded. This principle holds true for any interview, client, or witness.

---

4. Record Keeping

Once the initial client interview is complete and you have all the information, you need to organize it. Fact information sheets can be quite helpful. The example of a fact information or summary sheet in Figure 2.3 has been developed for a defense firm, but it can be easily adapted for use in a plaintiff-oriented firm as well.

FACT INFORMATION SHEET—FILE SUMMARY

Case:
File no.:

Plaintiff:	Our client:
Date of incident:	Phone:
DOB:	Claim no.:
Social Security no.:	Insured:

Opposing counsel: **Our experts:**

CIVIL ACTION

Cause no.:	Judge:	Phone:
Filed:	Judge's secretary:	Phone:
Served:	Judge's law clerk:	Phone:
Answered:		
Venue:		
Notes on court:		

DEADLINES

TRIAL:	Scheduling conf.:
Order dated:	Discovery complete:
Plaintiff's experts:	Settlement conf.:
Defendant's experts:	Final PT conf.:
Joinders & amendments:	SJ motions:
Discovery served:	All other motions:
TRIAL NOTES:	

Figure 2.3. Fact Information Sheet—File Summary

Fact information sheets provide all necessary information at your fingertips. Once prepared, the sheets are then placed in a three-ring notebook in alphabetical order by client. The person working on the file does not need to search for needed information and can easily answer a client's questions on dates and status of the case. Since paralegals deal with many experts, these sheets can be helpful reminders of what experts have been used in the past. In essence, they provide a history of cases the paralegal has worked on and can be utilized at evaluation time. Also, the sheets provide information on specific courts practiced in, changes in rules, types of equipment available, likes and dislikes of judges, and trial notes. The paralegal can also readily remember all clients the firm has represented. It is helpful to not only have hard copies of these sheets, but also to input them as a searchable database. Once again, computers streamline the process of using forms such as this when the sheet is set up as a form.

An example of a case track checklist—general is shown in Figure 2.4.

Case name and no.:

Date of last correspondence with client:

Plaintiff's discovery:
      Served:
      Responded to:

Defendant's discovery:
      Served:
      Responded to:

Depositions:
      Name and date taken:
      Summarized:
      Input into database:

Trial:
      Notebooks prepared:
      Exhibits prepared:

Figure 2.4. Case Track Checklist–General

5. Tips for Dealing with Clients

If your client appears to be quite shy or uncomfortable, an easy technique for dealing with the problem is to sit side-by-side or directly across from the client, with no desk (which symbolizes authority) between you. Just take care not to invade the person's space. Keep in mind as well that certain individuals from other countries or cultural backgrounds have strict rules and customs about seating, personal space, and deference to authority. If you are unsure, ask someone, or utilize the various Internet resources available to find answers to your questions.

Take the time to get to know the client before jumping right in with questions. Lay a foundation, get some background on the client, and determine if there is any common ground. For example, you both could be from the same hometown or you could both enjoy gardening. It is never a good idea to start firing questions before you build trust and confidence with the client.

Some cases can be very sensitive, and the information you need to obtain can be very difficult to elicit. Take, for example, the case of a battered wife. It can be traumatic for her to explain her injuries, cuts, and bruises. Although you would need to get background information about the abuser, including how many times she has been battered, it can be very difficult if not impossible for the client to relate the facts and relive the incidents giving rise to her need for an attorney. Think also about the death of a child. Nothing can be as traumatic as the death of a loved one, especially a child. Facts and details of an accident or injury can be very hard to relate to someone else. If you find that a particular client is having trouble discussing a certain aspect of the case, move to a neutral topic to allow the individual to regain composure. Let the client talk. You can easily determine the client's emotional state from how he or she tells the story. Always be as tactful as possible, especially in cases involving death, suicide, assault, rape, or sexual activities.

Older, nonadult, disabled, and foreign-born individuals all present unique challenges to the paralegal. Often the older client has difficulty getting around or using stairs. Hearing may be a concern. Make sure that the environment is quiet and easily accessible so that an older client will not be impaired in any way. A paralegal may be required to interview a bedridden client at home or a hospitalized client. Determine what medications are being taken and decide the mental capacity of the person you are interviewing. If there is any question, speak with your supervising attorney.

Children present another set of problems. Generally speaking, to interview a child, you need to obtain the permission of one of the child's parents. Oftentimes it is best to tailor the interview site to the child's interests or comfort level. Having a parent or older sibling with the child helps to put him or her at ease. If there is any question at all about the ability of a client to speak and understand English, arrange for a competent interpreter or a family member who can assist you.

PRACTICE TIP

Interviewing is a skill that is learned and developed over time. There is no perfect formula, no hard and fast rules. Use common sense and plan. Planning will take time but will pay off in the long run.

---

6. Subsequent Interviews and Keeping Clients Up-to-Date

It is extremely important for the paralegal to ensure that the client is kept informed and up-to-date on his or her case. There is nothing more frustrating than not understanding the legal process and procedures in the first place and then never hearing what the next step is. At a minimum, every client should hear from the paralegal assigned to the case once a month, either by phone or in writing. Even if the contact is a short one-paragraph letter explaining that nothing has occurred, the client knows he or she hasn't been forgotten. Think of this task as a status report. It keeps you on track and informs the client as well. These client status reports also jog the attorney's memory about things he or she has planned to accomplish.

When subsequent interviews are necessary, remember to schedule them in advance and at times and days that will be convenient for your client. Try to be mindful of the client's particular work schedule or home responsibilities when setting up meetings, depositions, conferences, or settlement negotiations.

C. INITIAL INVESTIGATION AND VERIFICATION OF FACTS

After the initial interview, it is time to start the process of investigation and verification of facts. Of course, there are many types of investigations and many different techniques employed. Interviewing witnesses, as with interviewing clients, can be a challenging task. However, when the paralegal takes the time to think through the process, the type of interview, and the information needed, the process can be quite simple, successful, and productive. Either the lawyer or the paralegal should explain the investigative process to the client and inform him or her what to expect. If the client learns that others are being interviewed about the case without his or her prior knowledge, the client might infer that you did not believe his or her story. Explain that you need to corroborate the facts and to obtain additional information. Explain the importance of input from others and how the information obtained might be used at trial.

1. Type of Individual to be Interviewed

Keep the following various witness types in mind when deciding how to verify facts and obtain further information. Will this person be a neutral third party, a hostile witness, or a friendly witness? Does this individual have a specific specialty or knowledge base? Perhaps the individual is a treating physician, an expert witness, or a law enforcement officer. Is this witness necessary in an official capacity?

a. Friendly Witnesses

A **friendly witness** is an individual with case information who generally is open and willing to help and answer questions. These types of witnesses can be family members, witnesses who came forward without prompting, or people who feel they have relevant helpful information.

b. Hostile Witnesses

A **hostile witness** is an individual with case information who generally is not open and not willing to help and answer questions. These types of witnesses do not want to get involved or possibly have unfavorable impressions of your client.

c. Neutral Third-Party Witnesses

A **neutral third-party witness** is an individual with case information but no interest in the lawsuit who generally is open and willing to help and answer questions. These types of witnesses have no vested interest in the case and are simply providing pertinent facts to your particular case.

d. Official Witnesses

An **official witness** is an individual with case information usually as a result of the witness's official capacity. Official witnesses are easy to work with and are usually contacted because of their official capacity. These types of witnesses could be police officers who investigated an accident, city or county officials, government employees, or any other similar witness who acts in some related official capacity. It is important to remember with these witnesses are bound by certain rules and regulations in answering questions or meeting with you. Determine in advance if that is the case. For example, typically police officers charge a per hour rate, with a minimum amount, for meeting with attorneys regarding their specific investigations.

e. Specialty Witnesses

A **specialty witness** is an individual with case information usually as a result of his or her specialized knowledge. Specialty witnesses are almost always willing to answer questions but may have an hourly fee to answer your questions. These witnesses generally answer background questions, provide an overall picture of a problem, and are a wealth of information when you need to better understand a problem or claim presented by your client. An example of a specialty witness would be a biomechanical engineer or an environmental engineer.

f. Expert Witnesses

An **expert witness** is an individual hired by one of the parties to provide an opinion regarding his or her specialized knowledge. These witnesses provide opinions and testify at trial. (See Chapters 8 and 10 for more on expert witnesses, disclosures, and reports.)

2. Methods of Conducting the Interview

Interviews can be conducted in person or over the telephone. Care should be given to the decision to interview over the telephone. Telephone interviews can be difficult. Hearing clearly can be a problem, it can be hard to build enough of a rapport with the witness to get the information needed, and it is difficult to control. The person on the phone can be plagued by interruptions and have difficulty focusing on the questions presented. Obviously, body language cannot be assessed over the telephone either, as can be done in person.

When interviewing a witness in person, be cognitive of body language. Does the individual look you in the eye? Sit slightly forward in the chair when listening to you or relating the story (indicating interest and truth)? Fold both arms across his or her chest in a defensive posture? Fidget? Wring his or her hands, blush, blink nervously, or act defensive in any way? What clues can you discern from the individual's posture, presence, and style? Think about it. Do you feel more comfortable when someone shakes your hand firmly or when someone shakes your hand in a timid fashion?

Think about the type of interview you will conduct and the type of questions you will ask. There are many different types of interviews and interviewing techniques. A few different types of interviewing techniques follow.

a. Lead-Taking Interviews

A **lead-taking interview** is a discussion controlled by the person asking questions of a witness. These type of interviews determine the direction of the interview or indicate what the interviewee should be talking about. The interviewer can structure this type of interview in numerous ways.

i. Structuring

Structuring is making remarks that define the interviewing situation, indicate what the purpose the interview is expected to accomplish, or outline the responsibilities of both individuals, that is, telling "what we can do here." This technique includes remarks setting the time and limits of the interview, but not those relating to the end of the interview (for example, "I see we've come to the end of the hour").

ii. Directive and Specific Types of Questions

In this technique, the interviewer asks an outright question that requires a factual answer. It does not include interrogative statements, which are merely intended to redefine, clarify, or repeat a feeling. Questions used with this approach would include "What do you think of that?" and "How old are you?"

iii. Nondirective Leads and Questions

In this technique, the interviewer makes statements that encourage the interviewee to state the problem further. This excludes leads that would greatly limit what the client could bring out about the problem or any feelings about it. In general, this type of lead is one that encourages a statement without limiting the nature of the response except in a very general way. It would include "Tell me more about it" or "Would you like to tell me how you feel about it?"

b. Nondirective Response to Feeling

This technique involves attempts to restate a feeling that the interviewee has expressed, but not to interpret or to offer advice, criticism, or suggestions. There are various subcategories in the use of this technique.

i. Simple Acceptance*
This technique should never imply approval or criticism.

ii. Restatement of Content or Problem
This technique is a simple repeating of what the interviewee has said without any effort to organize, clarify, or interpret it, or any effort to show that the interviewer is appreciating the feeling of the interviewee's statement by understanding it.

iii. Clarification or Recognition of Feeling
This is a statement by the interviewer that puts the client's feeling or affective tone in somewhat clearer or more recognizable form.

c. Semidirective Response to Feeling

This category include those responses that are interpretive in character—responses in which the interviewer points out patterns and relationships in the material presented. This category is always used when causation is implied or indicated: "You did this because . . ."

d. Directive Counseling

These are categories of responses that imply a relationship in which the interviewer attempts to project his or her attitudes onto the interviewee or client. In most cases, this kind of directive interviewing is overstepping the role of a good interviewer and generally should never be used in the paralegal's role as interviewer.

e. Minor Categories

This category relates to any other technique that does not seem to be related to the principle problem.

i. Ending of the Contact
These include any responses dealing with the close of the contact or with the setting of a time for a future contact.

ii. Ending of the Series
These responses relate to the ending of the series of interviews or to statements that no further contact is necessary.

iii. Friendly Discussion
These exchanges involve material unrelated to the problem and serve only the purpose of establishing good rapport.

---

*Simple acceptance can be denoted by a yes response, or a response such as "mmm."

iv. Unclassifiable
These are responses that cannot be classified in one of the above categories.

3. Basic Helping Skills

There are ways in which you can assist the witness or client with basic helping skills to elicit the information you need through various types of questions asked:

i. Open-ended questions
These types of questions encourage the person to develop an answer and talk at greater length and in more detail.

ii. Closed questions
These types of questions usually call for a simple "yes" or "no" and are typically phrased so that the answers are limited to a few words.

iii. Paraphrasing
A **paraphrase** is a restatement in fewer words of a statement previously made. Paraphrasing is a method of restating the interviewee's basic message in similar but usually fewer words. The main purpose of paraphrasing is to check out your understanding of what the interviewee has said. You are also communicating to the interviewee that you are trying to understand his or her basic message.

iv. Reflecting and Understanding
Reflecting feelings involves more than a simple restatement of words. The reflecting or understanding of feelings response should echo the feeling that may not have been expressed openly but was clearly a part of the response.

v. Summarization
Summaraziation is the process of reviewing and condensing information obtained during an interview. Summarization is used to review, condense, or clarify what the interviewee has said. It puts together a number of interviewee statements, a phase of an interview, or an entire interview. Summaries can be used during a session or at the end.

4. To Tape or Not to Tape

Always ask the attorney if he or she wants the interview tape-recorded. There are some circumstances in which an attorney might not want an interview taped due to concerns over whether the tape would be discoverable. Some attorneys feel that taping an interview will inhibit a witness, making him or her concentrate more on how the words sound than on what they say. Some witnesses do not like to be taped and feel very uncomfortable, thus setting an undesirable tone for the interview.

However, some attorneys believe the advantages to taping an interview outweigh any possible disadvantages. For example, taping an interview will ensure that all information is remembered, retained, and accurate. Taping an interview will ensure that the person interviewed will be honest. Most people when they know they are being taped are more cautious about the facts given and will try to be more honest. Also, taped interviews will reflect the interviewee's mood, voice, inflections, nervousness, poise, and ability to articulate—all areas that notes will not capture.

Last, but not least, with a taped interview, the paralegal can assess his or her performance and learn from the experience to become a better or more polished interviewer.

If taping the interview, the paralegal should adhere to the following eight specific rules.

1. State his or her name, title, date, purpose of the interview, and location.
2. Have the witness identify him- or herself by name, address, and phone number.
3. Ask for permission to record the interview.
4. Identify others in the room.
5. Explain interruptions and state times of conclusion and restart.
6. Ask if the witness wants to receive a transcript of the tape.
7. State the conclusion time, that the statement was given freely and that the witness will be given an opportunity to make any changes.
8. Have the witness verify in his or her own voice that the statement was voluntary.

D. CONFLICTS CHECKING

Conflicts can arise in many different areas and in many different ways. Although this section is not meant as a complete discussion or treatise on the subject, it is very important that the paralegal be cognizant of situations in which conflicts arise and what sources are available to provide solutions and answers to pertinent questions.

There are literally hundreds of books written on this subject. Although there are rules and guidelines written to assist lawyers and their staff with these concerns, there are always exceptions to the rules and gray areas that you as the paralegal will face. As the individual charged with obtaining and gathering facts, the paralegal must always be mindful of the situations in which conflicts can and do arise. Furthermore, it is part of the paralegal's responsibility to ensure that the attorneys they work for are aware of potential conflicts. In order to fullfill that responsibility, the paralegal needs to be aware of areas in which common conflicts of interest arise.

1. Conflicts of Interest

A **conflict of interest** is a conflict between public and private interests in which a person's duty could lead to the disregard of another person's duty. The eight most common conflicts of interest follow.

1. **Fees paid.** There are instances when someone other than the client may pay the attorneys' fees. For example, a third party may pay fees in the instance of the insurance

contract. The dilemma raised then becomes to whom does the attorney have a duty to. Both the insured and the insurer, or one of them?

2. **Aggregate settlements.** When representing two or more clients, an attorney cannot accept an aggregate settlement of claims until and unless he or she informs all parties and receives their consent.

3. **Financial assistance to clients.** Lawyers are prohibited from providing financial assistance to clients. They may, however, advance court costs and litigation expenses.

4. **Former clients.** A lawyer cannot represent a person in the same or a very similar matter in which that lawyer formerly had represented a client whose interests are materially adverse to the potential client or about whom the lawyer has protected information.

5. **Multiple representations.** An attorney cannot represent two or more parties who have adverse interests. This particular problem arises usually in the areas of family law and real estate transactions, although it can be an issue elsewhere.

6. **Gifts.** Substantial gifts are prohibited when a lawyer drafts an instrument on behalf of an unrelated client due to the concern that the lawyer would be in a position to exert undue influence.

7. **Business transactions with clients.** Business transactions between a lawyer and a client are not prohibited, but there are guidelines to provide protection to the client.

8. **Acquiring interests in litigation.** Lawyers generally are prohibited from acquiring a proprietary interest in any litigation in which they are involved.

2. Conflicts Checks

One of the first things that a paralegal should do after a new client comes in the door and any adverse parties have been identified is to run a conflicts check. This check will determine whether the firm has ever represented a client or adverse party in the past and will indicate possible conflicts of interest. Of course, your supervisory attorney will make the final call as to whether to accept or reject a case, but it is the paralegal's job to assist the attorney in making that determination. Conflicts checks are done in different ways, and each firm or attorney has a specific system in place. Mainly, though, information on clients is kept on computer and the names and other pertinent information are archived. The computer database in Figure 2.5 carries at a minimum the information shown to help eliminate any possible conflicts.

3. Role of the ABA Model Code and Model Rules

The American Bar Association (ABA) is a voluntary association of lawyers that has played a major role in the development of ethical rules and guidelines. It even issues opinions interpreting the rules. Although the ABA's rules are not binding on any state bar or bar association, the ABA is a highly respected body and is very influential. Most states and bar associations have adopted the ABA ethical rules, of which there are two sets: the ABA

CONFLICT CHECK SHEET

Date:

Name of client:
(Alternative spellings if applicable)

Relationship of client:

All possible adverse parties:

Description of case:

Conflict? Yes: ☐ No: ☐

Figure 2.5. Conflict Check Sheet

Model Code of Professional Responsibility and the ABA Model Rules of Professional Conduct. Both are excellent resources when an ethical issue arises or when there is a question as to a conflict of interest.

We will look next at a couple of the rules and comments addressing the conflicts enumerated in section D1 above.

Rule 1.7   *Conflict of Interest: General Rule*

(a) A lawyer shall not represent a client if the representation of that client will be directly adverse to another client, unless:

(1) the lawyer reasonably believes the representation will not adversely affect the relationship with the other client; and

(2)each client consents after consultation.

(b) A lawyer shall not represent a client if the representation of that client may be materially limited by the lawyer's own interests, unless:

(1) the lawyer reasonably believes the representation will not be adversely affected; and

(2) the client consents after consultation. When representation of multiple clients in a single matter is undertaken, the consultation shall include explanation of the implications of the common representation and the advantages and risks involved.[1]

Rule 1.8   *Conflict of Interest: Prohibited Transactions*

(a) A lawyer shall not enter into a business transaction with a client or knowingly acquire an ownership, possessory, security, or other pecuniary interest adverse to a client unless:

---

1. ABA Ann. Model Rules of Prof' Conduct, (1999).

(1) the transaction and terms on which the lawyer acquires the interest are fair and reasonable to the client and are fully disclosed and transmitted in writing to the client in a manner which can be reasonably understood by the client;

(2) the client is given a reasonable opportunity to seek the advice of independent counsel in the transaction; and

(3) the client consents in writing thereto.

(b) A lawyer shall not use information relating to representation of a client to the disadvantage of the client unless the client consents after consultation, except as permitted or required by Rule 1.6 or Rule 3.3.

(c) A lawyer shall not prepare an instrument giving the lawyer or a person related to the lawyer as parent, child, sibling, or spouse any substantial gift from a client, including a testamentary gift, except where the client is related to the donee.

(d) Prior to the conclusion of representation of a client, a lawyer shall not make or negotiate an agreement giving the lawyer literary or media rights to a portrayal or account based in substantial part on information relating to the representation.

(e) A lawyer shall not provide financial assistance to a client in connection with pending or contemplated litigation, except that:

(1) a lawyer may advance court costs and expenses of litigation, the repayment of which may be contingent on the outcome of the matter; and

(2) a lawyer representing an indigent client may pay court costs and expenses of litigation on behalf of the client.

(f) A lawyer shall not accept compensation for representing a client from one other than the client unless:

(1) the client consents after consultation;

(2) there is no interference with the lawyer's independence of professional judgment or with the client-lawyer relationship; and

(3) information relating to representation of a client is protected as required by Rule 1.6.

(g) A lawyer who represents two or more clients shall not participate in making an aggregate settlement of claims of or against the clients, or in a criminal case an aggregated agreement as to guilty or nolo contendere pleas, unless each client consents after consultation, including disclosure of the existence and nature of all the claims or pleas involved and of the participation of each person in the settlement.[2]

Rule 1.9   *Conflict of Interest: Former Client*

(a) A lawyer who has formerly represented a client in a matter shall not thereafter represent another person in the same or a substantially related matter in which that person's interests are materially adverse to the interests of the former client unless the former client consents after consultation.

(b) A lawyer shall not knowingly represent a person in the same or a substantially related matter in which a firm with which the lawyer formerly was associated had previously represented a client

2. *Id.*

(1) whose interests are materially adverse to that person; and

(2) about whom the lawyer had acquired information protected by Rules 1.6 and 1.9(c) that is material to the matter.

(c) A lawyer who has formerly represented a client in a matter or whose present or former firm has formerly represented a client in a matter shall not thereafter:

(1) use information relating to the representation to the disadvantage of the former client except as Rule 1.6 or Rule 3.3 would permit or require with respect to a client, or when the information has become generally known; or

(2) reveal information relating to the representation except as Rule 1.6 or Rule 3.3 would permit or require with respect to a client.[3]

Rule 4.2 of the ABA Model Rules states:

In representing a client, a lawyer shall not communicate about the subject of the representation with a party that the lawyer knows to be represented by another lawyer in the matter, unless the lawyer has the consent of the other lawyer or is authorized by law to do so.[4]

The comment to ABA Model Rule 4.2 states:

In the case of an organization, this Rule prohibits communications by a lawyer for one party concerning the matter in representation with persons having a managerial responsibility on behalf of the organization, and with any other person whose act or omission in connection with that matter may be imputed to the organization for the purposes of civil or criminal liability or whose statement may constitute an admission on the part of the organization.[5]

Here are a few final admonitions.

- Paralegals must always identify themselves as such. Make sure that the individual or individuals you are dealing with know that you are not an attorney.
- Paralegals are not authorized to practice law or provide legal advice.
- Paralegals can never communicate directly with an adverse party when they are represented by an attorney. That party's attorney will handle all communications.

This is an area fraught with peril, but easily navigable when you rely on your supervising attorney and remember to utilize the references and resources available to you. Take the time to thoroughly review and familiarize yourself with the appendix in the back of this book. The appendix contains full reprints of the NAL Code of Ethics and Professional Responsibility and the NALA Model Standards and Guidelines for Utilization of Legal Assistants.[6]

---

3. *Id.*
4. *Id.*
5. ABA Compendium of Prof' Responsibility, Rules and Standards, (1999).
6. *See also http://www.nala.org/stand.htm.*

E. STATUTE OF LIMITATIONS CONSIDERATIONS

Statute of limitations is defined as the time period legislatively allowed for bringing litigation against another party. If the action is not brought within the proscribed period of time, it can be barred. Therefore, the paralegal must be meticulous in gathering information and facts relevant to the case, especially the relevant dates. For example, if a client has a potential claim against the United States, the paralegal would look to 28 U.S.C.A. §2401:

> 28 U.S.C.A. §2401. *Time for commencing action against United States.*
>
> (a) Except as provided by the Contract Disputes Act of 1978, every civil action commenced against the United States shall be barred unless the complaint is filed within six years after the right of action first accrues. The action of any person under legal disability or beyond the seas at the time the claim accrues may be commenced within three years after the disability ceases.
>
> (b) A tort claim against the United States shall be forever barred unless it is presented in writing to the appropriate federal agency within two years after such claim accrues or unless action is begun within six months after the date of mailing, by certified or registered mail, of notice of final denial of the claim by the agency to which it was presented.

This book deals only with federal law, so remember that state laws vary. Be sure to check on the statutes in your particular state. An excellent resource available on the Internet is *http://www.findlaw.com.* This site provides links to every state's statutes.

F. OVERVIEW OF GENERAL LEGAL THEORIES

The purpose of this section is to expose the paralegal to the various types of legal theories we will work with in this book. We have all heard the buzz words *theory of the case, legal theory, cause of action, claim, liability.* What do they all mean? Although the terms are different, they can be used interchangeably to test facts obtained and to determine whether it is appropriate to seek assistance from a court and file a complaint. It is helpful for the paralegal to be aware of the basis for these various legal theories.

Certainly the theory of the case can be discussed prior to the client coming in if enough information is given at the outset, or after the client has left when more facts have been gathered. Knowing and understanding the basics of various legal theories will aid the paralegal in doing a better job of assisting the attorney. The paralegal student will take other courses outlining in depth various legal theories. Attorneys take years in law school devoting time to understanding and comprehending legal theory.

Claims or causes of action—that is, legal theories—have several sources: courts, legislatures, common law, and torts. Remember, however, that it is the job of the attorney to determine the legal theory under which to file a complaint.

The next sections describe the basic legal theories used in this book.

1. Fraud

Fraud is the intentional misrepresentation of a fact or facts meant to induce someone to do something. Fraud may be induced by words or behavior. Allegations of fraud, like negligence, must be made with particularity. A pleading that merely claims fraud but states no facts to support it is insufficient.

2. Strict Liability

Strict liability is the failure to use the care that a reasonably prudent and careful person would use under similar circumstances. Strict liability is "liability without fault" or liability without a showing of criminal intent to case harm. It is a stricter standard than that imposed by an allegation of simple negligence. Strict liability is generally implied in product liability cases in which the law imposes a higher standard on sellers and manufacturers of consumer products that may be defective and therefore unsafe or unreasonably dangerous to the consuming public. In such instances, the law imposes a strict standard of performance on the defendant that will preclude defenses such as ignorance, waiver, contributory negligence, and the like.

3. Misrepresentation

Misrepresentation is defined as an intentionally false statement that is unjustifiably relied on by another. Misrepresentation may be conveyed through words or action.

4. Negligence

Negligence is not doing something that a reasonable man, under ordinary circumstances, would do or doing something that a reasonable man would not do. Negligence actions include

- Contractual claims
- Statutory rights
- Medical malpractice actions
- Wrongful discharge
- Criminal actions
- Personal injury actions

Negligence covers harm due to conduct that was unreasonable under the circumstances. There are four elements of a negligence cause of action:

1. Duty
2. Breach of duty
3. Proximate cause
4. Damages

5. Wrongful Death

Wrongful death is a lawsuit brought on behalf of the deceased by his or her beneficiaries alleging that his or her death is attributable to the willful or negligent act of another.

6. Contract Law

A **contract** is a legally enforceable agreement between two or more parties. It may be oral or written and is a promise by one party between two or more parties. The law recognizes a duty to perform these promises and allows recovery of damages for the lack or failure of performance of said agreements or promises. Generally, to create a valid contract, the following six elements must be present:

1. Offer
2. Acceptance
3. Consideration
4. Capacity of the parties to contract
5. Intent of the parties to contract
6. Object of the contract

Let's take a look at each element separately. An offer is a definite expression or overt action that starts a contract; it is what is offered to another for the return of another's promise to act. It must be identified specifically and with certainty. Acceptance of the offer creates the contract which is then legally enforceable. Generally an acceptance cannot be withdrawn and cannot modify the terms of the offer. If any terms are modified, the acceptance would be termed a counteroffer. Consideration for a contract may be money or may be another right, interest, or benefit. It can even be a detriment, loss, or responsibility given up to another. The general rule is that a promise to perform an act that you are already legally bound to do is not a sufficient consideration for a contract. The law presumes the parties have the capacity to enter into a contract. A person who is trying to avoid a contract would have to plead his lack of capacity to contract, that is, he was a minor at the time, under the influence of drugs or alcohol, or mentally incompetent. There must be a mutual assent or a meeting of the minds of the parties on all essential elements and terms of the proposed contract. There can be no contract unless the parties involved intended to enter into one. Finally, a contract is not enforceable if its object is illegal or against public policy.

In most civil cases, a party suffering harm is seeking money awards to alleviate their loss or pain and suffering, though there are times when a money damage award does not and will not make the individual whole. In such an event the party may file a complaint in equity. A court hearing in an equity case may order the return or delivery of property or the performing or refraining from performing some act.

Courts of equity consider the equitable rights of both parties. They weigh what is and what is not fair. The most important prerequisites to filing an action in equity are as follows.

- The plaintiff does not have an adequate remedy at law.
- The plaintiff is suffering, or is about to suffer, an irreparable harm.

A plaintiff may be entitled to equitable relief if he or she does not have a remedy at law. Therefore, if a money award alone will satisfy the damages caused, do not file your lawsuit in a court of equity. You do not have a cause of action in equity in such case. Another consideration of the equity courts may be whether the court decree, if ordered, will be feasible to enforce.

In an equity case, the court hears the case without a jury. The court makes findings of both fact and law as the basis for its final order. The court may, in some cases, allow a jury to hear a certain factual phase of the case if the judge believes it would be necessary, on his or her own motion or on the motion of a party to the case. The basic relief that an equity court may give, if a cause of action is stated entitling him to such relief, may be one of more of the following:

- Injunction
- Specific performance
- Rescission
- Reformation

An injunction is an order of the court directing a party to a cause of action in equity to do some act or to refrain from doing some act.

Specific performance is the usual equitable remedy available to a plaintiff in cases arising from a contractual relationship. The overriding consideration is still whether the legal remedy (money damages) is adequate and, furthermore, whether the consideration bargained for is unique and thereby irreplaceable.

Rescission is an equitable remedy whereby plaintiff seeks to avoid the existence of a contract. The primary consideration of rescission is whether the grounds for rescission occurred at or before the time the contract was entered into by the parties. The usual basis for a complaint for rescission are

- Mistake (the facts constituting the mistake must be stated) in the complaint
- Misrepresentation or fraud (the facts constituting the fraud must be stated in the complaint)

The mistake can be either "bilateral" or "unilateral," a mistake on both parties' side or a mistake by one party. The courts will not order a rescission of a contract for a unilateral mistake unless the nonmistaken party knows, or should have known, of the mistaken party's mistake.

Reformation is the equitable remedy for reforming or changing a written contract by decree to conform to the original intent of the parties. This occurs when the writing does not state exactly what the parties meant it to state. The difference between reformation and rescission is that in rescission there is a finding that no original valid contract existed, as it was entered into only because of a mistake, misrepresentation, or fraud. In reformation there is a valid original contract that simply does not conform to the true intent of the parties.

There are numerous defenses to causes of action stated. A summary analysis of typical affirmative defenses include accord or satisfaction, arbitration and award, assumption of risk, contributory negligence, comparative negligence, discharge, duress, estoppel, illegality, laches, license/privilege, res judicata, statute of limitations, statute of frauds, and waiver. (See Chapter 8 for a thorough discussion and explanation of each of these defenses.)

ETHICS

A common problem for paralegals is the one of being asked for "legal advice." So often family member, acquaintances, and friends will say, "You work in the legal field, what should I do about . . .". You may hear, "My husband is paying his ex-wife $500 a month in child support. We think it is too much. What do the child support guidelines say?" As a paralegal you will oftentimes know the answers to these questions, or you will actually be the employee at the firm who runs the child support calculations for the attorneys. However, providing legal advice, any legal advice, to any person is illegal and unethical. The best way to approach such questions is to say that you are not allowed to give legal advice and to tell those asking them to seek the advice of an attorney. Making statements like that will not make you sound silly or stupid. Answering the questions and getting in trouble will. Most practicing paralegals have heard of the story of the paralegal who helped a family member in a divorce action by preparing the petition and other necessary paperwork. All the couple wanted was to save money, and they really didn't have any disputes. However, the couple soon turned from a friendly parting of the ways to a very antagonistic parting of the ways. They both felt they "could have gotten more" and eventually sued the paralegal for giving incorrect and inappropriate legal advice. The rest is history, and the paralegal is no longer a practicing paralegal.

If you are ever in doubt about whether answering a client's question would be crossing the line into legal advice, ask your attorney. No one will fault you for saying "I will have to get back to you or I must refer you to Mr. Jones, the attorney." Not providing legal advice is a thin line to walk and an issue that will come up continually during your career as a professional, practicing paralegal. Don't let one mistake ruin your career.

CONCLUSION

Initial client contact and commencement of a case can be an exciting time. It can also be overwhelming to the new paralegal, or even the experienced paralegal, if he or she is not well organized and has not planned an approach. Take the time to prepare. It will be worth it in the end. Gather all paperwork at least a day prior to the scheduled contact or interview. Review the type of case and issues as presented by the client on the phone. Meet with your attorney to define your role and responsibility. Discuss with him or her the information and facts needed to commence work on the case. Prepare your interview area and greet the client at the appointed time with a smile and a handshake.

If you are interviewing witnesses, remember to think through the purpose of the interview and how you will conduct the interview. Will it be by phone or in person? How will you best get the information needed? Consider the comfort of the witness, his or her schedule and ability to get around. Determine if there are any unusual circumstances such as a disabled witness, a foreign-born witness who does not speak English, or a hearing-impaired witness. When considering the comfort of the witness include some thought as to how to present yourself. Should you dress casually or should your attire be more formal?

As with anything, practice and experience are the best teachers. As you develop your interviewing skills, do not let yourself become too overconfident. Always keep an edge and plan for any encounter.

USING TECHNOLOGY IN THE LAW OFFICE

A. CALENDARING OR TICKLING SYSTEM

One of the most important deadlines an attorney deals with is the statute of limitations deadline, or the time required by statute for a party to file his or her claim. This deadline, along with several others, needs to be calendared or tickled so that it is not forgotten or missed. In fact, most attorneys' malpractice insurance coverage requires the utilization and maintenance of a calendaring or tickling system. Further, most insurance companies require that attorneys have two resources for their calendar or tickler systems—themselves and their secretaries or paralegals. The calendaring or tickling system can be created manually, but many legal professionals find it more efficient to use an electronic calendaring system.

There are several electronic calendaring programs that have a tickler feature, allowing for the tracking of important deadlines. Many of these programs have an alarm option, which will appear on the computer screen according to the time designated. If you are using a network version for your calendaring program, any changes made by you, the secretary, or the attorney are visible to all parties immediately, as are any designated alarms. The network version provides important deadline information to several sources at one time, thereby decreasing the likelihood of missed or forgotten deadlines. Of course, as with any calendaring software, there should be a means for backup in case of system failure. Attorneys will often choose to maintain both an electronic and a manual calendar or tickler system, the idea being that there is no harm in maintaining calendared or tickled deadlines in more than one place.

PRACTICE TIP

Carefully keep track of all approaching deadlines in the cases you are working on. Provide reminders to the attorney sufficiently in advance of the due dates to allow time to prepare any documents or schedule anything that could be required to meet the deadline. It really is not enough to simply rely on the firm's calendaring system because reminders a day or two in advance might not allow enough time to complete the required task. A litigation paralegal who carefully watches the calendar and reminds the attorney at several intervals about trial-related and other deadlines is especially valuable to a busy trial attorney.

Figure 2.6 depicts an example of the Microsoft Outlook 97 calendar or tickling software with a set alarm.

Another technology tool that can be used if you or the attorney you are working with travels frequently is a **Personal Digital Assistant (PDA),** handheld, satellite accessible computer device. One of the most popular brands of PDA is the Palm Pilot. A PDA allows individuals to access their e-mail, as well as their office calendar or tickling system, and have at their fingertips important phone numbers and addresses while away from the office.

B. CONFLICT OF INTEREST

When your attorney decides to represent a client, the first thing that must be done is a conflict check. Ethically, the attorney cannot represent the same two clients in a matter because it would create a conflict of interest. There is also a conflict issue if your attorney has represented a client in a previous matter and now decides to represent an adverse party in the same or similar matter. Another primary question that surfaces is, "Can a party receive equal and fair representation if the attorney on the opposing side has previously represented that party?" Ethically, the answer is no unless both parties agree to waive such a conflict. For a further explanation regarding the ethical considerations concerning a conflict of interest check, see the appendix in the back of this book.

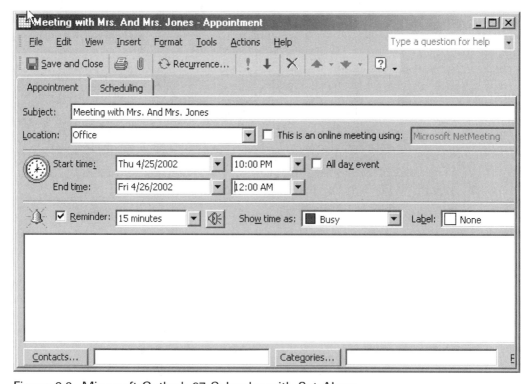

Figure 2.6. Microsoft Outlook 97 Calendar with Set Alarm

Attorneys who do not adhere to their ethical obligations can be reprimanded, sanctioned, or disbarred. That is why it is so important that a thorough conflict check be done *prior* to any agreement of representation. This conflict of interest check can be done any number of ways, manually or, more and more frequently, through the use of technology.

If you are hired to work in a larger firm, your firm most likely will have a department that handles conflict checks and maintains a client database. However, if you are hired to work in a smaller firm, you may end up being one of the individuals responsible for such conflict checks. If you do not have the resources to maintain and utilize an electronic database, then such information can be stored manually in a card-catalog-type system similar to a reference library. The principles of good database management remain the same.

Suggested categories for a manual client database include the following:

- Full name
- Spouse's full name
- Corporation name, if any
- Address(es)
- Telephone number(s)
- Matter(s) of representation
- File location for previous matter(s) of representation
- Attorney(s) responsible for previous matter(s) of representation

These categories would allow you to obtain information regarding prior representation from several sources of information. It is important to note that this system is only as good as those who create and utilize it. The information entered needs to be accurate and complete for this system to work. Normally this system would be stored alphabetically by the client's last name but the information can be stored alphabetically by one of the other categories. Maintaining a consistent sorting system needs to be of primary importance when you create the conflict of interest card catalog or database.

Figure 2.7 is an example of the manual card catalog system for your reference.

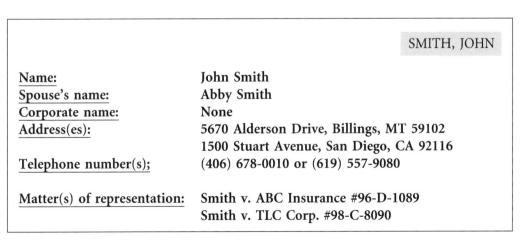

	SMITH, JOHN
Name:	John Smith
Spouse's name:	Abby Smith
Corporate name:	None
Address(es):	5670 Alderson Drive, Billings, MT 59102
	1500 Stuart Avenue, San Diego, CA 92116
Telephone number(s);	(406) 678-0010 or (619) 557-9080
Matter(s) of representation:	Smith v. ABC Insurance #96-D-1089
	Smith v. TLC Corp. #98-C-8090

Figure 2.7. Manual Card Catalog System

The other method for checking conflicts of interest involves the use of an electronic client database. There are advantages to this type of system when compared to the manual system; however, as stated above, the system is only as good its creator and utilizers.

The first advantage to a **computerized conflicts database,** a database created to confirm whether conflicts of interest exist, is that it can be accessed on your computer while you are sitting at your desk. The time it takes to do a database search is substantially less than manually searching a card-catalog-type system. If your attorney is on the telephone with a potential client, you can quickly run a conflict check for him or her before the call is complete.

Second, a database system requires minimal storage space. The conflict information usually is stored on a computer network or station. It does need to be periodically backed up on a **CD-ROM,** a device for recording digital information on computer disc, or a **tape backup,** a device for recording digital information on tape. There are several different types of databases on the market. The most readily available is Microsoft Access, which comes with the Microsoft Office software package. There are other litigation-based database programs such as Concordance and Summation.

As with any database software, searchable fields can be set up. These fields are similar to the categories discussed in the previous paragraphs. One thing to be aware of with database fields is that each field can be set up with designated parameters. For example, the name database field can require that names are entered last name first with a comma and space followed by the first name. The address field can be split into three fields, one for the street address and the other two for city/state and zip code. This type of field setup would allow you to search separately by city or zip code. Another extremely important field is the matter(s) of representation field. This field must list *all* parties involved in prior cases. The accuracy of this field is crucial for an adequate conflict check to be done. If it's possible, the case number should be referenced with the case name. Additional fields that should be created include a location field for previous files and a field referencing the responsible attorney.

C. ELECTRONIC CLIENT COMMUNICATION

It is always important that the client be kept informed about case progress and status. One way to keep the client informed electronically is through the use of **e-mail,** or electronic mail. E-mail has become more and more prevalent as a means of communication. The primary reason for the popularity of e-mail communication is due to its easy access and rapid exchange of information between parties. A client does not have to wait several days for the mail to be updated regarding the status of his or her case. E-mail communication is sometimes even faster than a telephone call.

The negative side to using e-mail as a means of communication with a client is that such confidential communication could be mistakenly sent to the wrong person. E-mail could be accessed by outside parties equating to a possible breach in the attorney-client confidentiality. E-mail is also a written form of communication stored on the computer and, as a result, can be retrieved by others. A default signature with a disclaimer message should be inserted below any signature names to ensure that no waiver of the attorney-client communication occurs. Below is an example of some disclaimer language that could be inserted following any e-mail signature:

> This electronic mail transmission may constitute an attorney-client communication that is privileged at law. It is not intended for transmission to, or receipt by, any unauthorized persons. If you have received this electronic mail transmission in error, please delete it from your system without copying it, and notify the sender by reply e-mail or by calling the _____ Law Firm so that our address record can be corrected.

If e-mail communication is to be utilized, then the client should be fully informed of the potential security risks associated with this communication tool. If e-mail is used properly, it can be an incredibly powerful communication tool.

KEY TERMS

Case law	Interview	Open-ended questions
Closed questions	Investigation	Paraphrase
Conflict of interest	Leading questions	Specialty witness
Contract	Lead-taking interviews	Statutes
Empathy	Litigation	Statute of limitations
Expert witness	Misrepresentation	Strict liability
Fraud	Negligence	Summarization
Friendly witness	Neutral third-party witness	Wrongful death
Hostile witness	Official witness	

TECHNOLOGY TERMS

CD-ROM	Personal Digital Assistant	Tape backup
E-mail	(PDA)	

USEFUL WEB SITES

http://www.ipl.org   The Internet Public Library, a reference library with links to sites on the Web, links to newspapers, and resources and references.

http://www.loc.gov   The Library of Congress, a research section with numerous research tools. You can look up a book using a simple word and title search.

http://www.mapquest.com   Mapquest, provides a detailed map and directions for any address and street in the United States.

chapter 3

Determining Case Strategy—Filing the Complaint

---

chapter objectives

In this chapter, we will discuss

- The basics of the court system
- An overview of the litigation process, including venue, jurisdiction, the complaint and summons, and discovery
- Case strategy
- How to develop a discovery plan
- Automation for the law office and an overview of technology software available for case management, document management, and litigation support
- An overview of electronic legal research tools

A. THE COURT SYSTEM—FEDERAL AND STATE COURTS

Jurisdiction is required in every kind of judicial action. It is the power of a court to hear a particular cause and to tender a binding decision as to the cause before it. To hear and determine a cause the court must have two kinds of jurisdiction:

1. **In personam** ("of the person") is the court's power to bind the parties to the court's judgment.
2. **In rem** ("of the subject matter") is the court's power to adjudicate rights regarding property located within the state in which the court sits.

A plaintiff must always affirmatively plead a proper jurisdictional basis when forming the complaint. In other words, the complaint must show that federal jurisdiction exists.

While jurisdiction refers to the power of the court to hear the subject matter and render a judgment concerning it, **venue** refers to the proper place for the trial of the particular action. It is regulated by statute and/or rules of court. Jurisdiction of the case is determined by the allegations of fact and the prayer of the **complaint.** The complaint is a statement of the dispute and describes what the plaintiff is asking for. It limits what the court can award by way of damages or other relief sought.

Jurisdiction of a court may be original or appellate. The state trial courts have **original jurisdiction**—that is, the power to try a case—except for some appeals from inferior trial courts and administrative agencies.

Generally, the attorney will make the ultimate decision to file a cause of action in state versus federal court. However, it is necessary for the paralegal to have a basic understanding of the reasons the choice is made.

1. U.S. Federal Courts

The U.S. federal courts include the Supreme Court, appellate courts, trial courts, federal courts in each state, and other entities. Figure 3.1 is a picture of the U.S. Supreme Court in Washington, D.C.

The three branches of the federal government—legislative, executive, and judicial—operate within a constitutional system known as checks and balances. This means that although each branch is formally separate form the other two, the Constitution often requires cooperation among the branches. Federal laws, for example, are passed by Congress and signed by the President. The judicial branch, in turn, has the authority to decide

Figure 3.1. Supreme Court of the United States

the constitutionality of federal laws and resolve other disputes over federal laws, but judges depend on the executive branch to enforce court decisions.

Article III of the U.S. Constitution establishes the judicial branch. The federal courts often are called the guardians of the Constitution because their rulings protect rights and liberties guaranteed by the Constitution. Through fair and impartial judgments, the federal courts interpret and apply the law to resolve disputes. The courts do not make the laws. That is the responsibility of Congress. Nor do the courts have the power to enforce the laws. That is the role of the President and the many executive branch departments and agencies.

The Constitution gives Congress the power to create federal courts other than the Supreme Court and to determine their jurisdiction. It is Congress, not the judiciary, that controls the type of cases that may be addressed in the federal courts. Congress has three other basic responsibilities that determine how the courts will operate. First, it decides how many judges there should be and where they will work. Second, through the confirmation process, Congress determines which of the President's judicial nominees ultimately become federal judges. Third, Congress approves the federal courts' budget and appropriates money for the judiciary to operate. The judiciary's budget is a very small part—substantially less than 1 percent—of the entire federal budget.

Under the Constitution, the President appoints federal judges with the "advise and consent" of the Senate. The President usually consults senators or other elected officials concerning candidates for vacancies on the federal courts.

The President's power to appoint new federal judges is not the judiciary's only interaction with the executive branch. The Department of Justice, which is responsible for prosecuting federal crimes and for representing the government in civil cases, is the most frequent litigator in the federal court system. Several other executive branch agencies affect the operations of the courts. The U.S. Marshals Service, for example, provides security for federal courthouses and judges, and the General Services Administration builds and maintains federal courthouses.

Within the executive branch there are some specialized subject-matter courts, and numerous federal administrative agencies that adjudicate disputes involving specific federal laws and benefits programs. These courts includes the U.S. Tax Court, the U.S. Court of Military Appeals, and the U.S. Court of Appeals for Veterans Claims. Although these courts and agencies are not part of the judiciary established under Article III of the Constitution, appeals of their decisions typically may be taken to the Article III courts.

An individual citizen who wishes to observe a court in session may go to the federal courthouse, check the court calendar, and watch a proceeding. Anyone may review the pleadings and other papers in a case by going to the court clerk's office and asking for the appropriate case file. Unlike most of the state courts, however, the federal courts generally do not permit television or radio coverage of trial court proceedings.

The right of public access to court proceedings is partly derived form the Constitution and partly from court tradition. By conducting their judicial work in public view, judges enhance public confidence in the courts and allow citizens to learn firsthand how our judicial system works.

In a few situations, the public may not have full access to court records and court proceedings. In a high-profile trial, for example, there may not be enough space in the courtroom to accommodate everyone who would like to observe. Access to the courtroom also may be restricted for security or privacy reasons, such as the protection of a juvenile or a confidential informant. Finally, certain documents may be placed under seal by the judge, meaning that they are not available to the public. Examples of sealed information include confidential business records, certain law enforcement reports, and juvenile records.

The Supreme Court is the highest court in the federal judiciary. Congress has established two levels of federal courts under the Supreme Court: the trial courts and the appellate courts.

a. Trial Courts

The U.S. district courts are the trial courts of the federal court system. Within limits set by Congress and the Constitution, the district courts have jurisdiction to hear nearly all categories of federal cases, including both civil and criminal matters. There are 94 federal judicial districts, including at least 1 district in each state, the District of Columbia, and Puerto Rico. Each district includes a U.S. bankruptcy court as a unit of the district court. Three territories of the United States—the Virgin Islands, Guam, and the Northern Mariana Islands—have district courts that hear federal cases, including bankruptcy cases. A list of U.S. district courts is shown in Table 3.1.

There are two special trial courts that have nationwide jurisdiction over certain types of cases. The U.S. Court of International Trade addresses cases involving international trade and customs issues. The U.S. Court of Federal Claims has jurisdiction over most claims for money damages against the United States, disputes over federal contracts, unlawful "takings" of private property by the federal government, and a variety of other claims against the United States.

According to 28 U.S.C. §1331, "district courts shall have original jurisdiction of all civil actions arising under the Constitution, laws, or treaties of the United States." The basic requirements for jurisdiction under §1331 are that the claim be based on federal law, which must be demonstrated in the complaint, and that the federal claim be substantial rather than frivolous. There are several other sections of Title 28 that grant federal courts jurisdiction to hear particular matters:

§1333   Admiralty
§1334   Bankruptcy
§1336   Interstate commerce
§1337   Commerce/antitrust
§1338   Patent, copyright, trademark
§1339   Postal
§1340   Internal Revenue Service

The general venue statute for federal district courts is 28 U.S.C. §1391, which has two basic provisions. Under §1391(a), if jurisdiction is based solely on diversity—that is, where the parties reside—venue is proper in the district (1) where "any defendant resides, if all defendants reside in the same state," or (2) where a substantial part of the events or omissions giving rise to the claim occurred or a substantial part of the property

TABLE 3.1.   U.S. DISTRICT COURTS

State	District	Number of Authorized Judgeships	Location
Alabama	Northern District	7	Birmingham, AL 35203
	Middle District	3	Montgomery, AL 36101
	Southern District	3	Mobile, AL 36602
Alaska		3	Anchorage, AK 99513
Arizona		9	Phoenix, AZ 85025
Arkansas	Eastern District	5	Little Rock, AR 72201 (5 divisions)
	Western District	6	El Dorado, AR 71730 (6 divisions)
California	Northern District	14	San Francisco, CA 94102
	Eastern District	6	Sacramento, CA 95814
	Central District	27	Los Angeles, CA 90012
	Southern District	8	San Diego, CA 92189
Colorado		7	Denver, CO 80294
Connecticut		8	New Haven, CT 06510
Delaware		4	Wilmington, DE 19801
District of Columbia		15	Washington, DC 20001
Florida	Northern District	4	Tallahassee, FL 32301
	Middle District	11	Jacksonville, FL 32201
	Southern District	17	Miami, FL 33128
Georgia	Northern District	11	Atlanta, GA 30335
	Middle District	4	Macon, GA 31202
	Southern District	3	Savannah, GA 31412
Guam		1	Agana, GU 96910
Hawaii		3	Honolulu, HI 96850
Idaho		2	Boise, ID 83724
Illinois	Northern District	22	Chicago, IL 60604
	Southern District	3	East St. Louis, IL 62202
	Central District	3	Springfield, IL 62705

continued on next page

State	District	Number of Authorized Judgeships	Location
Indiana	Northern District	5	South Bend, IN 46601
	Southern District	5	Indianapolis, IN 46204
Iowa	Northern District	2	Cedar Rapids, IA 52401
	Southern District	3	Des Moines, IA 50309
Kansas		5	Wichita, KS 67202
Kentucky	Eastern District	13	Lexington, KY 40596
	Western District	2	Louisville, KY 40202
	Eastern and Western	7	
Louisiana	Eastern District	13	New Orleans, LA 70130
	Middle District	2	Baton Rouge, LA 70821
	Western District	7	Shreveport, LA 71101
Maine		3	Portland, ME 04101
Maryland		10	Baltimore, MD 21201
Massachusetts		13	Boston, MA 02109
Michigan	Eastern District	15	Detroit, MI 48226
	Western District	4	Grand Rapids, MI 49503
Minnesota		7	St. Paul, MN 55101
Mississippi	Northern District	3	Oxford, MS 38655
	Southern District	6	Jackson, MS 39201
Missouri	Eastern District	6	St. Louis, MO 63101
	Western District	5	Kansas City, MO 64105
	Eastern and Western	2	
Montana		3	Billings, MT 59101
Nebraska		3	Omaha, NE 68101
Nevada		5	Las Vegas, NV 89101
New Hampshire		3	Concord, NH 03301
New Jersey		17	Newark, NJ 07102
New Mexico		6	Albuquerque, NM 87103

continued on next page

State	District	Number of Authorized Judgeships	Location
New York	Northern District	4	Syracuse, NY 13261
	Eastern District	15	Brooklyn, NY 11201
	Southern District	28	New York, NY 10007
	Western District	4	Buffalo, NY 14202
North Carolina	Eastern District	4	Raleigh, NC 27611
	Middle District	4	Greensboro, NC 27402
	Western District	3	Asheville, NC 28801
North Dakota		4	Bismarck, ND 58502
North Mariana Islands		1	Saipan, N. Mar. I. 96950
Ohio	Northern District	11	Cleveland, OH 44114
	Southern District	8	Columbus, OH 43215
North Dakota		4	Bismarck, ND 58502
Oklahoma	Northern District	3	Tulsa, OK 74103
	Eastern District	1	Muskogee, OK 74401
	Western District	6	Oklahoma City, OK 73102
	Northern, Eastern, and Western	1	
Oregon		6	Portland, OR 97205
Pennsylvania	Eastern District	22	Philadelphia, PA 19106
	Middle District	6	Scranton, PA 18501
	Western District	10	Pittsburgh, PA 15230
Puerto Rico		7	Hato Rey, PR 00918
Rhode Island		3	Providence, RI 02903
South Carolina		10	Columbia, SC 29201
South Dakota		3	Sioux Falls, SD 57102
Tennessee	Eastern District	5	Knoxville, TN 37901
	Middle District	4	Nashville, TN 37203
	Western District	5	Memphis, TN 38103
Texas	Northern District	12	Dallas, TX 75242
	Southern District	19	Houston, TX 77208
	Eastern District	7	Tyler, TX 75702
	Western District	11	San Antonio, TX 82061

continued on next page

State	District	Number of Authorized Judgeships	Location
Utah		5	Salt Lake City, UT 84101
Vermont		2	Burlington, VT 05402
Virginia	Eastern District	10	Alexandria, VA 22320
	Western District	4	Roanoke, VA 24006
Washington	Eastern District	4	Spokane, WA 99210
	Western District	7	Seattle, WA 98104
West Virginia	Northern District	3	Elkins, WV 26241
	Southern District	5	Charleston, WV 25329
Wisconsin	Eastern District	5	Milwaukee, WI 53022
	Western District	2	Madison, WI 53701
Wyoming		3	Cheyenne, WY 82001

involved in the action is located, or (3) where "any defendant is subject to personal jurisdiction" at the time the action is commenced. Under §1391(b), if jurisdiction is based other than solely on diversity, venue is proper on the same terms as parts (1) and (2) of §1391(a). However, if there is no other district, venue is also proper in the district "in which any defendant may be found."

Once the applicable statutes are determined, the question of a party's residence arises since §1391 is based on residence. For venue purposes, residence is viewed in much the same way as citizenship. An individual's citizenship is where the individual had permanent residence. A corporation under §1391 is considered a resident of any district "in which it is incorporated or licensed to do business or is doing business." Where a defendant is the United States or its agencies, officers, or employees, §1391(e) controls and provides that venue is generally proper—unless law provides otherwise—where the defendant resides, where a substantial portion of the events or omissions giving rise to the action occurred or a substantial part of the property involved in the action is located, or where the plaintiff resides if no property is involved.

b. Appellate Courts

The 94 judicial districts are organized into 12 regional circuits and 1 federal circuit, each of which has a U.S. court of appeals. A court of appeals hears appeals from the district courts located within its circuit, as well as appeals from decisions of federal administrative agencies. In addition, the Court of Appeals for the Federal Circuit has nationwide jurisdiction to hear appeals in specialized cases, such as those involving patent laws and cases decided by the U.S. Court of International Trade and the U.S. Court of Federal Claims.

A list of the 13 U.S. courts of appeals and the state district courts within their individual jurisdictions is shown in Table 3.2. A map showing the 13 federal circuit courts is shown in Figure 3.2.

c. U.S. Supreme Court

The **U.S. Supreme Court** consists of the Chief Justice of the United States and associate justices. At its discretion, and within certain guidelines established by Congress, the

TABLE 3.2. U.S. COURTS OF APPEALS

Federal Circuit **Washington, D.C.**	United States
District of Columbia Circuit **Washington, D.C.**	District of Columbia
First Circuit **Boston, MA**	Maine Massachusetts New Hampshire Puerto Rico Rhode Island
Second Circuit **New York, NY**	Connecticut New York Vermont
Third Circuit **Philadelphia, PA**	Delaware New Jersey Pennsylvania Virgin Islands
Fourth Circuit **Richmond, VA**	Maryland North Carolina South Carolina Virginia West Virginia
Fifth Circuit **New Orleans, LA**	Louisiana Mississippi Texas
Sixth Circuit **Cincinnati, OH**	Kentucky Michigan Ohio Tennesee
Seventh Circuit **Chicago, IL**	Illinois Indiana Wisconsin

continued on next page

Eighth Circuit **St. Louis, MO**	Arkansas Iowa Minnesota Missouri Nebraska North Dakota South Dakota
Ninth Circuit **San Francisco, CA**	Alaska Arizona California Guam Hawaii Idaho Montana Nevada North Mariana Islands Oregon Washington
Tenth Circuit **Denver, CO**	Colorado Kansas New Mexico Oklahoma Utah Wyoming
Eleventh Circuit **Atlanta, GA**	Alabama Florida Georgia

Supreme Court each year hears a limited number of the cases it is asked to decide. Those cases may begin in the federal or state courts, and they usually involve important questions about the Constitution or federal laws.

d. Jurisdiction of Federal Courts

Before a federal court can hear a case or "exercise its jurisdiction," certain conditions must be met. First, under the Constitution, federal courts exercise only judicial powers. This means that federal judges may interpret the law only through the resolution of actual legal disputes, referred to in Article III of the Constitution as "Cases or Controversies." A court cannot attempt to correct a problem on its own initiative or to answer a hypothetical legal question.

Second, assuming there is an actual case or controversy, the plaintiff in a federal lawsuit also must have legal "standing" to ask the court for a decision. That means the plaintiff must have been aggrieved, or legally harmed in some way, by the defendant.

Third, the case must present a category of dispute that the law in question was designed to address, and it must be a complaint that the court has the power to remedy.

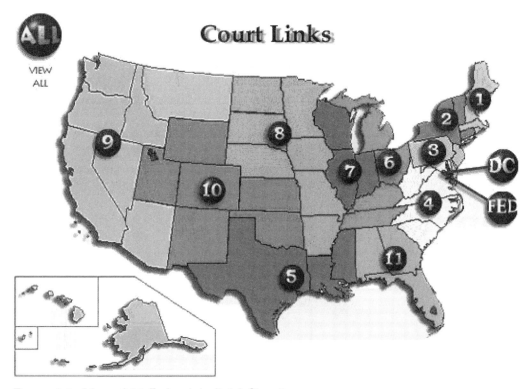

Figure 3.2. Map of 13 Federal Judicial Circuits
Reprinted from the Internet at *http://www.uscourts.gov/links.html.*

In other words, the court must be authorized, under the Constitution or a federal law, to hear the case and grant appropriate relief to the plaintiff. Finally, the case cannot be moot, that is, it must present an ongoing problem for the court to resolve. The federal courts, thus, are courts of limited jurisdiction because they may decide only certain types of cases as provided by Congress or as identified in the Constitution.

Although the details of the complex web of federal jurisdiction that Congress has given the federal courts is beyond the scope of this book, it is important to understand that there are two main sources of the cases coming before the federal courts:

1. Federal question jurisdiction
2. Diversity jurisdiction

In general, federal courts may decide cases that involve the U.S. government, the U.S. Constitution or federal laws, or controversies between states or between the United States and foreign governments. A case that raises such a "federal question" may be filed in federal court. Examples of such cases might include a claim by an individual for entitlement to money under a federal government program such as Social Security, a claim by the government that someone has violated federal laws, or a challenge to actions taken by a federal agency.

A case also may be filed in federal court based on the "diversity of citizenship" of the litigants, such as between citizens of different states, or between Untied States citizens and those of another country. To ensure fairness to the out-of-state litigant, the Constitution provides that such cases may be heard in a federal court. An important limit to diversity jurisdiction is that only cases involving more than $75,000 in potential damages may be filed in a federal court. Claims below that amount may only be pursued in state court. Moreover, any diversity jurisdiction case regardless of the amount of money involved may be brought in a state court rather than a federal court.

Federal courts also have jurisdiction over all bankruptcy matters, which Congress has determined should be addressed in federal courts rather than the state courts. Through the bankruptcy process, individuals or businesses that can no longer pay their creditors may either seek a court-supervised liquidation of their assets, or they may reorganize their financial affairs and work out a plan to pay off their debts.

Although federal courts are located in every state, they are not the only forum available to potential litigants. In fact, the great majority of legal disputes in American courts are addressed in the separate state court systems. For example, state courts have jurisdiction over virtually all divorce and child custody matters, probate and inheritance issues, real estate questions, and juvenile matters, and they handle most criminal cases, contract disputes, traffic violations, and personal injury cases. In addition, certain categories of legal disputes may be resolved in special courts or entities that are part of the federal executive or legislative branches, and by state and federal administrative agencies.

2. State Courts

Generally, in state court, an action is commenced when the first pleading is filed with the clerk of court by the person bringing the action. The person bringing the action is referred to as the plaintiff and the person against whom the action is filed is referred to as the defendant. To commence the action, the plaintiff prepares a complaint and files it with the clerk of court. Also, the plaintiff requests that a summons be issued. A summons is a notice that a legal action has been started. It is served on the defendant along with a copy of the complaint.

Thereafter, the defendant answers the complaint, files the answer with the clerk of court, and mails a copy to the plaintiff or the plaintiff's attorney. In the answer, the defendant defends against the allegations contained in the complaint by admitting or denying the facts stated therein. The defendant may also allege further facts, affirmative defenses that deny recovery to the defendant, or a counterclaim. After the answer is filed, there are other pleadings, motions, and discovery documents filed, which will be discussed in Chapter 7 and Chapter 8.

PRACTICE TIP

Knowledge of the courts and their official rules can be a timesaver in preparing, filing, amending, and obtaining copies of court documents. Knowing the names, addresses, and phone numbers of the various courthouses, clerks of court, judges, judges' clerks, and other court officials can make the paralegal's job so much easier.

B. IDENTIFYING LEGAL CLAIMS

There are no specific rules on drafting your **statement of claims,** a written declaration of the claims made against another party, but there are guidelines to follow. Rule 8(a) of the Federal Rules of Civil Procedure states the following:

> (a) Claims for Relief. A pleading which sets forth a claim for relief, whether an original claim, counterclaim, cross-claim, or third-party claim, shall contain (1) a short and plain statement of the grounds upon which the court's jurisdiction depends, unless the court already has jurisdiction and the claim needs no new grounds of jurisdiction to support it, (2) a short and plain statement of the claim showing that the pleader is entitled to relief, and (3) a demand for judgment for the relief the pleader seeks. Relief in the alternative or of several different types may be demanded.

All this is actually good news for the drafter. The statement should be "short and plain" of the grounds for jurisdiction. For individual parties involved in a lawsuit, jurisdiction would be alleged as follows:

> Jurisdiction herein is based on diversity of citizenship of the parties and the amount in controversy. Plaintiff is a citizen of the State of Montana, Defendant is a citizen of the State of California.

Rule 8(e) continues:

> *Pleading to be Concise and Direct; Consistency.*
>
> (1) Each averment of a pleading shall be simple, concise, and direct. No technical forms of pleading or motions are required.
> (2) A party may set forth two or more statements of a claim or defense alternately or hypothetically, either in one court or defense or in separate counts or defenses. When two or more statements are made in the alternative and one of them if made independently would be sufficient, the pleading is not made insufficient by the insufficiency of one or more of the alternative statements. A party may state as many separate claims or defenses as the party has regardless of consistency and whether based on legal, equitable, or maritime grounds. All statements shall be made subject to the obligations set forth in Rule 11.

It is a good idea to follow the guidelines below when drafting your statement of claims.

1. Stay away from legalese such as "the party of the first part." The idea is to state your claim, not impress the reader with your legal prowess. Use plain English, everyday language that can be easily understood.
2. Keep it short, simple, and concise. Your statement of claims does not have to be a long diatribe or a learned treatise. Make it as short as possible. Make it very simple, easy to follow, and try to keep events in chronological order.
3. Tell your story by providing pertinent facts. Identify your parties and provide pertinent facts such as dates, times, locations, and so on. A statement of claims is simply that—your client's story that led to the filing of the lawsuit.
4. Remember what you learned in English class. Use separate paragraphs, full sentences, and grouped thoughts.

Below is an example of a simple, well-written statement of claims in a personal injury case.

1. Plaintiff Mary Doe is a resident of Anytown, California, and defendant John Brown is a resident of Pleasantville, Oregon.
2. On January 1, 2000, at approximately 11:00 P.M., plaintiff Mary Doe was driving her 1993 Chevy Impala eastbound on I-93 near Anytown, California.
3. On January 1, 2000, at approximately 11:00 P.M. defendant John Brown was driving his 1999 Dodge Durango westbound on I-93 near Anytown, California.
4. Doe negligently crossed the center lane of I-93 and struck Brown's vehicle, seriously injuring Mr. Brown.

Separate counts should be used when pleading different theories of recovery. **Theories of recovery** are defined as the bases of recovery against the opposing party. This enables the drafter to set out each theory clearly and is accomplished through the use of counts. Counts in a pleading are individual claims made by plaintiff against the defendant. Counts are separate causes of action alleged in the same complaint. Each cause of action alleged can be based on the same set of circumstances or same occurrence. An example of separate counts follows. Note that each legal theory is labeled in the heading of each count.

COUNT I—Breach of Warranty

COUNT II—Strict Liability

Plaintiff restates and realleges the allegations contained in paragraphs 1-15 of Count I as if fully restated herein.
[Drafter goes on to state cause of action on different theory of strict liability.]

COUNT III—Negligence

Plaintiff restates and realleges the allegations contained in paragraphs 1-15 of Count I as if fully restated herein.

C. CHOICE OF FORUM, JURISDICTION, AND VENUE

1. Choice of Forum

Choice of forum is very important and involves the process of choosing the suitable court for resolution of a legal matter. Sometimes this process is also referred to establishing jurisdiction. Jurisdiction is the location in which a case belongs, or the power or authority of a court to hear or decide a given case of question of fact or law. The forum, then, is the place where plaintiffs and defendants can litigate their claims. Therefore, attorneys have a choice as to where to file their client's claims or cause of action. In choosing a forum, attorneys are mindful of procedural differences in the various courts. The eventual choice of a forum will depend on jurisdiction and venue.

2. Jurisdiction

There are different types of jurisdiction. However, there are two main types, subject matter and personal.

1. **Subject matter jurisdiction** is the power of a court to hear particular matters, while **general subject matter jurisdiction** is the court's power to hear and determine cases of the proceeding's general category.
2. **Personal jurisdiction** is the court's power over the person.

State courts have general subject matter jurisdiction and generally can hear any type of case. However, that has been changing from state to state. For example, many states now have domestic courts, probate courts, or small claims courts.

Federal courts have limited subject matter jurisdiction. There are two types of subject matter jurisdiction for federal courts:

1. Federal question
2. Diversity/amount in controversy

Federal question jurisdiction is discussed in section A1d above. Diversity refers to the citizenship of the parties. More simply, it means where the parties reside. Therefore, diversity of citizenship refers to citizens of different states. 28 U.S.C. §1332 states:

> (a) The district courts shall have original jurisdiction of all civil actions where the matter in controversy exceeds the sum or value of $75,000, exclusive of interest and costs, and is between—
> (1) citizens of different states;
> (2) citizens of a state and citizens or subjects of a foreign state;
> (3) citizens of different states and in which citizens or subjects of a foreign state are additional parties; and
> (4) a foreign state, defined in section 1603(a) of this title, as plaintiff and citizens of a State or different States.

As outlined in 28 U.S.C. §1251, the U.S. Supreme Court has what is known as original jurisdiction in certain cases such as controversies between two or more states, actions involving ambassadors, controversies between the United States and a state, and actions by a state against the citizen of another state.

Federal court jurisdiction is based on the following four types of cases:

1. Cases presenting questions arising under the Constitution, laws, or treaties of the United States.
2. Cases involving sums of more than $75,000.
3. Cases involving diversity of citizenship.
4. Cases of original jurisdiction.

3. Venue

Venue statutes control where plaintiff files the initial complaint against the defendant. Again, venue is the geographic location where a case can be heard. It is a concept aligned to jurisdiction, which determines

- The court that should hear the case based on convenience of the parties
- Location of witnesses and evidence
- Place where the event in question happened
- Fundamental fairness

Generally, in federal courts, if jurisdiction is based solely on diversity, venue is proper in one of the three districts stated in 28 U.S.C. §1391(a):

1. In the district where the defendant resides
2. In the district in which a substantial part of the property is situated, or a substantial amount of the events occurred
3. In the district in which any defendant is subject to personal jurisdiction at the time the action is commenced

> **Venue generally.** (a) A civil action wherein jurisdiction is founded only on diversity of citizenship may, except as otherwise provided by law, be brought only in (1) a judicial district where any defendant resides, if all defendants reside in the same State (2) a judicial district in which a substantial part of the events or omissions giving rise to the claim occurred, or a substantial part of the property that is the subject of the action is situated, or (3) a judicial district in which any defendant is subject to personal jurisdiction at the time the action is commenced, if there is no district in which the action may otherwise be brought.

Generally, if jurisdiction is not founded solely on diversity of citizenship, venue is proper in one of the three districts stated in 28 U.S.C. §1391(b):

> (b) A civil action wherein jurisdiction is not founded solely on diversity of citizenship may, except as otherwise provided by law, be brought only in (1) a judicial district where any defendant resides, if all defendants reside in the same State, (2) a judicial district in which a substantial part of the events or omissions giving rise to the claim occurred, or a substantial part of property that is the subject of the action is situated, or (3) a judicial district in which any defendant may be found, if there is no district in which any defendant may be found, if there is no district in which the action may otherwise be brought.

There are, of course, additional venue considerations if the defendant is a corporation. For purposes of this discussion, that information can be found at part 28 U.S.C. §1391(c). Additional special venue statutes can be found in 28 U.S.C. §1394 and elsewhere in the Code. It is always good practice to review the statutes to see if a special venue statute applies to your case and overrides the general provisions discussed above.

A motion can be made for a change in venue. Motions can be made for venue changes due to improper venue, prejudicial publicity, or convenience of the parties. The federal statute dealing with change of venue can be found at 28 U.S.C. §1412, which states:

> A district court may transfer a case or proceeding under Title 11 to a district court for another district, in the interest of justice or for the convenience of the parties.

The decisions regarding jurisdiction and venue can be complicated and involve much discussion on case strategy. A lengthy discussion with your supervising attorney should be carried out prior to drafting the complaint. All states have their own jurisdictional and venue statutes, so be sure to check the particular state's codes prior to drafting your complaint.

D. DRAFTING THE COMPLAINT

After the questions concerning jurisdiction, venue, and forum have been determined, the paralegal will draft the complaint. The **complaint** is a pleading that commences an action and seeks relief based on a particular set of facts and circumstances. All complaints, whether filed in state or federal court, have the following components:

1. Caption
2. Jurisdiction
3. Identification of parties
4. Body of complaint
5. Prayer for relief
6. Signature
7. Verification
8. Demand for jury trial

The caption identifies the court and parties.

ATTORNEY NAME, ADDRESS, PHONE

IN THE UNITED STATES DISTRICT COURT
FOR THE DISTRICT OF MONTANA
BILLINGS DIVISION

MARY DOE,		
	Plaintiff,	)))) Case No. CV 97 114 BLG JDS
vs.		))) TITLE OF PLEADING
ABC CORPORATION, a Foreign Corporation,		)))
	Defendant.	)

The parties are briefly described in the introductory paragraphs of the complaint.

1. Mary Doe resides in Montana.
2. ABC Corporation is a foreign corporation with its principal place of business in the State of Delaware.

The body of the complaint contains the factual allegations pertaining to the specific cause of action and various legal theories of the case. Here is where the drafter will tell the "story" of the case.

The prayer for relief contains what the plaintiff is requesting the court to do. Here is where the drafter states the remedy and types of relief requested. For example, in a personal injury case, the drafter may request monetary damages for medical bills, pain and suffering, loss of enjoyment of life, and future medical bills.

The signature component contains the signature of the attorney representing the plaintiff. The Federal Rules of Civil Procedure states that the pleading must be signed by one attorney of record. That signature indicates the attorney has read the pleading, that the facts contained therein are true to the attorney's best knowledge and belief, and that the cause of action is well grounded in fact. It is good practice, if at all possible, to have the plaintiff sign the complaint as well. Since the plaintiff has provided the facts on which the complaint was based, his or her signature attests to the same facts as the attorney. Ideally, initial investigation and verification of facts has already occurred, providing further evidence of the plaintiff's cause of action.

The verification indicates that the party to the lawsuit has read the complaint and that all the facts contained therein are true and correct to the best of his or her knowledge and belief. The demand for jury trial is simply that, the plaintiff is demanding a trial by jury. Note that the defendant can also demand a jury trial when he files his or her answer.

According to Rule 3 of the Federal Rules of Civil Procedure, "A civil action is commenced by filing a complaint with the court."

E. DRAFTING THE SUMMONS

Once the complaint is prepared, a summons is drafted. The **summons** is both a pleading used to commence a civil action and a process directed to the person named that an action has been commenced against him or her. The **summons** is issued by the clerk of court, and a separate summons is issued for each defendant. Federal courts also require a civil cover sheet when filing the cause of action. The cover sheet is self-explanatory and covers the areas previously discussed in this chapter.

Rule 4 of the Federal Rules of Civil Procedure deals with drafting the summons.

Rule 4.   *Summons*

(a) Form.

The summons shall be signed by the clerk, bear the seal of the court, identify the court and the parties, be directed to the defendant, and state the name and address of the plaintiff's attorney or, if unrepresented, of the plaintiff. It shall also state the time within which the defendant must appear and defend, and notify the defendant that failure to do so will result in a judgment by default against the defendant for the relief demanded in the complaint. The court may allow a summons to be amended.

(b) Issuance.

Upon or after filing the complaint, the plaintiff may present a summons to the clerk for signature and seal. If the summons is in proper form, the clerk shall sign, seal, and issue it to the plaintiff for service on the defendant. A summons, or a copy of the summons if addressed to multiple defendants, shall be issued for each defendant to be served.

(c) Service with Complaint; by Whom Made.

(1) A summons shall be served together with a copy of the complaint. The plaintiff is responsible for service of a summons and complaint within the time

allowed under subdivision (m) and shall furnish the person effecting service with the necessary copies of the summons and complaint.

(2) Service may be effected by any person who is not a party and who is at least 18 years of age. At the request of the plaintiff, however, the court may direct that service be effected by a United States marshal, deputy United States marshal, or other person or officer specially appointed by the court for that purpose. Such an appointment must be made when the plaintiff is authorized to proceed in forma pauperis pursuant to 28 U.S.C. §1915 or is authorized to proceed as a seaman under 28 U.S.C. §1916.

(d) Waiver of Service; Duty to Save Costs of Service; Request to Waive.

(1) A defendant who waives service of a summons does not thereby waive any objection to the venue or to the jurisdiction of the court over the person of the defendant.

(2) An individual, corporation, or association that is subject to service under subdivision (e), (f), or (h) and that receives notice of an action in the manner provided in this paragraph has a duty to avoid unnecessary costs of serving the summons. To avoid costs, the plaintiff may notify such a defendant of the commencement of the action and request that the defendant waive service of a summons. The notice and request

(A) shall be in writing and shall be addressed directly to the defendant, if an individual, or else to an officer or managing or general agent (or other agent authorized by appointment or law to receive service of process) of a defendant subject to service under subdivision (h) ;

(B) shall be dispatched through first-class mail or other reliable means;

(C) shall be accompanied by a copy of the complaint and shall identify the court in which it has been filed;

(D) shall inform the defendant, by means of a text prescribed in an official form promulgated pursuant to Rule 84, of the consequences of compliance and of a failure to comply with the request;

(E) shall set forth the date on which request is sent;

(F) shall allow the defendant a reasonable time to return the waiver, which shall be at least 30 days from the date on which the request is sent, or 60 days from that date if the defendant is addressed outside any judicial district of the United States; and

(G) shall provide the defendant with an extra copy of the notice and request, as well as a prepaid means of compliance in writing. If a defendant located within the United States fails to comply with a request for waiver made by a plaintiff located within the United States, the court shall impose the costs subsequently incurred in effecting service on the defendant unless good cause for the failure be shown.

(3) A defendant that, before being served with process, timely returns a waiver so requested is not required to serve an answer to the complaint until 60 days after the date on which the request for waiver of service was sent, or 90 days after that date if the defendant was addressed outside any judicial district of the United States.

(4) When the plaintiff files a waiver of service with the court, the action shall proceed, except as provided in paragraph (3), as if a summons and complaint had been served at the time of filing the waiver, and no proof of service shall be required.

(5) The costs to be imposed on a defendant under paragraph (2) for failure to comply with a request to waive service of a summons shall include the costs subsequently incurred in effecting service under subdivision (e), (f), or (h), together with the costs, including a reasonable attorney's fee, of any motion required to collect the costs of service.

(e) Service Upon Individuals Within a Judicial District of the United States.
Unless otherwise provided by federal law, service upon an individual from whom a waiver has not been obtained and filed, other than an infant or an incompetent person, may be effected in any judicial district of the United States:

(1) pursuant to the law of the state in which the district court is located, or in which service is effected, for the service of a summons upon the defendant in an action brought in the courts of general jurisdiction of the State; or

(2) by delivering a copy of the summons and of the complaint to the individual personally or by leaving copies thereof at the individual's dwelling house or usual place of abode with some person of suitable age and discretion then residing therein or by delivering a copy of the summons and of the complaint to an agent authorized by appointment or by law to receive service of process.

(f) Service Upon Individuals in a Foreign Country.
Unless otherwise provided by federal law, service upon an individual from whom a waiver has not been obtained and filed, other than an infant or an incompetent person, may be effected in a place not within any judicial district of the United States:

(1) by any internationally agreed means reasonably calculated to give notice, such as those means authorized by the Hague Convention on the Service Abroad of Judicial and Extrajudicial Documents; or

(2) if there is no internationally agreed means of service or the applicable international agreement allows other means of service, provided that service is reasonably calculated to give notice:

(A) in the manner prescribed by the law of the foreign country for service in that country in an action in any of its courts of general jurisdiction; or

(B) as directed by the foreign authority in response to a letter rogatory or letter of request; or

(C) unless prohibited by the law of the foreign country, by

(i) delivery to the individual personally of a copy of the summons and the complaint; or

(ii) any form of mail requiring a signed receipt, to be addressed and dispatched by the clerk of the court to the party to be served; or

(3) by other means not prohibited by international agreement as may be directed by the court.

(g) Service Upon Infants and Incompetent Person.
Service upon an infant or an incompetent person in a judicial district of the United States shall be effected in the manner prescribed by the law of the state in

which the service is made for the service of summons or like process upon any such defendant in an action brought in the courts of general jurisdiction of that state. Service upon an infant or an incompetent person in a place not within any judicial district of the United States shall be effected in the manner prescribed by paragraph (2)(A) or (2)(B) of subdivision (f) or by such means as the court may direct.

(h) Service Upon Corporations and Associations.

Unless otherwise provided by federal law, service upon a domestic or foreign corporation or upon a partnership or other unincorporated association that is subject to suit under a common name, and from which a waiver of service has not been obtained and filed, shall be effected:

(1) in a judicial district of the United States in the manner prescribed for individuals by subdivision (e)(1), or by delivering a copy of the summons and of the complaint to an officer, a managing or general agent, or to any other agent authorized by appointment or by law to receive service of process and, if the agent is one authorized by statute to receive service and the statute so requires, by also mailing a copy to the defendant, or

(2) in a place not within any judicial district of the United States in any manner prescribed for individuals by subdivision (f) except personal delivery as provided in paragraph (2)(C)(i) thereof.

(i) Service Upon the United States, and its Agencies, Corporations, or Officers.

(1) Service upon the United States shall be effected

(A) by delivering a copy of the summons and of the complaint to the United States attorney for the district in which the action is brought or to an assistant United States attorney or clerical employee designated by the United States attorney in a writing filed with the clerk of the court or by sending a copy of the summons and of the complaint by registered or certified mail addressed to the civil process clerk at the office of the United States attorney and

(B) by also sending a copy of the summons and of the complaint by registered or certified mail to the Attorney General of the United States at Washington, District of Columbia, and

(C) in any action attacking the validity of an order of an officer or agency of the United States not made a party, by also sending a copy of the summons and of the complaint by registered or certified mail to the officer or agency.

(2) Service upon an officer, agency, or corporation of the United States shall be effected by serving the United States in the manner prescribed by paragraph (1) of this subdivision and by also sending a copy of the summons and of the complaint by registered or certified mail to the officer, agency, or corporation.

(3) The court shall allow a reasonable time for service of process under this subdivision for the purpose of curing the failure to serve multiple officers, agencies, or corporations of the United States if the plaintiff has effected service on either the United States attorney or the Attorney General of the United States.

(j) Service Upon Foreign, State, or Local Governments.

(1) Service upon a foreign state or a political subdivision, agency, or instrumentality thereof shall be effected pursuant to 28 U.S.C. §1608.

(2) Service upon a state, municipal corporation, or other governmental organization subject to suit, shall be effected by delivering a copy of the summons and of the complaint to its chief executive officer or by serving the summons and complaint in the manner prescribed by the law of that state for the service of summons or other like process upon any such defendant.

(k) Territorial Limits of Effective Service.

(1) Service of a summons or filing a waiver of service is effective to establish jurisdiction over the person of a defendant

(A) who could be subjected to the jurisdiction of a court of general jurisdiction in the state in which the district court is located, or

(B) who is a party joined under Rule 14 or Rule 19 and is served at a place within a judicial district of the United States and not more than 100 miles from the place from which the summons issues, or

(C) who is subject to the federal interpleader jurisdiction under 28 U.S.C. §1335, or

(D) when authorized by a statute of the United States.

(2) If the exercise of jurisdiction is consistent with the Constitution and laws of the United States, serving a summons or filing a waiver of service is also effective, with respect to claims arising under federal law, to establish personal jurisdiction over the person of any defendant who is not subject to the jurisdiction of the courts of general jurisdiction of any state.

(l) Proof of Service.

If service is not waived, the person effecting service shall make proof thereof to the court. If service is made by a person other than a United States marshal or deputy United States marshal, the person shall make affidavit thereof. Proof of service in a place not within any judicial district of the United States shall, if effected under paragraph (1) of subdivision (f), be made pursuant to the applicable treaty or convention, and shall, if effected under paragraph (2) or (3) thereof, include a receipt signed by the addressee or other evidence of delivery to the addressee satisfactory to the court. Failure to make proof of service does not affect the validity of the service. The court may allow proof of service to be amended.

F. TIME CONSIDERATIONS IN SERVICE

The Summons must be served within 120 days after the filing of the complaint. If it is not, the court may dismiss the action. Rule 4(m) of the Federal Rules of Civil Procedure states:

(m) Time Limit for Service.

If service of the summons and complaint is not made upon a defendant within 120 days after the filing of the complaint, the court, upon motion or on its own initiative after notice to the plaintiff, shall dismiss the action without prejudice as to that defendant or direct that service be effected within a specified time; provided that if the plaintiff shows good cause for the failure, the court shall extend the time for service for an appropriate period. This subdivision does not apply to service in a foreign country pursuant to subdivision (f) or (j)(1).

It is also important to look at Rule 6(a) of the Federal Rules of Civil Procedure which rules deals with how to compute time periods under the rules:

> In computing any period of time prescribed or allowed by these rules, by the local rules of any district court, by order of court, or by any applicable statute, the day of the act, event, or default from which the designated period of time begins to run shall not be included. The last day of the period so computed shall be included, unless it is a Saturday, a Sunday, or a legal holiday, or, when the act to be done is the filing of a paper in court, a day on which weather or other conditions have made the office of the clerk of the district court inaccessible, in which event the period runs until the end of the next day which is not one of the aforementioned days. When the period of time prescribed or allowed is less than 11 days, intermediate Saturdays, Sundays, and legal holidays shall be excluded in the computation. As used in this rule and in Rule 77(c), "legal holiday" includes New Year's Day, Birthday of Martin Luther King, Jr., Washington's Birthday, Memorial Day, Independence Day, Labor Day, Columbus Day, Veterans Day, Thanksgiving Day, Christmas Day, and any other day appointed as a holiday by the President or the Congress of the United States, or by the state in which the district court is held.

It is important to note that if the time period allowed is less than 11 days, Saturdays, Sundays and legal holidays are not included in the computation of time. The rule also set forth "legal holidays" considered in this Rule.

Note that according to Rule 4(b) the court can, on motion or by its own discretion, increase the time period allowed:

(b) Enlargement.

When by these rules or by a notice given thereunder or by order of court an act is required or allowed to be done at or within a specified time, the court for cause shown may at any time in its discretion (1) with or without motion or notice order the period enlarged if request therefor is made before the expiration of the period originally prescribed or as extended by a previous order, or (2) upon motion made after the expiration of the specified period permit the act to be done where the failure to act was the result of excusable neglect; but it may not extend the time for taking any action under Rule 50(b) and (c)(2), 52(b), 59(b), (d) and (e), 60(b), and 74(a), except to the extent and under the conditions stated in them.

G. DISCOVERY

1. Overview

Discovery is the disclosure of information previously unknown. Subject to certain limitations, discovery is a formal, pretrial process designed to give all parties access to the same evidence that will then be available at the time of trial. If each party knows what all other parties know about the case, a more accurate assessment of the case is possible, and pretrial settlement is more probable.

It is important to keep in the mind the purposes of discovery as well as the relationship that discovery has to the issues.

a. Purposes of Discovery

The purposes of discovery are

- To obtain evidence that might not be available at trial because of a witness's age, poor health, or absence from the jurisdiction
- To narrow the issues for trial
- To avoid unfair surprise during trial
- To encourage settlement before trial

b. Relationship to Issues

Early identification and clarification of issues is essential to meaningful and fair discovery control. Fundamental to control is that discovery be directed at the material issues of the case.

The general principle governing the scope of discovery is found in Federal Rule of Civil Procedure 26(b)(1):

> Parties may obtain discovery regarding any matter, not privileged, that is relevant to the claim or defense of the party. . . . Relevant information need not be admissible at the trial if the discovery appears reasonably calculated to lead to the discovery of admissible evidence.

Discovery sought must be "relevant to the subject matter [of] the action," and "[t]he information sought [must appear] reasonably calculated to lead to the discovery of admissible evidence." These are important considerations to remember.

Rule 26 of the Federal Rules of Civil Procedure states the following guidelines for discovery.

(a) Required Disclosures; Methods to Discover Additional Matter.
(1) Initial Disclosures.

Except to the extent otherwise stipulated or directed by order or local rule, a party shall, without awaiting a discovery request, provide to other parties:

(A) the name and, if known, the address and telephone number of each individual likely to have discoverable information relevant to disputed facts alleged with particularity in the pleadings, identifying the subjects of the information;

(B) a copy of, or a description by category and location of, all documents, data compilations, and tangible things in the possession, custody, or control of the party that are relevant to disputed facts alleged with particularity in the pleadings;

(C) a computation of any category of damages claimed by the disclosing party, making available for inspection and copying as under Rule 34 the documents or other evidentiary material, not privileged or protected from disclosure, on which such computation is based, including materials bearing on the nature and extent of injuries suffered; and

(D) for inspection and copying as under Rule 34 any insurance agreement under which any person carrying on an insurance business may be liable to satisfy part or all of a judgment which may be entered in the action or to indemnify or reimburse for payments made to satisfy the judgment.

Unless otherwise stipulated or directed by the court, these disclosures shall be made at or within 10 days after the meeting of the parties under subdivision (f). A party shall make its initial disclosures based on the information then reasonably available to it and is not excused from making its disclosures because it has not fully completed its investigation of the case or because it challenges the sufficiency of another party's disclosures or because another party has not made its disclosures.

(2) Disclosure of Expert Testimony.

(A) In addition to the disclosures required by paragraph (1), a party shall disclose to other parties the identity of any person who may be used at trial to present evidence under Rules 702, 703, or 705 of the Federal Rules of Evidence.

(B) Except as otherwise stipulated or directed by the court, this disclosure shall, with respect to a witness who is retained or specially employed to provide expert testimony in the case or whose duties as an employee of the party regularly involve giving expert testimony, be accompanied by a written report prepared and signed by the witness. The report shall contain a complete statement of all opinions to be expressed and the basis and reasons therefor; the data or other information considered by the witness in forming the opinions; any exhibits to be used as a summary of or support for the opinions; the qualifications of the witness, including a list of all publications authored by the witness within the preceding ten years; the compensation to be paid for the study and testimony; and a listing of any other cases in which the witness has testified as an expert at trial or by deposition within the preceding four years.

(C) These disclosures shall be made at the times and in the sequence directed by the court. In the absence of other directions from the court or stipulation by the parties, the disclosures shall be made at least 90 days before the trial date or the date the case is to be ready for trial or, if the evidence is intended solely to contradict or rebut evidence on the same subject matter identified by another party under paragraph (2)(B), within 30 days after the disclosure made by the other party. The parties shall supplement these disclosures when required under subdivision (e)(1).

(3) Pretrial Disclosures.

In addition to the disclosures required in the preceding paragraphs, a party shall provide to other parties the following information regarding the evidence that it may present at trial other than solely for impeachment purposes:

(A) the name and, if not previously provided, the address and telephone number of each witness, separately identifying those whom the party expects to present and those whom the party may call if the need arises;

(B) the designation of those witnesses whose testimony is expected to be presented by means of a deposition and, if not taken stenographically, a transcript of the pertinent portions of the deposition testimony; and

(C) an appropriate identification of each document or other exhibit, including summaries of other evidence, separately identifying those which the party expects to offer and those which the party may offer if the need arises.

Unless otherwise directed by the court, these disclosures shall be made at least 30 days before trial. Within 14 days thereafter, unless a different time is specified by the court, a party may serve and file a list disclosing (i) any objections to the use under Rule 32(a) of a deposition designated by another party under subparagraph (B) and (ii) any objection, together with the grounds therefor, that may be made to the admissibility of materials identified under subparagraph (C). Objections not so disclosed, other than objections under Rules 402 and 403 of the Federal Rules of Evidence, shall be deemed waived unless excused by the court for good cause shown.

(4) Form of Disclosures; Filing.

Unless otherwise directed by order or local rule, all disclosures under paragraphs (1) through (3) shall be made in writing, signed, served, and promptly filed with the court.

(5) Methods to Discover Additional Matter.

Parties may obtain discovery by one or more of the following methods: depositions upon oral examination or written questions; written interrogatories; production of documents or things or permission to enter upon land or other property under Rule 34 or 45(a)(1) or (C), for inspection and other purposes; physical and mental examinations; and requests for admission.

(b) Discovery Scope and Limits.

Unless otherwise limited by order of the court in accordance with these rules, the scope of discovery is as follows:

(1) In General.

Parties may obtain discovery regarding any matter, not privileged, which is relevant to the subject matter involved in the pending action, whether it relates to the claim or defense of the party seeking discovery or to the claim or defense of any other party, including the existence, description, nature, custody, condition, and location of any books, documents, or other tangible things and the identity and location of persons having knowledge of any discoverable matter. The information sought need not be admissible at the trial if the information sought appears reasonably calculated to lead to the discovery of admissible evidence.

(2) Limitations.

By order or by local rule, the court may alter the limits in these rules on the number of depositions and interrogatories and may also limit the length of depositions under Rule 30 and the number of requests under Rule 36. The frequency or extent of use of the discovery methods otherwise permitted under these rules and by any local rule shall be limited by the court if it determines that: (i) the discovery sought is unreasonably cumulative or duplicative, or is obtainable from some other source that is more convenient, less burdensome, or less expensive; (ii) the party seeking discovery has had ample opportunity by discovery in the action to obtain the information sought; or (iii) the burden or expense of the proposed discovery outweighs its likely benefit, taking into account the needs of the case, the amount in controversy, the parties' resources, the importance of the issues at stake in the litigation, and the importance of the proposed discovery in resolving the issues. The court may act upon its own initiative after reasonable notice or pursuant to a motion under subdivision (c).

(3) Trial Preparation: Materials.

Subject to the provisions of subdivision (b)(4) of this rule, a party may obtain discovery of documents and tangible things otherwise discoverable under subdivision (b)(1) of this rule and prepared in anticipation of litigation or for trial by or for another party or by or for that other party's representative (including the other party's attorney, consultant, surety, indemnitor, insurer, or agent) only upon a showing that the party seeking discovery has substantial need of the materials in the preparation of the party's case and that the party is unable without undue hardship to obtain the substantial equivalent of the materials by other means. In ordering discovery of such materials when the required showing has been made, the court shall protect against disclosure of the mental impressions, conclusions, opinions, or legal theories of an attorney or other representative of a party concerning the litigation.

A party may obtain without the required showing a statement concerning the action or its subject matter previously made by that party. Upon request, a person not a party may obtain without the required showing a statement concerning the action or its subject matter previously made by that person. If the request is refused, the person may move for a court order. The provisions of Rule 37(a)(4) apply to the award of expenses incurred in relation to the motion. For purposes of this paragraph, a statement previously made is (A) a written statement signed or otherwise adopted or approved by the person making it, or (B) a stenographic, mechanical, electrical, or other recording, or a transcription thereof, which is a substantially verbatim recital of an oral statement by the person making it and contemporaneously recorded.

(4) Trial Preparation: Experts.

(A) A party may depose any person who has been identified as an expert whose opinions may be presented at trial. If a report from the expert is required under subdivision (a)(2)(B), the deposition shall not be conducted until after the report is provided.

(B) A party may, through interrogatories or by deposition, discover facts known or opinions held by an expert who has been retained or specially employed by another party in anticipation of litigation or preparation for trial and who is not expected to be called as a witness at trial, only as provided in Rule 35(b) or upon a showing of exceptional circumstances under which it is impracticable for the party seeking discovery to obtain facts or opinions on the same subject by other means.

(C) Unless manifest injustice would result, (i) the court shall require that the party seeking discovery pay the expert a reasonable fee for time spent in responding to discovery under this subdivision; and (ii) with respect to discovery obtained under subdivision (b)(4)(B) of this rule the court shall require the party seeking discovery to pay the other party a fair portion of the fees and expenses reasonably incurred by the latter party in obtaining facts and opinions from the expert.

(5) Claims of Privilege or Protection of Trial Preparation Materials.

When a party withholds information otherwise discoverable under these rules by claiming that it is privileged or subject to protection as trial preparation material, the party shall make the claim expressly and shall describe the nature of the documents, communications, or things not produced or disclosed in a manner that, without revealing information itself privileged or protected, will enable other parties to assess the applicability of the privilege or protection.

(c) Protective Orders.

Upon motion by a party or by the person from whom discovery is sought, accompanied by a certification that the movant has in good faith conferred or attempted to confer with other affected parties in an effort to resolve the dispute without court action, and for good cause shown, the court in which the action is pending or alternatively, on matters relating to a deposition, the court in the district where the deposition is to be taken may make any order which justice requires to protect a party or person from annoyance, embarrassment, oppression, or undue burden or expense, including one or more of the following:

(1) that the disclosure or discovery not be had;

(2) that the disclosure or discovery may be had only on specified terms and conditions, including a designation of the time or place;

(3) that the discovery may be had only by a method of discovery other than that selected by the party seeking discovery;

(4) that certain matters not be inquired into, or that the scope of the disclosure or discovery be limited to certain matters;

(5) that discovery be conducted with no one present except persons designated by the court;

(6) that a deposition, after being sealed, be opened only by order of the court;

(7) that a trade secret or other confidential research, development, or commercial information not be revealed or be revealed only in a designated way; and

(8) that the parties simultaneously file specified documents or information enclosed in sealed envelopes to be opened as directed by the court.

If the motion for a protective order is denied in whole or in part, the court may, on such terms and conditions as are just, order that any party or other person provide or permit discovery. The provisions of Rule 37(a)(4) apply to the award of expenses incurred in relation to the motion.

(d) Timing and Sequence of Discovery.

Except when authorized under these rules or by local rule, order, or agreement of the parties, a party may not seek discovery from any source before the parties have met and conferred as required by subdivision (f). Unless the court upon motion, for the convenience of parties and witnesses and in the interests of justice, orders otherwise, methods of discovery may be used in any sequence, and the fact that a party is conducting discovery, whether by deposition or otherwise, shall not operate to delay any other party's discovery.

All parties are under a duty to supplement their responses upon learning new information or uncovering new documents not previously disclosed.

c. Types of Discovery

There are five types of discovery. Generally interrogatories, requests to produce, and depositions are used on a routine basis. Requests for physical and mental examination of persons and requests for admissions are also used in specific circumstances. The five types of discovery are

1. Interrogatories
2. Requests to produce documents or things for inspection
3. Requests for physical and mental examination of persons
4. Requests for admission of facts
5. Depositions

Every paralegal should take the time once a year to review the Rules of Civil Procedure, both state and federal. If you are like most of us, we seldom have the time—or make the time—to perform such a review. Yet it is absolutely essential to our jobs. Most state rules of civil procedure mirror the federal rules.

Interrogatories are written questions prepared and sent to the opposite party before trial. They usually must be answered within 30 days. The answers are signed by the client, and the attorney signs if there are any objections to the questions asked.

Requests to produce documents or things are written questions asking that the party produce certain documentation relevant to the cause of action that could lead to the discovery of admissible advice. Again, the client signs, as does the attorney if there are any objections.

Requests for physical or mental examination of persons requests that the party who has put his or her mental or physical condition at issue be required to submit to an independent medical examination to determine the extent of injury, or the physical or mental condition of that party. They may also request to inspect property. Usually the parties can agree on this issue, and this formal request does not become necessary.

Requests for admissions of fact ask a party to admit or deny the truth of a particular statement. If an admission is not specifically denied, it will be deemed admitted. Therefore, it is extremely important that the paralegal docket when the requests come in and make sure they are responded to in a timely fashion. Usually the time within which you must answer is 30 days.

Depositions are oral questions asked by one party to another in a formal process. The attorneys for the parties ask the questions before a court reporter, and the court reporter records the responses. Then the court reporter transcribes the recording into a hardcopy and provides the parties with copies of the deposition. Most court reporters today have the ability to provide not only a hardcopy of the transcript, but also a disk copy. It is best if you, when scheduling depositions, request that the court reporter also provide an ASCII disk so that the full text of the deposition can be loaded into your specific database. Be sure you know what format the ACSII disk must be in so that it will be compatible with your database. The attorney and paralegal then have full-text capacity to search the transcript. Not only does it aid in searching, but it will also aid in digesting the deposition. Digesting a deposition consists of summarizing or outlining the key facts or issues.

Many law firms now use combined discovery requests—discovery requests that include interrogatories, requests for production, and requests for admission. This is an efficient and cost-effective way of conducting discovery by combining everything into one pleading. However, again, caution must be used when you are served with such a document to make sure the requests for admission are denied, if appropriate, in a timely manner.

The rules governing the various types of discovery are listed below.

Rule 30.   *Deposition Upon Oral Examination.*

(a) When Depositions May Be Taken; When Leave Required.

(1) A party may take the testimony of any person, including a party, by deposition upon oral examination without leave of court except as provided in paragraph (2). The attendance of witnesses may be compelled by subpoena as provided in Rule 45.

(2) A party must obtain leave of court, which shall be granted to the extent consistent with the principles stated in Rule 26(b)(2), if the person to be examined is confined in prison or if, without the written stipulation of the parties.

(A) a proposed deposition would result in more than ten depositions being taken under this rule or Rule 31 by the plaintiffs, or by the defendants, or by third-party defendants;

(B) the person to be examined already has been deposed in the case; or

(C) a party seeks to take a deposition before the time specified in Rule 26(d) unless the notice contains a certification, with supporting facts, that the person to be examined is expected to leave the United States and be unavailable for examination in this country unless deposed before that time.

(b) Notice of Examination: General Requirements; Method of Recording; Production of Documents and Things; Deposition of Organization; Deposition by Telephone.

(1) A party desiring to take the deposition of any person upon oral examination shall give reasonable notice in writing to every other party to the action. The notice shall state the time and place for taking the deposition and the name and address of each person to be examined, if known, and, if the name is not known, a general description sufficient to identify the person or the particular class or group to which the person belongs. If a subpoena duces tecum is to be served on the person to be examined, the designation of the materials to be produced as set forth in the subpoena shall be attached to, or included in, the notice.

(2) The party taking the deposition shall state in the notice the method by which the testimony shall be recorded. Unless the court orders otherwise, it may be recorded by sound, sound-and-visual, or stenographic means, and the party taking the deposition shall bear the cost of the recording. Any party may arrange for a transcription to be made from the recording of a deposition taken by nonstenographic means.

(3) With prior notice to the deponent and other parties, any party may designate another method to record the deponent's testimony in addition to the method specified by the person taking the deposition. The additional record or transcript shall be made at that party's expense unless the court otherwise orders.

(4) Unless otherwise agreed by the parties, a deposition shall be conducted before an officer appointed or designated under Rule 28 and shall begin with a statement on the record by the officer, that includes (A) the officer's name and business address; (B) the date, time, and place of the deposition; (C) the name of the deponent; (D) the administration of the oath or affirmation to the deponent; and (E) an identification of all persons present. If the deposition is recorded other than stenographically, the officer shall repeat items (A) through (C) at the beginning of each unit of recorded tape or other recording medium. The appearance or demeanor of deponents or attorneys shall not be distorted through camera or sound-recording techniques. At the end of the deposition, the officer shall state on the record that the deposition is complete and shall set forth any stipulations made by counsel concerning the custody of the transcript or recording and the exhibits, or concerning other pertinent matters.

(5) The notice to a party deponent may be accompanied by a request made in compliance with Rule 34 for the production of documents and tangible things at the taking of the deposition. The procedure of Rule 34 shall apply to the request.

(6) A party may in the party's notice and in a subpoena name as the deponent a public or private corporation or a partnership or association or

governmental agency and describe with reasonable particularity the matters on which examination is requested. In that event, the organization so named shall designate one or more officers, directors, or managing agents, or other persons who consent to testify on its behalf, and may set forth, for each person designated, the matters on which the person will testify. A subpoena shall advise a non-party organization of its duty to make such a designation. The persons so designated shall testify as to matters known or reasonably available to the organization. This subdivision (b)(6) does not preclude taking a deposition by any other procedure authorized in these rules.

(7) The parties may stipulate in writing or the court may upon motion order that a deposition be taken by telephone or other remote electronic means. For the purposes of this rule and Rules 28(a), 37(a)(1), and 37(b)(1), a deposition taken by such means is taken in the district and at the place where the deponent is to answer questions.

(c) Examination and Cross-Examination; Record of Examination; Oath; Objections.

Examination and cross-examination of witnesses may proceed as permitted at the trial under the provisions of the Federal Rules of Evidence except Rules 103 and 615. The officer before whom the deposition is to be taken shall put the witness on oath or affirmation and shall personally, or by someone acting under the officer's direction and in the officer's presence, record the testimony of the witness. The testimony shall be taken stenographically or recorded by any other method authorized by subdivision (b)(2) of this rule. All objections made at the time of the examination to the qualifications of the officer taking the deposition, to the manner of taking it, to the evidence presented, to the conduct of any party, or to any other aspect of the proceedings shall be noted by the officer upon the record of the deposition; but the examination shall proceed, with the testimony being taken subject to the objections. In lieu of participating in the oral examination, parties may serve written questions in a sealed envelope on the party taking the deposition and the party taking the deposition shall transmit them to the officer, who shall propound them to the witness and record the answers verbatim.

(d) Schedule and Duration; Motion to Terminate or Limit Examination.

(1) Any objection to evidence during a deposition shall be stated concisely and in a nonargumentative and nonsuggestive manner. A party may instruct a deponent not to answer only when necessary to preserve a privilege, to enforce a limitation on evidence directed by the court, or to present a motion under paragraph (3).

(2) By order or local rule, the court may limit the time permitted for the conduct of a deposition, but shall allow additional time consistently with Rule 26(b)(2) if needed for a fair examination of the deponent or if the deponent or another party impedes or delays the examination. If the court finds such an impediment, delay, or other conduct that has frustrated the fair examination of the deponent, it may impose upon the persons responsible an appropriate sanction, including the reasonable costs and attorney's fees incurred by any parties as a result thereof.

(3) At any time during a deposition, on motion of a party or of the deponent and upon a showing that the examination is being conducted in bad faith or in such manner as unreasonably to annoy, embarrass, or oppress the deponent or party, the court in which the action is pending or the court in the district where the deposition is being taken may order the officer conducting the examination to cease forthwith from taking the deposition, or may limit the scope and manner of the taking of the deposition as provided in Rule 26(c). If the order made terminates the examination, it shall be resumed thereafter only upon the order of the court in which the action is pending. Upon demand of the objecting party or deponent, the taking of the deposition shall be suspended for the time necessary to make a motion for an order. The provisions of Rule 37(a)(4) apply to the award of expenses incurred in relation to the motion.

(e) Review by Witness; Changes; Signing.

If requested by the deponent or a party before completion of the deposition, the deponent shall have 30 days after being notified by the officer that the transcript or recording is available in which to review the transcript or recording and, if there are changes in form or substance, to sign a statement reciting such changes and the reasons given by the deponent for making them. The officer shall indicate in the certificate prescribed by subdivision (f)(1) whether any review was requested and, if so, shall append any changes made by the deponent during the period allowed.

(f) Certification and Filing by Officer; Exhibits; Copies; Notices of Filing.

(1) The officer shall certify that the witness was duly sworn by the officer and that the deposition is a true record of the testimony given by the witness. This certificate shall be in writing and accompany the record of the deposition. Unless otherwise ordered by the court, the officer shall securely seal the deposition in an envelope or package indorsed with the title of the action and marked 'Deposition of [here insert name of witness]' and shall promptly file it with the court in which the action is pending or send it to the attorney who arranged for the transcript or recording, who shall store it under conditions that will protect it against loss, destruction, tampering, or deterioration. Documents and things produced for inspection during the examination of the witness, shall, upon the request of a party, be marked for identification and annexed to the deposition and may be inspected and copied by any party, except that if the person producing the materials desires to retain them the person may (A) offer copies to be marked for identification and annexed to the deposition and to serve thereafter as originals if the person affords to all parties fair opportunity to verify the copies by comparison with the originals, or (B) offer the originals to be marked for identification, after giving to each party an opportunity to inspect and copy them, in which event the materials may then be used in the same manner as if annexed to the deposition. Any party may move for an order that the original be annexed to and returned with the deposition to the court, pending final disposition of the case.

(2) Unless otherwise ordered by the court or agreed by the parties, the officer shall retain stenographic notes of any deposition taken stenographically or a copy of the recording of any deposition taken by another method. Upon

payment of reasonable charges therefor, the officer shall furnish a copy of the transcript or other recording of the deposition to any party or to the deponent.

(3) The party taking the deposition shall give prompt notice of its filing to all other parties.

(g) Failure to Attend or to Serve Subpoena; Expenses.

(1) If the party giving the notice of the taking of a deposition fails to attend and proceed therewith and another party attends in person or by attorney pursuant to the notice, the court may order the party giving the notice to pay to such other party the reasonable expenses incurred by that party and that party's attorney in attending, including reasonable attorney's fees.

(2) If the party giving the notice of the taking of a deposition of a witness fails to serve a subpoena upon the witness and the witness because of such failure does not attend, and if another party attends in person or by attorney because that party expects the deposition of that witness to be taken, the court may order the party giving the notice to pay to such other party the reasonable expenses incurred by that party and that party's attorney in attending, including reasonable attorney's fees.

Rule 31. *Depositions Upon Written Questions.*

a) Serving Questions; Notice.

(1) A party may take the testimony of any person, including a party, by deposition upon written questions without leave of court except as provided in paragraph (2). The attendance of witnesses may be compelled by the use of subpoena as provided in Rule 45.

(2) A party must obtain leave of court, which shall be granted to the extent consistent with the principles stated in Rule 26(b)(2), if the person to be examined is confined in prison or if, without the written stipulation of the parties.

(A) a proposed deposition would result in more than ten depositions being taken under this rule or Rule 30 by the plaintiffs, or by the defendants, or by third-party defendants;

(B) the person to be examined has already been deposed in the case; or

(C) a party seeks to take a deposition before the time specified in Rule 26(d).

(3) A party desiring to take a deposition upon written questions shall serve them upon every other party with a notice stating (1) the name and address of the person who is to answer them, if known, and if the name is not known, a general description sufficient to identify the person or the particular class or group to which the person belongs, and (2) the name or descriptive title and address of the officer before whom the deposition is to be taken. A deposition upon written questions may be taken of a public or private corporation or a partnership or association or governmental agency in accordance with the provisions of Rule 30(b)(6).

(4) Within 14 days after the notice and written questions are served, a party may serve cross questions upon all other parties. Within 7 days after being served with cross questions, a party may serve redirect questions upon all other

parties. Within 7 days after being served with redirect questions, a party may serve recross questions upon all other parties. The court may for cause shown enlarge or shorten the time.

(b) Officer to Take Responses and Prepare Record.

A copy of the notice and copies of all questions served shall be delivered by the party taking the deposition to the officer designated in the notice, who shall proceed promptly, in the manner provided by Rule 30(c), (e), and (f), to take the testimony of the witness in response to the questions and to prepare, certify, and file or mail the deposition, attaching thereto the copy of the notice and the questions received by the officer.

(c) Notice of Filing.

When the deposition is filed the party taking it shall promptly give notice thereof to all other parties.

Rule 33.   *Interrogatories to Parties.*

(a) Availability.

Without leave of court or written stipulation, any party may serve upon any other party written interrogatories, not exceeding 25 in number including all discrete subparts, to be answered by the party served or, if the party served is a public or private corporation or a partnership or association or governmental agency, by any officer or agent, who shall furnish such information as is available to the party. Leave to serve additional interrogatories shall be granted to the extent consistent with the principles of Rule 26(b)(2). Without leave of court or written stipulation, interrogatories may not be served before the time specified in Rule 26(d).

(b) Answers and Objections.

(1) Each interrogatory shall be answered separately and fully in writing under oath, unless it is objected to, in which event the objecting party shall state the reasons for objection and shall answer to the extent the interrogatory is not objectionable.

(2) The answers are to be signed by the person making them, and the objections signed by the attorney making them.

(3) The party upon whom the interrogatories have been served shall serve a copy of the answers, and objections if any, within 30 days after the service of the interrogatories. A shorter or longer time may be directed by the court or, in the absence of such an order, agreed to in writing by the parties subject to Rule 29.

(4) All grounds for an objection to an interrogatory shall be stated with specificity. Any ground not stated in a timely objection is waived unless the party's failure to object is excused by the court for good cause shown.

(5) The party submitting the interrogatories may move for an order under Rule 37(a) with respect to any objection to or other failure to answer an interrogatory.

(c) Scope; Use at Trial.

Interrogatories may relate to any matters which can be inquired into under Rule 26(b)(1), and the answers may be used to the extent permitted by the rules of evidence.

An interrogatory otherwise proper is not necessarily objectionable merely because an answer to the interrogatory involves an opinion or contention that relates to fact or the application of law to fact, but the court may order that such an interrogatory need not be answered until after designated discovery has been completed or until a pretrial conference or other later time.

(d) Option to Produce Business Records.

Where the answer to an interrogatory may be derived or ascertained from the business records of the party upon whom the interrogatory has been served or from an examination, audit, or inspection of such business records, including a compilation, abstract or summary thereof, and the burden of deriving or ascertaining the answer is substantially the same for the party serving the interrogatory as for the party served, it is a sufficient answer to such interrogatory to specify the records from which the answer may be derived or ascertained and to afford to the party serving the interrogatory reasonable opportunity to examine, audit, or inspect such records and to make copies, compilations, abstracts, or summaries. A specification shall be in sufficient detail to permit the interrogating party to locate and to identify, as readily as can the party served, the records from which the answer may be ascertained.

Rule 34. *Production of Documents and Things and Entry Upon Land for Inspection and Other Purposes.*

(a) Scope.

Any party may serve on any other party a request (1) to produce and permit the party making the request, or someone acting on the requestor's behalf, to inspect and copy, any designated documents (including writings, drawings, graphs, charts, photographs, phonorecords, and other data compilations from which information can be obtained, translated, if necessary, by the respondent through detection devices into reasonably usable form), or to inspect and copy, test, or sample any tangible things which constitute or contain matters within the scope of Rule 26(b) and which are in the possession, custody or control of the party upon whom the request is served; or (2) to permit entry upon designated land or other property in the possession or control of the party upon whom the request is served for the purpose of inspection and measuring, surveying, photographing, testing, or sampling the property or any designated object or operation thereon, within the scope of Rule 26(b).

(b) Procedure.

The request shall set forth, either by individual item or by category, the items to be inspected, and describe each with reasonable particularity. The request shall specify a reasonable time, place, and manner of making the inspection and performing the related acts. Without leave of court or written stipulation, a request may not be served before the time specified in Rule 26(d).

The party upon whom the request is served shall serve a written response within 30 days after the service of the request. A shorter or longer time may be directed by the court or, in the absence of such an order, agreed to in writing by the parties, subject to Rule 29. The response shall state, with respect to each item or category, that inspection and related activities will be permitted as requested, unless the request is objected to, in which event the reasons for the objection shall be stated. If objection is made to part of an item or category, the part shall be specified and inspection permitted of the remaining parts. The party submitting the request may move for an order under Rule 37(a) with respect to any objection to or other failure to respond to the request or any part thereof, or any failure to permit inspection as requested.

A party who produces documents for inspection shall produce them as they are kept in the usual course of business or shall organize and label them to correspond with the categories in the request.

(c) Persons Not Parties.

A person not a party to the action may be compelled to produce documents and things or to submit to an inspection as provided in Rule 45.

Rule 35. *Physical and Mental Examination of Persons.*

(a) Order for Examination.

When the mental or physical condition (including the blood group) of a party or of a person in the custody or under the legal control of a party, is in controversy, the court in which the action is pending may order the party to submit to a physical or mental examination by a suitably licensed or certified examiner or to produce for examination the person in the party's custody or legal control. The order may be made only on motion for good cause shown and upon notice to the person to be examined and to all parties and shall specify the time, place, manner, conditions, and scope of the examination and the person or persons by whom it is to be made.

(b) Report of Examiner.

(1) If requested by the party against whom an order is made under Rule 35(a) or the person examined, the party causing the examination to be made shall deliver to the requesting party a copy of the detailed written report of the examiner setting out the examiner's findings, including results of all tests made, diagnoses and conclusions, together with like reports of all earlier examinations of the same condition. After delivery the party causing the examination shall be entitled upon request to receive from the party against whom the order is made a like report of any examination, previously or thereafter made, of the same condition, unless, in the case of a report of examination of a person not a party, the party shows that the party is unable to obtain it. The court on motion may make an order against a party requiring delivery of a report on such terms as are just, and if an examiner fails or refuses to make a report the court may exclude the examiner's testimony if offered at trial.

(2) By requesting and obtaining a report of the examination so ordered or by taking the deposition of the examiner, the party examined waives any privilege the party may have in that action or any other involving the same controversy, regarding the testimony of every other person who has examined or may thereafter examine the party in respect of the same mental or physical condition.

(3) This subdivision applies to examinations made by agreement of the parties, unless the agreement expressly provides otherwise. This subdivision does not preclude discovery of a report of an examiner or the taking of a deposition of the examiner in accordance with the provisions of any other rule.

(c) Definitions.

For the purpose of this rule, a psychologist is a psychologist licensed or certified by a State or the District of Columbia.

Rule 36.   *Requests for Admission.*

(a) Request for Admission.

A party may serve upon any other party a written request for the admission, for purposes of the pending action only, of the truth of any matters within the scope of Rule 26(b)(1) set forth in the request that relate to statements or opinions of fact or of the application of law to fact, including the genuineness of any documents described in the request. Copies of documents shall be served with the request unless they have been or are otherwise furnished or made available for inspection and copying. Without leave of court or written stipulation, requests for admission may not be served before the time specified in Rule 26(d).

Each matter of which an admission is requested shall be separately set forth. The matter is admitted unless, within 30 days after service of the request, or within such shorter or longer time as the court may allow or as the parties may agree to in writing, subject to Rule 29, the party to whom the request is directed serves upon the party requesting the admission a written answer or objection addressed to the matter, signed by the party or by the party's attorney. If objection is made, the reasons therefor shall be stated. The answer shall specifically deny the matter or set forth in detail the reasons why the answering party cannot truthfully admit or deny the matter. A denial shall fairly meet the substance of the requested admission, and when good faith requires that a party qualify an answer or deny only a part of the matter of which an admission is requested, the party shall specify so much of it as is true and qualify or deny the remainder. An answering party may not give lack of information or knowledge as a reason for failure to admit or deny unless the party states that the party has made reasonable inquiry and that the information known or readily obtainable by the party is insufficient to enable the party to admit or deny. A party who considers that a matter of which an admission has been requested presents a genuine issue for trial may not, on that ground alone, object to the request; the party may, subject to the provisions of Rule 37(c), deny the matter or set forth reasons why the party cannot admit or deny it.

The party who has requested the admissions may move to determine the sufficiency of the answers or objections. Unless the court determines that an objection is justified, it shall order that an answer be served. If the court determines that an answer does not comply with the requirements of this rule, it may order either that the matter is admitted or that an amended answer be served. The court may, in lieu of these orders, determine that final disposition of the request be made at a pretrial conference or at a designated time prior to trial. The provisions of Rule 37(a)(4) apply to the award of expenses incurred in relation to the motion.

(b) Effect of Admission.

Any matter admitted under this rule is conclusively established unless the court on motion permits withdrawal or amendment of the admission. Subject to the provision of Rule 16 governing amendment of a pretrial order, the court may permit withdrawal or amendment when the presentation of the merits of the action will be subserved thereby and the party who obtained the admission fails to satisfy the court that withdrawal or amendment will prejudice that party in maintaining the action or defense on the merits. Any admission made by a party under this rule is for the purpose of the pending action only and is not an admission for any other purpose nor may it be used against the party in any other proceeding.

2. Time- and Cost-Saving Measures for Specific Types of Discovery

a. Depositions

Here is where a paralegal can be most valuable. Paralegals usually are charged with setting depositions. Setting a deposition entails preparing a notice of taking deposition; determining the location, time, and date; locating a court reporter; and serving the notice. It can also entail requesting the issuance of a **subpoena**, a court-issued (or, in some states, an attorney-issued) document compelling a person to appear at a certain place and time to provide testimony regarding a specific matter. It can be a time-consuming process when trying to coordinate schedules of multiple attorneys, but the paralegal should always contact opposing counsel before setting the deposition to make sure the time and date are convenient. All attorneys appreciate this courtesy and have come to expect it. It can be very difficult to change schedules or reset depositions.

There are some cost-saving measures that the paralegal can keep in mind when setting depositions. Every paralegal should give consideration to the following.

- Informal interviews: Think about using informal interviews as opposed to the more formal deposition process.
- Nonstenographic depositions: In certain circumstances it would be appropriate to simply have the deposition taped and not to use a court reporter.
- Telephonic depositions: To save travel cost and time, depositions can be done over the telephone.
- Conference depositions: Videoconferencing can be cost-effective when there are multiple attorneys or parties in multiple states.
- Written questions: Use of written questions can be cost-effective. The written questions can be asked by the court reporter, so that the attorney does not have to attend, or written questions such as interrogatories can be used.

b. Interrogatories

Paralegals are also charged with drafting interrogatories, and this is an area in which considerable time and expense can be saved with a little planning through the use of master interrogatories. Master interrogatories cover a specific area such as background, wrongful death, personal injury, and so on. Also, interrogatories from previous litigation can be used. It is quite helpful to have a discovery notebook of forms and questions used previously that is separated by area.

PRACTICE TIP

Practices to save time and expense: Remember to review carefully and make sure what you are sending is relevant to your case. Everyone has heard about the legal assistant that mistakenly sent out stock interrogatories without reviewing first to see if the questions pertained to the parties and issues of the current case. Master interrogatories can be a big timesaver, but must be tailored to the specific case each time sent out. Interrogatories from other litigation can be used as well, tailoring for the specific issues.

There are further ways to save time and expense in the discovery process. Give some thought to what they are and how they may be utilized.

c. Further Practices to Save Time and Expense

Here are some additional suggestions for time- and cost-saving measures.

- Stipulations under Federal Rule of Civil Procedure 29: The rule gives parties authority to alter procedures, limitations, and time limits on discovery so long as they do not interfere with times set by court order.
- Informal discovery: Counsel should be encouraged to exchange information, particularly relevant documents, without resort to formal discovery.
- Automatic disclosure: Rule 26(a)(1), and some local rules, require the parties to identify relevant witnesses and categories of documents early in the litigation.
- Reducing deposition costs: Savings may be realized when depositions are taken, when feasible, by telephone, by electronic recording devices, or by having deponents come to central locations.
- Information from other litigation and sources: When information is available from public records (such as government studies or reports), from other litigation, or from discovery conducted by others in the same litigation, the parties may be required to review those materials before additional discovery is undertaken.
- Joint discovery requests and responses: In multiparty cases in which no lead counsel has been designated, parties with similar positions may be required to submit a combined set of interrogatories, requests for product, or requests for admission.
- Modified discovery responses: When a response to a discovery request can be provided in a form somewhat different from that requested, but with substantially the same information and at a savings in time and expense, the responding party should make that fact known and seek agreement from the requesting party.
- Combined discovery requests: Several forms of discovery can sometimes be combined into a single request.
- Conference depositions: When knowledge, of a subject is divided among several people and credibility is not an issue, a conference deposition may be feasible.

H. PLANNING CASE STRATEGY

Planning the case strategy is an ongoing process. It is helpful, however, if you visit with your supervising attorney immediately after the case comes in, and then at least monthly as the case progresses. Planning case strategy is closely aligned to preparing an outline and planning. Case strategy takes into account the client's objectives and concerns and his or her cost constraints. From there, you commence laying an outline for litigation and discovery planning.

I. LAYING AN OUTLINE FOR LITIGATION AND DISCOVERY PLANNING

A discovery plan should be designed to facilitate the orderly and cost-effective acquisition of relevant information and materials and the prompt resolution of discovery disputes. Adoption of a discovery plan is the principal purpose of the initial conference, which is preceded by meeting of counsel for the purpose of developing a discovery plan for submission to the court.

When planning discovery you should determine the least expensive way to conduct the discovery you need. Plan an outline of the following areas:

Elements of the claim
Sources of proof
    Records
    Witnesses
Investigation
    Facts obtained
Formal discovery
Trial preparation
Trial

At this point you should always look to a quick and final resolution of the matter whether through settlement, arbitration, or mediation. Decide then which methods—interrogatories, requests for production, depositions, and so on—would be the best discovery forum.

Then develop a litigation timeline that will serve the client's objectives, meet his or her needs, and cost-effectively settle the dispute. Your timeline should include all pertinent dates for filing the complaint, getting the summons and complaint served, propounding discovery, answering discovery, setting depositions, conducting investigations, filing motions, conferences, disclosures, and trial preparation. The last date on your timeline should be the trial date, and all preparation should be completed at a minimum two weeks in advance of that date.

Chapter 5 will address more fully the role of technology in document production and management. However, a short overview of automation for the law office will be helpful when you make discovery considerations.

J. OVERVIEW OF AUTOMATION FOR THE LAW OFFICE

1. Case Management Software

Case management software programs organize the litigation practice by tracking information central to the case, like important deadlines, budgets, and client information. This type of software can be very helpful in managing the discovery process. The main features of this type of software include the following:

- Organizes case data in an easily searchable and customizable format
- Creates and outputs many reports
- Logs the date pleadings arrive (or are filed) and subsequently calculates upcoming court appearances and deadlines
- Acts as an electronic daily planner, letting you keep track of all your court appearances, meetings, filing dates, and other important events
- Has basic word processing functions that allow you to create letters, memoranda, and even short briefs or pleadings
- Has database functions that provide a place where data is stored.

The ease with which data can be searched and retrieved is an important element in determining the effectiveness of a case management system.

2. Document Management Software

Document management software is used to track documents produced in disparate formats, from word processing files to spreadsheets to scanned images. Document management systems provide search tools that let you instantly locate documents without becoming lost in a complex directory structure. These systems can also perform more complex operations, including archiving or deleting older documents and establishing security rights to restrict access to certain documents and version control, which allows multiple generations of a document to coexist. See Chapter 5 for additional information on document management.

3. Litigation Support Software

Litigation support is a broad category of software that emphasizes the storage and management of the large quantities of documents produced in litigation. Litigation support packages usually include the following features.

- **Imaging software:** Along with a scanner, imaging software lets you convert the stacks of paper common to just about every litigation into electronic images. This makes the transport, indexing, and retrieval of important documents much easier.
- **Database capabilities:** Once all the paper has been digitized, you need to be able to track and manipulate the documents. The database feature of most litigation support programs allows you to do this.

- **Full-text search capabilities:** It's great to reduce the amount of paper in a law office, but only if you can find and retrieve important documents quickly and easily. Full-text searching helps you find the proverbial needle in the haystack. Litigation support programs let you search for information in a variety of ways.

Many of these litigation support programs are also designed for use in a courtroom, where fast access to key information and documents is often a key factor in whether your side wins or loses.

Summation Blaze for Windows provides sophisticated transcript and document management tools in one easy-to-use program. Summation is an industry leader and has been used by over 30,000 clients in law firms, corporations, and government agencies worldwide. Because Summation is a truly integrated system, you can search through all transcripts and documents in one easy operation, then quickly zoom from an outline detailing the search results to testimonial or documentary evidence in full context. Summation also lets you display search results sorted by issue category or date.

Summation: can be used to do the following:

1. Make effective use of transcripts
   a. Review a transcript provided on disk by a court reporter
   b. Preserve ideas as you go through transcript
   c. Flag and isolate key lines of testimony
   d. Issue and date code-flagged excerpts so they can be analyzed in conjunction with other key documentary and testimonial evidence
2. Create reports:
   a. Deposition digest
   b. List of follow-up questions for upcoming depositions
   c. Integrated chronology of key testimony and key documents
   d. Integrated report of key deposition excerpts and document summaries sorted alphabetically by issue code
3. Carry out simple searches under pressure situations such as cross-examination and deposition-taking
4. Preserve the results of searches in hardcopy reports for a three-ring binder, computer files that can be easily transferred into a word processor, a case outline, or an outline to prepare for an individual deposition
5. Carry out a finely focused database search of a large, document-intensive case

4. Considerations for Litigation Support Databases

There are seven key decisions to make with respect to equipment (hardware) for a computer-based litigation support database, and each decision has an important impact on the output of your litigation support database. However, you must consider both hardware and software.

- **Computer:** Personal preference and costs.
- **Memory:** The main memory (RAM) is where the computer does its work. The

RAM must be sufficiently large to hold both currently active software and any temporary files or portions of files used by the software.
- **Storage:** Governed primarily by size of database.
- **Backup:** Maintains nearly current copy of the database to protect against catastrophic data loss on the computer containing the working version of the database.
- **Monitor:** Personal preference and costs.
- **Printer:** Printing an entire database may require thousands of pages of output. You need adequate legibility, speed, reliability, and color.
- **Mobile units (if needed).**

For database management software, there are four generic types that can be used for litigation support. You need to determine the best type to meet your firm's needs.

1. Simple database
2. Relational database
3. Hierarchical database
4. Free-standing full-text retrieval software

There are two principal costs to any database management system: document handling costs and data entry costs. The document handling costs include: screening, numbering, copying, coding, quality control, and proofreading.

By far, the most significant cost in any database system is the cost to input data into the database. The input cost depends very heavily on the level of complexity of the database design. The input costs also depend on the salary level of the personnel used for each of the tasks in the input process.

The data entry costs include entry by keying and entry by scanning or imaging. Keying simply means entering abstracts of the documents into predetermined database fields. Scanning or imaging is the best approach for data entry because it is easy, is not very costly, can be done in-house, and complete copies of the documents are made a part of the database and therefore are scanned onto a CD. When using personal computer systems, the costs of conducting searches and running printouts from the database are primarily personnel costs. When deciding the best approach to take, whether to enter the document by keying or by imaging, you need to take into consideration your time constraints. How soon does the project need to be accomplished?

Remember: A great deal of knowledge about the case comes from working closely with the documents. If the firm personnel do the database work in-house, not only will the overall cost usually be lower for the client, but the staff will be closer to the facts of the case.

To make imaging work well for you, you need to consider the following elements.

- Timing: Don't wait until the last minute to send your case to a service bureau for imaging and coding.
- Document preparation: Thoroughly review the documents before passing them on to the service bureau.
- Database development (service bureau): If objective database coding is also being performed by the service bureau, communicate with the coders about what you want.
- Database development (in-house): Database development is a time-intensive and personnel-consuming project.

- Get expert help: If you have the right technical people, you don't have to be a techno-wizard to take advantage of imaging.

Finally, a last word on imaging. The final test for imaging is the courtroom. Here are some suggestions that should make your courtroom experience easier when using imaged documents.

- Do not go into court on the day of trial intending to surprise opposing counsel with a high-tech show.
- Well in advance of the trial date, visit the courtroom and confirm it has all the necessary outlets and electrical power to handle the computer equipment.
- Do not go into court with 20 CD-ROMs holding all of the discovery documents.
- Be aware of duplicate trial images.
- Use a combination of monitors and projection panels to display your evidence.
- Do a dry-run.
- Always keep a paper set of your exhibits.
- Make extra copies of the exhibit bar code labels.
- Prepare, Prepare, Prepare!

ETHICS

Ethical considerations are a challenge for the new paralegal. Where does the paralegal turn? There are so many things a paralegal cannot do. A paralegal cannot engage in the unauthorized practice of law. In other words, a paralegal cannot give legal advice, cannot take clients or establish an attorney/client relationship, cannot set fees, and cannot share in legal fees directly attributable to a specific case. As a paralegal, these "cannots" must be heeded at all times.

However, there are many things that a paralegal can accomplish. A paralegal can assist attorneys in the performance of their work, a paralegal can maintain integrity, a paralegal can display competency through his or her work and through continuing legal education. There are also the "musts." A paralegal must protect the interests of the client, must disclose his or her identity and position, must use discretion and professional judgment, and must adheed to high ethics and standards.

Whenever concerned about what you can, must, or cannot do, turn to the ethical guidelines available to you through the state bar associations, professional associations, attorney associations with paralegal members, and your supervising attorney. There are even Web sites exclusively devoted to the topic of ethics. One excellent site is Cornell's legal ethics by state, *http://www.law.cornell.edu/ethics*. Another good source for answers on ethical considerations is *http://www.legalethics.com/ethicsites.htm*. This particular site offers a list of ethics resources. Always remember to tap into the resources of your fellow coworkers and colleagues. Make sure that you network with the other paralegals working in your area and develop good working relationships that foster the give and take of supporting each other.

CONCLUSION

Laying an outline for planning litigation really starts when you identify legal claims, determine jurisdiction and venue, and draft your complaint. Once an action is commenced, your main objective should be a speedy and cost-efficient settlement of the dispute. To accomplish that objective, you need to carefully plan your discovery, what types to discovery to use, and when to use it.

Remember to utilize your available resources when planning discovery, disclosures, and motions, and refer to them often. Make sure your disclosures are complete and thorough and include all items required by the Federal Rules of Civil Procedure. It is further helpful to check the local rules of the particular court in which you filed the action to determine if there are any other rules you need to be mindful of.

USING TECHNOLOGY IN THE LAW OFFICE

The preceding text provides a general overview of the technology software available to the paralegal in case management, document management, and litigation support. This section focuses on expanding the discussion of technology to provide information on specific tools and software applications that can be utilized to increase law office effectiveness and efficiency with regard to performing legal research and developing a case outline and strategy.

A. ELECTRONIC LEGAL RESEARCH TOOLS

At the onset of a case, you need to identify three things: legal claims, jurisdiction, and venue. To identify these three items as they relate to your case, some preliminary legal research will need to be done. On-line legal research is legal research done on the World Wide Web. The online legal research software such as Lexis and Westlaw can be expensive and ineffective. The preference of many practicing paralegals is to perform the preliminary legal research on the Internet through various Web sites. The following legal sites can be useful in this process:

> *http://www.findlaw.com*
> *http://www.law.cornell.edu*
> *http://www.law.und.nodak.edu/lawweb/thormodsgard/library.html*

Most of the sites listed above will provide you access to federal and state statutes, as well as pertinent case law regarding the issue you are researching. There are two advantages to performing your preliminary research on the Internet. First, the Internet can be accessed for a nominal monthly fee with unlimited hours. Second, your searches can start out broadly and end narrowly without concern as to cost, resulting in comprehensive preliminary research. If you do not find all the information you need on the Internet, then further specific legal research can be done through Lexis or Westlaw.

Legal research in the twenty-first century is not only easy to access, it's easy to use. If you can't afford the expensive legal research software, then your preliminary research can be done on the Internet with more extensive research to be performed at the law library.

B. SOFTWARE FOR ESTABLISHING A CASE OUTLINE AND STRATEGY

There are several software programs on the market today that allow you to electronically establish a case outline, strategy, and statement of claims. The database software Summation contains a feature called Case Organizer, which can be effectively used to create case outlines, strategies, and statement of claims.

In Case Organizer, you can label tabs for the legal claims and witnesses of your case. Case Organizer also has a unique copy-and-paste option, allowing you to paste information from loaded deposition transcripts or database forms into the organizer. To copy use (CTRL & C) and to paste use (CTRL & V).

This program also contains a jump-back arrow for deposition testimony. If specific testimony is pasted into Case Organizer, then an automatic jump-back arrow can be clicked on, simultaneously placing the user back into the loaded deposition transcript. The amount of information placed in Case Organizer is completely determined by you and your attorney. Figures 3.3 and 3.4 demonstrate a sample case outline, as well as the jump-back arrow feature.

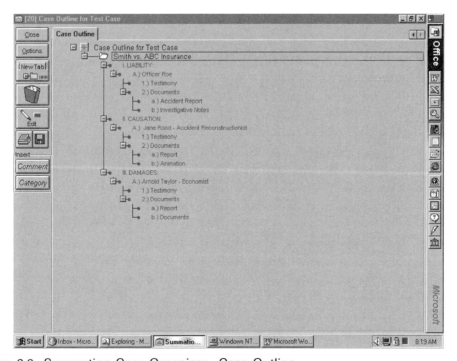

Figure 3.3. Summation Case Organizer—Case Outline

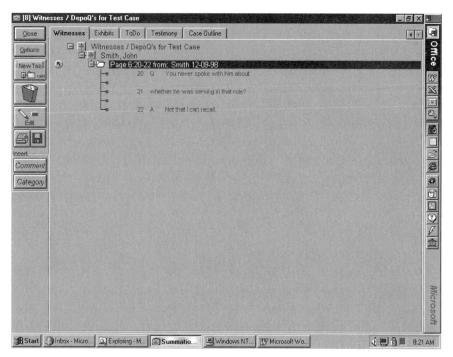

Figure 3.4. Summation Case Organizer—Jump-Back Feature

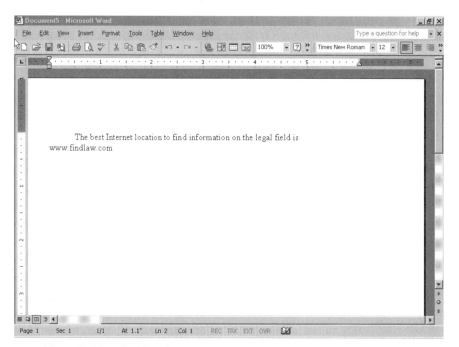

Figure 3.5. Hyperlinking in Word

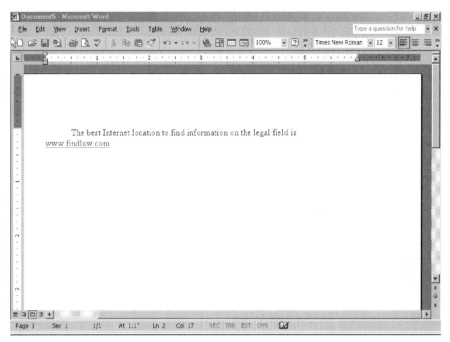

Figure 3.6. Hyperlinking in Word

Figure 3.7. Findlaw Web page accessed by hyperlinking.

Other software programs can be used to create a case outline, strategy, and statement of claims. For example, Microsoft Word has an outline view format that allows for numerous levels of subordination. Each of the outline levels created can be expanded or collapsed as you deem necessary. Word also contains the cut-and-paste feature, allowing you to paste information into your case outline and strategy. Although Word does not contain a jump-back arrow feature, it does contain a **hyperlink** feature that allows you to link to other documents or files.

Hyperlinking in Word is done by highlighting the desired text and pressing Ctrl-K to initiate the hyperlink. Once the hyperlink feature has been initiated, you browse out to the file you want linked. This process is visually demonstrated in Figures 3.5, 3.6, and 3.7

KEY TERMS

Choice of forum	Interrogatories	Requests to produce documents or things for inspection
Complaint	Jurisdiction	
Counts	Original jurisdiction	
Deposition	Personal jurisdiction	Statement of claims
Discovery	Requests for admission of facts	Subject matter jurisdiction
District courts		Subpoena
General subject matter jurisdiction	Requests for physical and mental examination of persons	Summons
		Theories of recovery
In personam		Venue
In rem		

TECHNOLOGY TERMS

Case management software	Full-text search capability	Imaging software
Database capability	Hyperlink	Litigation support software
Document management software		

USEFUL WEB SITES

http://www.fedworld.com   Government and business sites by category
http://www.law.emory.edu/FEDCTS   Federal Courts Finder
http://www.lawsource.com   American Law Sources On-line
http://www.llrx.com/columns/litigat.htm   Rules of court
http://www.lawguru.com/search/lawsearch.html   Legal search engines

chapter 4

Investigation

chapter objectives

In this chapter, we will discuss

- A general overview of investigation
- Steps involved in any good investigation
- Tips to ensure a successful investigation
- Various Web resources available to help with investigation
- Admissibility
- Introduction to evidence

A. NATURE OF INVESTIGATION

Investigation is the part of the legal process that involves the verification of facts. Investigation and interviewing are closely related and guided by the same principles. An investigator, even more than the interviewer, needs to be open-minded, receptive, and yet quite skeptical. The starting point for any investigation will be the supervisor's instructions and the facts already gathered from the client at the initial interview. Every investigation needs to have a clear idea of the type of investigation, the facts to prove or disprove, and a plan or outline.

The nature of investigation is to accomplish the following four purposes:

1. To obtain a complete factual picture
2. To locate evidence for trial
3. To obtain impeachment material
4. To verify the facts and obtain admissions

Your investigation enables you to test the legal theories of the case, come up with new ones, and locate further leads. The facts surrounding the event determine what the legal issues are; the legal issues then determine what evidence is material to the case. Logic and the rules of evidence determine what evidence is relevant and admissible at trial. Attorneys, however, will ultimately decide the admissibility of any evidence. But it is necessary for the paralegal to understand evidence, relevancy, and admissibility. At the end of this chapter we briefly explore those elements. Chapter 10, however, discusses evidence at length.

It remains that the paralegal's job is to obtain all the evidence available—keeping in mind relevancy and admissibility. How is that done?

B. BLUEPRINT OF A GOOD INVESTIGATION

There are four steps to any good investigation

1. Obtain preliminary information from the client
2. Physically inspect the scene or evidence
3. Determine appropriate legal theories
4. Prepare your blueprint or outline for investigation

The first step in any investigation is to speak with the client and obtain as much information as possible. An investigation cannot be planned without basic facts. How much the client can contribute varies. The widow of a decedent in a wrongful death action, for example, often will only know or remember the basics of the tragedy. You may have to get the start-up data from others. As discussed previously, emotions, past experiences, and health all are factors in the way a witness or claimant perceives a particular event or occurrence. See Chapter 2 for more information on interviewing.

The second step is to visit the scene and inspect the objects involved. A knowledge of the physical aspects of the case put it into context, which helps to orient your thinking and evaluate the facts. It is very helpful to actually be at the scene of an accident to determine the physical layout of the area. In a personal injury accident, for example, you might look for things such as:

Do trees block the driver's view of the intersection?
What signs are posted in the area?
Is there a lot of traffic at that particular location?

Oftentimes viewing the scene will enable you to think of other leads to follow in assessing the case. For example, if there appears to be a lot of traffic, both pedestrian and automobile, it might be good to check with the city on traffic regulation investigations and studies, or the highway patrol to see if they have accident statistics for that area.

If you are looking at physical evidence, it helps to be able to actually touch it. The opportunity to physically inspect an object allows you to look for defects, safety devices, and condition or wear. However, caution should be taken when doing so. Evidence or potential evidence should never be tampered with or changed in any way.

When you are at the scene of an accident or event, you should note and record a number of things:

- Topography
- Lines of vision
- Measurements of distances
- Physical evidence of the event

Similarly, when inspecting an object, you should note as much as possible about it: how it operates, where it was damaged, its safety features. In both cases, the paralegal should make sure that at a minimum they carry a good camera, one with a zoom lense. Other essential tools are tape measures, walking sticks, diagrams, and the notepad. Often it is helpful to take a tape recorder to quickly and easily tape your measurements and impressions.

The third step is to pin down each principle of law involved. You plan your investigation to find facts that satisfy or rebut these principles. How do you do that? By a thorough discussion with your attorney. If your investigation reveals facts that rebut or disprove your original theories, adjust your case accordingly. Complaints can be amended under certain circumstances.

All of this preliminary work prepares you for the fourth step, blueprinting the investigation. When preparing your blueprint, six topics should be covered in detail:

1. General areas to be investigated
2. Specific questions to be answered
3. Leads to explore
4. Sources to be tapped
5. Methods of investigation
6. Roles of the people involved

Your investigation blueprint might look something like Table 4.1.

TABLE 4.1. INVESTIGATION BLUEPRINT

Legal Theory	Facts to Support Legal Theory	Areas of Investigation	Sources	Person Assigned
Negligence				Paralegal

CASE SCENARIO

In the case of the sailboat owner, a decedent had been a guest on a small tour ship. One evening, after the vessel had tied up at a pier, the decedent and several others had gone ashore. They had dinner, shot some pool, and drank heavily. The others left for the ship. He stayed behind.

The next morning he was missing and not aboard ship. Ashore, the tavern people only recalled that he had left the tavern. No one saw him after that.

Then one of the other guests spotted his hat floating between the ship and the pier near the foot of a ladder built into the side of the pier. The renewed search found his body submerged at the same spot.

The official reports fleshed out the witnesses' brief accounts of the tragedy. Diagrams in the reports gave counsel a good grasp of the scene. Counsel and his paralegal had even gone to the scene to thoroughly familiarize themselves with the area, the ship, and the pier. They had the basic facts but had to work up the facts on negligence or causation.

The paralegal and attorney spent some time on research. A line of authority as found held that circumstantial evidence could support a prima facie case for an unwitnessed death. The cases also furnished guidelines for the type of circumstantial evidence that would stand up at trial.

The paralegal and attorney swiftly drew up a blueprint for the investigation:

Areas of investigation and specific questions:
The dock. Condition. Lighting. Structures on it. Materials on it.
The ladder. Condition. Defects. Marine growth on rungs exposed to water.
The ship. Any gangway or mode of egress. Railings. Lighting. Structures. How tied up.
The weather. Tide. Wind. How far ship from dock. Relationship of railing/ship to pier/ladder.
Decedent's activity ashore.
Customary and available modes of egress on tour ships.

Sources:
The captain and crew.
The tavern people and patrons.
Other guests.
Other possible witnesses.
Other vessels.
Charts, tide tables, and weather reports.

Leads: None as yet.

Method of investigation: Much of the information will come from potential defendants. The investigation of the pier and the vessel depends on them.

Investigator: Paralegal assigned to background research, photographs of ship and scene, obtaining documentation. A professional investigator might do better with the crew and tavern people than a paralegal. Paralegal assigned to interview other witnesses.

As you can see, there is much work to be done, and a blueprint will help keep the investigation on track.

C. SIX TIPS TO GUARANTEE A SUCCESSFUL INVESTIGATION

The key to a successful investigation is planning. There are six tips that will enable you to be successful in your endeavors:

1. Start right away
2. Interview all witnesses
3. Collect documents as you go along
4. Put everything in writing
5. Assume nothing
6. Keep control of the investigation process

1. Start Right Away

Promptness pays off. If you get started on your investigation right away, the witnesses will still be around and files will be complete. Evidence will not have disappeared and memories will be fresh. Painful or embarrassing events will not have had as much time to color recollection. Opposing counsel will not have had the opportunity to have schooled the witnesses.

Remember the main purpose of investigation is to get witness statements for use at trial. The closer these statements are in time to the event, the more powerful they are for impeachment or refreshing recollection at trial.

2. Interview All Witnesses

You should interview all the witnesses you can, whether they appear to be friendly, neutral, or hostile. Don't shy away from hostile witnesses. Even hostile witnesses can be very helpful for the following reasons.

- You might discover that the witness is not really hostile at all.
- You might be able to explain the hostility away.
- You might be able to use an absolute refusal to talk as a basis for impeachment.
- You might pick up useful information.

3. Collect Documents as You Go Along

Collect everything you can get your hands on. Examine all documents carefully. In modern litigation, physical things and demonstrative evidence play a central role. You must be aggressive about getting everything. Make sure you review all materials and documents as you get them. It has happened in the past that an individual injured in an automobile accident filled out some medical form or refused medical treatment stating that were no injuries, when later, after the person had time to think things through or talk to other people, he or she alleged injuries later.

4. Put Everything in Writing

Record each step in the investigation. Your memorandum should cover at least six points:

1. Date and place of the interview or investigative step
2. Circumstances
3. Names, addresses, capacities of everyone present
4. Information and data obtained
5. Background of the witness
6. Your appraisal of the witness

You should include any other relevant material to your specific investigation.

5. Assume Nothing

Don't take anything for granted or assume anything. All the facts need to be checked and rechecked. Follow your instincts. If you feel uncomfortable about something, check it out. Remember that you also can never assume that your client is telling you the truth or the complete truth. A healthy dose of doubt will enable you to keep an edge and remind you to verify your facts.

6. Keep Control of the Investigation Process

Keep up-to-date on the facts and circumstances of the case as well as the issues and legal theories. Maintain your records. Make sure your supervisor ultimately controls the investigation to preserve attorney-client privilege.

Determine if it would be best to outsource any type of investigation, or keep the investigation in-house using associates and paralegals. Ask yourself the following questions.

- What are your time constraints?
- What are you hoping to accomplish?
- What is your experience level and level of resources available?
- What are your cost constraints?
- What will work best for your client?
- What are you most comfortable doing?

D. WHAT TO DO IF YOU RUN INTO A BRICK WALL

If you run into a brick wall and cannot think of anywhere to turn, first discuss it with the attorney handling the case. Engage in some free-thinking and map out your investigation in the form of an outline. Start with the theory of the case, the facts, and possible leads or witnesses. Rework your blueprint. Oftentimes it is also helpful to check with other paralegals on how they have handled similar cases. However, a caveat: You should never under any circumstance discuss the specific facts of your case or the parties involved. Just speak in generalities.

E. ALTERNATIVE SOURCES OF INFORMATION

1. The Internet

a. Introduction

The Internet has changed forever our world—the way we communicate, the way we use computers, and the way we work. The Internet provides a medium for interaction and collaboration between individuals without regard to geographic location. It has provided access to information previously unavailable to millions of people. What started as an idea for file sharing, resource sharing, and collaboration has become an essential tool for doing business through the use of electronic mail and information sharing.

So what exactly is the **Internet**? It is a group of computers from around the world connected to one another sharing a common computer language: TCP/IP (Transmission Control Protocol/Internet Protocol). The Internet has become an essential part of doing business in a myriad of areas, but nowhere more so than in the legal arena. Use of the Internet by members of the legal community is no longer a luxury, it is fast becoming a part of professional competence. This is true even more so for paralegals than for the attorneys they work for.

The Internet has three principal uses for the legal profession:

1. Communications
2. Information collection, including research
3. Marketing

The area of communications includes e-mail, discussion groups, and publications. Information collection would include posting, legal research, medical research, organized databases, and access to medical information and hundreds of links to legal Web sites. Marketing is a tool for advertising the services available and the practice areas of a particular firm or attorney.

Though the Internet will continue to transform the legal profession, especially the way paralegals do their jobs, different members of the legal community will utilize the three principal uses of Internet in different ways. As a paralegal, you will most probably utilize the communications and information aspects of the Internet. Used correctly, the Internet can be the paralegal's "best friend" for locating information.

When using the information aspect of the Internet, it is important to keep in mind that there is a distinct difference between searching versus surfing the Net. When you surf, you simply click on links and go where they take you. Searching, on the other hand, makes you plan and helps you stay focused. Planning helps you to understand how to choose keywords and how to best work with Boolean operators such as *and, or, not,* or *near.* You need to keep in mind the difference among search engines. Remember that search engines do not index sites equally, they may not index information for months, and no one search engine indexes more than about one-third of the total composition of the Web.

PRACTICE TIP

No single search tool serves all research purposes. Know the source of the information obtained. Obtaining consistently useful search results means you must select the appropriate tools, think about potential information sources, and enter correctly formulated queries.

In this section and the exercises that follow we will work with *searching* the Internet and not simply *surfing.* Surfing can be great fun, but it is a tremendous drain on time and efficiency. Surfing is best saved for off-hours and having fun at home. We will not delve into substantive legal research using the Internet. That subject should be covered in your legal research and writing classes. Instead, we will focus on the basics of using the Internet as an alternative investigative search tool.

When using the Net or the Web, you need to be able to evaluate the accuracy of its resources. To help you do that, here are a few things to keep in mind when using the Internet.

1. There is virtually no quality control or accountability. So, although we may get a site for free, we cannot be assured of the quality, reliability, and accuracy of the information included there.

2. There are cost factors to consider. Some are obvious and direct such as the growing number of sites beginning to charge fees. Some are indirect such as time, hardware, software, and so on.

3. Sites are constantly moving. Web sites, especially good ones, seem to drop out of cyberspace altogether. Or they are under construction and not accessible. One day you get the perfect site, the next day you click on the link only to discover that the site has moved. If you are lucky, you will be automatically forwarded to the new location or at least provided with the new URL (Uniform Resource Locator). If you are unlucky, you will end up searching for the site all over again.

4. The distribution of all these pieces of information to millions of locations around the globe can be viewed as both a plus and a minus. The information you seek may be out there, but by the time you find it, it may have been quicker to pick up the phone and ask!

5. Sometimes, gaps are not easily discerned because of the Web's unstructured nature: Web directories, such as Yahoo!, have attempted to provide subject arrangement, but they include only a fraction of Web resources. There has been much discussion of cataloging the Web, but the information and transient nature of the resources make updating a nightmare.

6. The Web can be an especially powerful medium for the quick and relatively inexpensive access to vast quantities of research information for even the most

remote areas of the world. But there is still much that is unavailable electronically, and it may remain that way. Unfortunately, researchers, attorneys, and paralegals are starting to expect everything to be "on the Web." This can lead to dangerous conclusions by the uninformed—"if it's not there, the information must not exist." The mere existence of the Internet seems to stifle full and complete research.

7. Everything you ever wanted to know is not on the Internet. Things show up and disappear for no rational reason. You can't do anything about it. Remember, even as wonderful as it is, the Internet is just one legal research tool.

b. Overview of Online Legal Research

As most everyone knows, court information is widely available on the Internet, including opinions, cases, statutes, codes, and legislation. However, generally only fairly recent information is available. Legal information on the Internet can be divided into the same categories as we find in print:

PRIMARY SOURCES
Court opinions
Court rules
Codes and statutes
Legislation
Administrative law: agency rules and agency judicial opinions
Attorney general opinions
SECONDARY SOURCES
Treatises
Law review articles
Pathfinders, guides, and bibliographies
Law library catalogs and indexes
NONLAW MATERIALS USEFUL IN FACT FINDING
Accident reconstruction
Encyclopedias
Writing tools—dictionaries, quotations, literature
Forensic and other scientific information
Expert witnesses
People directories
Statistical data

We will focus on the Internet resources available for the paralegal that fall outside of the legal research categories listed above. As a paralegal, you will be requested to use the Internet for many things:

• Locating persons or corporations
• Obtaining statistical data
• Performing medical research
• Locating expert witnesses
• Finding public records information

- Getting background information on expert witnesses
- Locating consultants
- Other nonlegal research

Locating persons is relatively easy to do, but sometimes requires that you check several different Web sites. A good plan is to keep a log of all the places you have searched, with the date you searched. That way, you can get back on track if you are interrupted, and you have a record for your file. Also, a log enables you to commit to paper those comments you do not want to forget, such as the quality and quantity of the specific site. You may want to enter on your log all the facts you know about the person, such as full name, age, last known address, job/career/business information, education, hobbies, and so on. Corporations may often be located by using one of the excellent business search pages such as CEO Express (see Table 4.1).

Statistical information is issued by the government (federal and all 50 states). In addition, statistics are issued by trade associations, professional societies, think tanks, university centers, and other groups. There are numerous statistics on criminal law, such as sentencing statistics and death penalty statistics. The government collects all types of data including census, economic indicators, industrial reports, and consumer information. Numerous sites point you to expert witnesses, both public and private (*http://www.hierosgamos.com*). Medical research can be conducted on several excellent sites (*http://www.mdexpress.com*). See Table 4.1 for a list of additional Web sites.

PRACTICE TIP

A plethora of knowledge can also be uncovered by utilizing other areas of the Internet besides the Web. Posing questions or contacting authorities via e-mail, interactive seminars, newsgroups, or even subject-specific chat rooms may also be effective research tools. Remember to access paralegal specific sites such as the National Association of Legal Assistants or the National Federation of Paralegal Associations. Not only can you network, you can find useful links and post questions.

---

c. Getting Started

How do you start? The best advice to anyone interested in the wealth of information available on the Internet is to educate yourself, develop a plan, and stay abreast of the multitude of sites available. Once you become comfortable with searching and then targeting your search, finding information you need will be quick, easy, and painless.

Basically, there are three steps to working with the Internet and eventually becoming the firm Internet guru, an envious position:

1. Familiarity with Internet terminology
2. Experience
3. Organization

i. Familiarity with Internet Terminology

The first step is to become familiar with basic Internet terminology. We have defined the Internet. What is the **World Wide Web**? It is a network of different documents connected to each other through hypertext embedded in the documents. The Web works by using a client-server system, where the computer stores files and then downloads them to client computers. Think of the Web as a resource and research library.

You will encounter all types of new words and language. It is extremely important to become familiar with those words and their meanings. A few of the words you need to know to get started follow. See the Glossary for additional definitions.

Hypertext links. Words, pictures, or phrases in a document that can be selected using the mouse, which causes a new document to be displayed.

Adobe Acrobat Reader. A software application used to download and view PDF (Portable Document Format) documents, a common type of file found on the Internet.

Search engine. Software that looks for and finds Web and other Internet sites based on the search criteria you provide.

URL (**Universal Resource Locator**) is an address for a resource on the Internet.

Web browser. Free software, usually provided by an Internet Service Provider, that enables the user to look at, interact with, and generally browse files on the Internet. It is used to navigate the World Wide Web. It translates computer programming into text, pictures, sound, and video, all at the same time. Examples include Netscape or Internet Explorer.

Internet Service Provider. The company or organization that provides an Internet connection.

It is also important to keep in mind the **domain name**, the part of the URL that identifies the server and the filename you are looking for. The top level domain (the three letters at the end of the domain) acts as an area code or zip code. It allows more than one user to use the same name. The top level also identifies the type of institution that is responsible for the content of the page.

.com commercial
.edu educational
.gov government
.net computer network
.org nonprofit organization
.mil military

After deciding to give the Web a try, you need to develop some strategy for your searches. There are a few things to think about. What information do you need? Do you need a lot of information or basic background information? How long do you have to search?

Basically, there are two very different types of search services available: search engines and directories. **Search engines** are full-text indexes of Web pages that are compiled daily by software "robots" that locate and store millions of pages into the index. As you search an index, you are hoping to find a good match between the keywords you type in and all of the words contained in the index. You are relying on a computer to do simple pattern-matching between your query words and the words in the index.

Some of the major search engines found as of this writing follow.

AltaVista *(http://www.altavista.com)*   Size, speed, low rate of dead links, and multiple search options make it one of the most popular search engines.

HotBot *(http://hotbot.lycos.com)*   HotBot has one of the largest indexes of Web pages and offers lots of advanced search features to help you narrow your queries.

Excite *(http://www.excite.com)*   Excite is unique because in addition to regular search features, it offers concept searching. For instance, if your search includes the term *'film'*, Excite will also search for *'movie'*.

Lycos *(http://www.lycos.com)*   Lycos has easy pop-up menus to select search options. Its search engine focuses on popular sites, so if you are looking for a scientific or technical topic, try another search tool.

Infoseek *(http://www.infoseek.com)*   Infoseek has everything and is broken down into categories.

Yahoo! *(http://www.yahoo.com)*   This site has been around since 1994 and has a huge subject database, which is a great place to browse for Internet resources. A very useful starting place.

Directories, on the other hand, are collections of links to Web sites compiled by people, not software "robots." Directories are organized by category or topic and have the advantage over search engines in that they can be very precise in how they categorize pages. Examples of directories are LookSmart (*http://www.look smart.com*) and About.com (*http://www.about.com*).

So which do you use for your search? One of the most important advantages to an index is its size. Indexes have information on millions of Web pages. However, this size can be a problem in itself, especially for common subjects. Also, it is difficult, if not impossible, to determine the originator of the information or the quality of the link in the results you obtain. Directories, on the other hand, will almost always be of much higher quality and are organized in a hierarchical format so you can burrow down through the subject trees. The scope of the results may be much smaller than that returned by an index, thus the possibility of missing some important information is likely. The basic rules of thumb are these:

✦ **Search engines are best when you want lots of results or are searching for unique terms, such as a drug name or medical procedure.**

✦ **Directories are better when you want focused results or for broad categories that you can browse, such as family law or intellectual property law.**

ii. Experience

Now that you are somewhat familiar with terminology and what is available, get to know the surroundings. The second step is to become comfortable with using the Internet and the Web; in other words, get some experience and experiment. How do you do that? Simply by using it. Take the time to have fun and explore the possibilities. Keep in mind the following six tips.

1. No one method is the "right" one.
2. The simplest search is often the best.

3. Do not stop with only one search tool.
4. Do not use the same search tools for every search.
5. Experiment.
6. Experience.

You need to know when to turn to the Internet for information and when other sources of information would be more productive. Generally, the Internet is very useful in researching topics in the following eight categories.

1. Government information: Both state and federal governments are publishing more and more information on the Internet, a much more cost-effective and efficient means
2. International material: cases, codes, country data, statistics.
3. Computer or technology-related information
4. Medical information
5. News: hot topics and what is happening in the world
6. Unique terms
7. Background information
8. Expert witnesses and consultants

iii. Organization

The third and last step is to become organized. Decide how you are going to manage all the information, and where you are going to store it. You can bookmark sites, add sites to your favorites, or simply use a word processing table. It is important to note that Corel Word Perfect 8 or Microsoft Word 7 can convert site references to hyperlinks to the Web. This is not only helpful in case citing in briefs, it is fast becoming mandatory by many judges. Also, this hyperlinking function is extremely helpful in managing your favorite sites. For example, you can use the word processing table function to build a table of useful sites, along with comments on what the site offers, as well as developing keyword functions. You can then use the table to search for what you are looking for, find it, then go immediately to the site found. Table 4.2 shows an example of such a

TABLE 4.2.   TABLE OF USEFUL WEB SITES

Address	Comments	Keyword
http://www.consumerlawpage.com	Accident and insurance claims; defective products: SUVs, cars, trucks, aircraft; birth defects caused by toxic chemicals; cancer caused by toxic chemicals; financial and corporate fraud; preserving evidence, time limits and more.	defective products

continued on next page

Address	Comments	Keyword
http://www.medoptionslegal.com	MediFocus guides are valuable new roadmaps that help trial attorneys get through the complex maze of authoritative medical information required for their cases. Each in-depth guide identifies the key medical journal articles for a specific medicolegal issue. Note: Some guides are free, others require payment.	medical
http://www2.homefair.com/calc/salcalc.html	Cost of living (salary) calculator.	cost of living
http://www.kbb.com	Kelley Blue Book.	blue book
http://www.mapquest.com	Airport maps; road trip planner; driving directions.	travel
http://www.fedworld.gov	Government and business sites by category.	government
http://www.ceoexpress.com	Links to various sources for research, newspapers, maps, business sources, law references.	research
http://owl.english.purdue.edu	Punctuation, spelling, sentence structure, tips on searching the Internet.	English
http://www.ecola.com	Newspapers and magazines worldwide.	research
http://www.cdc.gov/nchs/howto/w2w/ w2welcom.htm	State links for birth, death, marriage, divorce, records. Health statistics.	statistics
http://members.aol.com/ronin48th/hope.htm	10-hour law school.	legal
http://www.pueblo.gsa.gov	Federal Consumer Information Center.	consumer publications
http://www.mic.ki.se/Medimages.html	Karolinska Institutet, Library, Stockholm, Sweden. A medical/anatomy site.	medical anatomy

table. As you can see, it may take some time to develop, but it is well worth the effort in the end due to time savings and efficiency.

Once a system such as this is used, you will have no difficulty finding and locating the information and sites you need.

In more advanced searches, keyword searching can be a powerful search method, but it requires an understanding of some important principles and techniques to be used effectively. Since keyword searches are free text, meaning they can find any word in any text, they must be used carefully. A keyword search in database records that have large free-text fields may result in your search terms being used in contexts other than what you anticipated, resulting in irrelevant hits.

Even with this limitation, however, the flexibility of the keyword search can easily overcome this potential hazard. Using search operators, you can limit your search results to only those records that match multiple criteria, such as several topics, a particular author, a year or range of years, a specific publisher or publication, and more.

Keyword searching, and search operators, are available in nearly all electronic databases, so learning how they operate is essential to taking full advantage of the capabilities of this search method. An example of common search operators to assist you in keyword searching are shown in Table 4.3.

Last, we need to address how to site resources found on the Internet. According to Rule 18.2.1(a) of the 17th Edition of *The Bluebook* (2000), the elements to Internet citation.

The elements of Internet citation are: the available information about the authority being cited (rule 18.2.1.(b)); the appropriate explanatory phrase (if any) to indicate which source actually was used by the author (rule 18.2.1); the provider responsible for the Internet site, where not apparent from the Uniform Resource Locator (URL) (Rule 18.2.1(c)-(d)); the URL (rule 18.2.1(c)); a date parenthetical (rule 18.2.1.(e)); and any explanatory parenthetical (rule 18.2.1(f)). the problems of pinpoint citations to Internet sources are addressed in rule 18.2.1(g).

The basic citation form states generally that "the citation of information to Internet

TABLE 4.3.   COMMON SEARCH OPERATORS

Operator	Function
AND	Finds records with both terms.
OR	Finds records containing either word.
NOT	Finds records containing the query word preceding it, without containing the word following it.
NEAR	Finds records with terms within a specified number of words of each other.
*	This is a wildcard operator for strings. A wildcard operator will enable you to search for names with different spellings, i.e. Smith or Smyth would be Sm*th.
" "	Finds records in which terms appear together as a group.

sources should indicate clearly and unambiguously the source actually used or accessed by the author of the citing work (rule 18.2.1)."

John Hiatt, *The Coolest Singer Ever,* available at *http://www.hiatt/com* (last modified April 24, 2000) .

Citations to journals that appear only on the Internet should include the volume number, the title of the journal, and the sequential article number; the explanatory phrase "at" to indicate an on-line journal (rule 18.2.1(b), and the Internet address. Pinpoint citations should refer to the paragraph number, if available:

> Dan L. Burk,*Trademark along the Infobah: A First Look at the Emerging Law of Cybermarks,* 1 RICH J.L. & TECH. 1, ¶ 12 (Apr. 10, 1997) at *http://urich.edu/~jolt/vlil/burk.html.*

One should not conclude that the Internet has now finished changing. The Internet, although a network in name and geography, is a creature of the computer, not the traditional network of the telephone or television industry. It will and it must continue to change and evolve at the speed of the computer industry if it is to remain relevant. It is now changing to provide such new services as real-time transport, in order to support audio an video streams. The availability of pervasive networking along with powerful affordable computing and communications in portable forms is making possible a new paradigm of nomadic computing and communications.

PRACTICE TIP

Successful searching on the Web requires planning, persistence, creativity, imagination and experience, and sometimes luck. Take the time to understand the basics of Web searching such as technology, sources, terms, strategy, and advanced searching techniques.

---

2. Commercial Databases

The burgeoning expanse of the cyberworld continues to reveal new resources for the legal researcher. While this is exciting and often helpful, it may be time for a reality check. The Internet may not have what you need; data may not be in a useful format and it may not be accurate. After all, there is little, if any, quality control of the Internet. Quoting *Law Technology Product News,*

> For certain types of information, the Internet cannot match the offerings of the commercial services. . . . . A common problem in litigation is finding information on a witness. . . . Although the Internet would appear to provide endless resources to assist in this task . . . the Internet falls far short when compared to commercial services.[1]

---

1. *Don't Cancel Your Database Accounts,* Apr. 1998.

Inexpensive development and negligible operational costs are two of the reasons for the plethora of new Internet sites and extranet networks. The reality is that you get what you pay for. In the case of many new collaborative extranets, what you get may not be very much. Consider IDEX Defense Network. IDEX has been in the business of tracking expert witness testimony for over 16 years. The network consists of over 3,200 member offices contributing case information that is compiled in a database approaching 800,000 records. With almost 90,000 experts in the network's database, IDEX finds case involvements on 75 to 80 percent of the experts requested. For many years, IDEX has added thousands of new records each month from requests and equally as many from a variety of other sources including published data, court reporting connections, and other outside sources. In contrast, extranet services rely solely on participants' voluntary contributions to build their databases. At the time of this writing, we are aware of no other sources that can compare to the quantity and quality of the data on expert testimony available from IDEX.

Much of the case information IDEX archives may never be found in other commercial databases or floating on the Internet. IDEX becomes aware of an expert's involvement early in the discovery process. Most claims settle. The expert may have provided a letter of opinion, a report, or perhaps a deposition prior to the settlement of the case. Often this type of case information may never be published, and therefore rarely found on the Internet. As a result, IDEX may be your best source for the following settled case information.[2]

- Backgrounds searches on experts
- Searches for medical and scientific literature
- Electronic document archive available online
- Testimonial history (case history) of plaintiff and defense experts

3. Public and Private Sources

In the quest for information, a paralegal must rely on both public and private sources. Any good investigator grows in his or her profession by developing individual and agency contacts that serve the purposes of providing information. Contacts are individuals willing to provide information to which an investigator would usually have a more difficult time obtaining or gaining access to.

a. Public Sources

Public sources are a public entity where information is found, taken, or derived. Public access to information is guaranteed under statutory and common law. That access, however, is not absolute and is subject to certain regulatory processes. Much information that the paralegal needs to obtain is of public record such as judgments, birth records, marriage records, divorce records, tax records, voter registrations, and motor vehicle

2. 8 IDEX Rev.; No. 1; Winter 2000.

licensing. There is a wealth of information from all kinds of agencies, both federal and state. To name a few:

- Census Bureau
- Department of Justice
- Federal Aviation Agency
- Internal Revenue Service
- National Board of Transportation Safety
- Occupational Safety and Health Administration
- Social Security Administration
- Veteran's Administration

Luckily for the paralegal, all these sites and more are now located on the Internet. All of these sites vary in the amount of information available, but they all are excellent sources of information. Many of these agencies offer needed forms online. With a simple download, a paralegal can have access to a needed document in a matter of minutes.

An excellent source available on the Internet is the Federal Web Locator (*http://www.infoctr.edu/fwl/*). The Federal Web Locator is a service provided by the Center of Information Law and Policy and is designed to be a "one stop shopping point for federal government information on the World Wide Web." All the investigative paralegal needs to do is simply click on the link provided and he or she is then instantly taken to the site needed. Take time to familiarize yourself with the content of the information available. It might be helpful to list the home page under your favorites on your computer. The site is something you will use often and the list of agencies at the site can jog your memory when you are investigating as possible information sources.

There are a myriad of state and local agencies with a wealth of information. Again, most of the agencies are available on the Internet. All states generally have some type of administrative bureaucracy dealing with records and other documentation. A paralegal worth his or her salt should be aware of these sites and be able to gain access to the information provided. Every state is different in the information they have online, however, most Secretary of State offices and government offices have online access and links to various state agencies. Generally, most states have the following state agencies available as public sources, both online and through the agency itself.

- County and local courthouses
- Department of Corrections
- Department of Highways
- Department of Labor and Industry
- Department of Motor Vehicles
- Secretary of State
- Traffic departments
- Workers Compensation

b. Private Sources

Private sources are private entities where information is found, taken, or derived. Although the public sources of information can yield excellent results, the paralegal should not neglect all the private sources available. Aside from utilizing the services of private investigators, detectives, process servers, and other private individuals or agencies, the paralegal can take advantage of a host of sources that are often bypassed in the investigative process. The following list describes five of the most useful ones.

1. ***Directories and databases.*** Historically, certain information has been collected in directories or other databases. With the advent of the electronic age, this data collection has been enhanced. Most of these types of private information are located on the Internet. Some examples of directories or databases follow.
   a. Lexis/Westlaw: case law, statutory and administrative decisions; available only to paid subscribers
   b. Medical indexes: indexes and abstracts of articles from major medical journals; a wealth of information is available online through the National Library of Congress Free Medline (*http://www.nlm.nih.gov*)
   c. Telephone directories: Available at most libraries in hardcopy and online at *www.switchboard.com*
   d. *Federal Register:* publication of notices, rules, and regulations of government offices
   e. City directories: Addresses, phone numbers, and cross-references based on name, street, or phone
   f. Professional listings: listings of professional associations, trades, groups, and specialty areas
2. ***Libraries.*** In this day and age, libraries are almost forgotten sources of investigative information. Most libraries have collections of legal books and publications, directories, and historical information. Research librarians can assist with research, answer questions, and provide guidance in the quest for information. Colleges and university libraries are generally participants in interlibrary loan programs affording access to every major library in the United States.
3. ***Newspapers.*** Old newspapers are now being filed under standardized classification systems and are generally on microfilm or microfiche. Stories or topical concerns are arranged chronologically or in some other order for appropriate indexing and cataloging.
4. ***Professional associations and groups.*** Many private foundations and associations can provide access to relevant information.
5. ***Commercial databases.*** There are numerous commercial databases that offer services on locating information on missing persons, credit histories, liens, judgments, and bankruptcies.

4. Other Investigative Sources and Techniques

a. Skip Tracing

Skip tracing is a process used to locate possible parties to a legal action through third-party contacts. Most often it is used to enforce debt collections, to find debtors who have default judgments against them and to locate the assets and sources of income of these judgment debtors. Skip tracing starts with basic information such as Social Security number, full name, most recent address, friends or relatives, a physical description, or a photograph. Skip tracing is very much an individual research technique developed over time. There is no one way to do it. There is much room for creativity.

b. FOIA Requests

Freedom of Information Act (FOIA) requests are those that fall under the Freedom of Information Act. They provide access to federal records in the executive branch. Figure 4.1 shows a sample FOIA request.

Although individuals can use the FOIA to obtain agency records relating to themselves, they should also be aware of their option to utilize the Privacy Act for this purpose. Unlike the FOIA, which merely enables you to obtain access to such records, the Privacy Act establishes your right to correct, amend, or expunge records in which the information about you is not accurate, relevant, timely, or complete. In fact, the Privacy Act permits you to sue the agency for refusal to correct or amend your record, as well as for refusal to give you access. Depending on the information sought, it may be advisable to request access jointly under both statutes when attempting to obtain certain information.

The 1966 Freedom of Information Act created a sweeping change in public access to federal records in the executive branch by allowing any person, regardless of nationality or need, to obtain documents not falling under one of nine exemptions. For the first time, the burden of proof was placed on the government to show why information should be withheld from the public.

The 1974 and 1976 amendments to the FOIA were passed to ensure easier and speedier access to documents. These amendments require agencies to publish in the *Federal Register* the procedures for filing FOIA requests and to make available policies and policy interpretations adopted by agencies but not published in the *Federal Register.*

The FOIA applies to all administrative agencies of the executive branch, including the armed forces, but not to Congress, the courts, or the President's immediate staff. The executive branch includes executive offices, departments, bureaus, councils, commissions, government corporations, government-controlled corporations, and regulatory agencies.

There are nine areas of exemptions to the FOIA specified in the law:

1. Exemption (b)(1): documents that are properly classified and, if disclosed, would harm the national defense or foreign policy
2. Exemption (b)(2): matters "related solely to the internal personnel rules and practices of an agency."
3. Exemption (b)(3): pertains to information that is "specifically exempted from disclosure by statutes" when the statute has established criteria for withholding that leaves no discretion in the matter
4. Exemption (b)(4): protects "trade secrets and commercial or financial information" obtained from a person who is privileged or confidential
5. Exemption (b)(5): applies to "interagency or intraagency memoranda or letters" that would not be available by law to a party other than an agency in litigation with the agency

Dear Mr. Smith:

We have been retained by John and Mary Doe to investigate the circumstances surrounding a fire that destroyed property on their private land south of Anywhere, Montana, on or about January 1, 2000. The fire became known as the "Very Windy Fire" following ignition at or near Jump Off Peak in the Rocky Mountains on National Forest land near Anywhere, Montana.

This Freedom of Information request to the United States Department of the Interior, Bureau of Land Management (BLM), shall include a request for information and documents from all BLM offices, agencies, and outposts under the Department of the Interior's direction, supervision, and control, including the state office, district offices, regional offices, resource area offices, and interagency fires dispatch centers or offices in Montana and Idaho that were involved in any aspect concerning the detection, dispatch, confinement, presuppression, or suppression, of the Very Windy Fire.

Every attempt has been made to narrow these requests so we do not obtain the same documentation that has been provided to Mr. and Mrs. Doe previously under their Freedom of Information request. For example, we do not wish to obtain the entire fire packet. We are primarily interested at the present time in information and documents that discuss or reflect the initial reports of smoke, ignition, or fire in the area where the Very Windy Fire originated.

Please provide us with the following information:

[List specific information requested. For example:]
    All documents or audio tapes, including but not limited to, telephone logs or tapes, dispatch logs or tapes, radio logs or tapes, telephone records or notes, as well as other documents, that reflect the date and time the ignition or fire was initially reported to any BLM office, agency, station, outpost, or any employee thereof, whether such report was an internal report or an external report, whether such report was oral or written, and whether any action was taken at that time of the report to dispatch or suppress the fire.

Please provide us with an estimate of the copying charges necessary to respond to the request for documents contained in this letter prior to providing the actual documents.

If you have any questions, please contact us at the direct dial number listed above. Thank you for your cooperation in this matter.

Figure 4.1. Sample FOIA Request Letter

6. Exemption (b)(6): covers "personnel and medical files and similar files, the disclosure of which would constitute a clearly unwarranted invasion of personal privacy"
7. Exemption (b)(7): prevents the disclosure of "investigatory records compiled for law enforcement purposes," but only to the extent that they are included in one or more of the six areas outlined in the Act
8. Exemption (b)(8): exempts information "contained in or related to examination, operating, or condition reports prepared by, on behalf of, or for the use of an agency responsible for the regulations or supervision of financial institutions"
9. Exemption (b)(9): applies to "geological and geophysical information and data, including maps, concerning wells"

F. GENERAL RULES OF ADMISSIBILITY

It is imperative that the paralegal start thinking in terms of evidence and admissibility very early in the case. **Evidence** is any item or fact that can be used to prove or disprove a case. The basic prerequisites of admissibility are relevance, materiality, and competence. In general, if evidence is shown to be relevant, material, and competent, and is not barred by an exclusionary rule, it is admissible. Fed. R. Evid. 402.

Relevant evidence is evidence used to prove a fact at issue in the case. Evidence is relevant when it has any tendency in reason to make the fact that it is offered to prove or disprove either more or less probable. Fed. R. Evid. 401. To be relevant, a particular item of evidence need not make the fact for which it is offered certain, or even more probable than not. All that is required is that it have *some* tendency to increase the likelihood of the fact for which it is offered. Weighing the evidence is for the finder of fact, and although a particular piece of evidence, standing by itself, may be weak, it will be admitted unless it is otherwise incompetent or it runs afoul of an exclusionary rule. For example, if the fact to be proved is that the defendant bit off the plaintiff's nose in a fight, testimony by an eyewitness to the act would clearly be relevant, but so would testimony by a witness who heard the plaintiff and the defendant exchange angry words on the day before the fight, or even testimony by a witness who sold the defendant a disinfectant mouthwash shortly afterwards.

Material evidence is evidence that tends to make a specific fact either more or less probable. Evidence is material if it is offered to prove a fact that is at issue in the case. For example, if testimony of an eyewitness is offered to prove that it was raining on the day of the signing of a contract, that evidence may be relevant to prove the fact for which it is offered, yet the fact that it was or was not raining may be immaterial to any of the issues in the case, which may turn entirely on whether one or both parties breached the contract. The issues in the case are determined by the pleadings, any formal stipulations or admissions, and the applicable law. For example, if, in a case of breach of contract, the defendant has conceded that the plaintiff performed all his covenants, proof of that performance would no longer be material unless it were relevant to some other issue.

Competent evidence is evidence said in the court by a competent witness. Evidence is competent if the proof that is being offered meets certain traditional requirements of reliability. The preliminary showing that the evidence meets those tests, and any other prerequisites of admissibility, is called the *foundational evidence*. When an objection is made that an answer to a question, a document, or a thing lacks a proper foundation, what the objector is really saying is that a showing of competence, or of another prerequisite of admissibility, has not yet been made. The modern trend in the law is to diminish the importance of the rules of competence by turning them into considerations of weight. Fed. R. Evid. 601.

In general, if competent evidence is offered to prove a relevant and material fact, it is admissible even if it would have been improper to receive it for another purpose. For example, while evidence of prior bad acts is generally not admissible to show that a person acted similarly in the present case, it may be admissible to show motive, plan, intent, or lack of mistake or, in federal court, to impeach a witness's credibility. When evidence is received for a limited purpose, the party who thinks a jury may make improper use of that evidence is entitled, upon request, to a limiting instruction.

However, where the value of evidence for its proper purpose is slight and the likelihood that it will be used for an improper purpose by a finder of fact is great, a court may, in its discretion, exclude the evidence even though it would otherwise be admissible. In this situation, the probative value of the evidence is said to be outweighed by its prejudicial effect.

Prejudice means improper harm. The fact that evidence may be extremely harmful to one party's case does not necessarily make it prejudicial. Courts also have discretion to exclude otherwise admissible evidence to prevent confusion, delay, waste of time, or the needless presentation of cumulative evidence.

G. EVIDENCE

Evidence is discussed more fully in Chapter 10; however, at this juncture the paralegal should be mindful of the rules applicable in federal courts that govern what evidence is admissible—the Federal Rules of Evidence. In order to assist fully with the investigative process, a paralegal must be aware of the four types of evidence:

1. Real
2. Demonstrative
3. Documentary
4. Testimonial

Some rules of evidence apply to all four types and some apply only to one or more of them. First, we will cover general rules of admissibility that apply to all evidence. Then, we will cover the four traditional types of evidence. Special topics, like the form of examination, the hearsay rule, and the lay opinion rule, are discussed in Chapter 10. However, this section will provide a good background and a referral resource for your investigative process.

1. Real Evidence

Real evidence is evidence meeting certain requirements or reliability. It is a thing the existence or characteristics of which are relevant and material. Real evidence is usually a thing that was directly involved in some event in the case. The written contract on which an action is based is real evidence both to prove its terms and to prove that it was executed by the defendant. If it is written in a faltering and unsteady hand, it may also be relevant to show that the writer was under duress at the time of its execution. The bloody clothes, the murder weapon, a crumpled automobile, the scene of an accident—all may be real evidence.

To be admissible, real evidence, like all evidence, must be relevant, material, and competent. Establishing these basic prerequisites, and any other special ones that may apply, is called *laying a foundation*. The relevance and materiality of real evidence are usually obvious. Its competence is established by showing that it really is what it is supposed to be. Proving that real or other evidence is what it purports to be is called *authentication*.

Real evidence may be authenticated in three ways:

1. By identification of a unique object
2. By identification of an object that has been *made* unique
3. By establishing a chain of custody.

The easiest and usually the least troublesome way to authenticate real evidence is by the testimony of a witness who can identify a unique object in court. For example, the curator of a museum may be able to testify that he is familiar with, say, a Picasso and that what has been marked as exhibit so-and-so is in fact that work. It is important to remember, however, that many more mundane objects may be amenable to this kind of identification. A unique contract, or one that has been signed, may be authenticated by a person who is familiar with the document or its signatures. A ring may have an inscription by which it can be identified. Even a manufactured object, like a wallet, may be identifiable by its owner after years of use have given it marks of distinction.

The second method—identification in court of an object that has been made unique—is extremely useful since it sometimes allows a lawyer or client to avoid the pitfalls of proving a chain of custody by exercising some forethought. If a witness who can establish an object's relevance to the case marks it with his signature, initials, or another mark that will allow him to testify that he can tell it from all other objects of its kind, that witness will be allowed to identify the object in court and thus to authenticate it. Often, if a member of the lawyer's staff such as the paralegal early in the chain of custody marks the evidence, big problems can be avoided if a later link in the chain turns out to be missing.

The third and least desirable way to authenticate real evidence is by establishing a chain of custody. Establishing a chain of custody requires that the whereabouts of the evidence at all times since the evidence was involved in the events at issue be established by competent testimony.

The proponent of the evidence must also establish that the object, in relevant respects, has not changed or been altered between the events and the trial. This can sometimes be a tall order, or can require the testimony of several witnesses. If there is any time from the events in question to the day of trial during which the location of the item cannot be accounted for, the chain is broken. In that case, the evidence will be excluded unless another method of authentication can be used.

2. Demonstrative Evidence

Demonstrative evidence is evidence used to illustrate verbal testimony. Demonstrative evidence is just what the name implies—it demonstrates or illustrates the testimony of a witness. It will be admissible when, with accuracy sufficient for the task at hand, it fairly and accurately reflects that testimony and is otherwise unobjectionable. Typical examples of demonstrative evidence are maps, diagrams of the scene of an occurrence, animations, and the like. Because its purpose is to illustrate testimony, demonstrative evidence is authenticated by the witness whose testimony is being illustrated. That witness will usually identify salient features of the exhibit and testify that it fairly and accurately reflects what he saw or heard on a particular occasion, such as the location of people or things on a diagram.

3. Documentary Evidence

Documentary evidence is evidence through documents, notes, writings, instructions, or any other similar type of object. Documentary evidence is often a kind of real evidence, as, for example, when a contract is offered to prove its terms. When a document is used this way, it is authenticated the same way as any other documentary evidence—by a witness who identifies it or, less commonly, by witnesses who establish a chain of custody for it. However, because they contain human language, and because of the historical development of the common law, documents present special problems not presented by other forms of real evidence, such as when they contain hearsay.

When dealing with documentary evidence, it is a good idea to ask yourself four questions:

1. Is there a parol evidence problem?
2. Is there a best evidence problem?
3. Is there an authentication problem?
4. Is there a hearsay problem?

The **parol evidence rule,** which bars the admission of extrinsic evidence to vary the terms of a written agreement, is usually considered a matter of substantive law, not of rule of evidence. Accordingly, we will not deal with it here. See Chapter 10 for a more thorough discussion of the parol evidence rule.

As has been noted above, documents can be authenticated the same way as any other real evidence. Material alterations must be accounted for. There are also specifically approved methods of authenticating documents listed in the Federal Rules of Evidence, including the submission to the finder of fact of a known exemplar of a signature for comparison with the signature on a disputed document, authentication by evidence of a reply, and authentication by content.

In addition, some documents, such as certified copies of public records, official documents, newspapers, periodicals, trade inscriptions, acknowledged documents to prove the acknowledgment, certificates of the custodians of business records, and certain commercial paper and related documents are, to one extent or another, self-authenticating under the federal rules. Fed. R. Evid. 901, 902.

The best evidence rule is a rule requiring that the original document be submitted to the court for admission. The best evidence rule provides that, where a writing is offered in evidence, a copy or other secondary evidence of its content will not be received in place of the original document unless an adequate explanation is offered for the absence of the original. Fed. R. Evid. 1002.

The best evidence rule arose during the days when a copy was usually made by a clerk or, worse, a party to the lawsuit. Courts generally assumed that if the original was not produced, there was a good chance of either an error or fraud. Now that "copy" usually means "photocopy," the chance of a copy being in error, as opposed to simply illegible, is slight. In addition, courts are reluctant to require needless effort and delay where there is no dispute about the fairness and adequacy of a photocopy.

Accordingly, the federal rules allow the use of mechanically produced duplicates unless a party has raised a genuine question about the accuracy of the copy or can show that its use would be unfair. Fed. R. Evid. 1003. However, there is always a danger of a party questioning a document, so it is important to remember that, unless you have a stipulation to the contrary, or your document fits one of the exceptions listed in the statute, you must be ready to produce originals of any documents involved in your case or to produce evidence of why you can't.

Under the federal rules, compilations or summaries of voluminous records may be received if the originals are available for examination by the other parties.

4. Testimonial Evidence

Testimonial evidence is evidence that is said in court at the proceeding by a competent witness. Testimonial evidence is the most basic form of evidence and the only kind that does not usually require another form of evidence as a prerequisite for its admissibility. In general, a witness is competent if he or she meets four requirements:

1. He must, with understanding, take the oath or a substitute.
2. He must have personal knowledge about the subject of his testimony. In other words, the witness must have perceived something with his senses that is relevant to the case.
3. He must remember what he perceived.
4. He must be able to communicate what he perceived.

There are other rules of competence that relate to special circumstances, such as the rule that a juror is generally incompetent to impeach his own verdict or that, at least in federal court, a judge is not competent to testify in a trial over which he is presiding, but these and other rules like them rarely come up in practice.

In addition, in keeping with the modern trend to view issues that were previously thought to involve questions of competence, the rules of competence are very liberally construed and rarely result in the exclusion of evidence. For example, the requirement that a witness take the oath or a substitute permits virtually any kind of affirmation by which the witness, in effect, promises to tell the truth. The understanding of the oath or affirmation that is required can be that of a small child or mentally disabled person. The communication that is required may be in writing or through an interpreter, whether of spoken or of sign language. In addition, deficiencies in knowledge generally affect only weight, so long as the witness perceived *something* relevant.

ETHICS

The area of investigation for paralegals can be a difficult one in terms of ethics. Some paralegals have been tempted in their zeal to obtain information, verify facts, and locate evidence for trial to manipulate the information to their client's favor. While paralegals should be zealous advocates of their firm's clients, they should take great care to obtain the facts and evidence—all the facts and evidence—whether good or bad for the client. It can be extremely embarrassing for an attorney to be surprised near trial by information or evidence that should have been readily apparent from the start of the case.

Whenever a paralegal is conducting investigation, he or she must take great care in identifying who they are, who they work for, who they represent (plaintiff versus defendant), and that they are a paralegal. Remember to ensure that the party you are interviewing understands your role and understands that you are not an attorney. The same rule holds true for investigation. Never misrepresent your reason for the investigation. It is completely unethical for a paralegal to not disclose the law firm and the party they represent. The successful paralegal is one who holds truth as a premium and never compromises his or her high standards of ethical conduct.

CONCLUSION

Each client or witness is an individual person with unique needs, fears, personality traits, verbal abilities, intellectual skills, and motivations. Successful interviewing requires a willingness and capacity to discover, explore, and understand that unique perspective of the interview. Investigative skills can be developed over time. A successful investigation is one that has been planned and outlined ahead of time.

There is a wealth of information available, public and private. With the advent of the Internet, that information is becoming more and more accessible. The Internet makes investigation simple, quick, and more thorough. Background information is available to assist in understanding basic principles and concepts. Forms are available to assist in requesting the information needed.

The paralegal of today is smart to learn the resources available and keep updated on the new offerings. One easy way to do so is to review professional publications for sites used by others and tips on locating the information you need.

USING TECHNOLOGY IN THE LAW OFFICE

Investigation has become much less time-intensive since the advent of technology. The Internet allows for immediate access to information regarding individuals, corporations, and governmental entities. The only way for a paralegal to truly realize the potential of the Internet as an investigative tool is to use it.

A. INTERNET INVESTIGATION

The Internet has increased the efficiency and effectiveness of case investigation. It allows for immediate access to any information that is considered public record. It takes minutes to perform a national search to locate individuals, obtaining their current address, phone number, and a map to their residence. Research on medical and legal issues is at your fingertips, as is company or product research.

It takes time to establish a listing of favorite Web sites utilized for case investigation. However, once this listing is established it saves you numerous investigative hours. Most governmental bodies have **Web sites** (the address location of a Web page) that allow you to request records or information online. Further, several private corporations maintain extensive Web sites containing valuable information. Investigations regarding the opposing party's expert witnesses can be done online, as most professional experts maintain some type of Web site.

The Internet has become a primary source of information for case investigation and has the potential to replace other sources of information within the next five to ten years.

B. LOCATING EXPERT WITNESSES ON THE INTERNET

The next time you are asked to locate an expert witness for a case, think of the Internet. Through that connection you can locate names of potential witnesses, identify expert witness banks and databases, and verify credentials.

First, determine the specialty in which the expert needs to testify, (for example, medical, technical, business, corporate). Then, break that down into specific subcategories. For example, if you need an expert physician to testify in a medical malpractice case regarding cardiac surgery, first look to "medical," then look to "cardiology," then to "cardiac surgery."

It is always difficult to decide where to go on the Internet to find that expert. Once you have gone through the thought process above, start by looking at professional associations or published journals, articles, or books. Web sites of colleges and universities may lead to experts, as well as professional associations and societies. These sites can also be helpful in verifying credentials. Don't forget to use commercial databases and commercial referral services. An excellent commercial referral service is the Technical Advisory Service, Inc. (TASA). When using a service such as this, however, be sure to inquire into the fees charged and make sure that those fees are included in the litigation budget. There are many other sources on the Internet to go to find experts, such as directories of expert witnesses and consultants. Through experience you will determine the best sources to use. With a little forethought and experience you will become proficient at finding expert witnesses.

The Internet is also very useful in verifying an expert's credentials. Always be suspicious enough of an expert's credentials to investigate. If you fail to investigate an expert before making a commitment, chances are your neglect will come back to haunt you. You can verify that a particular expert has authored articles, obtain copies of those articles, and see what other areas the expert has written on. Not only should you investigate a potential expert you want to hire, you should investigate the expert hired by the opposing party. If the opposing party has not taken the time and care you have, you may be able to discover something adverse and not known to your opponent.

Always keep a list of Web sites found and visited to ensure that you do not backtrack and spend precious time revisiting certain sites. The list will also be useful in the future when again looking for experts.

C. ORGANIZING INVESTIGATIVE INFORMATION ELECTRONICALLY

If you are using the Internet for case investigation, it is advisable to save your favorite Web sites by their source. One way to do this is to set up **favorites folders** (items created within your Internet browser allowing you to organize your preferred Web sites) and under those folders place numerous Web sites. For instance, government sites would be placed in a government favorite folder and medical research sites would be placed in a medical favorite folder. Keeping favorites organized in this manner allows for quick and easy Web site access. Figure 4.2 depicts a favorites folder separating investigation Web site sources.

Further, investigative information specific to a case can be saved under that case folder's investigative subdirectory. Figure 4.3 depicts a case folder with an investigative subdirectory.

The Internet is a powerful tool, and the only way to fully realize its potential is to use it.

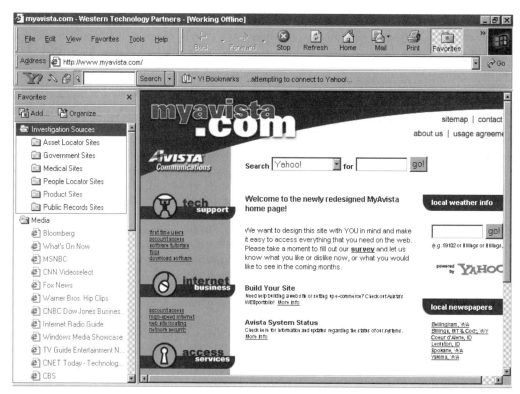

Figure 4.2. Microsoft Explorer–Investigation Sources

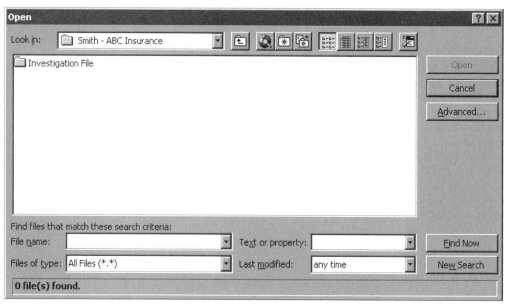

Figure 4.3. Microsoft Explorer–Favorites Folder

KEY TERMS

Best evidence rule	FOIA request	Public sources
Competent evidence	Investigation	Real evidence
Demonstrative evidence	Material evidence	Relevant evidence
Documentary evidence	Parol evidence rule	Skip tracing
Evidence	Private sources	Testimonial evidence

TECHNOLOGY TERMS

Directories	Search engines	World Wide Web
Domain names	URL (Universal Resource	
Favorites folders	Locator)	
Internet	Web sites	

USEFUL WEB SITES

Search engines:
http://www.google.com
*www.google.com/
    advanced_search*
http://www.altavista.com
http://www.excite.com
http://www.lycos.com
*http://www.hotbot.lycos.
    com*

*http://www.northernlight.
    com*
Specialty search engines:
*http://www.searchgov.
    com*
http://www.searchedu.com
*http://www.pandia.com/
    news/*

**Online legal research re-
sources:**
http://www.westlaw.com
http://www.lexisnexis.com
*http://www.american
    legalnet.com*
http://www.loislaw.com

Managing Documents

A paralegal working in civil litigation will be given the difficult task of managing documents and organizing information. Creation and maintenance of a—**document management system**—is a crucial part of the paralegal's duties. One of the most important skills a paralegal possesses involves being able to anticipate document management issues *before* they become issues. What type of document management system you choose will depend on resources available at your firm. Most attorneys you work for will rely on the document and information management skills you implement.

There are five primary groups of documents involved in litigation:

1. Client documents: documentation provided by an individual who has retained your attorney for legal representation
2. Third-party/other source documents: documentation provided by an entity not named in the lawsuit
3. Produced documents: documentation submitted in response to discovery requests
4. Privileged documents: documentation withheld from production
5. Documents produced by the opposing party

How you as the paralegal manage these five primary groups of documents determines to a great degree how smoothly the case will proceed from investigation through discovery and on to trial. Every document management system should address the following five areas:

1. Organizing documents
2. Indexing documents
3. Establishing document identifiers
4. Separating key documents in a case
5. Compiling documents in a searchable database

A. ORGANIZING DOCUMENTS

The attorney(s) you work for may have specific systems established for the organization of records. Before organizing or reorganizing files, communicate with the attorney about what system you plan to use. Remember, you are working as a team and your success will depend upon good communication. It does you no good to spend hours organizing documents within a file only to discover that the attorney wants something other than what you have done. Your efforts should be focused on making the attorney's job easier, not more difficult. If you do not understand the attorney's document organizing system, ask him or her to explain why they employ such a system. You both may realize the benefits that result from combining your ideas.

As a general rule, attorneys usually organize documents in two ways: by date and by issue. During trial, the litigator undertakes the task of telling a story from beginning to end while addressing several issues as the story is told. One way for the attorney to tell their client's story is through a timeline of events. If the paralegal organizes documents chronologically by document category, the attorney should be able to quickly review and compile documents for an event timeline, which assists in simplifying the story to be told.

When documents are being received from several different sources on a file, the paralegal must be able to organize these documents in some semblance of order. These documents need to be separated and organized according to their source category. Documents will likely be organized within the following five categories:

1. Client documents
2. Third-party/other source documents
3. Produced documents
4. Withheld documents
5. Documents received during discovery production

Each of these categories of documents should be organized separately.

1. Client Documents

Client documents are those documents your attorney receives from the client. Client documents should be organized in a file separate from the main file so that the attorney you are working with knows what documents the client provided. The client may have done internal research and investigation. If there are internal client documents resulting from investigation or research, such documents should be separated and organized chronologically. Client documents are easily organized chronologically according to the date they are created. It should always be noted on the client files when the information was received by the client. Dating the information received provides the attorney with a system for separating documents received from a client. In most cases clients continually will be locating and producing information. To respond adequately to discovery requests for documents, your attorney will need to know what has been produced to opposing counsel and what has yet to be produced. The best way to do this is by separating documents received from the client by date of receipt.

PRACTICE TIP

Create an index that tracks the date your attorney received client documents and the date client documents were produced or withheld from discovery. Remember to bates-number these documents so that you can identify them by bates number on your index. The index would be set up in a table with three columns: Bates Range, Date Received, and Date Produced/Withheld.

---

2. Third-Party/Other Source Documents

Third-party/other source documents include documents received from individuals or entities who are *not* named in the legal action. These items are another category of documents that need to be organized. Examples of third-party documents include

- Medical records
- Workers' compensation records: documents generated by the workers' compensation carrier as a result of an on-the-job injury
- Law enforcement records—documents generated by federal, state, or local law enforcement agencies
- Witness statements

These documents normally are organized by their source chronologically. For example, if you have received medical records, these documents would be considered third-party/other source documents, and you would organize them by the healthcare provider putting them in order chronologically by date (oldest to newest). You may wonder why it is suggested the records be organized in ascending order, that is, from earliest event to most-recent event? The primary reasons for organizing records in **ascending order,** by date is to allow for a continuing numbering system if additional records are obtained at a later date. You can simply add the additional documents to the end of the original set of records without having to change your numbering system.

3. Produced Documents

Produced documents are those documents your attorney produces to the opposing party in response to discovery requests. Pursuant to Federal Rule of Civil Procedure 34(b), this category of documents needs to be produced as it is kept in the usual course of business or otherwise organized in response to discovery requests from opposing counsel. Discovery requests consist of written questions asking for information or documents regarding the civil action. Specifically, a request for production of documents should be created utilizing the procedure defined in Rule 26 of the Federal Rules of Procedure. This rule allows parties to request the production of any nonprivileged relevant documents within the opposing party's possession, custody, or control.

The documents that are produced from a written discovery request will most likely come from several different sources: the client, third parties, and other entities. The documents that are produced must be organized in response to written discovery requests.

PRACTICE TIP

Insert colored tabbed sheets identifying which discovery request the sets of documents are in response to. In addition, number or label the documents consecutively using an alpha identifier and number identifier.

For instance, if the client production is for John Smith, label the production JSP 00001 and up for John Smith Production. For further reference, you will need to refer to certain numbered documents in your responses to request for production. By doing this, opposing counsel knows that JSP 00001 through 00007 are documents responsive to discovery request number one and so forth. If you also insert colored index sheets between each document production, you will further categorize which documents respond to certain written document requests. The discovery responses then can be easily traced back to the corresponding documents.

---

4. Privileged Documents

Privileged documents are those documents *not* produced by your attorney to opposing counsel due to one of two protected privileges:

1. **attorney-client privilege:** evidentiary privilege provided to a client allowing him or her to refuse to disclose and to prevent any other person from disclosing confidential communications between the client and the attorney
2. **work product doctrine privilege:** evidentiary privilege provided to any documentation prepared in the anticipation of litigation

Priviledged documents will also need to be organized separately. Pursuant to Rule 26 of the Federal Rules of Procedure, requested documents can only be withheld if (1) the documents fail to fall within the scope and/or limitations of discovery, or (2) the documents can be classified to fall within a protected privilege.

Rule 26(b)(2)of the Federal Rules of Procedure limits discovery as follows:

The frequency or extent of use of the discovery methods otherwise permitted under these rules and by any local rule shall be limited by the court if it determines that: (i) the discovery sought is unreasonably cumulative or duplicative, or is obtainable by from some other source that is more convenient, less burdensome, or less expensive; (ii) the party seeking discovery has had ample opportunity by discovery in the action to obtain the information sought; or (iii) the burden or expense of the proposed discovery outweighs its likely benefit, taking into account the needs of the case, the amount in controversy, the parties' resources, the importance of the issues at stake in the litigation, and the importance of the proposed discovery in resolving the issues.

The production of any documents that fall under (i), (ii), or (iii) of Rule 26(b)(2) can be objected to and withheld from production.

As previously stated, Rule 26 also affords parties protected privileges regarding the production of discovery documents. The privileges that are normally asserted in withholding documents include the attorney-client privilege and the attorney work product privilege.

The documents protected by the attorney-client privilege include those documents involving any communication between the attorney and his orher client.

As for the attorney work product doctrine, Rule 26(b)(3) of the Federal Rules of Civil Procedure indicate that the following constitutes documentation within the scope of the attorney work product doctrine:

(3) Trial Preparation Materials. Subject to the provisions of subdivision (b)(4) of this rule, a party may obtain discovery of documents and tangible things otherwise discoverable under subdivision (b)(1) of this rule and prepared in anticipation of litigation or for trial by or for another party or by or for that other party's representative (including the other party's attorney, consultant, surety, indemnitor, insurer, or agent) only upon a showing that the party seeking discovery has substantial need for the materials in the preparation of the party's case and that the party is unable without undue hardship to obtain the substantial equivalent of the materials by other means. In ordering discovery of such materials when the required showing has been made, the court shall protect against disclosure of the mental impressions, conclusions, opinions, or legal theories of an attorney or other representative of a party concerning the litigation.

The attorney work product privilege applies to all documents that demonstrate the thoughts or mental impressions of the attorney or other representatives working on the litigation case.

As with most procedural rules, each attorney interprets these discovery limitations and privileges in a different manner. Some attorneys employ a narrow interpretation, while other attorneys extend their interpretation to include a much broader scope. It is important for you to fully understand how the attorney you are working for interprets the privileges afforded to them, as you may be called on by that attorney to review documents and pull those documents deemed privileged under the procedural rules. As a paralegal, I have learned that this task can vary tremendously when working with different attorneys. As always, make sure that your communication with the attorney is clear and precise regarding what constitutes a privileged document.

> PRACTICE TIP
>
> Before you begin drafting responses to discovery requests, meet with your attorney and ask what types of documents he or she considers to be privileged pursuant to the attorney-client privilege or the attorney work product privilege. Specifically, ask about what he or she considers to be "prepared in anticipation of litigation."

Privileged documents should also be copied, separated, and labeled. Normally, I will label privileged documents for John Smith, JS PRIV 00001 and up. However, let's assume you have several documents were were numbered JS 00001 through 01000 and this numbering occurred prior to any review and omission of privileged documents. In this case, another approach to organizing and separating the numbered documents would involve pulling those number documents that are privileged and inserting in their place colored sheets indicating the document number, the identity of the document and the privilege asserted in withholding the document. Utilizing this approach explains any gap that may occur in the numbering system when documents are withheld from production.

Pursuant to Rule 26(b)(5) of the Federal Rules of Procedure, an index or log must be produced to opposing counsel regarding any documents withheld from production. Typically, this log is entitled a privilege log. A **privilege log** is a document pertaining to information protected from production. This rule requires that the following information be provided in the index or log:

> When a party withholds information otherwise discoverable under these rules by claiming that it is privileged or subject to protection as trial preparation material, the party shall make the claim expressly and shall describe the nature of the documents, communications, or things not produced or disclosed in a manner that, without revealing information itself privileged or protected, will enable other parties to assess the applicability of the privilege or protection.

Normally the number identifier is included along with the document description and privilege asserted to allow for the quick location of each privileged document. Table 5.1 is an example of a privilege log done through the use of a word processing table.

5. Documents Produced by Opposing Party

Documents produced by the opposing party are the documents your attorney receives from the opposing party in response to written discovery requests. Hopefully, these documents will be organized and labeled upon production to you. If the documents are not labeled upon receipt, then you should label them according to the party producing them. For example, if ABC Insurance produces these documents, they should be labeled ABC 00001 and so forth. You should also maintain an index of the labeled documents responsive to your discovery requests. If several sets of discovery requests are sent, then you need to know which documents were produced to which set of discovery.

TABLE 5.1.   PRIVILEGE LOG

Document Identifier	Document Date	Document Description	Privilege Asserted
JS 00001-00015	10/15/1997	Letter from John Smith to attorney, Scott Arnold, re: representation	Attorney-client privilege
JS 00024-00029	11/15/1997	E-mail from attorney, Scott Arnold, to John Smith re: status of case	Attorney-client privilege
JS 00056-00059	10/06/1998	Claim notes re: status of dispute and potential for suit	Attorney work product–generated in anticipation of litigation
JS 00090-00095	01/08/1998	Legal research memo re: litigation	Attorney work product

---

PRACTICE TIP

If the opposing party's production documents are not labeled and you label them upon receipt, provide the opposing party with a labeled set so they will have identically numbered documents to use during depositions. This reduces any confusion that may be encountered by both counsel during depositions. Numbered documents are easy to identify and locate during a deposition.

B. INDEXING DOCUMENTS

1. Creating an Entire File Index

Another task that exists in every document management system is indexing. Indexing of an entire file involves the creation of primary categories for that file. Normally, there are seven categories to every file:

1. Correspondence: documentation generated as a result of case communications
2. Pleadings: documentation containing formal allegations submitted by the parties involved in a lawsuit
3. Discovery: the process of discovering what was previously unknown
4. Investigation: the process of inquiring into or tracking down through questioning, inspecting or observing facts and other information

5. Notes: any documentation generated by an individual to to track information and refresh recollection
6. Legal research: information obtained through the review of legal treatises or past cases
7. Experts: individual with specialized knowledge obtained from personal or educational experiences

These primary categories will most likely contain subcategories within them. Figure 5.1 demonstrates a possible file index with subcategories.

PRACTICE TIP

The file folder labels should contain the category name and the index number assigned to that category for easy identification and location by all. The labels can also be color coded by category.

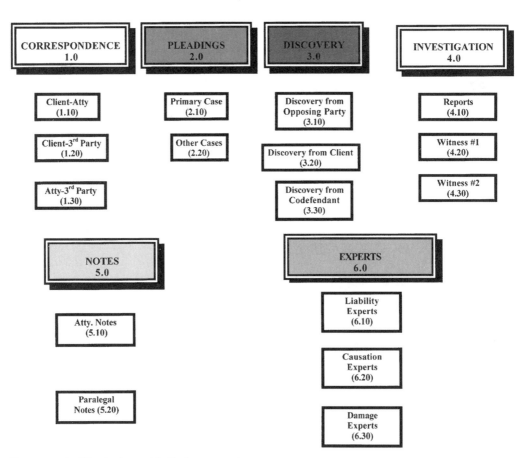

Figure 5.1. File Index with Subcategories

2. Color Coding

Color coding can be employed to designate which primary category of the file you are within: for example, Correspondence—White, Pleadings—Red, Discovery—Blue, Investigation—Yellow, Notes—Gray, and Experts—Green. On each of the file folders for these primary categories, the label used can have a colored bar on it for quick identification by category. Color-coding the primary categories ensures that all of those working on the file will have quick and easy access.

3. Assigning Index Numbers to the File Index

Depending on how detailed you want the file index to be, the numbers assigned to each file can be expanded by 1/10, 1/100, or 1/1000. Normally you assign the primary file categories with whole numbers from 1 through 6 or higher, if necessary. Any subcategories are then numbered consecutively by tenths. For example, different types of correspondence would be placed in subcategories and numbered 1.10, 1.20, 1.30, and so forth. As always, this file index can be numbered as simply or complexly as necessary. The larger the file, the more complex your index numbering system will become.

4. Location Identifier within the File Index

Another item always included within the index is a location identifier. This informs anyone in the office of the actual physical location for each category and subcategory of the file. This becomes extremely important when multiple individuals are working on a file or when you are working in a larger office, as different portions of the file can be located in various places throughout the office. If at all possible, try to keep the file in one central location to avoid confusion that may arise when fragments of the file are located throughout the office.

5. Completed File Index

When the index has been drafted, copies of it should be made for all the attorneys, paralegals, and other staff working on the case so that it can be effectively utilized within the office. Figure 5.2 is an example of a file index.

6. Creating an Index for Categories within the File

Individual small indexes can be created for the seven primary categories of a file and the numerous subcategories.

INDEX TO FILE MATERIALS

Smith vs. ABC Insurance Co.
Cause No. 95-K-1400
U.S. DISTRICT COURT, BILLINGS, MONTANA
File No. 20-136-201

LOCATION

1. **CORRESPONDENCE:**   4th Floor File Cabinet

VOLUME NUMBERS:

1	04/07/98—06/04/98
2	06/05/98—08/31/98
3	09/01/98—Present

1.10—CLIENT DOCUMENTS:

BOX# 1.10	Smith's Document Box #1	**(BATES SP 00001 to 01939)**
BOX# 1.20	Smith's Document Box #2	**(BATES SP 01940 to 02500)**
BOX# 1.30	Smith's Document Box #3	**(BATES SP 02501 to 03100)**
BOX# 1.40	Smith's Document Box #4	**(BATES SP 03101 to 04200)**
BOX# 1.50	Smith's Document Box #5	**(BATES SP 04201 to 04900)**
BOX# 1.60	Smith's Document Box #6	**(BATES SP 04901 to 05700)**
BOX# 1.70	Smith's Document Box #7	**(BATES SP 05701 to 06300)**
BOX# 1.80	Smith's Document Box #8	**(BATES SP 06301 to 08302)**

2. **PLEADINGS:**   (Blue 3-ring notebooks)   **SMITH WAR ROOM**

DOCKET NUMBERS—PRIMARY CASE:

1	1-55
2	56-95
3	96-119
4	120-

DOCKET NUMBERS—SECONDARY CASE:

1	1-30
2	31-50
3	51-70
4	71-

Figure 5.2. File Index

3. <u>DISCOVERY:</u> (Blue 3-ring notebooks) **SMITH WAR ROOM**

VOLUME NUMBERS:

1 06/07/98—09/10/98
2 09/11/98—12/27/98
3 12/28/98—02/14/99
4 02/15/99—Present

DISCOVERY DOCUMENTS: **SMITH WAR ROOM**

3.10—DOCUMENTS PRODUCED BY SMITH:

BOX# 3.10	Smith's Original Box #1	**(BATES SP 00001 to 01939)**
BOX# 3.11	Smith's Original Box #2	**(BATES SP 01940 to 02500)**
BOX# 3.12	Smith's Original Box #3	**(BATES SP 02501 to 03100)**
BOX# 3.13	Smith's Original Box #4	**(BATES SP 03101 to 04200)**
BOX# 3.14	Smith's Original Box #5	**(BATES SP 04201 to 04900)**
BOX# 3.15	Smith's Original Box #6	**(BATES SP 04901 to 05700)**
BOX# 3.16	Smith's Original Box #7	**(BATES SP 05701 to 06300)**

3.20—DOCUMENTS RECEIVED FROM OPPPOSING PARTY:

BOX# 3.20	AB Insurance Box #1	**(BATES ABP 00001 to 01800)**
BOX# 3.21	AB Insurance Box #2	**(BATES ABP 01801 to 02500)**
BOX# 3.22	AB Insurance Box #3	**(BATES ABP 02501 to 03300)**
BOX# 3.23	AB Insurance Box #4	**(BATES ABP 03301 to 04500)**

3.30—PRIVILEGED DOCUMENTS:

BOX# 3.30	JS PRIV 00001 to 01003
BOX# 3.31	JS PRIV 01050 to 02001

4. <u>INVESTIGATION:</u>

4.10—DOCUMENTS RECEIVED FROM THIRD-PARTY/OTHER SOURCES:

SMITH WAR ROOM

4.10	Police Investigation and Accident Report
4.20	Medical Records

Figure 5.2. (Continued)

4.20-1   St. Patrick Hospital Records   (BATES SPH 00001 to 00304)
4.20-2   Joseph's Rehabilitation Records (BATES JR 00001 to 00104)
4.20-3   EMS Ambulance Records   (BATES EMS 00001 to 00023)

4.30—WITNESS FILES: **SMITH WAR ROOM**

4.30 Witnesses
    4.30-1   John Smith   **(DEPOSITION EXHIBITS #__ to __)**
    4.30-2   Robert Daniels   **(DEPOSITION EXHIBITS #__ to __)**
    4.30-3   Jane Murray   **(DEPOSITION EXHIBITS #__ to __)**
    4.30-4   Scott Black   **(DEPOSITION EXHIBITS #__ to __)**

5.   NOTES: **SMITH WAR ROOM**

5.1 Attorney Notes
5.2 Paralegal Notes

6.   EXPERTS: **SMITH WAR ROOM**

6.1 Liability Experts
    6.1.1   Jeff Roe -   Highway Patrolman
6.2 Causation Experts
    6.2.1   Jane Rood-   Accident Reconstruction
6.3 Damages Experts
    6.3.1   Arnold Taylor   Economist

7.   LEGAL DOCUMENTS: **4th FLOOR FILE CABINET**
7.1 Executed Protective Order
7.2 Stipulations

8.   LEGAL RESEARCH AND MEMOS: **4TH FLOOR FILE CABINET**

8.1 Attorney Legal Research
8.2 Paralegal Legal Research
8.3 Attorney Memorandums
8.4 Paralegal Memorandums

Figure 5.2. (Continued)

a. Correspondence

The correspondence category should have an index that includes the following information:

- Client–Attorney Correspondence
- Client–Third-Party Correspondence
- Attorney–Third-Party Correspondence

This method allows you to easily locate correspondence between different entities. The correspondence is typically organized in ascending order by the date. Not all attorneys will want to separate correspondence into the three categories listed above. If the attorney you are working for wants to keep everything together, your index should just list the volume of correspondence and the dates included within that volume; for example: *Correspondence Volume I:* 10/23/92 through 11/04/1994, *Correspondence Volume II:* 11/05/1994 through 12/23/1996, and so forth.

b. Pleadings

The pleadings category should have an index that includes the following information:

- Docket Number
- Date
- Pleading Title
- Pleading Source

Another common name for this type of index is a pleading docket sheet. Some attorneys prefer to number their pleadings file pursuant to the court's docket number. This approach allows the attorney to cite quickly to court docket numbers during any briefing. The primary reason for utilizing the court's docket numbers during briefing would be to facilitate your reader's, (the judge's,) ability to easily retrieve and review the documents cited to by docket number. This method makes sense primarily because it ensures citing consistency between the attorneys and the court. However, some attorneys prefer to index their pleadings sequentially by date, assigning docket numbers pursuant to such dates. Check with the attorney you work with to ascertain which method should be employed when indexing pleadings.

PRACTICE TIP

Suggest the idea of utilizing the court's docket to index pleadings. Provide your attorney with the advantages in doing this.

---

c. Discovery

Discovery is another primary category that usually needs to be indexed. Since most courts do not allow for the filing of discovery responses or the documents responsive to discovery requests, the index created for discovery requests or responses and documents are indexed chronologically by date. Normally, the index sheet, or discovery docket sheet, contains the following information:

- Docket number
- Date
- Document title
- Document source

Normally you would separate the discovery file from the pleadings file; however, there are some attorneys that prefer the discovery requests and responses be included within the pleadings. If this method is preferred, the index created needs to be organized chronologically by date. Since discovery is not normally filed with the court, it does not have an assigned docket number and subsequently the index you create cannot be organized by docket number.

d. Investigation

Under the investigation category, an index can be created for each witness and investigative report. Usually, each witness will have provided certain documents, reviewed certain documents, and given a statement and a deposition. The witness index should be indexed with the following information:

- Documents provided
- Documents reviewed
- Statement testimony
- Deposition testimony
- Documents referencing witness

You may have documents within the witness files that also appear in the discovery files; however, this method allows for effective and efficient retrieval of documents pertaining to a specific witness. At the time of trial or deposition, this type of indexing will prove tremendously useful.

e. Notes

The notes file usually contains internal memorandums and notes made by the attorneys or paralegals working on the case. This file can be indexed by the individual creating the information. For example, you might want quick access to your notes without having to go through the entire notes file. Indexing the file by specific attorney or paralegal will allow for quick access to the information needed. The notes within this file can also be indexed by the legal issue they address. A negligence action has three primary legal elements: liability, causation, and damages. The notes file could be separated by these three legal elements, including a fourth miscellaneous index tab for notes that do not pertain to these three elements.

PRACTICE TIP

Keep your notes in a paralegal notes folder in your office. This practice provides quick and easy access when the attorney, client, or witness calls for a status report or additional information.

---

f. Experts

It is very important to index the expert files in a case because any documents generated or reviewed by an expert are discoverable by opposing counsel. Rule 26(a)(2)(B) of the Federal Rules of Civil Procedure regarding expert disclosures requires the following:

> Except as otherwise stipulated or directed by the court, this disclosure shall, with respect to a witness who is retained or specially employed to provide expert testimony in the case or whose duties as an employee of the party regularly involve giving expert testimony, be accompanied by a written report prepared and signed by the witness. The report shall contain a complete statement of all opinions to be expressed and the basis and reasons therefor; *the data or other information considered by the witness in forming opinions;* any exhibits to be used as a summary of or support for the opinions; the qualifications of the witness, including a list of all publications authored by the witness within the preceding ten years; the compensation to be paid for the study and testimony; and a listing of any other cases in which the witness has testified as an expert at trial or by deposition within the preceding four years. (Emphasis added.)

When setting up expert files for the attorneys you work for, create an index that includes the following information:

- Expert curriculum vitae
- Expert report
- Expert publications
- Documents reviewed by expert
- Documents created by expert
- Sworn statement
- Expert deposition
- Past testimony

If the case you are working on requires that the expert review several boxes of documentation, it may work best to create a "documents reviewed" list identifying the documents reviewed by number identifier. This list can then be filed under the "documents reviewed by expert" index category and referred to or produced when opposing counsel inquires as to which documents the expert has reviewed in generating his or her written report.

Other categories you will need to obtain information for are expert publications and expert past testimony. It is routine that, prior to taking your expert's deposition, opposing counsel will have reviewed this information for any inconsistencies. You don't want the attorney you work for to find out during the expert's deposition that he or she has written or testified differently on a previous occasion. Obtaining past publications should also be done to ensure the accuracy of your expert's curriculum vitae and written report.

Depending on what party you represent, there are several resources available to assist you in obtaining past publications and past testimony. The Association of Trial Lawyers of America (ATLA) will supply this information to attorneys representing the plaintiff in an action. IDEX (the Collaborative Defense Network for Expert Witness Research) and the Defense Research Institute (DRI) will provide this information to attorneys representing the defendants in an action. Another source that should not be overlooked is the Internet. Several experts have Web sites that contain their written materials or sources to obtain such materials. As far as past testimony, if you know the past cases your expert has testified in, contact the attorney who used him or her as an expert and request a copy of sworn statements, depositions, and trial testimony.

g. Documents

As previously discussed, there are five primary categories of documents: client documents, third-party/other source documents, documents produced in response to discovery, documents withheld from discovery production, and documents produced by the opposing party. Under each of these primary categories are subcategories of documents. How these documents are indexed as a group and separately depends on the method of indexing your attorney wishes to employ. Normally these documents are indexed by their number identifier. For example, if you have several boxes of documents that fall under the "documents produced" category, each of these documents should have a document identifying number assigned to them and should be indexed by this identifying number, as well as the box number.

Subcategories of documents located within the primary categories of documents usually are organized chronologically and assigned document identifying numbers. These subcategories of documents are indexed by their assigned document identifying numbers and by the party supplying such documents. An example of this would be medical records. In any personal injury case, there will be medical records obtained from different health care providers. These medical records probably will be assigned document identifiers with three alpha characters designating the health care provider followed by a numerical bates number. When these records are indexed, include the name of the health care provider and the range of bates numbers.

C. ESTABLISHING DOCUMENT IDENTIFIERS

Document identifiers are numerical or alphabetical characters, or a combination of the two, generated to identify documentation. How documents are identified or labeled is critical to maintaining an efficient document management system. For example, if your attorney has several documents that must be produced and he or she fails to number these documents prior to production, as a result, those same documents when used during deposition or trial will be difficult to sort through and to identify because they have no document identifiers.

In addition, there are times when the opposing counsel will number or label documents produced to him or her without any document identifier. The problem is compounded when your attorney decides to label those same documents according to his or her document identifier. This results in the same documents having several different numbering systems—and in massive confusion during depositions and trial. A simple way to avoid such confusion is to develop a system of assigning document identifiers to all documents produced.

Finally, when documents have assigned identifying numbers they can always be returned to their original order even if they get misplaced. Frequently, during preparation for hearings, depositions, and trials, the attorneys will review documents and fail to place them back in their original order. The paralegal who has assigned identifying numbers to all documents can quickly return a group of documents to their original order without having to reorganize them chronologically or otherwise.

Normally the easiest way to identify documents is by a three- or four-letter identifier and number identifier. For instance, if your attorney's client is John Smith, the documents produced would be labeled: JSP 00001. In assigning the numeric identifier, make sure you have plenty of space within your number system. If you think you will be producing several thousand documents, include enough zeros in your numerical system to support a production of several thousand documents.

By utilizing the previously discussed approach, only the documents produced would be numbered. Any privileged documents that were withheld would need to be labeled separately from the produced documents. Normally, this is done as follows: JS PRIV 00001 and up.

If you receive documents from the opposing party that have not been assigned document identifiers, you should consider assigning document identifiers. Unless the number of documents produced by the opposing party is fairly small, these documents should be assigned document identifiers. What approach you utilize in numbering these documents should be discussed with your attorney and possibly opposing counsel to ensure minimal confusion.

Establishing number identifiers for client documents and third-party/other source documents should be accomplished as discussed above. The only consideration that should be made with client documents includes copying an extra set of documents *prior* to numbering the documents. This will allow for a clean set of documents to be labeled during discovery production. The last thing you want is documents with several different document identifiers. Use the same method for third-party/other source documents if those documents are also going to be produced in response to discovery requests.

D. SEPARATING KEY DOCUMENTS IN A CASE

Another task that may be accomplished when managing documents in a case includes separating out key documents in a case. These documents can be referred to as "hot documents" or "smoking guns." As always, it is imperative that you fully discuss the important issues of a case with your attorney so that you know which documents are key to your case. There is no easy way to accomplish this task; you simply have to review all of the documents within the file and copy those documents key to your case. These copied documents should then be placed in a file and organized either chronologically or by issue. If you have properly assigned document identifiers, copies of these key documents should be easily traced back to their original source. A "key" document file simply provides you with yet another avenue for retrieving important documents.

ETHICS

There are certain ethical considerations that need to be addressed regarding a document management system. Maintaining the confidentiality of the documentation you are managing needs to always be a primary focus. Some or all of the information managed may be protected by a confidentiality agreement or protective order. **A confidentiality agreement** is a contract entered between parties that protects private information. A **protective order** is a decree from the court generated to protect a person from further harassment or abusive service of process or discovery. In order to be ethically prudent in your position, it is always recommended that the paralegal review all confidentiality agreements or protective orders prior to commencing any document management.

Another item that may need to be considered by the paralegal, is restricted access to the file and the establishment of a security system. If the paralegal is maintaining a computer database document management system, then access can be restricted through restricted password access. If a manual document management system is being employed, then the paralegal may be responsible for locking the file cabinets that house case documents.

If you are going to maintain a computerized document management system, it is your ethical and professional responsibility to maintain a reliable backup copy of the computer files for your case. Depending on your resources, files can be backed up onto diskette, CD-ROM, or tape. These backup files should be stored in a place separate from the original file to prevent simultaneous damage or destruction of both files.

Another item that may need to be considered is the archival or deletion of document information once the case is completed. Normally, the attorney will want some documentation archived and will allow for other documentation to be deleted. This decision should be made by the attorney in charge of the case and *not* by the paralegal working on the case. If a computerized document management system is being employed, archival of all file documents should be accomplished by saving the information onto diskette or CD-ROM. If your attorney has limited storage space, all of the case documents can be scanned and saved onto CD rom, allowing for the destruction of all hard copies. Any deletion or destruction of case documents should be authorized by the attorney for the case.

PRACTICE TIP

Organize the documents with an eye toward trial. Make sure the system of organization will allow any paralegal or attorney to retrieve any document at trial quickly and efficiently. Communicated frequently with the attorney about this issue and make sure he or she is familiar with the organization system.

Have a system for tracking and replacing documents removed from the master set. This might be as simple as a folder or as complex as checkout sheets. Ideally, you should have a duplicate set so the attorney never touches the master set.

CONCLUSION

As stated previously, one of your primary duties as a paralegal involves the management of case documents. To excel in these duties, you must develop a routine system of document management. This system can be manual, computerized, or a combination of both. Your success or failure in document management depends on your ability to address document management issues *before* they become issues. Developing and customizing your document management skills to fit the needs of the attorneys you work for should be your primary goal. You are employed to make the attorney's job easier, not more difficult. Maintaining a good line of communication with the attorneys will help to ensure that the document management system developed will be effective and efficient.

USING TECHNOLOGY IN THE LAW OFFICE

The following section includes a detailed discussion of the technology tools and software applications commonly utilized in document management, including definitions for database terminology. This information is invaluable to any paralegal whose document management system involves the use of a database, word processing, spreadsheet, or other software program.

A. DATABASE DOCUMENT MANAGEMENT

Technology has provided the paralegal with some amazing resources when it comes to document management. The primary technology resource utilized in document management is database software. **Databases** allow for the searching of specific information. Database software was created for the following purposes to categorize, organize, and sort information placed within a database. There are three primary components to every database:

1. **Fields:** a primary database component including data pertaining to a specific topic or issue
2. **Forms:** a primary database component that allows for the collection of specific information through the use of fields
3. **Reports:** a primary database component generated as a result of a database search or sort

These components can allow the user to perform these four software applications:

1. **Database sorting:** a software application available to arrange database fields in chronological, numerical, or alphabetical order
2. **Database queries:** a database application that allows for combined or single field searching

3. **Macros/lookup tables:** a database application developed to shorten a computer application process for the user
4. **Database reports:** documents generated from a database sorting or search

A database is only as efficient and effective as the person creating it. For this reason, it is imperative that the paralegal understand what each component is and how its applications function.

1. Fields—What Are They

Fields are comprised to include data dealing with a specific topic or issue. For instance, a date field contains the specific date of the document being summarized, while a document type field contains data indicating the type of document being summarized. A database form normally will contain several fields created by you and customized for the document management system you employ. Prior to creating fields in a database, you should meet with the attorney working on the case to determine what data is important to the case.

PRACTICE TIP

The process of determining how to categorize and organize information in a database is *critical* to the success of the database. This needs to be accomplished through a lengthy discussion with your attorney to determine how he or she wants to utilize the database.

Figure 5.3 depicts several fields that have been created within the database program Summation. Figure 5.4 depicts several fields that have been created within the database program Microsoft Access.

2. Field—Applications

Every field you create can be done so with specific limitations. For instance, a date field can be specifically created to only allow information to be entered in date format, and a document identifier field/table can be created to only allow for the entry of numerical values. There are several types of field limitations, including: note text, multientry, date, currency, and integer. When you are creating your database fields try to always consider the length of the data to be entered into the field, as well as the type of data being entered.

Another application to be utilized regarding fields includes the process of sorting your fields. Normally, database programs will allow for sorting in four different ways: ascending order, descending order, alphabetical order, or numerical order. The majority of sorting will occur in your date or bates number fields. These fields usually will be sorted chronologically in ascending or descending order. The technological advantage to using the sorting application is obvious, in that information being entered into a database does not have to be organized chronologically by date prior to entry, as it can be sorted

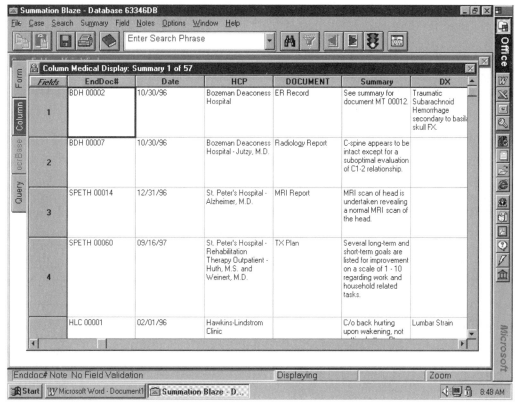

Figure 5.3. Summation—Creating Fields

within seconds once it has been entered into the database. Alphabetical sorting normally is used on fields that include names, document types, or issues. Numerical sorting is used on fields created for document identifiers or bates numbers.

Fields can also be queried, which involves searching for specific information within a field. For instance, if you were working on a personal injury case that occurred due to a motor vehicle accident dated October 26, 1997, then you could query the date field for all entries dated October 26, 1997.

Macros and lookup tables are another software application that can be used with fields. When entering data into the fields inevitably there will be certain terms that you will enter repetitively. Macros or lookup tables allow you to use "quick keys" to enter the entire term quickly. For example, if you are creating a medical chronology and your summary field contains several lengthy medical terms that are being entered repetitively, you can set up a macro or lookup table for these terms. The quick key for degenerative disc disease, for example, could be set up as "ddd"; entering these three letters would result in the insertion of the medical term. Basically, macros or lookup tables have been created to allow the user to shorten some application tasks.

The final application that can be utilized with fields is the process of generating

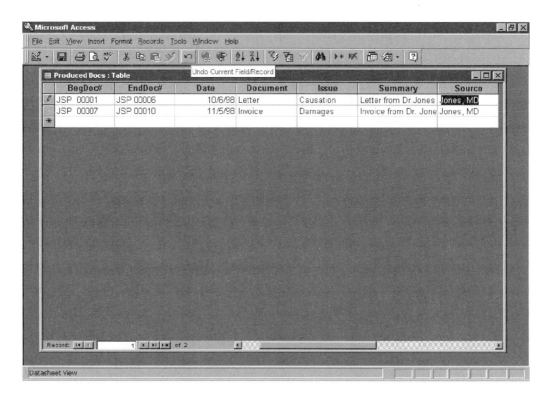

Figure 5.4. Microsoft Access–Creating Fields

reports. Reports are normally generated from the result of a query on a particular field or several fields. A query is simply a search of the data within fields adhering to specific parameters. For instance, if you wanted all letters of correspondence between Mr. Smith and AB Insurance from October 1998 through December 1999, you would query three fields: the source field for Smith or ABC Insurance, the document field for all letters, and the date field for records equal to or greater than October 1998 and less than or equal to December 1999. Once this query has been run, only documents fitting these particular parameters will appear, and a report can be generated from this query. Reports could also be generated after sorting a certain field.

3. Forms–What Are They

Database forms are best described as components of a database that allow for the collection of specific information through using fields. For example, a medical records summary or medical chronology could be set up as a database form containing only medical information, while a produced documents database form would contain information regarding only those documents produced. These two forms could be located within the same *case* database but would be separate *forms* distinguished by the information they contained. Figure 5.5 depicts a form that has been created within the database software Summation. Figure 5.6 depicts a form that has been created within the database software Microsoft Access.

4. Forms—Applications

Database forms can also be sorted. Normally sorting in multiple database forms is done in ascending or descending order by date. Generally, when working in litigation the order that things occurred becomes a central focus of the case. Timelines usually are generated and can be easily created through the use of a database sorting application.

Another application that can be utilized with database forms is queries. You can query multiple database forms for a certain name or term. For example, let's assume you have a medical records database form and a produced documents database form that you need to query for the term *degenerative disc disease*; the query application will allow for such a search to be done.

Macros and lookup tables can also be utilized with database forms. An example of this would include creating a macro that prepopulates certain fields. Normally, this is done in the bates number field to reduce the amount of database entry necessary. The macro would automatically continue the numbering system where the ending bates number for the last record left off. Of course, this entry could be edited if necessary but would substantially reduce the time it takes to enter data into the database form.

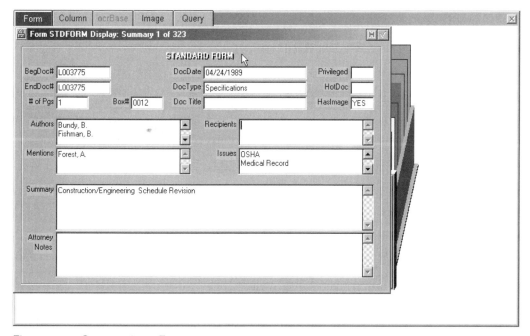

Figure 5.5. Summation—Form

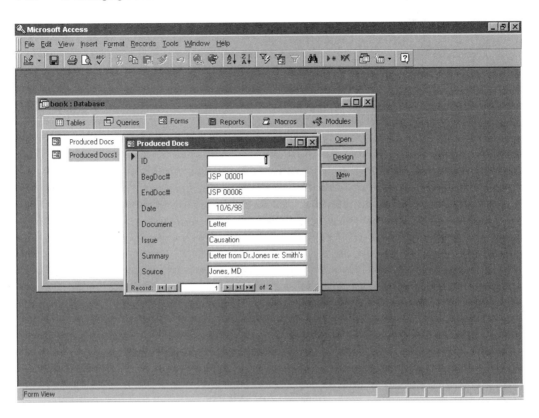

Figure 5.6. Microsoft Access—Form

Once again, reports can be generated from performing queries or sorting on multiple database forms. Reports are the best way for you to demonstrate to the attorney you are working with just how useful a database software program can be to his or her practice, simply because it allows you to filter massive amounts of information into very specific parameters. A litigation attorney's job is to filter through the details to present the big picture.

5. Reports—What Are They

Reports are documents generated from the data you compile into the case database. Reports can be created from queries and sorted in any format specified by you or the attorney you work for. Reports create a quick, concise synopsis of the data contained within a database according to the parameters you specify. Figure 5.7 depicts a report generated from the database software Summation. Figure 5.8 depicts a report generated from the database software Microsoft Access.

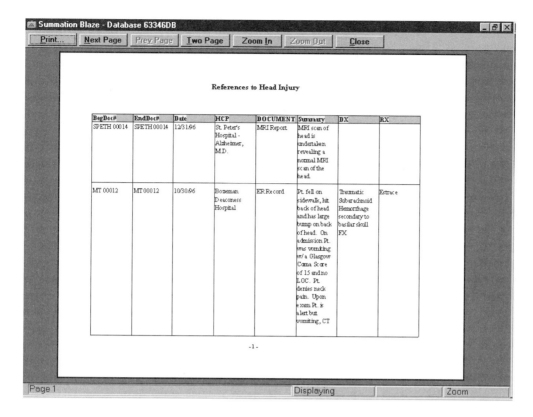

Figure 5.7. Summation—Report

6. Reports—Applications

Reports are normally the result of performing different software applications within the database software. For example, when a query is performed or fields are sorted, a report can be generated from such queries or field sorting. These reports can be formatted in any manner specified by the user. When your attorney requests specific information to be sorted in a particular order, you can perform a query, sort it, and rely on it in compiling the documents requested. The reports generated can be used by you to compile the documents requested or given to the attorney for his or her use. Reports simply allow you to further filter out data and present that information in a visually satisfying manner.

B. DETERMINING WHAT DATABASE FORMS ARE NEEDED

The first step in managing documents within a database is determining which database forms are needed for the case. This determination depends on the different types of

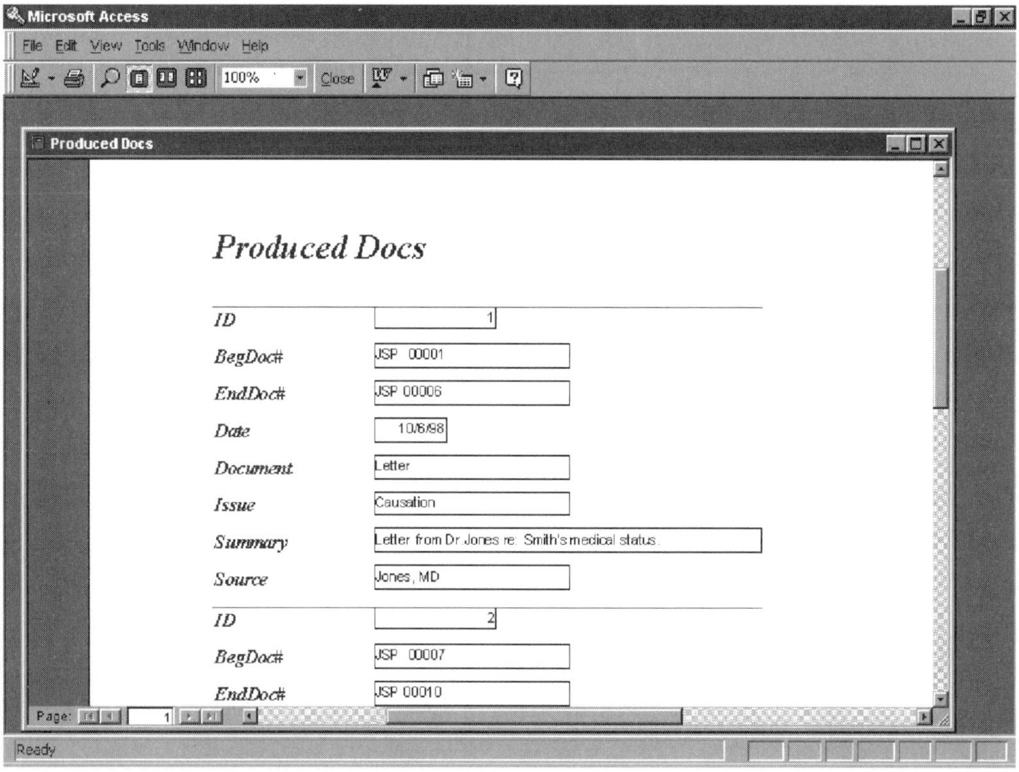

Figure 5.8. Microsoft Access–Report

documents you have in the case—that is, client documents, third-party/other sources documents, produced documents, privileged documents, and documents produced by the opposing party.

One common database form in a personal injury case includes a medical records database form. This form, of course, would contain summaries of the medical records regarding the personal injury action. Other examples of database forms include the following:

- Produced Documents: including documents produced by both sides and containing a field to identify which side produced the information
- Privileged documents: including all documents deemed privileged by either side and identified by bates numbers and document type
- Event chronology: including all the critical events of the case, as well as the date of occurrence and a document reference

Selecting which forms you will create and utilize is a very important process, as this determines how you will organize the information within a case. As always, you should sit down with the attorney working on the case to determine which forms would be most beneficial in presenting the case.

C. CREATING FIELDS WITHIN A DATABASE FORM

Once you have determined which database forms you are going to utilize, fields for each of these forms need to be created. Most database software will include several preformatted fields that you may choose to use. Normally, I set up my fields independently from any preformatted fields so that I can set the field parameters and limitations as I see fit. Prior to creating any fields within a database form, I always meet with the attorney working on the case to ascertain the critical issues of the case and obtain any suggestions on fields that he or she feels need to be created.

There are several different types of parameters and limitations that can be placed on fields. When creating fields, you should consider the following:

- The type of data being entered
- The length of the data being entered
- The function the data being entered will be required to perform

Figure 5.9 below depicts the types of field parameters and limitations available within Summation. Figure 5.10 depicts the types of field parameters and limitations available within Microsoft Access.

1. Data Type

The type of data being entered into a field determines some of the parameters and limitations that will be placed on it. A date field should be created so that it will only allow for the entry of a date, and more specifically, so that it will only accept a date entered in a specific format: that is, mm/dd/yy or mm/dd/yyyy.

The document identifier field usually will be split into two fields, a beginning document number field and an ending document number field; this allows for multiple-paged documents to be summarized and entered into a database. Further, limits can be placed on the document number fields, requiring that the number entered have a certain number of alphabetical characters and numerical characters, that is, AAA00000 or aaa00000. One can also create these document number fields to only allow for numerical entries.

Other data type specific fields could be currency, integer, and decimal type fields. Once you have determined the type of data being entered within a field, you can determine the parameters and limitations these fields need to adhere to.

2. Length of Data

How many characters a field will need is extremely important, as you do not want to begin entry into a field only to discovery that its length limitation is too small for the

Data Type	Purpose
Note Text	For alphanumeric data. Maximum length is 4,000 characters.
Date	For dates. The default format is MM/DD/YYYY. Dates are checked for validity. "Fuzzy" dates where the month, day, or year is unknown are acceptable. Field size: up to 30 characters.
Multientry	For multiple alphanumeric entries. Searches can be done on individual entries. Each entry is contained on a separate line and cannot exceed 80 characters.
Integer	For whole numbers in the range −999,999,999 to 999,999,999. Field size: up to ten digits.
Currency	For currency values in the range $0.00 to + or − $999,999,999,999.99. Field size: up to 20 characters.
Time	For times; specify hours, minutes, and "a.m." or "p.m."
Real	For numbers including decimal portions. Field size: up to 8 digits.
Fixed Length Text	For alphanumeric data. The default size is 8 characters; the maximum length is 1,500 characters. This is a fixed-length field that is declared when defined (unlike the Note Text field, which varies depending on the number of characters entered).

Figure 5.9. Summation Blaze Data Types

data you are inserting. Fields that normally contain a large amount of text include abstract or summary fields. Every database is going to have a maximum character limit even within its longest data type field. In Summation, the field type that allows for the largest number of characters is the text field type.

Another field parameter or limitation available is the multientry field type, which is normally used for a field containing several names, parties, or issues. An example of this would be a legal issues field indicating which legal issues pertain to a particular document. A multientry field type allows for entries of numerous issues or parties. If you feel that there is potential for a field to contain more than one issue or party name, then you should set the field up as a multientry field.

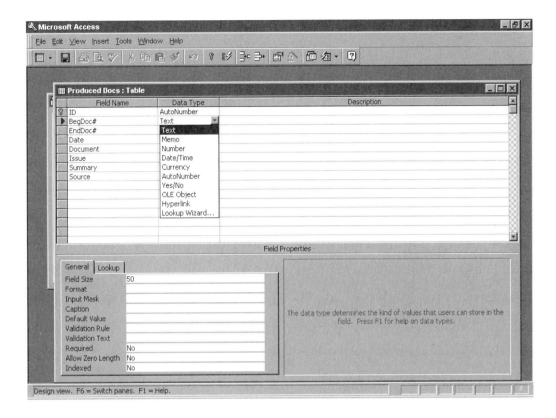

Figure 5.10. Microsoft Access—Field Parameters and Limitations

3. Function Data Is Required to Perform

Some data you enter into a field will be required to perform particular functions. For example, a total normally will need to be calculated for a currency, integer, or decimal field. These fields are created with parameters that allow for calculating totals. Several of the other fields types available will not allow for calculating totals; therefore, it is imperative that you determine whether the data to be entered will need to be calculated. The function your data is required to perform should determine the type of field you designate for it.

D. COMPILING DOCUMENTS IN A SEARCHABLE DATABASE

Once database forms have been set up and fields have been created for each form, the process of entering data can commence. Depending on the resources available in your office, entry of data can be done in two different ways: dictated coding of documents or manual entry of coded documents. Coding of documents is simply the process of pulling pertinent information from the documents and inserting this information into a sortable medium, a database. If you are without support staff to assist in the entry of document summaries or coding of documents, then you will most likely be entering the pertinent information manually on your own. If you have access to support staff, then you can dictate the pertinent information and have support staff manually enter it. If you are planning to utilize support staff for data entry, then it again becomes extremely important to set strict limits regarding the entry format of each field. Another good idea would be to create a spelling list of names and other lengthy terms for the data entry individual so that he or she is consistent when entering data. Further, lookup tables can be created for lengthy terms so that the person entering data doesn't have to repetitively type in the full term every time it is mentioned. Utilization of these suggested processes helps to reduce the occurrence of data entry errors. Such errors become very detrimental to the reliability of your database if they are not recognized and corrected. For instance, if you perform a search for the name "Joe Balzick" but the name is misspelled in some places, only the occurrences specifically spelled "Joe Balzick" will be queried up when you run the search. Some errors can be reduced by running what is called a "fuzzy search," which would reveal any names similar to "Joe Balzick"; however, the most efficient way to search your database is by using precise terminology. Proofreading your document coding is crucial to assure quality control of the database.

E. SORTING INFORMATION WITHIN A DATABASE

One of the applications you will use extensively once your database is created includes that of sorting the database. As indicated previously, sorting can be done in four different manners:

1. Ascending order
2. Descending order
3. Numerical order
4. Alphabetical order

The process involves accessing the field you want sorted and indicating the order to sort information in that field.

Normally you will only be sorting one field in a particular order; however, there will be occasions when you will need to sort multiple fields consecutively. Most database programs allow for multiple field sorting, as well as individual field sorting. This option allows you to sort several fields in a particular order while also sorting each of these fields in a specific order. For example, you may want your database sorted first by the date field in ascending order, then by the bates number in ascending order, and finally by the document type field in ascending order. This sorting would result in all documents being placed in chronological date order, numerically by bates numbers and alphabetically by document type.

F. PERFORMING QUERIES

Queries are searches performed on the database information. When you are looking for specific information or "the needle in the haystack," you perform a query to locate this information as effectively and efficiently as possible. When a query is performed on a database, a query report is generated and can be printed for the attorney or paralegal requesting the information.

Queries can be basic or advanced depending on the information to be retrieved. Basic queries require that the information sought only adhere to one parameter. For instance, if you were looking for all documents dated October 16, 1997, you would perform a query for all coded documents dated October 16, 1997. Advanced queries require that the information sought adhere to multiple parameters. An example of an advanced query would request (1) all letters (2) from Mr. Smith (3) dated October 16, 1997.

Connectors must be used if you plan to perform an advanced query; some of these connectors include

- and
- or
- not
- equal to
- less than and
- greater than

G. UTILIZING MACROS AND LOOKUP TABLES

Macros and lookup tables have been created for one primary purpose, to shorten a computer application process for the user. The best example for this involves the creation of "quick keys" for entering lengthy terminology. If you are continually entering "John Smith," a quick key of "JS" could be designated through a macro or lookup table to equate to "John Smith." If this process is utilized effectively, data entry time could be reduced substantially through macros or lookup tables.

H. GENERATING REPORTS

Reports can be generated from the entire database, multiple database forms, sorting of fields, or querying of fields. When you are formatting a report, you have the ability to select which fields are printed in the report through a field selection process. In Summation's column format, the fields shown are the fields that will print when you request a report. In Microsoft Access, you can customize your report to include or exclude particular fields in a report.

What format the report is printed in—columnar, tabular, or table view—depends on which format you specify prior to printing. You will need to experiment with these different report formats to determine which format the attorney you are working for prefers. However, keep in mind that the presentation style of any report should be created to impress and influence the reader. Frequently, database reports will be attached as exhibits to legal briefs or discovery responses, and can ultimately assist in the settlement negotiation process if utilized effectively.

I. THE ADVANTAGE OF DATABASE DOCUMENT MANAGEMENT

Database document management allows the paralegal to perform document management duties more effectively and efficiently. The concept of searching and researching entire boxes of documents manually for information has become unnecessary if documents are coded into a computer database. Even the process of chronologically organizing documents can be postponed if the documents are coded into a database. The sorting application allows for coded documents to be entered in random order only to be sorted within seconds through the database. The query application allows the paralegal to filter out specific information from voluminous pages of documents. You can find "the needle in the haystack" and you can find it within minutes *not* days. Reports afford the paralegal an avenue for presenting the information requested in a visually enhanced format.

The one thing every paralegal learns when it comes to document management is that when an attorney wants something, he or she usually wants it immediately. Computer database programs provide the paralegal with a document management system that is extremely efficient and effective, making his or her job that much easier. As with any new medium, the paralegal will be required to take the initiative and learn how to utilize the database software; however, the time is well spent considering the hours that will be saved manually searching and researching the same documents for different information. I would encourage all paralegals to experiment with some type of computer database software in the implementation of their document management system.

J. OTHER SOFTWARE FOR MANAGING DOCUMENTS

If you do not have database software available in your office, spreadsheet and word processing programs can be utilized in managing documents and information. **Spreadsheets** are software-generated documents consisting of columns and rows that allow for mathematical calculations. **Word processing tables** are software-generated documents containing text and consist of tables and rows. However, word processing and spreadsheet programs were not created specifically for sorting and organizing data and, as a result, have more data entry limitations than database software.

1. Spreadsheet Software

Spreadsheet software is created to calculate numerical values through the use of formulas, *not* to manage and sort data; therefore, spreadsheets are limited in the amount of information that they can contain. Nonetheless, if you do not have access to database software, spreadsheets can be used to create the following:

- Document summaries
- Case chronologies
- Timelines

a. Creating Fields

Spreadsheets contain cells that can be used as fields for the purpose of data entry. **Cells** are text boxes within a spreadsheet containing pertinent data or information. Each cell can be labeled with a field name, and the data information pertaining to this field can be entered in the cells below the field name. The format of each cell can be established prior to data entry. Most spreadsheets contain cell formatting for text, dates, currency, and integers. Summary fields or any lengthy text field needs to be limited in character size, as most spreadsheets were not created to contain extensive amounts of text data within a single cell.

b. Field Applications

A spreadsheet can sort in ascending and descending order, alphabetically or numerically. As long as you have formatted your cell correctly, you should be able to sort it in ascending or descending order.

The only queries that can be performed within a spreadsheet involve the use of a "find" option; Boolean search options are not available in most spreadsheets. The "find" application allows you to find only each individual occurrence of a particular phrase or word. Another limit regarding queries involves generating reports. A query report cannot be generated in a spreadsheet as it can be in a database.

2. Word Processing Software

Word processing software is created for generating typed documents and reports, *not* to manage or sort data; therefore, word processing documents are limited when it comes to querying and searching for data information. Nonetheless, if you do not have available database software, then a table created through a word processing program can provide some of the applications available in a database. When establishing a table, you will utilize **rows**, the horizontal section of a table, and, **columns**, the vertical section of a table.

a. Creating Fields

A table can be created with header columns serving the same purpose as database fields. Data specific to each of the columns can be entered directly below these headers. These columns will allow for an extensive amount of text to be entered into them but cannot be formatted specifically as to date, currency, integer, or text columns.

b. Field Applications

A word processing table can provided limited sorting in ascending or descending order for text, number, and date columns. Two columns can be sorted simultaneously in the order you determine. If the document you create is not in a table, then it cannot be sorted.

The only searches or queries that can be performed in word processing tables involves the "find" option mentioned above in the spreadsheet software section. Once again, only simple word searches can be performed; Boolean searches are not possible with a word processing table.

Although word processing tables are limited in the electronic document management, they are a resource that can be used if database software is not available. Word processing tables can be used to create document summaries, case chronologies, and timelines. Another word processing application that can be used to create a timeline is text boxes. However, one must realize that a timeline created with text boxes cannot be sorted. Normally, a timeline created with text boxes is used for demonstrative purposes at trials or hearings, not for the electronic management of documents.

KEY TERMS

Attorney-client privilege	Privilege log	Work product doctrine
Client documents	Privileged documents	privilege
Confidentiality agreement	Produced documents	
Document identifiers	Protective order	
Document management system	Third-party/other source documents	

TECHNOLOGY TERMS

Ascending order	Database reports	Rows
Cells	Database sorting	Spreadsheets
Columns	Fields	Word processing tables
Databases	Forms	
Database query	Macros and Lookup Tables	

USEFUL WEB SITES

http://www.summation.com and *http://www.casesoft.com*   Litigation support software
http://www.microsoft.com and *http://www.windows.com*   Microsoft Corporation
http://www.DocsEngine.com   Document assembly
http://www.thinkdocs.com   Document assembly software
http://www.worldox.com   Document management software

chapter 6

Damages

chapter objectives

In this chapter, we will discuss

- The basics of tort law
- Types of affirmative defenses
- An overview of various types of damages
- Damage analysis and tracking of damages
- Use of focus groups to effectively determine the reaction of a jury to a particular case
- Use of technology for jury verdict research and for calculating and updating damage information

A. INTRODUCTION

There are many areas of legal practice in which a paralegal can be invaluable, but none more so than in the area of damages. **Damages** are compensation that can be recovered in a court by a person who has suffered loss or injury. Damages are a part of many types of causes of action such as breach of contract, products liability, wrongful death, and personal injury. It is the paralegal who can track those damages and be indispensable in keeping them current. In plaintiff's cases, the paralegal obtains initial information from the client, develops discovery requests such as interrogatories, assists in locating damage experts, and organizes all the documentation necessary to support the damage claim. In a defense case, the paralegal similarly develops discovery requests (although with a different focus than in a plaintiff's case), assists in locating damage experts, and organizes all the documentation. In the former, the paralegal is proactive, in the latter reactive. In either case, the paralegal obtains records and documentation, ensuring that all aspects of the damage claim are supported. However, to get started, the paralegal needs to have a basic understanding of tort law. This chapter is not meant to be an exhaustive treatise on tort law but an overview, providing a basis for further study and the catalyst for discussing damages.

B. TORT LAW

Most torts are part of the common law of a state. **Common law** is judge-made law. In deciding cases, judges create common law in areas not covered by the legislature. The statutes of the legislature are superior in authority to the common law of courts.

What is a tort? A tort is a civil wrong causing harm to a person or property. Every tort is a cause of action, which is simply a legally acceptable reason for bringing a suit. To state a cause of action a party must allege facts that support every component of the cause of action. Those components are called *elements*, or the component parts of a rule.

There are three main categories of torts:

1. Intentional
2. Negligence
3. Strict liability

In intentional torts, the defendant either desired to bring about the result or knew with substantial certainty that the result would follow from what he or she did or failed to do. Examples of intentional torts are assault, battery, and false imprisonment. The elements in a cause of action for civil battery are

- The act
- Intent to cause harmful or offensive contact
- Harmful or offensive contact with the plaintiff's person
- Causation of the harmful or offensive contact
- Damages

The general meaning of **strict liability** is liability without fault. If the defendant engages in a certain kind of conduct that causes harm, liability will result irrespective of intent, negligence, or innocence. An example would be carrying on an abnormally danger-ous activity such as blasting. If the plaintiff is injured because of the explosion of the defendant's dynamite, the latter will be responsible or liable regardless of whether the defendant desired to injure the plaintiff (intent) and regardless of whether the defendant acted reasonably in setting off the explosives (negligence). It is sometimes very difficult to distinguish strict liability from negligence, especially in the area of product liability. The elements of a cause of action in strict liability for abnormally dangerous conditions or activities are

- The existence of an abnormally dangerous condition or activity
- Knowledge of the condition or activity
- Proximate causation
- Damages

Negligence covers harm due to conduct that was unreasonable under the circumstances. The elements of a negligence cause of action are

- Duty: an obligation to use reasonable care to avoid injuring the person or damaging the property of others
- Breach of duty: unreasonable conduct
- Proximate cause: produces injury without which the result of the act would not have occurred
- Damages: compensation that can be recovered in a court by a person who has suffered loss or injury.

Negligence has been called a catch-all tort in that it encompasses a very wide variety of unreasonable actions and inactions that cause injury. The word *negligence* is used in two different senses. First, it refers to the entire tort that cannot exist unless all four elements of the cause of action are present (duty, breach of duty, proximate case, and damages). Second, the word *negligence* is often used in the same sense as unreasonableness, which is the breach-of-duty element of the tort. Hence, you will see the word *negligence* used to mean the entire tort or one of the elements of the tort—the breach-of-duty-element. In this book, the word usually refers to the entire tort, rather than to one of its elements. However, always carefully determine the usage of the term in your studies and work.

The hallmark of negligence is fault, sometimes referred to as *culpability* or *wrongfulness*. We are not liable under the law of negligence for every injury we cause. For example, a driver is not considered negligent simply because he or she causes an injury. Negligence law will make us pay only for those injuries we wrongfully cause. In the vast majority of negligence cases that are litigated, the questions before the court are

- Was the defendant's conduct unreasonable?
- Did the defendant cause the plaintiff's injury?

It is important that you remember this. A short definition of negligence is injury caused by unreasonable conduct. Remember, in a negligence cause of action, the elements are

- Duty
- Breach of duty
- Proximate cause
- Damages

We will analyze each element. But, before we do that, we need to understand the concept of *foreseeability*, an ability to see or know beforehand. Foreseeability is a critical concept in tort law. In three of the elements of negligence—duty, breach of duty, and proximate cause—foreseeability often plays a major role.

The word *foresee* means "to see or know beforehand." *Foreseeable*, the adjective, therefore means "that which one can see or know beforehand." From a legal perspective, the emphasis is on the extent to which something can be known beforehand. It is important to understand that the question is, "how foreseeable is it, if at all?" That is the question you are dealing with when you look at foreseeability. It is primarily a question of the extent to which something is predictable. Also, it is important to understand that foreseeability is to be determined *before* the fact, not after. If you want to know, for example, whether a fire was foreseeable, you mentally turn the clock back to the period of time before the fire occurred and ask, "how likely was it, if at all, that a fire would occur?" The determination is not made on the basis of what happens after the fact. An event or result is not foreseeable simply because it happened!

Now, let us look at each element of a negligence cause of action. The first element, **duty**, is an obligation or a requirement to conform to a standard of conduct prescribed by law. It is the obligation to use reasonable care to avoid risks of injuring the person or property of others. From there, the next questions become

- Who owes this duty?
- To whom is it owed?
- When does the duty arise?
- What is the standard of conduct to which there must be conformity?

All of these questions can be answered by the general rule on duty, that is, whenever one's acts or omissions create a foreseeable risk of injury to someone else's person or property, a duty of reasonable care arises to take precautions to prevent that injury.

We have discussed the first element of negligence, duty—that a duty exists. The concern then becomes a duty to do what? The answer in the vast majority of cases is to use reasonable care to avoid injuring others. A defendant breaches his or her duty by engaging in unreasonable conduct. *Reasonableness* then becomes the standard of care that we use in most cases to determine whether the second element of negligence—breach of duty—applies to a given fact situation. **Breach of duty** occurs when a defendant can foresee an accident causing serious injury, when the defendant taking precautions to prevent the injury causes the defendant neither undue burden or inconvenience, and the defendant fails to take those precautions.

To establish a breach of duty by showing unreasonable conduct on the part of the defendant in a negligence case, five steps are necessary:

1. State the injury that the plaintiff claims to have suffered because of the defendant.
2. Identify the specific acts or omissions of the defendant about which the plaintiff is complaining.
3. Turn back the clock at the time just before the acts and omissions you have identified took place. Ask yourself what a reasonable person would have done under the same or similar circumstances at that time.
4. Compare the specific acts and omissions of the defendant identified with what you said a reasonable person would have done above.
5. Reach your conclusion:
   a. If the comparison tells you that the defendant did exactly what a reasonable person would have done, you can conclude that the defendant acted reasonably and hence there is no breach of duty.
   b. If the comparison tells you that a reasonable person would have done the opposite of what the defendant did, you can conclude that the defendant acted unreasonably and hence that there was a breach of duty.

The third element of a negligence cause of action is proximate cause. In **proximate cause** the defendant is the cause in fact of the plaintiff's injury, the injury was the foreseeable consequence of the original risk, and there is no reason why the defendant should not be liable for what he or she caused in fact. The basic question in proximate cause is

- Did the defendant cause the plaintiff's injury?

However, you must also be aware that in some cases there is a second question that must be answered:

- At what point will the law refuse to hold the defendant responsible for the injury or injuries that he or she has in fact caused?

This question becomes critical in two main situations:

1. When the injury suffered by the plaintiff appears to be unusual or unexpected
2. When other causes join the defendant in a chain-type sequence

We will concern ourselves in this discussion, though, with the first question, "did the defendant cause the plaintiff's injury?"

The tests of proximate cause are

- The cause-in-fact test—cause which produces an occurrence and without which the occurrence would not have happened.
- The cut-off test—only when the incidents are independent of each other that the nearest is to be charged with the disaster.

Two alternative tests are often used to determine whether the defendant was the cause in fact of the plaintiff's injury:

- The but-for test
- The substantial factor test

In the but-for test the question is, "is it more likely than not that but for what the defendant unreasonably did or failed to do, the injury would not have been suffered by the plaintiff?" In the substantial factor test the question is, "is it more likely than not that the defendant's unreasonable acts or omissions were a substantial factor in producing the injury suffered by the plaintiff?" The latter test is fully adequate and often easier for a plaintiff to establish. However, one should always keep in mind the but-for test as well.

As stated, it is usually easier for a plaintiff to establish cause in fact by the substantial factor test than by the but-for test, but in most cases, both tests will lead to the same result. The important point is that in tort law, it is sufficient if the plaintiff proves cause in fact by the broader substantial factor test. In analyzing any tort problem on the issue of cause in fact, you should apply both tests, but always keep in mind that the substantial factor test will be sufficient. Plaintiff will have a stronger case if he or she can show cause in fact by the but-for test. Hence, you should determine whether this could be done on the facts before you. If not, move on to the substantial factor test, particularly when more than one causal entity has contributed to the plaintiff's injury.

Note that the substantial factor test only requires that the defendant be a substantial factor. It is not necessary that the defendant be the sole or only cause of the plaintiff's injury to be able to say that the defendant was the cause in fact of the injury. It is not even necessary to show that the defendant was the dominant factor in producing the injury. Being a substantial factor is enough.

What do we mean when we say that there is evidence of causation? How does one establish a connection between cause and effect? For the vast majority of cases, the best tool in assessing causation is our common sense based on everyday experience, depending heavily on time and space. With time we ask, "did the injury occur after the defendant's acts or omissions?" The shorter the time between the plaintiff's injury and the acts or omissions of the defendant, the more convinced we are that those acts or omissions caused the injury. The more time that elapses between the defendant's acts or omissions and the injury of the plaintiff, the more skeptical we are that those acts or omissions caused the injury. With space we ask, "did the injury occur in the same area or vicinity where the defendant was acting or failing to act?" The closer we can pinpoint the defendant's acts or omissions to the area or vicinity of the plaintiff's injury, the more convinced we are that those acts or omissions caused the injury. The greater the distance between the area or vicinity of the injury and the area or vicinity of the defendant's acts or omissions, the more skeptical we are that those acts or omissions caused the injury.

Last, the basic cut-off rule to determine when the defendant will not be liable for what he or she has caused is that the injury must be the foreseeable consequence of the original risk created by the defendant's unreasonable acts or omissions. Let's look at an example. Peter speeds through a red light. He hits another car in the intersection, which was proceeding on a green light. The plaintiff in the other car, Dave, suffers a broken leg from the collision, and the car is completely demolished. Using the but-for test, but-for the way Peter drove, the plaintiff would not have suffered property damage to his car or a broken leg. Peter was certainly a substantial factor in producing the personal and property damages. Peter is the cause of both. Peter is also the proximate cause of the personal and property damage. Dave's broken leg and demolished car are foreseeable consequences of the original risk Peter created. Therefore, there is no need for a cut-off rule. Peter is the proximate cause of what he caused in fact.

Suppose that the plaintiff suffers a second or third injury that are all causally related to the first. For example, the defendant carelessly pushes the plaintiff who breaks an arm. Two months later, while walking on crutches, the plaintiff falls and further injures her arm or leg. Soon thereafter the plaintiff catches pneumonia because of her general run-down condition. Assuming that the defendant is the cause in fact of these injuries, defendant will be liable for *all* injuries. They are all foreseeable consequences of the original risk defendant created. Defendant proximately caused them all. This conclusion is subject to the general principle that the plaintiff must take reasonable steps to mitigate the consequences of the original injury caused by the defendant. Plaintiff, for example, cannot refuse all medical attention and then hold the defendant responsible for the aggravation of the injury that resulted from the plaintiff's refusal to see a doctor. There are, however, exceptions to the general cut-off rule, but a discussion of those lies beyond the scope of this book.

Now we will look at the fourth and last element of a negligence cause of action, damages. **Damages** are the actual harm or loss suffered by the plaintiff. The plaintiff must suffer actual harm or loss to person or property for a negligence cause of action to be viable. It is not enough that the defendant has engaged in unreasonably or even reckless conduct. Without actual harm or loss, the negligence action fails. While we will focus in this chapter on damages in a negligence action, most of the principles apply also to intentional and strict liability torts.

When a party has alleged facts that cover every element of the cause of action, that party has stated a prima facie case. A **prima facie case** is defined as a case in which each element of the plaintiff's case can be proven. In other words, in a negligence cause of action, the four elements—duty, breach of duty, proximate cause, and damages—can all be proven. Therefore, the following points are needed to establish a prima facie case in a negligence action.

- Was there a duty of care owed to the plaintiff by the defendant, which was violated?
- Was the defendant's breach of duty the result of his or her failure to act or not to act as a reasonable, prudent person?
- Did the defendant violate a statute at the time he or she breached this duty of care?
- Did plaintiff, in fact, sustain damages or injury as a result of the breach of duty?
- Was the defendant's breach of duty the actual and proximate case of the plaintiff's injury or damage?
- Was the plaintiff in any way negligent, thereby contributing to the breach?
- Are there any affirmative defenses to defendant's breach of duty, if owed?

C. AFFIRMATIVE DEFENSES

Affirmative defenses raise new issues concerning the allegations contained in plaintiff's complaint. **Affirmative defenses** are pled by the defendant and dispute the plaintiff's legal right to bring a claim; they can deny recovery to the plaintiff if proven. Rule 8(c) of the Federal Rules of Civil Procedure list affirmative defenses. When answering a complaint, an affirmative defense might look like this:

FIRST AFFIRMATIVE DEFENSE

Plaintiff's complaint fails to state a claim upon which relief can be granted.

SECOND AFFIRMATIVE DEFENSE

Plaintiff was contributorily negligent . . .

Concerning negligence, there are two major defenses to negligence:

1. Contributory negligence doctrine
2. Assumption of risk doctrine

There are also two related doctrines:

3. Last clear chance doctrine
4. Comparative negligence doctrine

These defenses will be defined and enumerated here for your reference, but will not be thoroughly discussed.

1. Contributory Negligence

Contributory negligence acts as a complete defense to the plaintiff's negligence action against the defendant. If the plaintiff was unreasonable in avoiding risks for his or her own safety, and if this unreasonableness was a substantial factor in producing the plaintiff's own injury, the defendant is not liable. This is true even though the defendant also was negligent by acting unreasonably in creating risks for the plaintiff's safety and even though the defendant's unreasonableness was a substantial factor in producing the plaintiff's injury.

2. Assumption of the Risk

Assumption of risk acts as a complete defense to the plaintiff's negligence action against the defendant. If the plaintiff knowingly and voluntarily exposes him- or herself to a known danger and thereby accepts the risks of being injured by the negligence of the defendant, the latter is not liable for the injury he or she negligently caused the plaintiff.

3. Last Clear Chance

Last clear chance acts to offset the impact of contributory negligence. Last clear chance is a doctrine designed to benefit the plaintiff only. If the defendant had the last clear chance to avoid the injury, the plaintiff wins even though the plaintiff was contributorily negligent.

4. Comparative Negligence

Comparative negligence acts to apportion the damages between the plaintiff and the defendant. This doctrine measures negligence in percentages and allows for a reduction in damages assessed to the plaintiff.

D. DAMAGES

The common thread throughout all torts is that the plaintiff has suffered damages. Damages are an element of every cause of action. So what does the word *damages* mean? Damages are the dollars lost, paid, or owed as the result of the accident. Damages include such things as the cost of first aid, ambulances, medical or hospital care and treatment, drugs and appliances (for example, crutches, braces), nurses, lost income or wages, property damages (for example, automobile, personal effects, clothing, luggage), therapy treatments, transportation expense to and from the doctors, and special help at home during the period confined.

Damages are actual harm or loss. The plaintiff must suffer actual harm or loss to person or property. It is not enough that the defendant has engaged in unreasonable or even reckless conduct. Remember, without actual harm or loss, the negligence action fails. In this chapter we will focus on damages in a negligence action; however, most of the principles discussed apply to intentional and strict liability torts as well.

We need to first look at some very basic definitions:

Damages: A pecuniary compensation—a money award for a legally recognized wrong—or indemnity that can be recovered in a court by any person who has suffered loss or injury. Damages are considered a *legal* remedy.

General damages: Those compensatory damages that usually and naturally result from the kind of wrong that the defendant has commited. Pain and suffering, for example, naturally are expected to follow from an assault to the head or a negligent fall into a ditch. The complaint does not have to specifically plead the components of general damages as a condition of the plaintiff's right to prove those damages at trial.

Special damages: Those compensatory damages that are peculiar to the particular plaintiff, for example, medical expenses, funeral expenses, or loss of earnings resulting from a tort. Special damages usually must be specifically pled in a complaint.

Consequential damages: Damages that do not flow directly and immediately from the act of the party, but only from the consequences or results of an act. Means the same as special damages.

Punitive damages: A noncompensatory form of damages to punish the defendant and to deter similar conduct by others. Punitive damages are an exception to the rule that tort law is designed to make the plaintiff whole. Punitive damages are awarded when the defendant has acted with actual malice, ill will,, or conscious disregard for others. Mere negligence is not enough. Nor is intentional conduct enough unless a court can conclude that the defendant has acted in a morally reprehensible way.

Exemplary damages: Damages given as an enhancement of compensatory damages because of wanton reckless, malicious, or oppressive character of acts complained of. Means the same as punitive damages.

Compensatory damages: Damages that consist of both special and general damages. Damages designed to make the plaintiff whole, to compensate him or her for actual loss or injury. The primary purpose of tort law is to provide compensatory damages for harm caused by recognized torts. Through the vehicle of a money payment, the plaintiff is placed in the position he or she was in before the injury or an effort is made to return to the status quo through compensatory damages. Out-of-pocket or clear economic losses are covered, for example, medical bills, loss of wages. An attempt is also made to provide a money payment for noneconomic losses, for example, pain and suffering.

Nominal damages: A small amount of money awarded when the defendant has committed a tort but when no actual loss is shown. Nominal damages can never be awarded in a negligence action since actual damages are required for the existence of the tort. Nominal damages are awarded in intentional and strict liability cases when the tort has been committed but no actual harm has resulted other than the technical commission of the tort.

The typical paralegal will not encounter every category of damages in every case. However, it is helpful to be aware of the various types. Let's take a closer look at each category of the more common types of damages.

1. General Damages

General damages are damages accruing from a wrong that are its immediate, direct, and proximate result. They are anything that generally flows from the wrongful act. General damages include such things as pain and suffering. Pain and suffering can be difficult to quantify, and consideration must be given to a number of items, such as intensity of pain, duration of pain, impact of pain on future enjoyment, and so on. This element of damages is best discussed with the supervising attorney. It is also helpful to seek information from similar cases and the awards and jury verdicts rendered.

2. Economic Damages

Economic damages include such things as medical expenses and loss of income from time missed at work. Calculating medical damages, and other matters related to the costs of medical care and rehabilitation is merely one facet of damages evaluation. Relying on economic valuation experts is a wise practice; the paralegal should not muddle through these types of complicated calculations. Damage calculations, to be convincing, cannot be the result of conjecture but rather must result from hard and fast economic data. Financial experts will be able to gauge and calculate a client's earning capacity. Evaluation firms and even computer-driven software will produce the present and projected wage losses for a given client.

The age of a claimant is another analytical component in determining the amount of damages. A higher life expectancy should inevitably produce a higher damage award. The U.S. Department of Health and Human Services publishes annually a life expectancy chart. The paralegal must also differentiate the client's life expectancy based on race and gender. Higher damage awards can be expected in the first three decades of a person's life. For information on life expectancy, see statistics published by the U.S. Government. (*http://www.cdc.gov/nchs/fastats/lifexpec.htm* and *http://www.cdc.gov/nchs/data/nvs47_28.paf*).

3. Punitive damages

Punitive damages are meant to punish the wrongdoer for his or her conduct. Punitive damages may be awarded in addition to compensatory damages. They are awarded in cases in which the defendant's conduct is willful or malicious.

4. Special or Specific Damages

Specific or special damages are peculiar to that plaintiff. They include such things as medical expenses incurred, physical therapy, diagnostic testing, and funeral expenses. Again, the paralegal must be cognizant of the damages incurred and dutifully compile documentation of all special damages incurred by the client. In certain cases this will entail ensuring that all medical bills and expenses are current and up-to-date. Sometimes clients will need to be specifically asked about the special damages they have incurred. Many clients do not realize the full financial impact of a cause of action until they have thoroughly discussed how the wrongful act has affected their lives with someone such as a paralegal or attorney.

Rules 9(g) of the Federal Rules of Civil Procedure requires that

"[w]hen items of special damage are claimed, they shall be specifically stated." In other words, you must set those items of special damages out in the complaint providing sufficient detail of type and amount.

5. Compensatory Damages

Compensatory damages are all those that "compensate" the injured party. Compensatory damages may be either general such as pain and suffering or specific such as payment of medical expenses incurred.

Pain is often experienced at the time the tort is committed, during the medical treatment, and during recovery. During these periods, mental suffering and distress can also occur, resulting in the injured party experiencing

- Fright
- Humiliation
- Fear
- Anxiety
- Loss of companionship
- Unhappiness
- Depression
- Inconvenience

The amount recovered for such pain and suffering will depend on the amount of time it was experienced and the intensity of the experience. Also considered are the age, sex, and condition of life of the plaintiff. It is, of course, very difficult to assign a dollar amount to compensate the plaintiff for pain and suffering. The main guide available is the amount a reasonable person would estimate as fair. Again, this should be discussed with your supervising attorney.

Consortium is the companionship, love, affection, sexual relationship, and services that one spouse provides another. There can be a recovery for a tortious injury termed "loss of consortium." There must be an underlying tort to recover for loss of consortium.

PRACTICE TIP

Remember to keep the case moving. Plan ahead and map out the expected medical treatment of your client, when to order medical records or updated medical reports, when to order medical bills and lost wage information, and when to provide status reports to the client, the adjuster, or your supervising attorney. Promptly complete tasks as they come up. Follow up on all leads and calendared dates.

E. DOCTRINE OF AVOIDABLE CONSEQUENCES

The doctrine of avoidable consequences is that which imposes a duty on the person injured to minimize his or her damages. Once a plaintiff has been injured, he or she must take reasonable steps to avoid further injury. The defendant will not be liable for those damages that could have reasonably been avoided by the plaintiff. The doctrine of avoidable consequences refers to unreasonable conduct by the plaintiff after the defendant has wronged the plaintiff. The most obvious example is the plaintiff who fails to obtain medical help after being injured by the defendant. The plaintiff has aggravated his or her own injury. The defendant will be liable for the initial injury, but not for the aggravation of that injury if the failure to seek medical assistance was unreasonable under the circumstances.

The same principles apply to harm to property. Suppose that the defendant negligently sets fire to a small portion of the plaintiff's barn. The plaintiff cannot sit by and watch the entire farm burn up if some reasonable steps by the plaintiff could have mitigated or lessened the loss, such as throwing an available bucket of water on the fire or calling the fire department.

F. DAMAGE ANALYSIS AND TRACKING OF DAMAGES

Many personal injury cases never go to trial; in fact, the majority of them settle out of court. However, that does not mean that you don't have to prove your client's case or defend your client against allegations set forth by the plaintiff. Supporting documentation regarding damages is extremely important. Documents should be ordered as soon as the case commences. It is the responsibility of the paralegal to obtain and verify the facts, and this responsibility covers three distinct areas:

1. Legal interviewing
2. Investigation
3. Fact analysis

We have covered interviewing and investigation in the previous chapters of this book. However, this section will cover those areas specifically dealing with obtaining damage information.

The basic objective of the legal interview in a negligence cause of action is to obtain the facts from the client. In this initial process, it is helpful to utilize a background information checklist. Such a checklist for an automobile accident might include such information as

- Name of client, address, and phone number
- Other names and addresses used
- Current work address and phone number
- Job title, length of employment, salary
- Date of birth and social security number
- Martial status and name of spouse
- Children, names and ages
- Prior marriages and divorces
- Education
- Health status prior to accident and medical history
- Names and addresses of doctors currently treating client
- Nature of treatment
- Medical problems
- Hospital treatment, operations, diagnostic testing
- Name of every insurance company that covered care
- Nature of accident including date, time, other specifics
- Other facts related to accident
- Names, addresses, and phone numbers of witnesses
- Copies of medical bills, accident report, police reports, tickets issued
- Names, addresses, and phone numbers of other attorneys consulted about this matter

Other techniques for identifying facts you need to inquire about are formulation of questions, discovery requests, legal analysis to show how to identify further facts that need to be pursued, and legal research to identify further facts that need to be pursued and to determine the damages elements of the particular jurisdiction.

Once the background information is obtained, the interviewer prepares a written report or intake memo. Intake memos have different purposes, but contain the same basic information:

- From
- To
- Date of interview
- Case name and file number
- Re: line indicating the memo outlines an intake interview

The memo would start "Mr. Doe was interviewed in my office on January 1, 2002. He was involved in an automobile accident that occurred . . ." The remainder of the memo outlines the facts obtained from the client.

Therefore, the memo might look something this:

INTAKE MEMO

TO:	**John Doe**	**FROM:**	**Mary Johns, Paralegal**
DATE:	**January 1, 2002**	**FILE:**	**Smith v. Johnson**
FILE NO.:	**88-204-001**		
RE:	**Outline of Intake Interview**		

Mr. Doe was interviewed in my office on January 1, 2002. He was involved in an automobile accident which occurred . . .

The intake memo should also

- Conform to the instructions of the supervisor
- Be readable, neat, comprehensive, and devoid of spelling or grammatical errors
- Accurately reflect what the client said
- Present the facts of the case chronologically
- Be organized by subject headings, such as "Background," "Facts of the Accident," and "Medical Care."

After the initial intake, the next step is the investigation. The objective of investigation, of course, is to uncover facts. More specifically, investigation helps in deciding whether to take a case, provides many of the facts that need to be researched, provides a way to verify what the client has said, helps in deciding whether to settle a case and for how much, and helps in preparing for trial.

The paralegal needs to give careful thought to the type and source of damage documentation and information. Both plaintiff and defense need to review medical records, medical bills, pharmacy records, employment records, accident reports, witness statements, medical reports, photographs, and receipts. Potential sources for this information would be medical care providers, pharmacies, physical therapists, counselors, mental health professionals, employers, friends, family members, coworkers, police officials, adjuster, claimant, and, not least, the client.

PRACTICE TIP

Be sure to request a declaration or certificate signed by the custodian of the records that authenticates the client's medical records and bills. The insurer or defendant will usually require authenticated copies of the medical records. Settlement negotiations cannot begin until all medical records and bills have been received by either the adjuster or the defendant.

Although the paralegal usually does fact gathering and investigation, in complex cases, the office may also utilize an outside expert to help investigate as well as to provide testimony at trial. There are a wide variety of such experts available, such as economic experts, medical experts, forensic experts, technical consulting experts, and private investigators.

The hallmark of a professional investigator is to view people, objects, things, and events as unique, a lesson to be learned by all paralegals. The focus of the investigator is on differences and individuality. Professionalism in investigation means to analyze the facts so that there is an exploration of all the details that make the facts unique. To analyze the facts simply means to collect all (or almost all) the details relating to those facts. During the process of analyzing facts, the investigator collects more facts to obtain a comprehensive picture of what happened. Your major guide in accomplishing this is common sense. You need to design an investigation strategy consisting of questions that you would like answered to obtain a much more detailed picture of what happened. To do this, you elaborate on the facts already collected in terms of the following commonsense questions: who, what, where, when, when, and how. You must get your mind into the habit of generating factual questions. This particular habit is developed through experience, training, and conscious attention to the facts of the case.

One of the guides to investigation is the law of evidence. The investigator should have an eye on what rules of evidence apply to the facts covered in the field. See Chapter 10. Also, something that many investigators overlook is the preservation of evidence. Automobiles are wrecked and repaired. The car itself is of little use after it has been repaired as far as evidencing physical facts about the accident or about the damage. Generally, this evidence is preserved by the use of photographs. However, in some situations, particularly in cases involving defective products where the issue might be one of breach of implied warranty, the object should be preserved to prove the mechanics or workability of the subject matter to establish the case for either the defendant or the plaintiff. In the preservation of evidence for use at trial at a later date, the article in question must be maintained in the same condition that it was in at the time of the accident.

In many instances, experiments will be utilized to show that certain physical facts are or are not true. This is very effective in convincing the jury and often will turn the tide of a lawsuit. However, it is imperative that experiments be conducted under the identical circumstances of the accident itself and through use of some independent official who need not necessarily be a witness paid by the person using him or her. If experiments are to be done at the direction of the investigator, it is wise to consult the attorney who will be involved in the case. Of course, the person conducting the experiment must exercise the greatest of care to simulate the conditions under which the accident happened. Also, it is important to perform the experiment through the use of independent people and sources so no bias claims can be raised.

Remember, obtaining the essential facts without getting the witnesses or the evidence or the means to corroborate the facts at a later date is of little value to anyone. Investigators and paralegals should take the time early in their careers to sit in on a few jury trials and watch the procedure of evidence. Their investigations will improve, and thus the attorney's effectiveness for his client will be enhanced.

It is very helpful for the paralegal to prepare a summary of the medical treatment of the plaintiff in chronological order (whether you represent plaintiff or defendant). The paralegal must review each medical records entry to summarize the following elements:

- The plaintiff's subjective complaints of pain and medical problems
- The objective findings from the plaintiff's treating providers
- The provider's assessment of the subjective and objective findings
- Recommended treatment plan
- Drugs prescribed
- Diagnosis and prognosis

Preparing such a summary will allow the paralegal to identify gaps in treatment, other sources or providers through referrals, an indication of the plaintiff's compliance with recommended treatments, and any subjective statements made by the plaintiff. Once gaps or other sources are identified, the paralegal can continue the process of obtaining and tracking damage information.

G. ENSURING CURRENT DAMAGE FIGURES

Economic experts can assist the attorney and paralegal in arriving at current damage figures and quantifying them. The basic steps used in computing economic loss are

1. Establish an earnings base for a period prior to the accident
2. Establish current medical costs to serve as a base for future projections
3. Determine a historical earnings trend
4. Determine life expectancy and work expectancy
5. Reduce computed future earnings by the amount of income taxes levied
6. Reduce the resulting sum by a discount factor to compute present value

Economic experts can be found in a variety of ways. The paralegal can search on the Internet, contact local universities and colleges, check with other paralegals for experts used in the past, and tap the resources available at his or her firm. Caution should be used when hiring experts. Check their credentials. Ask for cases in which they have testified in the past. Obtain copies of their testimony and a copy of their economic analysis. See if their report makes sense and if the conclusions reached can be documented.

H. PRACTICAL SUGGESTIONS

As in all facets of paralegal practice and procedure, record keeping, administrative tracking, and forms serve the client well. It can be effective and efficient to adopt some type of damage summary and worksheet to help you in tracking and determining damages. An example of such a worksheet is shown in Figure 6.1. If the paralegal adopts the summary

Date: _____

Last update: _____

Paralegal: _____

Case _____

Cause no. _____

Court _____

SPECIAL DAMAGES

    1. Medical

        a. Ambulance

        Name _____

        Address _____

        Date of Service _____

                  Documentation ☐   **TOTAL:** _____

        b. Hospital (List for each hospital)

        Name _____

        Address _____

        Emergency care _____

        Surgery _____

        Diagnostic testing _____

                  Documentation ☐   **TOTAL:** _____

        c. Physicians (List for each physician seen)

        Name _____

        Address _____

        Treatment _____

        Date of Treatment _____

        Diagnosis/Prognosis _____

                  Documentation ☐   **TOTAL:** _____

        Name _____

        Address _____

Figure 6.1. Damage Summary and Work Sheet

Date of Treatment _____

Treatment _____

Diagnosis/Prognosis _____

Documentation ☐   **TOTAL:** _____

d. Pharmacy (List for each medication prescribed)

Medication _____

Prescribing physician _____

Purpose _____

Documentation ☐   **TOTAL:** _____

Over-the-counter medications _____

_____

_____

Documentation ☐   **TOTAL:** _____

e. Travel

Date: _____

Medical provider/treatment _____

Mileage _____ (Miles _____ × \$.345 cents per mile = _____)

Lodging _____

Meals _____

Documentation ☐   **TOTAL:** _____

f. Home Care

Number of days _____ × *Hourly rate* _____ = _____

g. Physical Therapy

Name _____

Address _____

Referring physician _____

Treatment modality _____

Goals _____

Documentation ☐   **TOTAL:** _____

Figure 6.1. (Continued)

    h. Psychologist, Psychiatrist, Counselor

        Name _____

        Address _____

        Diagnosis _____

                  Documentation □   **TOTAL:** _____

   i. Durable Medical Equipment (List for each device)

        Type of equipment _____

        Prescribing physician _____

        Name and address of provider Cost _____

        Type of equipment _____

        Prescribing physician _____

        Name and address of provider _____

        Cost _____

                  Documentation □   **TOTAL:** _____

        TOTAL MEDICAL EXPENSES: _____

 2. Economic Damages

    a. Past wage loss

        Current wage _____

        Days lost due to injury _____

        Expected date of return to work _____

                         TOTAL: _____

    b. Future wage loss

        Current wage _____

        Age _____

        Worklife expectancy _____

                         TOTAL: _____

    TOTAL ECONOMIC DAMAGES: _____

Other special damages: _____

Figure 6.1. (Continued)

sheet at Figure 6.1, he or she can be sure that the damage claim is believable, a factor most important to the case in chief. The organizational and administrative skills of the paralegal must afford the jury an easy-to-read, easily digestible synopsis of this maze of bills and medical documentation.

Many trial attorneys rely on a form of memorializing the influence of pain and suffering on a plaintiff's lifestyle through the use of film and videotape. These memorializations are called "day-in-the-life videos" and provide a formidable piece of evidence for the jury to consider in its determination of damages. This form of damage assessment gives the jury an appreciation of the injury's influence on the entire life of the plaintiff. From the time the individual arises in the morning until he or she retires at night, the multiple effects of injury relative to the plaintiff's ability to walk, eat, clean, shower, dress, and interact with family members is fully documented. A picture is truly worth a thousand words.

The basic, fundamental rule in preparing a day-in-the-life video is to not make it too long. You must not lose your audience's attention. You must not overexpose the client, an injured party. You will have hours of truly great material available to choose from if you have done your work, and the challenge is to cut it down to approximately 15 minutes.

There are several other techniques and guidelines to keep in mind. You should avoid making the video appear too "slick." Do not overdramatize or overplay the emotional aspects. Let the facts speak for themselves. You can expect to take several hours of film to come up with a good settlement brochure film or day-in-the-life video for use at trial. Remember to retain all original film intact so you can use all or part of it in trial if a settlement is not accomplished. You can splice and assemble a settlement brochure film without altering any of the original tapes by reproducing parts on a second tape. Audio often makes a powerful impact, and explanatory matter can accompany the settlement film. But do not overlook the value of silence with certain parts of the film. It is often helpful to prepare a script to use as an accompaniment to the video. The script is also helpful in allaying any fears of the plaintiff of what will be taped and in moving the video along.

I. TRACKING DAMAGES FOR THE PLAINTIFF

Interrogatories are perfectly suited for forcing an opponent to be candid about the calculation of damages. For example, if your firm represents the plaintiff, you should ask the defendant what he or she contends is the correct amount of damages in the event that plaintiff should win. If the response is too small, the firm can then use it to paint the particular defendant as a Scrooge in front of the jury.

The paralegal working for a plaintiff's firm needs to assist the client with the collection of relevant data and documentation to support the claim. No firm should ever simply take the client at his or her word. You need to verify what has been told to you. The easiest way to do so is to collect the information needed directly from the source such as the physicians, hospitals, therapists, and other health care providers. Carefully review the documents and prepare a total. There is nothing more embarrassing than making an unsubstantiated claim. Your attorney will rely on you to be accurate and attentive to details. Oftentimes clients will forget about an aspect of damages, but it will be delineated in the documentation you receive. You can then obtain that further documentation yourself.

The best thing to do is to obtain a release or authorization to obtain specific medical information for your client at the initial intake interview. The client does not then have to return to sign the authorizations and you can do your job by obtaining the needed materials quickly and efficiently. Medical authorizations can be short and simple or lengthy and detailed. Just make sure that you have accurately outlined the materials requested. Depending on the case, thought should also be given to other authorizations needed such as for employment records, payroll records, and income tax records.

J. VERIFYING DAMAGE FOR THE DEFENDANT

The same statement applies here as in Section I: Interrogatories are perfectly suited for forcing an opponent to be candid about the calculation of damages. For example, if your firm represents the defendant, you should always send out an interrogatory requiring plaintiff to state exactly how much money he or she is asking for and how the amount is calculated, and to explain every bit of supporting documentation such as receipts and bills. that the plaintiff has. This practically forces the plaintiff to provide a reasonable number. If plaintiff claims an unsupportably high amount, your firm can simply read plaintiff's answer to this interrogatory to the jurors so that they can see for themselves how greedy plaintiff is. Remember to also ask for copies of all supporting documentation through the use of requests for production.

When representing defendants, interrogatories also offer a useful way of getting the background information supporting plaintiff's damage claims. Using interrogatories, requests for production of documents, and requests for admissions, the defendant's attorney can obtain an itemization of the expenses and losses that comprise plaintiff's damage, and copies of the receipts, invoices, and other documents that underlie them. This information will allow defendant's attorney to verify the items claimed by plaintiff and may provide leads that will help in the search for evidence to disprove plaintiff's damage claims.

Again, the paralegal can be invaluable in assisting with this process. The defense paralegal should carefully review the materials and documentation provided. Oftentimes medical bills or records refer to other treating physicians. It is important to obtain that information as well and to see if the plaintiff is following his or her doctor's suggestions. Also, it is important for the paralegal to carefully review the damage claim to ensure that the numbers are supported. On occasion a plaintiff has made a claim for damages that have been unsupported by the facts or documentation. The only way to see if that has happened is to carefully review the materials provided.

> **PRACTICE TIP**
>
> In a case in which liability is certain or almost certain, discuss with your attorney the advantages of offering to meet the plaintiff's immediate needs prior to full resolution of the claim. For example, offer to provide (with the understanding the defendant will receive credit toward settlement) a powered wheelchair and converted van to the man who is now a quadriplegic and the sole support of his family. Early efforts in the process such as this ensure that financial pressures are eased and the medical and physical needs are being met to facilitate recovery.

K. DISCLOSURE OF DAMAGE COMPUTATIONS

Rule 26(a)(1)(C) of the Federal Rules of Civil Procedure requires a computation of damages and disclosure of the documents underlying the computation. The computation of damages is a part of the body of the disclosure statement itself. It is usually best presented in a tabular form, listing each item for which a claim is being made, giving the dollar amount of each, and indicating what documents support each other.

Rule 26(a)(1)(C) specifically states:

> (a) Required Disclosures; Methods to Discover Additional Matter.
>
> (1) Initial Disclosures. Except to the extent otherwise stipulated or directed by order or local rule, a party shall, without awaiting a discovery request, provide to other parties: . . .
>
> (C) a computation of any category of damages claimed by the disclosing party, making available for inspection and copying as under Rule 34 the documents or other evidentiary material, not privileged or protected from disclosure, on which such computation is based, including materials bearing on the nature and extent of injuries suffered; . . .

The items comprising a party's damage claims usually fall into one of three categories:

1. Items involving concrete, provable expenses that are easy to establish, for example, a medical bill for treatment services rendered.
2. Items such as damages for pain and suffering that are difficult if not impossible to quantify. There is no way to compute the amount to be claimed for pain and suffering: Instead, it will be up to the jury to decide how much to award after hearing evidence about how much pain plaintiff has suffered.
3. Items that are based on provable quantities, but nevertheless require estimates or computations, for example, a claim for future income lost due to an injury.

As stated, in addition to the computation of damages, Rule 26(a)(1)(C) requires disclosure of the documents supporting the damage claims. This can be done either by accompanying the disclosure statement with copies of the documents or, as the rule suggests, by making the documents available for inspection and copying as would be done with a Rule 34 request for production of documents. The virtue of attaching copies is that doing so makes it easy to prove exactly what documents were disclosed. However, particularly with claims requiring evidence of the extent and severity of personal injuries, the group of possibly relevant documents may be quite large. Therefore, attaching copies of all relevant documents may be impracticable.

Remember to always bates stamp the documents, that is, to number them with an identifying alpha and numeric code. This simple process will allow you to track all documents produced with the disclosure, with discovery responses, or through making the documents available for inspection and copying. Documents are not lost with this process and are easily referred to. Today numbering is easier than ever. Microsoft Word provides an easy-to-use template for preparing labels to accomplish this task.

L. SETTLEMENT

The vast majority of legal disputes are settled without the need for trial. In fact, the moment a case is initiated, the opposing attorneys are usually thinking about the possibilities of settlement. There are substantial incentives for the parties to settle, such as the tremendous costs of a trial and the length of time needed to complete the litigation process.

More and more lawyers like to present settlement brochures to the attorneys on the other side and to the insurance company in an effort to settle the case. The primary purpose of a settlement brochure is to present the claim in as persuasive a fashion as possible. The preparation of such a brochure has two secondary advantages:

1. It disciplines the lawyer and the paralegal to analyze liability, marshal evidence, and appraise the case
2. It provides a dress rehearsal for trial in the event efforts at settlement are fruitless.

There are a number of reasons why the brochure will enhance the likelihood of a satisfactory settlement. The brochure presents the case in an orderly, dramatic, and persuasive manner. The typical claim is presented by the plaintiff's lawyer to the claims representative as an oral argument, more emotional than logical, more conclusionary then factual. Too often the settlement negotiation descends to a shouting match with each party becoming more partisan as the exchange continues with a lessening of a chance of settlement. The oral, face-to-face confrontation is not the most effective vehicle for settlement negotiations. Each side feigns an air of confidence in his case. The plaintiff's lawyer claims that there is "good" liability, the defendant insists it's "questionable."

A settlement brochure eliminates these problems. The plaintiff's case is presented in a written documentary form. It is based on facts—statements, reports, exhibits. There is no oratorical flourish or emotional argument. The claims representative receives the information factually and can appraise the case rationally.

There are additional benefits as well. A well-ordered, carefully planned brochure carries with it an aura of importance. The bulk alone suggests value. The preparation of a brochure demonstrates that the plaintiff has sufficient confidence in the magnitude of his or her case to warrant a detailed presentation. It immediately creates an impression of importance.

The following are elements found in a typical settlement brochure:

- A preface, setting out the conditions under which the brochure is being submitted
- Personal history of plaintiff
- Medical history of plaintiff—summary
- Medical history and physical report by initial attending physician
- Operative record of initial attending physician
- Consultation reports
- Additional operative records
- X ray interpretations
- Discharge summary
- Additional medical reports
- Medical expenses
- Effects of injuries
- Evaluation of claims
- Conclusion

Of course, the form varies to meet the particulars of the case, but this is the basic format used. Another type of settlement brochure might include:

- Preface, setting out the conditions under which the brochure is being submitted
- Summary of liability facts
- Summary of injuries
- Compilation of special damages
- Projected future damages and losses
- Legal authorities, together with a discussion of any novel issues of law
- A demand, setting out how it was arrived at

Also, a settlement brochure should include as exhibits some or all of the following:

- Photographs of injured victims
- Photographs of the scene of the accident if liability is an issue
- Hospital records, excerpts, or summaries
- Reports of experts such as economists, doctors, or liability experts
- Any official reports of the accident such as a police report
- The curriculum vitae of any special doctor or expert whose testimony is critical to the case

Often in smaller cases, a settlement letter, much like a settlement brochure, is just as effective. It should follow the same general outline so far as setting out a summary of the facts, both liability and damages, and have attached to it the appropriate photographs and documents.

How do you decide the appropriate vehicle to use? Discuss it with your supervising attorney. Talk about the case, the facts and strategy, and from there decide what you want the settlement letter or brochure to accomplish. How much do you want to say? How much do you want to keep to yourself for the time being? There will be times when you do not want to tip your hand and alert the opposing parties to your strategy. Let the attorney you work for decide with you the way to handle this aspect of the case.

Figure 6.2 is an example of a settlement brochure outline.

M. USE OF FOCUS GROUPS

Focus groups have been used effectively in determining the reaction of a jury to a particular case. **Focus groups** are groups of individuals used by attorneys to gain feedback on a case. They can help in letting counsel know if the range of damages set forth is reasonable. The paralegal is responsible for getting a focus group together, and there are many things to keep in mind:

1. Determine the number for the focus group. The usual focus group consists of between 7 and 11 individuals.
2. Determine the demographic makeup of your group. The best way to determine that is to obtain jury questionnaires from the local clerk of court and review and summarize them on an annual basis. Jury questionnaires will provide background information such as age, marital status, occupation, education, and jury experience.
3. Start making calls. Oftentimes it is easier to see if someone you know is aware of an individual who would fit your profile and would be willing to serve. Sometimes you simply need to use the phone book and make "cold calls."
4. Once you have your group together, confirm in writing the date, time, and location of the focus group. The location should be easy to find and get to. It should be well lighted and comfortable, as well as quiet. Let them know that a light snack will be provided and breaks will be taken. Each participant should be provided some monetary compensation. Discuss this with your attorney.
5. Determine if your attorney wants the proceeding videotaped. If so, locate a reliable videographer and meet him or her at the designated location to make sure it will meet your needs. Remember: If the proceedings are to be videotaped, you must let the participants know in advance. Many people object to being videotaped for a variety of reasons.
6. Prepare name cards for all participants.
7. Prepare confidentiality agreements for each participant to sign.
8. Prepare checks to compensate the individuals for their time.
9. Determine how the presentation will be conducted. Typically one attorney presents a summary of the facts of the case, then the plaintiff's side and then the defendant's case. Another attorney answers any legal questions. Once the case is presented, the group deliberates and then presents its findings.

Focus groups are a lot of work and sometimes quite expensive, but they can be valuable to the case. They help you look at your case from all angles and help to refine

Date:

Re: Settlement Brochure—Doe v. Johnson

Dear _____:

This brochure is submitted upon the following conditions:

Respectfully submitted,

SUMMARY

On January 2, 2002, at approximately 9:00 a.m. in clear, dry weather . . .

Liability is clear.

INJURIES AND DAMAGES

Mary Doe, born January 8, 1971, sustained a severe, closed-head injury, pelvic fractures, broken ribs, and a broken arm in the collision of January 2, 2002. Her medical condition is described in summary form in the Admission and History and Physical Notes made at ABC Hospital (Exhibit 1). . . .

All of the written words and evidence found in the medical records of Ms. Doe cannot adequately describe her injuries and the catastrophic nature of the effect those injuries have had on her life. Therefore, we have prepared a 15-minute day-in-the-life video for your consideration. See Exhibit 2. . . .

PAST MEDICAL COSTS

As of March 30, 2002, the following list summarizes the reasonable and necessary charges made by the various health care providers and hospitals for the care and treatment of Ms. Doe. All supporting documents and bills are attached as Exhibit 3.

ABC Hospital	$
Surgeon	
Physicians	
Lab work	
Clinic of the Valley	
	_____
TOTAL	$_____

Figure 6.2. Settlement Brochure Outline

FUTURE MEDICAL COSTS

We have retained Dr. Charles Rickman of XYZ Health Services Institute, who is a specialist in health care costs, to determine future medical costs of Ms. Doe. Dr. Rickman's report, including his Curriculum Vitae, is contained here as Exhibit 4.

The cost of Ms. Doe's future medical care, reduced to present value as reflected in Dr. Rickman's report, is $325,822.00.

EDUCATIONAL BACKGROUND AND POTENTIAL OF MARY DOE

Mary Doe was a normal, healthy individual prior to the collision of January 2, 2002. She attended . . .

LOSS OF EARNING CAPACITY

Had Ms. Doe not had these injuries inflicted upon her, she could have expected to live a normal life expectancy of _____ years from the date of occurrence. Based on her education attainments and work history, Ms. Doe . . .

LOSS OF ENJOYMENT OF LIFE, PAIN AND SUFFERING

In evaluating this case for settlement purposes, we have looked to the prospective damage issues that would be submitted to the jury at trial . . .

Past medical expenses
Future medical expenses
Loss of earning capacity
Past pain and suffering
Future pain and suffering

MARY DOE'S PRESENT CONDITION

At this time, Ms. Doe . . .

DEMAND

Our evaluation and research show the jury verdict range is from _____ to _____, calculated as set forth above.

We are authorized to settle this claim . . .

APPENDIX

Exhibits and photographs.

Figure 6.2. (Continued)

your arguments. Oftentimes questionnaires are used after the presentation of the plaintiff's case and then again after the presentation of the defendant's case to determine how the "jurors" feel after each argument. The jurors can be allowed to take notes, but be sure to retrieve all written notes to preserve confidentiality.

Be sure to have your focus group members sign confidentiality agreements stating the case they will be hearing, that they have no connection to any of the parties, have no interest in the case, and agree to keep all communications and deliberations confidential.

Preparing for a focus group review is not difficult. Just remember to plan and think through each stage. It is amazing what information can be garnered from the use of such a group. Focus groups can help settle your case, alert you to problem areas, and help you be better prepared for trial.

PRACTICE TIP

For the focus group, draft a short user-friendly form for feedback focused specifically on the issues that concern the attorney the most and discuss it with the attorney at least two weeks in advance of the focus group. This will allow the attorney to fine-tune the presentation of evidence to address the issues most impressive to jurors. Remember that focus groups often can provide better analogies for use at trial than the lawyers.

ETHICS

This chapter would not be complete without a short discussion on obtaining damages information ethically. What acts and behaviors are specifically prohibited in the area of damages? Where is the line drawn when obtaining damage information? For answers to these questions, you need to refer to the ABA Model Code of Professional Reponsibility, *Rules*, ABA Model Rules of Professional Conduct, and the National Association of Legal Assistants Model Code of Ethics and Professional Responsibility.

Let's look at the following two examples:

1. A paralegal who is conducting the initial intake interview of the client discusses what medical treatment the client has received. The client states that she has seen only two doctors and has spent approximately $2,500 in medical treatments for doctors, the hospital visit, and physical therapy. At this time she is still sore and stiff, but seems to be feeling better. The paralegal then states to the client that, as a general rule of thumb, an insurance company will assign a settlement value to an injury claim depending in large part on the total amount of medical bills. Settlements usually compute to three times the amount of medical bills. The

paralegal then tells the client to seek further medical treatment. What ethical rules have been violated?

2. A paralegal is working on an automobile accident case representing the defendant. During the course of his investigation and interviewing he finds that the defendant was informed three days prior to the accident that the brakes on the defendant's car were defective and needed to be replaced. Due to financial constraints, the defendant did not make the recommended repairs. Federal Rule of Civil Procedure 26(a)(1)(A) requires that each litigant disclose the "name and, if known, the address and telephone number of each individual likely to have discoverable information relevant to disputed facts alleged with particularity in the pleadings, identifying the subjects of the information." While preparing the Rule 26(a) disclosure, the paralegal determines in his own mind that this fact does not relate to any disputed facts, and the paralegal does not mention the advice to get the brakes fixed. Can the paralegal ethically withhold that information?

CONCLUSION

Remember that basic case preparation is essential when it comes to damages, whether your firm represents the plaintiff or the defendant. The paralegal can play a key role in the process of gathering damages information. That process should start immediately on commencement of the case and not wait until trial looms on the horizon. Immediate gathering of damage information is essential to setting forth damages or defending against them. Therefore, the initial step in any damage preparation should be to gain a full understanding for all damages elements allowable in the jurisdiction in which the case is filed.

The paralegal should list all the damages elements and provide a corresponding list of the sources to prove those elements. For example, the paralegal should be sure to order tax returns to learn about prior earnings history and thereby have documentation concerning that history. In addition to the tax returns, the W-2 statements, supplements, and schedules showing other sources of income can also be helpful as potential verifications of previous earnings. In other words, don't think of just one area for documentation, but think through all potential sources.

The same goes for medical records. Far too often, medical records are obtained from the date of the occurrence forward, ignoring that all records could be obtained that might reveal significant preinjury information that minimizes damages for the defendant. For the plaintiff, the paralegal should be sure that all records are obtained from all treating health care providers, not just one or two.

For the plaintiff, day-in-the-life videos showing portions of the plaintiff's day and the challenges faced can be invaluable, but must be carefully planned. For the defendant, surveillance films are useful to contradict plaintiff's use of a day-in-the-life video. Again, careful planning is essential to eliminate any privacy concerns; all surveillance films should be made in public view. The key to the use of those films is to avoid any editing.

Surveillance films should be used only when they graphically show that the plaintiff is lying about physical or cognitive functioning.

Remember that the paralegal must use extreme care in compiling damages information so as not to overlook an area that should be documented. It is an ongoing process that starts from the initial client interview and continues through the entire litigation process. Each step of the way the paralegal must update damages information and ensure its accuracy. To aide in this process, checklists are strongly encouraged.

USING TECHNOLOGY IN THE LAW OFFICE

The use of technology can be particularly helpful in the area of damages through jury verdict research. This jury verdict research can be easily done through the use of Westlaw or other various research institutes.

The Microsoft program Excel is very useful in tracking damages. You can easily prepare summaries of the health care provider, dates of service, and amounts. Excel also will calculate and update damage information easily and effortlessly. Since the program automatically recalculates when new numbers are added, the paralegal does not have to spend countless hours reentering information or re-adding. The autosum function of that program will do that for you. Figure 6.3 shows an example of Excel.

Figure 6.3. Microsoft Excel

KEY TERMS

Affirmative defenses

Assumption of risk doctrine

Breach of duty

Common law

Comparative negligence doctrine

Compensatory damages

Consequential damages

Contributory negligence doctrine

Damages

Doctrine of avoidable consequences

Duty

Exemplary damages

Focus groups

General damages

Last-clear-chance doctrine

Negligence

Nominal damages

Prima facie case

Proximate cause

Punitive damages

Special damages

Strict liability torts

USEFUL WEB SITES

Medical resources

http://www.mayoclinic.com

http://www.medicineNet.com

http://www.medmedia.com

http://www.medscape.com

http://www.merck.com

http://www.nlm.nih.gov

http://www.searchpointe.com

http://www.webmd.com

chapter 7

Further Discovery and Depositions

---

chapter objectives

In this chapter, we will discuss

- The rules of discovery
- The process and purpose of discovery
- Different types of discovery
- Mandatory disclosure rules
- Disclosure and discovery of expert opinions
- Understanding the essentials of computer discovery

A. RULES OF DISCOVERY

1. Overview

Subject to certain limitations, **discovery** is a formal, pretrial process designed to give all parties access to the same evidence that will be available at the time of trial. If each party knows what all other parties know about the case, a more accurate assessment of the case is possible, and pretrial settlement is more probable. Discovery is the primary fact-finding process in litigation. It is available in both federal and state courts, and many state discovery rules mirror the federal rules very closely. The Federal Rules of Civil Procedure, specifically Rules 26 through 37, cover this discovery process. We will briefly review each rule in this chapter.

The paralegal should use caution and always check the local rules of court as many federal and state courts have their own special rules and requirements regarding format, filing, and responses to discovery requests. Litigation paralegals need to have a thorough understanding of the process of discovery and the rules that govern that process so that they can efficiently and effectively use this necessary tool throughout the litigation process.

2. **Limitations and Controls**

The scope of discovery is outlined in Rule 26 of the Federal Rules of Civil Procedure, which generally provides that parties may discover anything (not privileged) that is relevant to the subject matter of the action or that is reasonably calculated to lead to admissible evidence. A matter is relevant to the subject matter of the action if it makes the existence of a material fact more or less probable than it would be otherwise. Discovery is specifically designed to prevent trial by surprise, contrary to many things you see on television.

Parties can discover anything relevant to the action or that might lead to the discovery of admissible evidence—except that which is privileged. What do we mean by privilege? Typically, **Privilege** is an advantage enjoyed by an individual, company, or class beyond advantages of others. In the context of the discovery process, a privilege is a protection against compulsory disclosure that is given to certain types of information, such as

- Trade secrets
- Communication between certain categories of people
- Attorney-client
- Physician-patient
- Clergy-parishioner
- Husband-wife

The various privileges are defined as follows and limit or restrict discovery by one party to another:

- Attorney-client privilege: the right of a client to refuse to disclose or have disclosed communications between the client and the attorney
- Work product document privilege: any notes, papers, memoranda, or writings prepared by an attorney in anticipation of litigation or for trial
- Physician-patient privilege: the right of a patient to refuse to divulge or have divulged by the physician the communications between the client and the physician
- Husband-wife or marital privilege: the right of a spouse to refuse to divulge or have divulged by his or her spouse confidential communications made by a spouse during a legally valid marriage
- Clergy-parishioner privilege: the right of a parishioner to refuse to divulge or have divulged by his or her clergy, the communications between the client and the clergy

A person cannot be required to disclose privileged matters either at a deposition (Rule 26) or at trial (Federal Rules of Evidence 501 in federal question cases or state privilege rules in diversity cases). Privileges, according to Rule 501, are based on policy considerations. There are privilege rules that provide that certain communications are inadmissible because of confidentiality issues. Recognized privileges vary between jurisdictions, and it is necessary to research which privileges are recognized in the jurisdiction in which you are working. The most common privileges are the attorney-client, work product document, physician-patient, and marital.

The **attorney-client privilege** applies to confidential communications between a client and his or her attorney or the attorney's representative (such as the paralegal) in the rendering of legal services to that client. It is the client who holds this privilege. A paralegal must be very mindful of this privilege when responding to discovery to ensure that no confidential communications are disclosed since such disclosure would waive this privilege. Therefore, when providing documents requested, the paralegal needs to carefully review the documents produced to make sure no confidential communications are included in the production.

A paralegal is reviewing the documents provided by the client in order to prepare them for production. What happens when a confidential communication is uncovered? Is it simply ignored? The answer is no. That document is certainly pulled and withheld from the production, but in its place a sheet of paper is placed identifying "Privilege Pull." Thereafter the document is identified on a privilege log. A **privilege log** is a table providing information on what documentation is being withheld as a result of some privilege. The type of privilege claimed for withholding that document is identified along with a complete description of the document withheld. That privilege log is then produced with all the other documents. Figure 7.1 is an example of a privilege log.

The **work product document privilege** is a qualified privilege regarding the papers, notes, memoranda, and reports gathered or prepared in anticipation of litigation. The privilege applies equally to materials prepared by a paralegal or other agent of the attorney working under the direction of the attorney. It can also apply to materials, notes, papers, or memoranda prepared by the client in anticipation of litigation.

The **physician-patient privilege** is probably the most recognized privilege. A patient has a privilege to not disclose and to prevent the physician from disclosing any information acquired by the physician in confidence while treating the patient. There are exceptions, however. In the case of a patient putting his or her mental or physical health in issue, such as in a personal injury case, the privilege will not apply. The opposing attorney has a right to obtain that information relative to the injury claimed.

The **clergy-parishioner privilege** is similar in nature to the physician-patient privilege.

PRIVILEGE LOG

Plaintiff's Responses to Defendants' First Set of Combined Discovery Requests

BATES NOS.	DATE	AUTHOR	SUBJECT	RECIPIENT(S)	PRIVILEGE
ABC 00088	10/29/82	John Doe (Attorney)	Internal correspondence regarding settlement	Jane Doe	Attorney-client communication Attorney work product
ABC 00089	10/28/82	Jim Smith (Attorney)	Correspondence regarding settlement in litigation	Doug Little (Attorney)	Attorney-client communication Attorney work product

Figure 7.1. Privilege Log

It protects the right of a parishioner to refuse to disclose and to prevent a clergy from disclosing any commuunications held between the two.

To promote marital harmony and communication between spouses, there is the **husband-wife** or **martial privilege**. According to the martial privilege, a confidential communication made by one spouse to another during a legally valid marriage is protected from disclosure. The responding party can also object to the discovery request. **Objections,** an adverse reason or argument, to discovery requests may be properly grounded on the following five theories.

1. The information sought is not relevant to the case.
2. The information is privileged.
3. The information is for trial preparation, for which the necessary demonstration of substantial need and inability to obtain the equivalent has not been made.
4. The interrogatory seeks information about specially retained nonwitness experts concerning whom the necessary showing of need and inability to obtain the substantial equivalent has not been made.
5. The inquiry places unreasonable burden on the respondent.

These objections are discussed further in the chapter.

So then, how do you respond to discovery requests?

B. RESPONDING TO DISCOVERY

There are two ways to respond to discovery requests. First, the responding party can answer the question or request propounded. Second, the responding party, through his or her attorney, can object or request court intervention. Anyone (whether a party or nonparty) from whom discovery is sought may resist the discovery attempt by obtaining a protective order or by raising a timely objection to the question or request.

A **protective order** is an order issued from the court restricting or limiting discovery by one party to another. Federal Rules of Civil Procedure 26(c) and 30(d)(3) govern protective orders. A protective order always can be issued by the court in which the main case is pending. If a deposition is involved, the protective order can be issued either by the court in which the action is pending or by the court in which the deposition is scheduled to be taken. To obtain a protective order the moving party must show good cause.

This type of order can be obtained when a party against whom the discovery is sought feels that he or she is being embarrassed, harassed, or subjected to overly burdensome or expensive discovery requests. If a protective order is appropriate, Rule 26(c) provides a variety of remedies to protect the moving party. These remedies include barring the requested discovery, regulating the discovery, limiting persons present at the discovery, or regulating or barring disclosure of trade secrets and confidential information.

C. PURPOSES OF DISCOVERY

As the parties and their representatives—attorneys and paralegals—move toward the trial stage of a cause of action, many preliminary steps are necessary. The paralegal is continuously concerned with the processes of discovery and disclosure. Under both federal and state rules, the courts are not forums of tactical surprise. Instead, the rules of discovery and disclosure emphasize the free exchange of information long before a trial date, and hidden witnesses and surprise papers and documents are discouraged.

Under the Federal Rules of Civil Procedure, the scope of discovery is liberally construed as long as the request is relevant to the subject matter involved in the pending litigation.

Since the discovery process is liberally construed and the parties are encouraged and required to share information, what is the purpose of discovery? Is there only one purpose? The answer is no. Discovery serves many purposes:

- To obtain evidence that might not be available at trial because of a witness's age, poor health, or absence from the jurisdiction
- To narrow the issues for trial
- To determine opposing counsel's contentions
- To obtain basic and factual information
- To determine witnesses, both lay and expert witnesses
- To determine demonstrative evidence and other relevant documentation
- To determine or prove the amount of damages
- To avoid unfair surprise during trial
- To encourage settlement before trial

As the paralegal drafts discovery requests, it is important to keep these purposes in mind. It will help you to draft requests that will provide useful information in the representation of the firm's client.

Discovery is **self-executing,** that is, the parties implement discovery procedures on their own, with little court intervention (the exception being when a party requests a protective order). Once discovery is served on a party, that party has 30 days within which to respond. Other parts of the rule state further timelines and when court intervention is necessary. For example, Rule 26(f) discusses establishing an overall discovery plan, and Rule 35 specifies that prior court approval must be obtained for mental or physical examinations. We will look at these rules more carefully later in this chapter.

1. Relationship to Issues

Early identification and clarification of issues is essential to meaningful and fair discovery control. Fundamental to control is that discovery be directed at the material issues of the case. Rule 26(b)(1) states the general principle governing the scope of discovery, that the material requested be "relevant to the subject matter" of the action and appear "reasonably calculated to lead to the discovery of admissible evidence."

2. **Planning and Control**

A discovery plan should be designed to facilitate the orderly and cost-effective acquisition of relevant information and materials and the prompt resolution of discovery disputes. Adoption of a discovery plan is the principal purpose of the initial conference. The initial conference is preceded by a meeting of counsel for the purpose of developing a discovery plan for submission to the court.

There is no magic for deciding how discovery should be carried out or in what sequence it should be carried out. Discovery needs to be tailored to the specific needs and facts of each case. Just because the discovery process is available does not mean that you have to utilize it. Every discovery type must have a specific purpose in the overall discovery plan of that particular case.

The discovery process is an orderly process, governed by rules. Rule 26(a) of the Federal Rules of Civil Procedure covers required disclosures, both initial disclosures and disclosure of expert testimony, and requires the parties to disclose the following either at their discovery meeting or within 10 days thereafter:

- Names, addresses, telephone numbers, and subject matters for anyone "likely to have discoverable information" about disputed facts
- Description of all relevant documents, data complications, and so forth
- Computation of damages and supporting documents
- Liability policies, if any, related to the dispute

Then, at least 90 days before trial, the parties must disclose expert witnesses, including

- Their opinions
- Data
- Exhibits
- Qualifications
- Amount received for testifying

At least 30 days before trial, the parties must disclose all witnesses that will or may be called at trial and must provide a list of exhibits that will or may be used.

Paralegals are vested with the responsibility of ensuring that these deadlines are met in a timely fashion. In most law firms, the secretary will calendar the dates to be met. However, it is good practice for the paralegal to keep his or her own calendar with these dates. In that way, the paralegal can anticipate upcoming deadlines and prepare draft responses for attorney review with enough lead time to make sure the final product is prepared on the date due.

D. TYPES OF DISCOVERY

There are five types of discovery:

1. Depositions upon either oral or written questions
2. Interrogatories

3. Requests for physical or mental examination of persons
4. Requests for production of documents or things for inspection
5. Requests for admission of facts

Let's look at each one separately

1. Depositions

A **deposition** is a discovery device used to record the sworn testimony of a witness prior to trial. (See Figure 7.9 for a sample deposition transcript.) Depositions may be oral (Rule 30) or upon written questions (Rule 31). Customarily, depositions are oral exchanges whereby testimony is taken under oath through the examination of opposing counsel. The proceedings, questions, and answers are recorded either by videotape or by transcription by an official court reporter. Depositions can be taken in attorneys' offices, judges' offices, conference rooms, or other mutually agreed-on locations.

Paralegals usually will set up depositions, coordinate with opposing counsel, prepare the notice, obtain the stenographer, and ensure that the requirements of the Rules of Civil Procedure have all been met. When first embarking on your career as a paralegal, and even after you have been practicing for a time, it is helpful to develop a checklist of things to do when setting depositions. There is nothing more embarrassing (or expensive) than to have a deposition set and have all parties show up, only to find the paralegal forgot to hire the court reporter. A deposition checklist might look something like Figure 7.2.

PRACTICE TIP

When multiple attorneys are involved in a particular case, it can be extremely difficult to coordinate schedules. It is common courtesy not to arbitrarily set a deposition without checking with opposing counsel to see if it fits with their schedules. One way to make the process easier is to fax a calendar to opposing counsel for the month in which you desire to take the deposition. Ask that counsel to cross off days that are not available and then fax the calendar back. Once you have received calendars from all counsel, you can see which days are open for all and then set the deposition accordingly. There is nothing more frustrating than making numerous phone calls to schedule depositions. This practice eliminates that need.

As you can see, it is, therefore, extremely important that the paralegal be intimately familiar with the Federal Rules of Civil Procedure. We will look at Rule 30 and Rule 31 by examining the component parts of each rule.

Rule 30(a), concerning depositions upon oral examination, states:

(a) When Depositions May be Taken; When Leave Required.
(1) A party may take the testimony of any person, including a party, by deposition upon oral examination without leave of court except as provided in paragraph (2). The attendance of witnesses may be compelled by subpoena as provided in Rule 45.

DEPOSITION CHECKLIST

Party to be deposed: _____

Attorneys involved with phone numbers:

_____

_____

Dates available/confirmed: _____

Date, time, and location of deposition: _____

_____

Court reporter: _____

Confirmation letter sent to court reporter: _____

Notice prepared: _____   Notice served: _____

Subpoena/subpoena duces tecum prepared and served: _____

Witness fees and mileage necessary? _____

If so, prepared? _____

If necessary, obtain process server: _____

Return of service filed with court: _____

Notice filed with court: _____

Figure 7.2. Deposition Checklist

(2) A party must obtain leave of court, which shall be granted to the extent consistent with the principles stated in Rule 26(b)(2), if the person to be examined is confined in prison or if, without the written stipulation of the parties,

(A) a proposed deposition would result in more than ten depositions being taken under this rule or Rule 31 by the plaintiffs, or by the defendants, or by third-party defendants;

(B) the person to be examined already has been deposed in the case; or

(C) a party seeks to take a deposition before the time specified in Rule 26(d) unless the notice contains a certification, with supporting facts, that the person to be examined is expected to leave the United States and be unavailable for examination in this country unless deposed before that time.

This part of Rule 30 simply tells us that a party can take the deposition of any person, whether a party or not, by deposition upon oral examination without first obtaining leave of court. The attendance at that deposition may be compelled by subpoena, but the party does not have to be subpoenaed. The remainder of Rule 30(a) specifies when leave of court must be requested to take the deposition: If the party to be deposed is in prison, if the deposition requested would result in more than 10 depositions being taken, or if the person has already been deposed or if the deposition is sought prior to the time specified in Rule 26(d).

Rule 30(b) states:

> (b) Notice of Examination: General Requirements; Method of Recording; Production of Documents and Things; Deposition of Organization; Deposition by Telephone.
>
> (1) A party desiring to take the deposition of any person upon oral examination shall give reasonable notice in writing to every other party to the action. The notice shall state the time and place for taking the deposition and the name and address of each person to be examined, if known, and, if the name is not known, a general description sufficient to identify the person or the particular class or group in which the person belongs. If a subpoena duces tecum is to be served on the person to be examined, the designation of the materials to be produced as set forth in the subpoena shall be attached to, or included in, the notice.
>
> (2) The party taking the deposition shall state in the notice the method by which the testimony shall be recorded. Unless the court orders otherwise, if may be recorded by sound, sound-and-visual, or stenographic means, and the party taking the deposition shall bear the cost of the recording. Any party may arrange for a transcription to be made from the recording of a deposition taken by nonstenographic means.
>
> (3) With prior notice to the deponent and other parties, any party may designate another method to record the deponent's testimony in addition to the method specified by the person taking the deposition. The additional record or transcript shall be made at that party's expense unless the court otherwise orders.
>
> (4) Unless otherwise agreed by the parties, a deposition shall be conducted before an officer appointed or designated under Rule 28 and shall begin with a statement on the record by the officer that includes
>
> > (A) the officer's name and business address;
> > (B) the date, time, and place of the deposition;
> > (C) the name of the deponent;
> > (D) the administration of the oath or affirmation to the deponent; and
> > (E) an identification of all persons present.
>
> If the deposition is recorded other than stenographically, the officer shall repeat items (A) through (C) at the beginning of each unit of recorded tape or other recorded medium. The appearance or demeanor of deponents or attorneys shall not be distorted through camera or sound-recording techniques. At the end of the deposition, the officer shall state on the record that the deposition is complete and shall set forth any stipulations made by counsel concerning the custody of the transcript or recording and the exhibits, or concerning other pertinent matters.
>
> (5) The notice to a party deponent may be accompanied by a request made in compliance with Rule 34 for the production of documents and tangible things at the taking of the deposition. The procedure of Rule 34 shall apply to the request.
>
> (6) A party may in the party's notice and in a subpoena name as the

deponent a public or private corporation or a partnership or association or governmental agency and describe with reasonable particularity the matters on which examination is requested. In that event, the organization so named shall designate one or more officers, directors, or managing agents, or other persons who consent to testify on its behalf, and may set forth, for each person designated, the matters on which the person will testify. A subpoena shall advise a nonparty organization of its duty to make such a designation. The persons so designated shall testify as to matters known or reasonably available to the organization. This subdivision (b)(6) does not preclude taking a deposition by any other procedure authorized in these rules.

(7) The parties may stipulate in writing or the court may upon motion order that a deposition be taken by telephone or other remote electronic means. . . .

A Rule 30 deposition may be videotaped or may be taken by telephone if the parties agree. Court permission must be obtained if the deposition is taken either before the complaint is filed or before the Rule 26 discovery meeting.

After the discovery meeting, depositions of parties may be taken simply by providing notice to the party-deponent and to all other parties; court permission is not required. If there is concern that the party-deponent might fail to appear, his or her attendance can be compelled under Rule 37. Therefore, caution dictates that a subpoena be used to ensure attendance even though the Federal Rules do not require it. Failure to obey a subpoena subjects the nonparty to contempt of court.

What, then, is a subpoena? A **subpoena** is a document commanding an individual's appearance at a certain time and place to give testimony upon a certain matter. See Federal Rule of Civil Procedure 45. What is a subpoena duces tecum? A **subpoena duces tecum** is a court process compelling production of certain specific documents. It is a document that requires a person to appear to testify and bring documents, books, records, papers, or other tangible things to the examination. Figure 7.4 shows an example of a subpoena duces tecum.

Rule 30(g) states:

(g) Failure to Attend or to Serve Subpoena; Expenses.

(1) If the party giving the notice of the taking of a deposition fails to attend and proceed therewith and another party attends in person or by attorney pursuant to the notice, the court may order the party giving the notice to pay to such other party the reasonable expenses incurred by that party and that party's attorney in attending, including reasonable attorney's fees.

(2) If the party giving the notice of the taking of a deposition of a witness fails to serve a subpoena upon the witness and the witness because of such failure does not attend, and if another party attends in person or by attorney because that party expects the deposition of that witness to be taken, the court may order the party giving the notice to pay to such other party the reasonable expenses incurred by that party and that party's attorney in attending, including reasonable attorney's fees.

IN THE UNITED STATES DISTRICT COURT
FOR THE DISTRICT OF MONTANA
BILLINGS DIVISION

JOHN and MARY DOE,	)	
	)	
Plaintiff,	)	Case No. CV 97 114 BLG JDS
	)	
vs.	)	**SUBPOENA**
	)	
ABC COMPANY, a Foreign Corporation,	)	
	)	
Defendant.	)	

TO:

YOU ARE COMMANDED to appear at a deposition and testify at the place, date, and time specified below:

PLACE OF DEPOSITION	DATE AND TIME
ISSUING OFFICER SIGNATURE AND TITLE	DATE
ISSUING OFFICER'S NAME, ADDRESS AND PHONE NUMBER	

(See Rule 45, Federal Rules of Civil Procedure, Parts C& D on Next Page)

PROOF OF SERVICE

	DATE	PLACE
SERVED		
SERVED ON (PRINT NAME)		MANNER OF SERVICE
SERVED BY (PRINT NAME)		TITLE

DECLARATION OF SERVER

I declare under penalty of perjury under the laws of the United States of America that the foregoing information contained in the Proof of Service is true and correct.

Executed on _____

_____
SIGNATURE OF SERVER

_____
ADDRESS OF SERVER

_____

Figure 7.3. Subpoena

Rule 45, Fed.R.Civ.P. Parts (C) & (D):

(c) PROTECTION OF PERSONS SUBJECT TO SUBPOENAS.

(1) A party or attorney responsible for the issuance and service of a subpoena shall take reasonable steps to avoid imposing undue burden or expense on a person subject to that subpoena. The court on behalf of which the subpoena was issued shall enforce this duty and impose upon the party or attorney in breach of this duty an appropriate sanction, which may include, but is not limited to, lost earnings and a reasonable attorney's fees.

(2)(A) A person commanded to produce and permit inspection and copying of designated books, papers, documents or tangible things, or inspection of premises need not appear in person at the place of production or inspection unless commanded to appear for deposition, hearing or trial.

(B) Subject to paragraph (d)(2) of this rule, a person commanded to produce and permit inspection and copying may, within 14 days after service of the subpoena or before the time specified for compliance if such time is less than 14 days after service, serve upon the party or attorney designated in the subpoena written objection to inspection or copying of any or all of the designated materials or of the premises. If objection is made, the party serving the subpoena shall not be entitled to inspect and copy the materials or inspect the premises except pursuant to an order of the court by which the subpoena was issued. If objection has been made, the party serving the subpoena may, upon notice to the person commanded to produce, move at any time for an order to compel the production. Such an order to compel production shall protect any person who is not a party or an officer of a party from significant expense resulting from the inspection and copying commanded.

(3)(a) On timely motion, the court by which a subpoena was issued shall quash or modify the subpoena if it:

(i) fails to allow reasonable time for compliance;
(ii) requires a person who is not a party or an officer of a party to travel to a place more than 100 miles from the place where that person resides, is employed or regularly transacts business in person, except that, subject to the provisions of clause (c)(3)(B)(iii) of this rule, such a person may in order to attend trial be commanded to travel from any such place within the state in which the trial is held, or

(iii) requires disclosure of privileged or other protected matter and no exception or waiver applies, or
(iv) subjects a person to undue burden.

(B) If a subpoena

(i) requires disclosure of a trade secret or other confidential research, development, or commercial information, or
(ii) requires disclosure of an unretained expert's opinion or information not describing specific events or occurrences in dispute and resulting from the expert's study made not at the request of any party, or
(iii) requires a person who is not a party or an officer of a party to incur substantial expense to travel more than 100 miles to attend trial, the court may, to protect a person subject to or affected by the subpoena, quash or modify the subpoena or, if the party in whose behalf the subpoena is issued shows a substantial need for the testimony or material that cannot be otherwise met without undue hardship and assures that the person to whom the subpoena is addressed will be reasonably compensated, the court may order appearance or production only upon specified conditions.

(d) DUTIES IN RESPONDING TO SUBPOENA.

(1) A person responding to a subpoena to produce documents shall produce them as they are kept in the usual course of business or shall organize and label them to correspond with the categories in the demand.

(2) When information subject to a subpoena is withheld on a claim that it is privileged or subject to protection as trial preparation materials, the claim shall be made expressly and shall be supported by a description of the nature of the documents, communications, or things not produced that is sufficient to enable the demanding party to contest the claim.

Figure 7.3. (Continued)

IN THE UNITED STATES DISTRICT COURT
FOR THE DISTRICT OF MONTANA
BILLINGS DIVISION

JOHN and MARY DOE,	)	
	)	
Plaintiff,	)	Case No. CV 97 114 BLG JDS
	)	
vs.	)	**SUBPOENA DUCES TECUM**
	)	
ABC COMPANY, a Foreign Corporation,	)	
	)	
Defendant.	)	

Figure 7.4. Subpoena Duces Tecum

TO:

YOU ARE COMMANDED to appear, produce, and permit inspection and copying of the following documents or objects at the place, date, and time specified below:

PLACE OF PRODUCTION	DATE AND TIME

Any and all documents concerning _____ , including but not limited to:

Any and all records, whether generated by you or any other source, pertaining to any treatment or consultation with _____ , DOB: _____ , for any medical reason, including, but not limited to, office notes, doctors' notes, nurses' notes, lab and radiology reports, diagnostic testing results, consultation reports, hospital records, psychology reports, psychiatric reports/records, prescriptions, application forms, insurance forms, correspondence, and any other information relating to the cure, treatment, diagnosis, prognosis, or any other matters regarding

_____

ISSUING OFFICER SIGNATURE AND TITLE	DATE

ISSUING OFFICER'S NAME, ADDRESS AND PHONE NUMBER

(See Rule 45, Federal Rules of Civil Procedure, Parts C& D on Next Page)

PROOF OF SERVICE

	DATE	PLACE
SERVED		
SERVED ON	(PRINT NAME)	MANNER OF SERVICE
SERVED BY	(PRINT NAME)	TITLE

DECLARATION OF SERVER

I declare under penalty of perjury under the laws of the United States of America that the foregoing information contained in the Proof of Service is true and correct.

Executed on _____

Date   _____
                                      SIGNATURE OF SERVER

                                      _____
                                      ADDRESS OF SERVER

                                      _____

Figure 7.4. (Continued)

Rule 45, Fed.R.Civ.P. Parts (C) & (D):

(c) PROTECTION OF PERSONS SUBJECT TO SUBPOENAS.

(1) A party or attorney responsible for the issuance and service of a subpoena shall take reasonable steps to avoid imposing undue burden or expense on a person subject to that subpoena. The court on behalf of which the subpoena was issued shall enforce this duty and impose upon the party or attorney in breach of this duty an appropriate sanction, which may include, but is not limited to, lost earnings and a reasonable attorney's fees.

(2)(A) A person commanded to produce and permit inspection and copying of designated books, papers, documents or tangible things, or inspection of premises need not appear in person at the place of production or inspection unless commanded to appear for deposition, hearing or trial.

(B) Subject to paragraph (d)(2) of this rule, a person commanded to produce and permit inspection and copying may, within 14 days after service of the subpoena or before the time specified for compliance if such time is less than 14 days after service, serve upon the party or attorney designated in the subpoena written objection to inspection or copying of any or all of the designated materials or of the premises. If objection is made, the party serving the subpoena shall not be entitled to inspect and copy the materials or inspect the premises except pursuant to an order of the court by which the subpoena was issued. If objection has been made, the party serving the subpoena may, upon notice to the person commanded to produce, move at any time for an order to compel the production. Such an order to compel production shall protect any person who is not a party or an officer of a party from significant expense resulting from the inspection and copying commanded.

(3)(a) On timely motion, the court by which a subpoena was issued shall quash or modify the subpoena if it:

(i) fails to allow reasonable time for compliance;
(ii) requires a person who is not a party or an officer of a party to travel to a place more than 100 miles from the place where that person resides, is employed or regularly transacts business in person, except that, subject to the provisions of clause (c)(3)(B)(iii) of this rule, such a person may in order to attend trial be commanded to travel from any such place within the state in which the trial is held, or

(iii) requires disclosure of privileged or other protected matter and no exception or waiver applies, or
(iv) subjects a person to undue burden.

(B) If a subpoena

(i) requires disclosure of a trade secret or other confidential research, development, or commercial information, or
(ii) requires disclosure of an unretained expert's opinion or information not describing specific events or occurrences in dispute and resulting from the expert's study made not at the request of any party, or
(iii) requires a person who is not a party or an officer of a party to incur substantial expense to travel more than 100 miles to attend trial, the court may, to protect a person subject to or affected by the subpoena, quash or modify the subpoena or, if the party in whose behalf the subpoena is issued shows a substantial need for the testimony or material that cannot be otherwise met without undue hardship and assures that the person to whom the subpoena is addressed will be reasonably compensated, the court may order appearance or production only upon specified conditions.

(d) DUTIES IN RESPONDING TO SUBPOENA.

(1) A person responding to a subpoena to produce documents shall produce them as they are kept in the usual course of business or shall organize and label them to correspond with the categories in the demand.

(2) When information subject to a subpoena is withheld on a claim that it is privileged or subject to protection as trial preparation materials, the claim shall be made expressly and shall be supported by a description of the nature of the documents, communications, or things not produced that is sufficient to enable the demanding party to contest the claim.

Figure 7.4. (Continued)

In practice, most depositions are set by agreement of the parties, especially when the deponent is a party to the lawsuit. However, when it comes to nonparties or other witnesses, it is always the best practice to serve a subpoena on that party along with the Notice of Taking Deposition to ensure they will attend the deposition when set. Figure 7.5 shows an example of a Notice of Taking Deposition.

Let's take a look at Rule 45. Rule 45 discusses the form and issuance of a subpoena in part (a), service in part (b), protection of persons subject to subpoena in part (c), duties in responding to a subpoena in part (d), and contempt in part (e). We will look at a few of the important parts that paralegals need to be aware of.

In federal court, as in many state courts now, an attorney may issue the subpoena. No longer does the secretary or paralegal have to run to the court issuing the subpoena to pick it up; it can be done right in the office by the attorney. Rule 45(a)(3) states:

The clerk shall issue a subpoena, signed but otherwise in blank, to a party requesting it, who shall complete it before service. An attorney as officer of the court may also issue and sign a subpoena on behalf of

Attorney
Name
Address
Phone
Attorneys for Defendant

IN THE UNITED STATES DISTRICT COURT
FOR THE DISTRICT OF MONTANA
BILLINGS DIVISION

JOHN and MARY DOE,	)	
	)	
Plaintiff,	)	Case No. _____
	)	
vs.	)	**NOTICE OF TAKING DEPOSITION**
	)	
ABC COMPANY, a Foreign Corporation,	)	
	)	
Defendant.	)	

PLEASE TAKE NOTICE that the undersigned will take the deposition of the person herein named at the time and place herein stated before a court reporter or such other person authorized to administer oaths in the State of Montana. Said deposition will continue until completed. You are invited to attend and cross-examine.

NAME   PLACE   DATE & TIME

Dated this _____ day of August, 2002.

LAW FIRM

By _____
Name and address

Attorneys for Defendant

CERTIFICATE OF SERVICE

This is to certify that the foregoing was duly served by mail upon the following parties and/or counsel of record this _____ day of August, 2002.

_____

cc.: Court Reporter

Figure 7.5. Notice of Taking Deposition

(A) a court in which the attorney is authorized to practice; or

(B) a court for a district in which a deposition or production is compelled by the subpoena, if the deposition or production pertains to an action pending in a court in which the attorney is authorized to practice.

Rule 45(b) deals with service of the subpoena. It states that the subpoena

- Can be served by any person who is not a party
- Must be served personally on the person named therein
- Can be served by anyone who is 18 years or older
- Can be served at any place within the district of the court by which it is issued, or at any place without the district that is within 100 miles of the place of the deposition, hearing, trial, production or inspection
- Must be accompanied by the current witness fee and round-trip mileage (no witness fee or mileage accompanies a subpoena issued by a U.S. agency or official)
- Must include a proof of service when necessary, filed with the court issuing the subpoena stating the date and manner of service and the names of the persons served, and certified by the person who made the service. (Figure 7.6 shows an example of a proof of service.)

Service on a corporation can be accomplished by serving an officer, a managing or general agent, or to any other agent authorized by appointment or by law to receive service of process. It is important to remember that the proof of service is filed with the court, which shows that the party has been properly served and noticed.

Rule 30(c) deals with "Examination and Cross-Examination; Record of Examination;

PROOF OF SERVICE

	DATE	PLACE
SERVED		
SERVED ON		**MANNER OF SERVICE**
SERVED BY		**TITLE**

DECLARATION OF SERVER

I declare under penalty of perjury under the laws of the United States of America that the foregoing information contained in the Proof of Service is true and correct.

Executed on _____

           Date   SIGNATURE OF SERVER

                                         ADDRESS OF SERVER
                                         XYZ Firm
                                         P.O. Box 2222
                                         Anywhere, USA

Figure 7.6. Proof of Service

Oath; Objections." Rule 30(d) deals with "Schedule and Duration; Motion to Terminate or Limit Examination." Since these two parts of Rule 30 deal more with what attorneys will handle, those parts of the rule are not set forth here. However, it certainly would be time well spent reviewing those parts on your own.

Rule 30(e) deals with "Review by Witness; Changes; Signing." It states:

> If requested by the deponent or a party before completion of the deposition, the deponent shall have 30 days after being notified by the officer that the transcript or recording is available in which to review the transcript or recording and, if there are changes in form or substance, to sign a statement reciting such changes and the reasons given by the deponent for making them. The officer shall indicate in the certificate prescribed by subdivision (f)(1) whether any review was requested and, if so, shall append any changes made by the deponent during the period allowed.

It is the stenographer who is mandated to get the copy to the deponent to review and make changes. However, it is the paralegal's responsibility to ensure that the deponent has reviewed the transcript and identified changes within the specified time period (30 days). Usually the deponent will indicate on a separate piece of paper any changes, sign the transcript, and return it to the paralegal, who then fills in the errata sheet appropriately. See Figure 7.7 for an example of a Rule 30(b)(6) Deposition Notice, Figure 7.8 for a Certificate and Errata Sheet, and Figure 7.9 for a Deposition Transcript.

Rule 30(f) deals with "Certification and Filing by Officer; Exhibits; Copies; Notice of Filing." This part of the rule discusses how the finished transcript should be handled and states that the original will be sealed and identified. In most jurisdictions, the original sealed transcript is provided to the party setting the deposition along with a copy, but is not filed with the court unless leave of court is obtained. A copy is also provided to opposing counsel. Again, this part will not be reproduced herein, but should be reviewed.

Rule 31 states that a deposition upon written questions may also be used. A **deposition upon written questions** is sworn testimony of a witness in response to questions posed by the court reporter. A party may serve cross questions within 14 days after the notice and written questions are served, and within 7 days after being served with cross questions, a party may serve redirect questions upon all other parties. A stenographer then will take the notice and questions and take the testimony of the witness in response to the questions, much as a deposition upon oral examination. The use of written questions can be a time-saver and more cost-efficient than a deposition upon oral examination, but care should be used in utilizing this discovery method. The two biggest disadvantages to its use are the lack of flexibility and the absence of spontaneity.

a. Cost-Saving Measures

Depositions upon oral examination or upon written questions are not the only way to obtain relevant information from this type of discovery method. There are other methods that can be used as well that can be cost-saving measures. The paralegal should keep these alternatives in mind and utilize them when appropriate. A few of the alternatives follow.

	IN THE UNITED STATES DISTRICT COURT
	FOR THE DISTRICT OF _____
	_____ DIVISION

1
2
3   Plaintiffs,   )
4   )   Case No.
5   vs.   )
6   )   **RULE 30(B)(6) DEPOSITION NOTICE**
7   Defendant.   )
8   )
9
10   _____
11
12   Pursuant to Rule 30(b)(6) Fed. R. Civ. P., the attorney for Plaintiff will
13   take the deposition upon oral examination before a court reporter, a Notary
14   Public, or some other officer authorized by law to administer oaths as follows:
15
16   **Party**
17   **Date & Time**
18   **Method**   Video (sound-and-visual) and stenographic
19   **Place**
20   The matters on which examination is requested are listed on the attached
21   Exhibit A.
22   According to Rule 30(b)(6), the deponent is to designate on or more officers,
23   directors or managing agents, or other persons who consent to testify on its behalf,
24   and set forth, for each person designated, the matters on which the person will
25   testify.
26   Dated this _____ day of _____, 1999.
27
28   By _____
29
30   ATTORNEYS FOR _____
31
32
33   **CERTIFICATE OF SERVICE**
34
35   This is to certify that the foregoing was duly served by mail upon the
36   following parties and/or counsel of record this _____ day of _____,
37   1999.
38
39

Figure 7.7. Rule 30(b)(6) Deposition Notice

118

1	THE STATE OF	)
2		)
3	COUNTY OF	)

4

5   I hereby certify that I have read the foregoing deposition, and that this
6 deposition is a true record of my testimony given at this deposition, together with any
7 changes or corrections that I have indicated in the spaces provided below and the
8 reasons for the changes. (DO NOT MAKE CORRECTIONS ON THE TRANSCRIPTS.
9 USE BACK SIDE OF PAGE IF NECESSARY)

10

11   PAGE   LINE   CHANGE OR CORRECTION   REASON FOR CHANGE

12 _____-_____-_____-_____
12 _____-_____-_____-_____
13 _____-_____-_____-_____
14 _____-_____-_____-_____
15 _____-_____-_____-_____
16 _____-_____-_____-_____
17 _____-_____-_____-_____
18 _____-_____-_____-_____
19 _____-_____-_____-_____
20 _____-_____-_____-_____
21 _____-_____-_____-_____
22 _____-_____-_____-_____
23 _____-_____-_____-_____
24 _____-_____-_____-_____
25 _____-_____-_____-_____
26 _____-_____-_____-_____
27 _____-_____-_____-_____
28 _____-_____-_____-_____
29 _____-_____-_____-_____
30 _____-_____-_____-_____
31 _____-_____-_____-_____
32 _____-_____-_____-_____
33 _____-_____-_____-_____
34 _____-_____-_____-_____

36

37   _____

38

39   SUBSCRIBED AND SWORN TO before me ny the said witness on this the
40 day of _____, 19____.

41

42   _____
                                        NOTARY PUBLIC

Figure 7.8. Certificate and Errata Sheet

```
                                    1
          IN THE SUPERIOR COURT OF THE STATE OF CALIFORNIA IN AND FOR THE
 1        CITY AND COUNTY OF SAN FRANCISCO
 2
 3        ANN GREEN,              )
 4              Plaintiff,   )
 5        vs.          )  NO.012345
 6                     )  VOLUME I
 7        JOE JONES CORPORATION, T.S.   )  PAGES 1-97
 8        JOHNSTON, INC., MARY ANDERSONNY, )
 9        JAMES MICHAELS, W.J. WILSON,   )
10        AND DOES 1-50, INCLUSIVE,   )
11                Defendants.  )
12           Deposition of ANN GREEN, taken on behalf of JOE JONES CORPORATION, at
13        407 Gold Street, Room 500, San Francisco, California 94000, commencing at 9:40
14        a.m., Saturday, March 7, 1992, before David A. House, C.S.R. 0002, a Notary
15        Public, and Thomas Morris, C.S.R. 0003, pursuant to Notice and Request to
16        Produce Documents.
17
18                 BALL & QUINN BAY AREA
19               CERTIFIED DEPOSITION REPORTERS
20                1 QUAIL STREET, SUITE 900
21              SAN FRANCISCO, CALIFORNIA 94000
22                  (415) 555-9999
                                    2
 1
 2        APPEARANCES OF COUNSEL:
 3
 4        FOR PLAINTIFF:
 5
 6           HAUFMANN AND KELSEY
 7           BY: LEONARD HAUFMANN, ESQ.
 8              -AND-
 9           JOSEPH HAUFMANN, ESQ.
10           1234 Hardings Avenue, Suite B
11           Oakmont, California 95559
12
13        FOR DEFENDANT:
14
15           DOUGHERTY, ELLISON & HART
16           BY: DAVID P. MATSEN, ESQ.
17           407 Gold Street
18           San Francisco, California 94000
19
20              —oOo—
21
```

Figure 7.9. Deposition Transcript

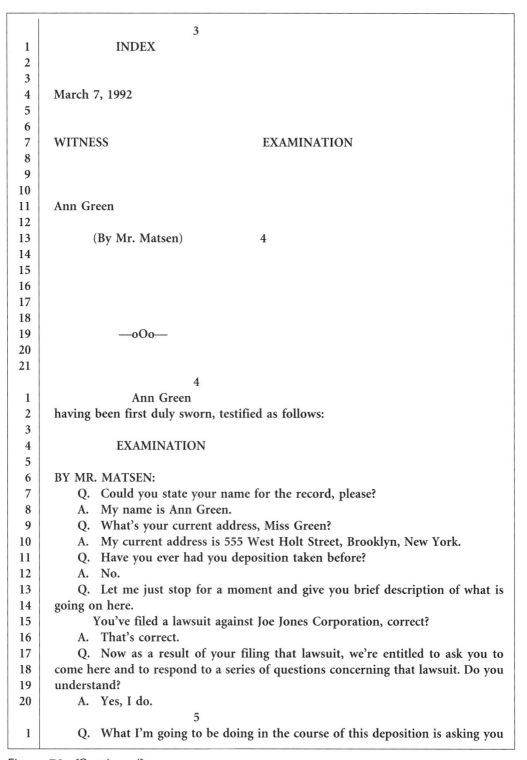

3

INDEX

March 7, 1992

WITNESS	EXAMINATION

Ann Green

   (By Mr. Matsen)   4

—oOo—

4

Ann Green
having been first duly sworn, testified as follows:

EXAMINATION

BY MR. MATSEN:

Q. Could you state your name for the record, please?

A. My name is Ann Green.

Q. What's your current address, Miss Green?

A. My current address is 555 West Holt Street, Brooklyn, New York.

Q. Have you ever had you deposition taken before?

A. No.

Q. Let me just stop for a moment and give you brief description of what is going on here.

You've filed a lawsuit against Joe Jones Corporation, correct?

A. That's correct.

Q. Now as a result of your filing that lawsuit, we're entitled to ask you to come here and to respond to a series of questions concerning that lawsuit. Do you understand?

A. Yes, I do.

5

Q. What I'm going to be doing in the course of this deposition is asking you

Figure 7.9. (Continued)

2	those questions. Your answers, my questions, anything that is said in this room is
3	going to be taken down by the court reporter sitting to your right. Okay?
4	A. Yes.
5	Q. What he will do with what comes out of that machine is type it up into a
6	transcript, what we call a transcript. Okay?
7	You will have an opportunity to review that transcript and to make any
8	changes that you wish to when you review it. do you understand?
9	A. Yes, I do.
10	Q. And please understand that I will be able to comment upon the changes
11	you make in the transcript and the transcript itself will be usable as evidence in
12	this case just as though you were testifying. Do you understand?
13	A. I do.
14	Q. Because you are testifying under oath here.
15	A. I know that.
16	Q. Good.
17	If in the course of this deposition you don't understand the question, or my
18	voice drops, you can't hear me, or something happens outside that makes
19	

Figure 7.9. (Continued)

- Informal interviews. These involve interviewing the party without utilizing the formal process of a deposition. Informal interviews can be taped, but the paralegal should discuss that with the attorney prior to taping any conversation.
- Nonstenographic depositions. These are depositions that are not recorded by a court reporter. This can be done by videotaping the questions and answers.
- Telephone depositions. These drastically cut down the costs of taking a deposition by eliminating travel expenses. This is particularly useful when there are numerous parties and attorneys involved or when the deponent lives far away from the jurisdiction.
- Conference depositions. These can be conducted through the use of video telecommunications. This eliminates the need for travel and cuts down on the time and expense involved. However, this technology is fairly new and its availability is not assured in all jurisdictions. This method is best utilized when multiple parties are involved who can share in the expense.
- Written questions. The use of written questions will be discussed later in this chapter. There are some distinct disadvantages to the use of this alternative and those disadvantages need to be carefully considered in the case at hand.
- Reduction in copies. Few people realize the expense involved in obtaining copies of lengthy depositions. Many court reporters now will provide ASCII disks at the request of the party setting the deposition. These disks (which contain the entire transcript) can then be used to print out multiple copies of the deposition, or simply used on the computer without the necessity of printing a hard copy.
- Limited attendance. Limited attendance means that not all parties or their attorneys will attend the deposition. Oftentimes when multiple parties are involved, attorneys

will designate one attorney to attend and take the deposition. However, this is only done when the attorneys can be assured that the interests of their client will be represented. Also, if travel is involved, many times it will only be the attorney attending the deposition; the party they represent will not attend.

b. Postdeposition

Paralegals engage in extensive postdeposition activity. Finished transcripts are often huge documents that can take a lot of time to review and digest. Therefore, to assist the attorney handling the case, it is the paralegal who develops indexes, digests, summaries, and other abbreviated techniques of deposition content. There are many methods of indexing or digesting depositions:

- Key points
- Key names of people, witnesses, or organizations
- Issues and subissues
- Key facts
- Key events

Digests enable the attorney or paralegal to quickly review the subject matter without having to read the entire deposition. Indexes are excellent tools in the preparation of trial exhibits, documents, appellate briefs, and evidence identification. There are many different ways of summarizing depositions, such as page, line and testimony; topic index, testimony and page; and, narrative form. When requested to summarize a deposition, ask the attorney how he or she likes to have the summary done and what he or she would find most useful. Figure 7.10 is an example of a deposition summary.

The use of ASCII disks with litigation support software can be invaluable in saving time. Most litigation support software programs allow you to search for key words such as names or dates. The programs also allow you to easily and quickly digest the depositions, although the need for that activity is diminished with the ability to search afforded by such programs.

Some attention to the integrity and accuracy of the deposition transcript is a necessary paralegal function. Inconsistencies in a witness's testimony should be noted. Such inconsis-

---

DEPOSITION SUMMARY
of Jane Doe
Dated: May 2, 2002
File No.

Topic	Testimony	Page
Background	Resides in Anywhere, Montana.	4
	Educated Harvard University. Masters Degree in Business 1990.	5

Figure 7.10. Deposition Summary

tencies can be used to later impeach the witness. A review may also reveal inaccuracies or omissions in the reporting. Given the liberal admissibility of a deposition, any inconsistencies or evidence that impeaches the deponent provides insight into credibility matters.

2. Interrogatories

Interrogatories are a series of written questions served by one party on another party, which must be answered under oath. Principles of discovery require that the questions be germane, relevant, sensible, not overly broad or burdensome and not represent a "fishing expedition." Interrogatories may relate to matters into which inquiry is permitted under Rule 26(b), and the answers may be used to the extent permitted by the rules of evidence. See Figure 7.11 for an example of defendant's first set of interrogatories to plaintiff.

Rule 33 sets forth guidlines for interrogatories. It states:

(a) Availability. Without leave of court or written stipulation, any party may serve upon any other party written interrogatories, not exceeding 25 in number including all discrete subparts, to be answered by the party served or, if the party served is a public or private corporation or a partnership or association or governmental agency, by any officer or agent, who shall furnish such information as is available to the party. Leave to serve additional interrogatories shall be granted to the extent consistent with the principles of Rule 26(b)(2). Without leave of court or written stipulation, interrogatories may not be served before the time specified in Rule 26(d).

(b) Answers and Objections.

(1) Each interrogatory shall be answered separately and fully in writing under oath, unless it is objected to, in which event the objecting party shall state the reasons for objection and shall answer to the extent the interrogatory is not objectionable.

(2) The answers are to be signed by the person making them, and the objections signed by the attorney making them.

(3) The party upon whom the interrogatories have been served shall serve a copy of the answer and objections if any, within 30 days after the service of the interrogatories. A shorter or longer time may be directed by the court or, in the absence of such an order, agreed to in writing by the parties subject to Rule 29.

(4) All grounds for an objection to an interrogatory shall be stated with specificity. Any ground not stated in a timely objection is waived unless the party's failure to object is excused by the court for good cause shown.

(5) The party submitting the interrogatories may move for an order under Rule 37(a) with respect to any objection to or other failure to answer an interrogatory.

(c) Scope; Use at Trial. Interrogatories may relate to any matters which can be inquired into under Rule 26(b)(1), and the answers may be used to the extent permitted by the rules of evidence.

An interrogatory otherwise proper is not necessarily objectionable merely because an answer to the interrogatory involve an opinion or contention that relates to fact or the application of law to fact, but the court may order that such an

```
                    IN THE UNITED STATES DISTRICT COURT
                    FOR THE DISTRICT OF _____
                                _____ DIVISION

  1
  2
  3          Plaintiffs,                    )
  4                                         )     Case No.
  5      vs.                                )
  6                                         )     DEFENDANT'S FIRST SET OF
  7                                         )     INTERROGATORIES TO PLAINTIFF
  8          Defendant.                     )
                                            )
  9
 10                      _____
 11
 12    TO:   Plaintiff, and his attorney _____,
 13
 14          COMES NOW the Defendant, _____, pursuant to Rule
 15    33, Federal Rules of Civil Procedure, submits the following interrogatories to
 16    the plaintiff, _____, for answer within thirty (30) days of service.
 17    Supplemental answers to these interrogatories are required pursuant to rule
 18    26(e), Federal Rules of Civil Procedure.
 19
 20          INTERROGATORY NO. 1: Please
 21
 22          Dated this _____ day of _____, 1999.
 23
 24                                     By _____
 25
 26                      ATTORNEYS FOR _____
 27
 28
 29                            CERTIFICATE OF SERVICE
 30
 31          This is to certify that the foregoing was duly served by mail upon the following
 32    parties and/or counsel of record this _____ day of _____, 1999.
 33
 34
 35
```

Figure 7.11. Defendant's First Set of Interrogatories to Plaintiff

interrogatory need not be answered until after designated discovery has been completed or until a pretrial conference or other later time.

(d) Option to Produce Business Records. Where the answer to an interrogatory may be derived or ascertained from the business records of the party upon whom the interrogatory has been served or from an examination, audit or inspection of such business records, including a compilation, abstract or summary thereof, and the burden of deriving or ascertaining the answer is substantially the same for the party serving the interrogatory as for the party served, it is a sufficient answer to such interrogatory to specify the records from which the answer may be derived or ascertained and to afford to the party serving the interrogatory reasonable opportunity to examine, audit, or inspect such records and to make copies, compilations, abstracts or summaries. A specification shall be in sufficient detail to permit the interrogating party to locate and to identify, as readily as can the party served, the records from which the answer may be ascertained.

Note that no party may serve more than 25 interrogatories including subparts, without a stipulation to serve more or permission of the court. With this limitation it is therefore extremely important to draft relevant interrogatories that will elicit the necessary information. The paralegal should carefully review the facts of the case, discuss the case and case strategy with the supervising attorney, and make a list of the facts, documents, or materials needed. From there the paralegal can draft effective interrogatories.

The responding party must answer the interrogatories in good faith and must supply the requested information unless a privilege or other basis for objection exists as discussed above. Rule 33 requires the responding party to answer interrogatories within 30 days of their service. The responses must be signed under oath by the party on which they are served, and objections to any particular questions must be signed by the responding party's attorney.

a. Objections

A party on whom interrogatories have been served has two possible responses, to answer the interrogatory or to object to the interrogatory. If the response is an objection, the objection simply needs to be stated as the answer to that particular interrogatory. There are several bases for objecting, such as the request is

- Outside the scope of discovery under Rule 26
- Too burdensome
- Too vague
- Too broad
- Requests information that is privileged or that is classified as attorney work document product

b. Practices to Save Time and Expense

There are several ways to save time and expense when propounding interrogatories to an opposing party. Here are some of them:

- Master interrogatories and precluding duplicate requests. Many firms use master interrogatories, interrogatories that have been made into form requests. Care should be used when utilizing master sets of interrogatories in that each set of discovery requests sent out must be tailored to the particular case at hand. There is nothing more embarrassing than sending interrogatories out that do not pertain to the facts of the case or refer to the wrong parties. It is also important to ensure that there are no duplicate requests especially due to the limitation of proprounding only 25 interrogatories.

- Use of interrogatories from other litigation. Sometimes it to helpful to keep copies of interrogatories used in other cases. These can then be used as a starting point for developing interrogatories specific to the case you are working on. It provides ideas and reminds you of what information is necessary to obtain.
- Successive responses. Successive responses are utilized when there are multiple parties and questions propounded are the same for each party.
- Computer responses. Many jurisdictions now require that the party propounding the interrogatories provide a disk to the opposing party of the questions. In this way the responding party does not have to retype the questions and can easily save the responses on disk. The disk and a hard copy of the response is then provided to the propounding party.
- Early resolution of disputes. Obviously early resolution of the dispute can eliminate the need for further discovery. This method encompasses settlement or some kind of agreement between the parties.

3. Request for Physical or Mental Examination

A Request for physical or mental examination is a request to the court that the party whose physical or mental condition is in issue be required to submit to a examination. Lawsuits frequently involve physical injuries. The amount of money requested as compensation for damages depends on how severe and how permanent the injuries are. Proof of these damages usually requires testimony by physicians. The plaintiff has his or her own treating physician who can give opinions as to the severity or permanency of an injury, but the defendant would certainly like to have his or her own expert or physician examine the plaintiff. Rule 35 of the Federal Rules of Civil Procedure allows for just that. Under this rule a defendant can request or file a formal written Notice of Independent Medical Examination or IME on the other party whose medical condition is in issue in the suit. The notice simply instructs the person to be examined to appear at the specified date, time, and doctor's office to be examined. Oftentimes the request for an IME is handled between counsel without the need for a form written notice. Counsel agree on the time and date, and the party then attends.

Rule 35 is not self-executing, that is the requesting party must file a motion to request it or initiate a phone call to opposing counsel. An order for examination will be entered if the requesting party can show the existence of both of the following conditions:

1. The physical or mental condition of a party (or a person in the custody or control of a party) is an issue in the case
2. There is good cause

However, in practice, counsel can usually agree on the IME. The constitutional right of privacy makes the scope of discovery under Rule 35 more narrow than it is under the other discovery rules.

Rule 35 covers "Physical and Mental Examinations of Persons." It states:

(a) Order for Examination. When the mental or physical condition (including the blood group) of a party, or of a person in the custody or under the legal control of a party, is in controversy, the court in which the action is pending may order the party to submit to a physical or mental examination by a suitably licensed or certified examiner or to produce for examination the person in the party's custody or legal control. The order may be made only on motion for good cause shown and upon notice to the person to be examined and to all parties and shall specify the time, place, manner, conditions, and scope of the examination and the person or persons by whom it is to be made.

Part (b) of Rule 35 covers the "Report of Examiner." It states that the party who has requested the examination shall, upon request, deliver a copy of the detailed written report of the examiner to the party requesting it. By requesting and obtaining a copy of the report, that party waives any privilege that party may have regarding the testimony of the person who examined them. A deposition may be taken of the examiner as well.

4. Request for Production

A request for production is a series of requests for documentation relevant to the lawsuit, served by one party on another party, which must be answered under oath. Rule 34 provides that any party may request any other party to produce documents and things or to allow inspection of land that is under the control of the responding party. The scope of Rule 34 is concerned with providing litigants with the opportunity to inspect and copy any designated documents, including writings, drawings, graphs, charts, photographs, phonorecords, and other data compilations and to inspect, test, or sample any tangible things that constitute or contain matters within the scope of Rule 26. See Figure 7.12 for an example of defendant's first request for production to plaintiff.

Paralegals can often have a difficult time determining what is a request with reasonable particularity and what is too broad an inquiry. Too often, lawyers make overly broad requests when they are not sure what documents exist. Often they use this devise as a "fishing expedition" to see what documents are out there. Paralegals who draft requests must refine their requests, narrow the scope of coverage, and specifically set forth those documents relevant to the case.

There are two ways to respond to a request to produce documents. The party can supply the documents requested or can respond by stating that the documents are available for inspection and copying. When the documents requested are voluminous, it is sometimes easier to make them available for inspection. The party with the documents and the party requesting the documents determine a mutually convenient time to review them. Prior to this inspection, the paralegal prepares and reviews the documents ensuring there are no privileged documents, and numbers each page of each document. The opposing party then reviews everything and indicates which documents he or she would like copies of. Again, the paralegal that the appropriate copies are made and that a record is kept of what copies were requested.

Remember that nonparties to the suit can be required to produce documents and

IN THE UNITED STATES DISTRICT COURT
FOR THE DISTRICT OF _____
_____ DIVISION

Plaintiffs,	)
	)
vs.	) Case No.
	)
	) **DEFENDANT'S FIRST REQUEST FOR**
	) **PRODUCTION TO PLAINTIFF**
Defendant.	)

_____

TO: Plaintiff, and his attorney _____,

COMES NOW the Defendant, _____, and pursuant to Rule 26(b) and Rule 34 of the Federal Rules of Civil Procedure, hereby requests the plaintiff to produce for inspection and copying the following categories of documents to be produced at the offices of _____, within thirty (30) days of the date of service. Inspection shall be by the undesigned, or other designated representative of defendant.

> *NOTE A:* "You" or "your" refers to the parties to whom this discovery request is directed, together with their representatives, agents, employees, insurers, and attorneys.

> **NOTE B:** the word "documents" shall be understood as defined in Rule 34(a), Mont.R.Civ.P.

> **NOTE C:** this request is directed to both plaintiffs and counsel representing plaintiffs and a joint response and/or production is contemplated.

> **NOTE D:** supplementation of responses to this request for production are required under Rule 26(e).

REQUEST FOR PRODUCTION NO. 1:

Dated this _____ day of _____, 1999.

By _____

ATTORNEYS FOR _____

Figure 7.12. Defendant's First Request for Production to Plaintiff

things under Rule 45 subpoena procedures. If there is an objection to a subpoena, objections must be made within 14 days after the subpoena is served. If the time for compliance is less then 14 days, objections must be served before the time for compliance.

Rule 34 deals with requests for production of documents and entry upon land for inspection. It states:

> (a) Scope. Any party may serve on any other party a request
>
> (1) to produce and permit the party making the request, or someone acting on the requestor's behalf, to inspect and copy, any designated documents (including writings, drawings, graphs, charts, photographs, phono records, and other data compilations from which information can be obtained, translated, if necessary, by the respondent through detection devices into reasonably usable form), or to inspect and copy, test, or sample any tangible things which constitute or contain matters within the scope of Rule 26(b) and which are in the possession, custody or control of the party upon whom the request is served; or,
>
> (2) to permit entry upon designated land or other property in the possession or control of the party upon whom the request is served for the purpose of inspection and measuring, surveying, photographing, testing, or sampling the property or any designated object or operation thereon, within the scope of Rule 26(b).
>
> (b) Procedure. The request shall set forth, either by individual item or by category, the items to be inspected and describe each with reasonable particularity. The request shall specify a reasonable time, place and manner of making the inspection and performing the related acts. Without leave of court or written stipulation, a request may not be served before the time specified in Rule 26(d).
>
> The party upon whom the request is served shall serve a written response within 30 days after the service of the request. A shorter or longer time may be directed by the court or, in the absence of such an order, agreed to in writing by the parties, subject to Rule 29. The response shall state, with respect to each item or category, that inspection and related activities will be permitted as requested, unless the request is objected to, in which event the reasons for the objection shall be stated. If objection is made to the part of an item or category, the part shall be specified and inspection permitted of the remaining parts. The party submitting the request may move for an order under Rule 37(a) with respect to any objection to or other failure to respond to the request or any part thereof, or any failure to permit inspection as requested.
>
> A party who produces documents for inspection shall produce them as they are kept in the usual course of business or shall organize and label them to correspond with the categories in the request.
>
> (c) Persons Not Parties. A person not a party to the action may be compelled to produce documents and things or to submit to an inspection as provided in Rule 45.

It is important to remember that the documents must be produced "as they are kept in the usual course of business" and the party producing the documents must "organize and label them to correspond with the categories in the request."

5. Stipulations of Fact and Requests for Admission

A request for admission is a series of written questions served by one party on another party seeking the admission of the truth of statements or opinions of fact, application of law to fact, or genuineness of a document. After the discovery meeting and initial disclosure, any party may serve upon any other party written requests for admission under Rule 36 seeking admission of the truth of

- Statements of fact
- Opinions of fact
- Application of law to fact
- The genuineness of any document

The purpose of requests for admission are to narrow the facts and issues to be proved at trial, not to obtain information (Rule 33, interrogatories) and not to inspect documents (Rule 34, request to produce). Answers or objections to requests for admission are due in 30 days or the requests are deemed admitted. If a party fails to admit the truth of any request and if the requesting party proves conclusively the subject matter of the request at trial, the court may require the nonanswering party to pay reasonable expenses connected with proving the matter. If used wisely, admissions are nothing more than a mechanism to reduce issues and eliminate the necessity of formalized proof. Admission response should be short, direct, and concisely stated, preferably with "admit" or "deny" comments. Any lengthy response could tend to open up secondary issues. The request for admission is continuous and ongoing. When evidence has been discovered and appears to be undisputed, a request for an admission regarding the newlyfound material is appropriate. Also, when a request for admission has been denied but the newlyfound material proves otherwise, the response must be amended stating the reasons for the amendment. See Figure 7.13 for an example of requests for admission.

Defense and plaintiff attorneys and their clients who can stipulate as to certain facts and events can make them a formal part of the court's record through a technique known as stipulation.

Rule 36, regarding requests for admissions, states:

> (a) Request for Admission. A party may serve upon any other party a written request for the admission, for purposes of the pending action only, of the truth of any matter within the scope of Rule 26(b)(1) set forth in the request that relate to statements or opinions of fact or of the application of law to fact, including the genuineness of any documents described in the request. Copies of documents shall be served with the request unless they have been or are otherwise furnished or made available for inspection and copying. Without leave of court or written stipulation, request for admission may not be served before the time specified in Rule 26(d).
>
> Each matter of which an admission is requested shall be separately set forth. The matter is admitted unless, within 30 days after service of the request, or within such shorter or longer time as the court may allow or as the parties may agree to in writing, subject to Rule 26, the party to whom the request is directed serves upon the party requesting the admission a written answer or objection addressed to the matter, signed by the party or the party's attorney. If objection is made, the reasons therefor shall be stated. The answer shall specifically deny the matter or set forth in detail the reasons why the answering party cannot truthfully admit or deny the matter. A denial shall fairly meet the substance of the requested admission, and when good faith requires that a party qualify an answer or deny only a party of the matter of which an admission is requested, the party shall specify so much of it as is true and qualify or deny the remainder. An answering party may not give lack of information

```
        IN THE UNITED STATES DISTRICT COURT
        FOR THE DISTRICT OF _____
                    _____ DIVISION
 1
 2                                  )
 3      Plaintiffs,                 )
 4                                  )   Case No.
 5   vs.                            )
 6                                  )   REQUESTS FOR ADMISSION
 7      Defendant.                  )
 8                                  )
 9
10              _____
11
12   TO:  Plaintiff, and his attorney _____,
13
14           COMES NOW the Defendant, _____, pursuant to Rule
15   36, Federal Rules of Civil Procedure, and submits the following requests for
16   admission to the plaintiff, _____, for answer within thirty (30)
17   days of service. Supplemental answers to these interrogatories are required pursu-
18   ant to Rule 26(e), Federal rules of Civil Procedure.
19
20           REQUEST FOR ADMISSION NO. 1:
21
22                         By _____
23
24           ATTORNEYS FOR _____
25
26
27              CERTIFICATE OF SERVICE
28
29           This is to certify that the foregoing was duly served by mail upon the
30   following parties and/or counsel of record this _____ day of _____,
31   1999.
32
33                                  _____
34
35
```

Figure 7.13. Request for Admission

or knowledge as a reason for failure to admit or deny unless the party states that the party has made reasonable inquiry and that the information known or readily obtainable by the party is insufficient to enable the party to admit or deny. A party who considers that a matter of which an admission has been requested presents a genuine issue for trial may not, on that ground alone, object to the request; the party may, subject to the provisions of Rule 37(c), deny the matter or set forth reasons why the party cannot admit or deny it.

The party who has requested the admissions may move to determine the sufficiency of the answers or objections. Unless the court determines that an objection is justified, it shall order that an answer be served. If the court determines that an answer does not comply with the requirements of this rule, it may order either that the matter is admitted or that an amended answer be served. The court may, in lieu of these orders, determine that final disposition of the request be made at a pretrial conference or at a designated time prior to trial. The provisions of Rule 37(a)(4) apply to the award of expenses incurred in relation to the motion.

(b) Effect of Admission. Any matter admitted under this rule is conclusively established unless the court on motion permits withdrawal or amendment of the admission. Subject to the provision of Rule 16 governing amendment of a pertrial order, the court may permit withdrawal or amendment when the presentation of the merits of the action will be subserved thereby and the party who obtained the admission fails to satisfy the court that withdrawal or amendment will prejudice that party in maintaining the action or defense on the merits. Any admission made by a party under this rule is for the purpose of the pending action only and is not an admission for any other purpose nor may it be used against the party in any other proceeding.

E. MANDATORY DISCLOSURE RULES

Mandatory disclosure rules are procedural rules that require parties who have information regarding the lawsuit to turn it over to the opposing party without being asked. The purpose behind these rules is to respond to the wastefulness and gamesmanship evidenced in the discovery process in the past. They reduce the use of discovery as a tactical weapon and minimize the time spent by judges in settling discovery disputes.

Most of the witnesses who testify in a trial are fact witnesses—people who describe some event they personally observed. However, there is another category of witnesses that is extremely important in the litigation process—expert witnesses, people who are employed to give opinions on specialized subjects that ordinary jurors might not be able to grasp on their own. Expert testimony may play a decisive role in the outcome of some lawsuits. So it goes without saying that each party will want to find out well before trial who the opposing party's experts are, what their opinions are, and how those opinions were arrived at.

F. DISCLOSURE AND DISCOVERY OF EXPERT OPINIONS

Management of the disclosure and discovery of expert opinions is essential to ensure adequate preparation by the parties, avoid surprise at trial, and facilitate rulings on the admissibility of expert evidence. An example of an expert disclosure statement is seen in Figure 7.14.

Rule 26(a)(2)(B) requires prediscovery disclosure of expert testimony. It states in pertinent part:

**IN THE UNITED STATES DISTRICT COURT
FOR THE DISTRICT OF MONTANA
BILLINGS DIVISION**

ABC COMPANY,	)	Cause No. _____
	)	
Plaintiff,	)	**EXPERT DISCLOSURE BY**
	)	
vs.	)	_____
	)	
JOHN DOE,	)	
	)	
Defendant.	)	

Pursuant to Rule 26(a)(2), Fed. R. Civ. P., and the Order dated September 16, 1998, concerning the deadlines for disclosing expert witnesses, defendant _____ hereby discloses its expert witnesses as follows:

1. Dr. Smith, 123 Maple Drive, Anytown, USA. Dr. Smith is a clinical psychologist who practices in _____. Dr. Smith may testify as _____.

The report of the foregoing expert is attached hereto in compliance with the court's order.

Respectfully submitted this 23rd day of June, 2000.

LAW FIRM

By _____
Name and Address

CERTIFICATE OF SERVICE

I, _____, one of the attorneys for the law firm of _____, hereby certify that on the 23rd day of June, 2000, I mailed a true and correct copy of the foregoing document, postage prepaid, to the following:

_____

Figure 7.14. Expert Disclosure Statement

Except as otherwise stipulated or directed by the court, this disclosure shall, with respect to a witness who is retained or specially employed to provide expert testimony in the case or whose duties as an employee of the party regularly involve giving expert testimony, be accompanied by a written report prepared and signed by the witness. The report shall contain a complete statement of all opinions to be expressed and the basis and reasons therefor; the data or other information considered by the witness in forming the opinions; any exhibits to be used as a summary of or support for the opinions; the qualifications of the witness, including a list of all publications authored by the witness within the preceding ten years; the compensation to be paid for the study and testimony; and a listing of any other cases in which the witness has testified as an expert at trial or by deposition within the preceding four years.

Figure 7.15 is an example of a prediscovery disclosure statement.

Oftentimes the task of preparing an expert witness disclosure falls to the paralegal to draft for the attorney's review. Therefore, the paralegal must keep in mind that the disclosure shall contain the following:

- Copy of the signed written report
- Bases of opinions
- Data or information considered
- Exhibits
- Qualifications
- Compensation
- List of other cases in which the expert witness testified in last four years

Discovery with respect to experts who will not testify at trial (consulting experts) is much more limited.

The time frame for preparing disclosures of expert testimony are set forth in Rule 26(a)(2)(C), which states "These disclosures shall be made at the times and in the sequence directed by the court. In the absence of other directions from the court or stipulation by the parties, the disclosures shall be made at least 90 days before the trial date or the date the case is to be ready for trial. . . ."

In preparation for the taking of a deposition upon oral examination of an expert witness, the paralegal is often responsible for preparing subpoenas duces tecum to the experts of opposing parties. It is extremely important that the paralegal specifically spells out all the necessary documentation requested. This documentation in the response provided will be the basis on which the attorney will prepare his or her questions for that expert. Thoroughness is hallmark to a good request. Therefore, some suggestions for use in subpoenas directed to experts follow.

Please provide your complete case file, including but not limited to:

1. Medical records, test protocol, test results, video and audio tapes, calculations, measurements, and/or photographs;
2. Any and all specialized literature, standards, manuals, brochures, photographs, and any other material generated by you or others that have been used by you in developing your opinions in this matter and/or on which you will rely to support your opinions in this matter;

Attorney
Attorneys for Defendant

IN THE UNITED STATES DISTRICT COURT
FOR THE DISTRICT OF MONTANA
BILLINGS DIVISION

JOHN DOE and MARY DOE,	)	
	)	
Plaintiff,	)	Case No.
	)	
vs.	)	**PREDISCOVERY DISCLOSURE**
	)	**STATEMENT OF DEFENDANT**
ABC COMPANY, a Foreign Corporation,	)	
	)	
Defendant.	)	
	)	

Pursuant to the Court's November 17, 1997, Order and Rule 200-5(a), Rules of Procedure of the United States District Court for the District of Montana, defendant ("Defendant") submits the following Prediscovery Disclosure Statement:

A.   Factual Basis for Claims and Defenses.
B.   Legal Theories Upon Which Defenses Are Based.
C.   Witness Disclosures.
D.   Relevant Documents.
E.   Computation of Damages.
F.   Insurance Coverage.

Dated this day of December, 1999.

LAW FIRM

By _____
    Name and Address

CERTIFICATE OF SERVICE

Figure 7.15. Prediscovery Disclosure Statement

3. Any and all documents provided to you by plaintiffs' counsel in this case;

4. Any and all correspondence between you and plaintiffs' counsel; and

5. Any and all invoices you submitted to plaintiffs' counsel.

Rule 26(a)(1) covers initial disclosures and states:

Except to the extent otherwise stipulated or directed by order or local rule, a party shall, without awaiting a discovery request, provide to other parties:

> (A) the name and, if known, the address and telephone number of each individual likely to have discoverable information relevant to disputed facts alleged with particularity in the pleadings, identifying the subjects of the information;
>
> (B) a copy of, or a description by category and location of all documents, data compilations, and tangible things in the possession, custody, or control of the party that are relevant to disputed facts alleged with particularity in the pleadings;
>
> (C) a computation of any category of damages claimed by the disclosing party, making available for inspection and copying as under Rule 34 the documents or other evidentiary material, not privileged or protected from disclosure, on which such computation is based, including materials bearing on the nature and extent of injuries suffered; and
>
> (D) for inspection and copying as under Rule 34 any insurance agreement under which any person carrying on an insurance business may be liable to satisfy part or all of a judgment which may be entered in the action or to indemnify or reimburse for payments made to satisfy the judgment.
>
> Unless otherwise stipulated or directed by the court, these disclosure shall be made at or within 10 days after the meeting of the parties under subdivision (f) [planning for discovery]. . . .

Rule 26(a)(3) covers pretrial disclosures and states:

[A] party shall provide to other parties the following information regarding the evidence that it may present at trial other than solely for impeachment purposes:

> (A) the name and, if not previously provided, the address and telephone number of each witness, separately identifying those whom the party expects to present and those whom the party may call if the need arises;
>
> (B) the designation of those witnesses whose testimony is expected to be presented by means of a deposition and, if not taken stenographically, a transcript of the pertinent portions of the deposition testimony; and
>
> (C) an appropriate identification of each document or other exhibits, including summaries of other evidence, separately identifying those which the party expects to offer and those which the party may offer if the need arises.
>
> Unless otherwise directed by the court, these disclosures shall be made at least 30 days before trial. . . .

G. PRACTICES TO SAVE TIME AND EXPENSE DURING DISCOVERY

There are many ways to save time and expense in the discovery process. Here is review of some of them.

- Stipulations under Federal Rule of Civil Procedure 29. The rule gives parties authority to alter procedures, limitations, and time limits on discovery so long as they do not interfere with times set by court order.
- Informal discovery. Counsel should be encouraged to exchange information, particularly relevant documents, without resort to formal discovery.
- Automatic disclosure. Rule 26(a)(1) and any other local rules require the parties to identify relevant witnesses and categories of documents early in the litigation.
- Reducing deposition costs. Savings may be realized when deposition are taken, when feasible, by telephone, by electronic recording devices, or by having deponents come to central locations.
- Information from other litigation and sources. When information is available from public records (such as government studies or reports), from other litigation, or from discovery conducted by others in the same litigation, the parties may be required to review those materials before additional discovery is undertaken.
- Joint discovery requests and responses. In multiparty cases in which no lead counsel has been designated, parties with similar positions may be required to submit a combined set of interrogatories, requests for product, or requests for admission.
- Modified discovery responses. When a response to discovery request can be provided in a form somewhat different from that requested, but with substantially the same information and at a savings in time and expense, the responding party should make that fact known and seek agreement from the requesting party.
- Combined discovery requests. Several forms of discovery can be combined into a single request.
- Conference depositions. When knowledge of a subject is divided among several people and credibility is not an issue a conference deposition may be feasible.
- Subpoenas. Under Rule 45, an attorney may subpoena documents or other tangibles from nonparties, avoiding unnecessary depositions.

What other methods can you think of to save time and expense?

H. CHECKLISTS

The use of checklists in this area is of primary importance. It enables the parties to get and remain on track. At the least, a checklist regarding discovery should include:

- Obligations of the parties and counsel under Rule 26
- Filing and service
- Early discovery matters
- Discovery control
- Confidential and privileged information
- Special problems and concerns

Remember that checklists offer both advantages and disadvantages. The advantages are obvious. The disadvantages are that checklists need to be modified for each case, and people can become lazy when using them.

I. PRACTICAL SUGGESTIONS

Here are a few practical suggestions for the litigation paralegal to think about when handling documents.

1. Inventory documents as soon as possible after the suit is commenced or as soon as documents have been produced.
2. Identify and maintain corporate organizational charts. These charts will facilitate proof of employee responsibilities and reporting lines for privilege purposes and will assist you in identifying potential document holders.
3. Identify probable document generating activities. Use the logical sequence of a transaction, the persons involved and the flow of communication to identify potential relevant files. For example, in products liability litigation think about:
   a. Design: products planning documents, marketing feasibility studies, technical feasibility studies, tooling studies, regulatory review analysis, detailed imperative product studies, prototype tests and analysis, project approval documents, general corporate design procedures, general corporate design philosophy, specific design specifications.
   b. Testing: prospective regulatory testing, alternative design testing, detailed comparative analysis testing, certification testing, product validation testing, corporate testing procedure documents, corporate testing criteria.
   c. Production: specifications, production run analysis, quality control documents.
   d. Marketing: development of marketing campaign, instructions and warning development, complaint procedures, complaints.
   e. Standards Committee participation and regulatory activities: regulations, participation and industry standards committees, government recall campaigns, testimony before administrative or legislative bodies.
4. Identify all documents depositories.
5. Obtain all document indexes.
6. Establish a litigation index system.

J. ESTABLISHING A LITIGATION INDEX SYSTEM

When establishing a litigation index system you should keep the system simple and understandable. If you do not understand the system, no one will. Avoid the use of computerized litigation systems unless you understand how the system works. Use existing capabilities of your office. Word processing programs can work as well as sophisticated programs in maintaining a good litigation index. Identify what information is important to you and consult with your supervising attorney as well as your secretary. Include the following basic information whether using a word processing or a computerized database index system:

- Internal document number
- Deposition exhibit number

- Trial exhibit number
- Author
- Recipient
- Mentions
- Document title
- Date
- Relevant issue (issue codes)
- Witness (pertains to)
- Source of document

There are a number of computerized litigation support systems. Of these, there are several types:

1. Keyword-based systems: a system that allows you to attach a keyword to a document and search by that keyword. You might develop an issue as a keyword and attach that keyword to all documents involved in the issue. For example, in a products liability case, issues might be related to defect, warning, alteration of product, and so on. These systems are useful in searching for documents that are relevant to an issue or relevant to an examination of a particular witness.
2. Full-text recording systems: a system that puts entire documents into memory and allows word searches for relevant topics. They are generally extremely expensive but useful in proper cases.

Have the paralegal (someone knowledgeable with the lawsuit) review the documents and enter them in the system. Have only one person involved in data input to maintain consistency.

As soon as a litigation indexing system is developed, the paralegal should implement procedures for preserving the organization and integrity of files prior to commencing special file searches. You may consider using a logging system or an "out" card system. "Out" card systems simply utilize cards that are placed in the file system in place of the file taken. The card indicates the name of the person in possession of the file and the date the file was removed.

Establish a means of identifying and preserving claims to privilege. If any documents are removed from the file, a source of the document should be identified and placed with the removed document, including the file number and organization. If segregating privileged or work product documents, establish a clerical process for preparing a list of the documents withheld from production. If a large number of documents must be screened for privilege, consider preparing a list, in alphabetical sequence, of all attorneys involved during the relevant time frame. Establish a means for identifying authors, addresses, and persons to whom copies are directed, including some indicational scope of responsibilities so that the "control group test" can be met, if applicable. The "control group test" then enables you to correctly identify attorneys involved so the documents they authored can be removed as privileged. Do not permit the use of any privileged or work product documents for the purpose of refreshing witnesses' recollections or in connection with obtaining expert opinion testimony.

Establish a procedure for stamping documents to indicate a production history. For example, a stamp on the back of a document may indicate the internal document number, when it was produced, which discovery request it was produced in connection with, and a recordation of any claim of privilege. (Remember: This is most easily done with a computerized database.)

Maintain a system by index or otherwise of all documents produced pursuant to Rule 34 requests.

Agree to sequentially number all exhibits and keep a uniform identification of exhibits throughout the litigation. Coordinate combined discovery requests between cooperating parties.

Establish a system for document preservation with due regard for problems with document preservation and computer storage.

Establish a central document depository in complex cases.

Make provisions for discovery of any computerized data. If the data are to be presented in machine-readable form, lead time and procedure should be established for the production. Always check for viruses.

ETHICS

As discussed earlier in the chapter, communication between an attorney and a client is privileged. The attorney/client privilege means that the attorney cannot reveal to anyone else any information received from the client. This privilege extends to the paralegal as well. Any information the paralegal receives during the course of employment from the client or in connection with the case must be kept confidential and not disclosed to others. Be very careful in discussing the client's case with other firm members in public places. Never discuss a client's case with family members, friends, or acquaintances. It can be very tempting to divulge confidential or interesting information to others. Even disclosing that the firm represents a client is unethical. If your firm happens to represent a public figure, film star, or popular individual, never let others know. You must keep that information secret and confidential as well as keeping the details of the representation and case confidential. Never be drawn in by questions such as "What interesting cases are you working on?," "Whom do you represent?," or "I saw Mary Doe walking into your building, what was she there for?"

CONCLUSION

As stated, the paralegal has a primary responsibility when it comes to assisting with the discovery process. The process can be cumbersome as in document intensive cases, or it can be simple as in personal injury cases. However, in either case, one of the primary duties of the paralegal is document control. The paralegal must develop a document identification system, preserve the documents, and ensure that all areas have been adequately covered. The paralegal must be concerned with the evidentiary foundation for the documents and must consider the discovery of computerized data and data from nonparties.

The discovery process can be lengthy and complicated. But with a little forethought and imagination, the process can be exciting and interesting. The paralegal must at all times be mindful of deadlines and ensure that those deadlines are met. Also, it must be remembered that answering discovery is not the "end of the line." If new information is located or information changes, supplemental answers must be filed and served.

USING TECHNOLOGY IN THE LAW OFFICE

Since this chapter deals with further discovery and depositions, the technology section is an appropriate area to discuss the essentials of computer discovery. This often overlooked area is ripe for the discovery process. However, the paralegal needs to understand computer-based documents, evidence, the kinds of information that exist, and what to look for.

What distinguishes computer-based evidence from traditional paper documents in the discovery process? Electronic documents that were thought to be lost or destroyed usually can be recovered. Valuable information such as the time, date, and author's name may be embedded in the electronic version of a document. Comparisons or computer backups to existing documents can be used to show that a critical document was altered, and when the event occurred. In the case of electronic mail, casual and candid correspondence may be frozen in time.

Computer-based evidence exists in many forms and locations within any computer system. The key to finding and using this information is understanding the kinds of information that may exist and where within the system to look for each type of information.

A. DATA FILES

The primary function of most computer systems is to process and store information. Sources for data files include office desktop computers, notebook computers, home computers, palmtop devices, network file servers, mainframes, and computers of secretary of personal assistants. Information processed and stored electronically can be divided into four basic categories: active data, replicant data, backup data, and residual data. Let's take a look at each separate category.

1. Active Data

Active data are information readily available and accessible to users. Active data includes word processing documents, spreadsheets, databases, e-mail messages, electronic calendars, and contact managers. A listing of active data files could be easily viewed through file manager programs such as Microsoft Windows Explorer.

2. Replicant Data

Replicant data include file clones. Many software manufacturers build in automatic backup features that create and periodically save copies of the file being worked on by a user. These files are created and saved to help users recover data lost due to a computer malfunction such as system crash or power loss.

3. Backup Data

Backup data are information copied to removable media to provide users with access to data in the event of a system failure. Networks are normally backed up on a routine schedule, while individual users tend to back up (if at all) on an informal basis. Network backups normally capture only the data saved on the centralized storage media, the file server, and do not capture all the data stored on an individual's hard drive.

4. Residual Data

Residual data are information that appears to be gone, but is still recoverable from the computer system. It includes deleted files still on a disk surface and data existing in other system hardware such as buffer memories. How is deleted data recoverable? In most operating systems, the term *deleted* does not mean "destroyed." Rather, when a file is deleted, the computer makes the space occupied by that file available for new data. Reference to the deleted file is removed from directory listings and from the file allocation table, but the bits and bytes that make up the file remain on the hard drive until they are overwritten by new data. The result is that a file appears to be gone, but may still be recovered from the disk surfaces.

Residual data can be buried in a number of other places on disks and drives. Forensic specialists have tools that allow them to examine the entirety of a drive for residual data. It is therefore important to note that simple copy commands will not capture residual data.

B. E-MAIL

Electronic mail or e-mail is now commonplace, both as a business tool and as a personal way to stay connected with family and friends. E-mail has several characteristics that make it an excellent source of evidence:

1. Most people use e-mail informally and candidly.
2. Many people believe e-mail is not permanent.
3. E-mail is more difficult to get rid of than most users believe. Permanently deleting messages is usually a two-step process on most e-mail systems, and many users only complete the first step.
4. E-mail is easily copied and forwarded, thus making distribution of a message nearly impossible to control.

C. BACKUP INFORMATION

While data files and e-mail are often targeted for evidence, they are not the only information that can be obtained from a computer system. Computer systems can provide a wealth of background information that may be valuable evidence or that can be used to further develop the facts of a case.

Audit trails and computer logs create an electronic trail of network usage. Audit trails contain information about who the user was and when, where, and how long the user was on the system. Also recorded may be information about who modified a file last and when the modification was made. An audit trail may also indicate when and by whom files were downloaded to a particular location, copied, printed, or purged.

Access control lists limit user's rights to access, view, and edit various files. Access rights often depend on the employee's particular job duties and position in the company. If litigation centers on a particular file or group of files, identifying who had access rights to the files and the type of access each person was allowed can establish data ownership or authenticity of files.

Nonprinting information carried by most data files is another excellent source of information. The most common example is the date and time stamp that MS-DOS puts on every file. Some word processing documents store revisions to documents, allowing a viewer to follow the thought process of the author as a document is edited. Some word processing packages allow users to insert "hidden" or nonprinting comments.

Sources for backup information would be systemwide backups done on a weekly, monthly, or other scheduled time basis. Also look to disaster recovery backups, which are usually stored offsite to prevent catastrophic loss of information or recovery of information in the event of catastrophic damage. Backup information is also located on personal backup media such as diskettes, and those sources should not be overlooked. Also, remember to check for tape archives, replaced or removed drives, CD-ROMs, and zip cartridges.

There is no question that information stored on computers is discoverable. The Federal Rules of Civil Procedure include in their definitions of documents "data compilations from which information can be obtained" and permit parties to "copy, test, or sample any tangible things" within the scope of discovery. The courts have further held that deleted files on a party's hard drive are discoverable and that an expert must be allowed to retrieve all recoverable files.

To effectively gather computer-based evidence you need to preserve existing electronic evidence, get an overview of the systems and users, and preserve the chain of custody. To preserve the maximum amount of information, you must put all parties (including your own client) on notice that information contained on computer systems is relevant to the dispute and that all parties must take immediate steps to preserve such information. The notice should indicate the type of information to be preserved, that is, electronic mail or data files. Then explain that the information may exist in places such as network file servers, mainframes, or stand-alone PCs. Data may also reside on data storage media such as tapes or floppy disks. The second part of the notice should specify that no discoverable data should be deleted or modified. Make clear that the data to be preserved includes not only active data, but archival, backup, and residual data as well. Remember, your client is expected to follow the same steps you are instructing your opponent to follow.

Your notice will be more effective if you can gather information on your opponent's system beforehand through discovery. You need to know the system configuration, application software and utilities, backup procedures and frequency, and log-ons and passwords. In addition to the discovery directed at the computer system itself, every witness may be questioned about his or her computer use. Knowing how each witness uses his or her computer and organizes and stores data may lead to sources of data not revealed by the discovery directed at general system usage.

A chain of custody verifies that information copied was not altered in the copying process or during analysis. A solid chain of custody is essential. Ensure you have a complete copy and that no information has been added or changed. All copies should be tamper-proof, and any original media collected as evidence should be write-protected. Label copies by time, date, source, and storage location. Forensic analysis of the information collected should be done on a working copy created from the secure copy whenever possible.

Computer discovery does not require you to be a computer expert. What it requires is a fundamental understanding of what kinds of information exist, where this information is stored, and how to ask the questions that will lead you to it.

KEY TERMS

Attorney-client privilege
Clergy-parishioner privi-
    lege
Depositions
Deposition upon written
    questions
Discovery
Expert witnesses
Husband-wife or marital
    privilege

Interrogatories
Mandatory disclosure rules
Objections
Physician-patient privilege
Privilege
Privilege log
Protective order
Request for admission

Request for physical or
    mental examination
Request for production
Self-executing
Subpoena
Subpoena duces tecum
Work product document
    privilege

TECHNOLOGY TERMS

Active data	Replicant data	Residual data
Backup data		

USEFUL WEB SITES

Finding persons, addresses, and phone numbers
http://www.switchboard.com
http://www.bigyellow.com
http://www.usps.gov/ncsc
http://www.bigfoot.com
http://www.four11.com

Finding statistics
http://www.fedstats.gov

Consumer information
http://www.pueblo.gsa.gov

Car values
http://www.kbb.com

News
http://www.cnn.com
http://www.usnewswire.com

Business
http://www.ceoexpress.com
http://www.refdesk.com
http://www.companiesonline.com
http://www.hoovers.com

chapter 8

Defending the Lawsuit and Use of Motions

chapter objectives

In this chapter, we will discuss

- What it means to defend against claims made by a plaintiff
- Elements of an answer to a complaint
- How to use counterclaims and cross-claims
- The different types of motions and how to use them effectively
- Independent medical examinations
- Using expert witnesses
- Class action lawsuits and how to defend against them
- How to use presentation software to effectively present exhibits

This chapter focuses on defending against a lawsuit and using motions. The Federal Rules of Civil Procedure are cited throughout this chapter because the paralegal's ability to interpret such procedural rules is a key element in assisting attorneys who are defending a lawsuit. Attorneys need paralegals who accurately follow the procedural and statutory requirements while performing their duties. The only way to understand legal terminology is to read it over and over until you have a comprehensive understanding of it. There is no better time than the present to start fine-tuning your interpretation skills with regard to legal terminology.

A. ANSWERING PLAINTIFF'S COMPLAINT

As discussed in detail during Chapter 2, if the attorney you work with represents the plaintiff in a lawsuit, then the case strategy will primarily focus on establishing the claims to be made. If you work for the attorney who represents the defendant in a lawsuit, then your primary case strategy will focus on defending against the claims made by the plaintiff.

The first step in defending a lawsuit involves providing an answer to each of the plaintiff's claims.

1. Denials to Complaint

The first required pleading document to be filed by the defendant in a lawsuit is an answer to the complaint. An **answer** is a pleading that responds to the plaintiff's complaint. Rule 8(b) of the Federal Rules of Civil Procedure requires the following when the defendant answers a complaint:

> (b) Defenses; Form of Denials. *A party shall state in short and plain terms the party's defenses to each claim asserted and shall admit or deny the averments upon which the adverse party relies. If a party is without knowledge or information sufficient to form a belief as to the truth of an averment, the party shall so state and this has the effect of a denial.* Denials shall fairly meet the substance of the averments denied. When a pleader intends in good faith to deny only a part of a qualification of an averment, the pleader shall specify so much of it as is true and material and shall deny only the remainder. Unless the pleader intends in good faith to controvert all the averments of the preceding pleading, the pleader may make denials as specific denials of designated averments or paragraph or may generally deny all the averments except such designated averments, or paragraphs as the pleader expressly admits; but, when the pleader does so intend to controvert all its averments, including averments of the grounds upon which the court's jurisdiction depends, the pleader may do so by general denial subject to the obligations set forth in Rule 11. (Emphasis added.)

The above rule requires the defendant to admit, deny, or state that he or she does not have sufficient information to admit or deny each claim made by the plaintiff. In other words, the defendant is required to provide an answer to each of the plaintiff's claims.

If the attorney you are working with requires that you draft answers for his or her review, then be sure that you comply with the procedural rules that require the answer to state admissions or denials in short, plain terms with each admission or denial identifying the claim that it encompasses. Those who draft legal documents frequently make the mistake of assuming that the document needs to contain a plethora of confusing legal terminology and complex sentences. The rule itself instructs the author of an answer to keep the language simple.

The procedural rules also require that the author of the answer identify each claim encompassed by an admission or denial. The easiest way to identify which claim is denied or admitted is by referencing the paragraph in which the claim appears in plaintiff's complaint. For example, a typical answer could state, "Defendant denies paragraph one of Plaintiff's Complaint."

As stated in the procedural rules, if the defendant is denying only a portion of the plaintiff's claim in a particular paragraph, then the answer must specify this. For instance, the answer would need to state, "Defendant denies the first sentence of paragraph one in Plaintiff's Complaint, but admits the remainder of this paragraph."

Further, if the defendant is without sufficient information or knowledge to form a belief as to the truth of a claim made by the plaintiff, then the answer must indicate this. An example would include this: "Defendant is without sufficient knowledge or information to form a belief as to the truth of the claim made by Plaintiff in paragraph one; and therefore, Defendant denies this claim."

As a paralegal, one of your biggest challenges will involve drafting legal documents in a format acceptable to your attorney. Every individual has a personalized writing style. A good paralegal learns the individual style of each attorney they work for and drafts legal documents accordingly.

PRACTICE TIP

When you are drafting an answer for your attorney, pull an example of an answer he or she has written for another case. This way you will have an idea of your attorney's writing style *before* you begin drafting a legal document for him or her.

---

2. Failure to Deny Plaintiff's Claims

Rule 8(d) states the effect of defendant's failure to deny claims made by the plaintiff:

(d) Effect of Failure to Deny. *Averments in a pleading to which a responsive pleading is required, other than those as to the amount of damage, are admitted when not denied in the responsive pleading.* Averments in a pleading to which no responsive pleading is required or permitted shall be taken as denied or avoided.
Emphasis added.

Essentially, if the defendant fails to deny a claim made by the plaintiff, then the claim is deemed admitted by the court.

3. Defenses and Affirmative Defenses

In addition to answering the plaintiff's claims, the defendant should also always include defenses and affirmative defenses within the answer. A **defense** is an allegation made by the defendant that provides a reason why the plaintiff should not receive what he or she is claiming. A defense does not assume that the plaintiff's claims are true. Essentially, a **denial defense** is a statement of denial provided as a reason in law or fact why the plaintiff should not recover or establish what he or she seeks. An **affirmative defense** constitutes the defendant's response to the plaintiff's claim, which disputes the plaintiff's legal right to bring the claim. An affirmative defense assumes that the claims made by the plaintiff are true, but not legally justified.

Rule 12(h) provides for a waiver of certain defenses if the defendant does not assert them by motion or responsive pleading. You must be very careful when you are drafting the answer to plaintiff's complaint that you do not waive any possible defenses. Rule

12(h) provides a listing of the defenses that can be waived for failure to plead or file a motion:

> (h) Waiver or Preservation of Certain Defenses.
>
> (1) *A defense of lack of jurisdiction over the person, improper venue, insuffi-ciency of process, or insufficiency of service of process is waived (A) if omitted from a motion in the circumstances described in subdivision (g), or (B) if it is neither made by motion under this rule nor included in a responsive pleading or an amendment thereof* permitted by Rule 15(a) to be made as a matter of course.
>
> (2) *A defense of failure to state a claim upon which relief can be granted, a defense of failure to join a party indispensable under Rule 19, and an objection of failure to join a party indispensable under Rule 19, and an objection of failure to state a legal defense to a claim may be made in any pleading permitted or ordered under Rule 7(a),* or by motion for judgment on the pleadings, or at the trial on the merits.
>
> (3) Whenever it appears by suggestion of the parties or otherwise that the court lacks jurisdiction of the subject matter, the court shall dismiss the action. (Emphasis added.)

Not only does this rule discuss waiver and preservation of defenses, it also indicates that subject matter jurisdiction is a defense that can always be raised at any time during the litigation process according to Rule 12(h)(3).

The defenses included in Rule 12(h) are lack of jurisdiction, improper venue, insuffi-ciency of process, insufficiency of service of process, lack of subject matter jurisdiction, and failure to state a claim on which relief may be granted. Make sure when you are drafting the answer to plaintiff's complaint that you include these defenses if they are applicable, preventing any potential waiver.

There are other defenses that can be raised in the answer, such as **assumption of risk**, **contributory negligence,** and **estoppel**.

- Assumption of risk: when a person is not allowed to recover for an injury if the person voluntarily exposed him- or herself to a known danger
- Contributory negligence: conduct by the plaintiff that is below the standard required and contributes to the negligence action that caused the plaintiff's harm
- Estoppel: a principle barring an individual from denying or alleging a certain fact because of previous conduct, allegation, or denial.

Rule 12(b) allows certain defenses to be made by motion; however, these same defenses can be asserted in the answer. You should always consult with your attorney regarding any additional defenses that need to be made. If additional defenses are not provided in the original answer, then your attorney will have to request an amendment of the answer from the court.

The final item that needs to be included within the answer is any potential affirmative defenses. As indicated above, this type of defense assumes that the plaintiff's claims are true, but not legally justified. Rule 8(c) provides a partial listing of affirmative defenses:

> (c) Affirmative Defenses. In pleading to a preceding pleading, a party shall set forth affirmatively accord and satisfaction, arbitration and award, *assumption of risk, contributory*

negligence, discharge in bankruptcy, duress, estoppel, failure of consideration, fraud, illegality, injury by fellow servant, latches, license, payment, release, res judicata, statute of frauds, statute of limitations, waiver, and any other matter constituting an avoidance or affirmative defense. When a party has mistakenly designated a defense as a counterclaim or a counterclaim as a defense, the court on terms, if justice so requires, shall treat the pleading as if there had been a proper designation. (Emphasis added.)

Please keep in mind that the above listing is not a complete listing of affirmative defenses. Any defense that assumes the truth of the claim, but argues the claim is not legally justified, can be asserted as an affirmative defense. Be sure to discuss all potential defenses and affirmative defenses with your attorney prior to filing the answer.

4. Deadlines for Answering Complaint

Civil litigation is focused on meeting the deadlines established by the court; therefore, as a paralegal, you need to be aware of all pertinent deadlines. If you work for a defense attorney, one deadline will be answering the complaint. This deadline should be included in a tickler system and calendared for at least two weeks before the due date. A **tickler system** is a system created to manage deadlines. Please refer to Chapter 2 for methods on creating a tickler system and calendaring.

Normally, the deadline for service of the answer on plaintiff is 20 days after defendant's receipt of the summons and complaint. This is discussed in Rule 12, which also allows for exceptions to the standard 20-day deadline:

> (a) When Presented.
> (1) Unless a different time is prescribed in a statute of the United States, a defendant shall serve an answer
> (A) within 20 days after being served with the summons and complaint, or
> (B) *if service of the summons has been timely waived on request under Rule 4(d), within 60 days after the date when the request for waiver was sent, or within 90 days after that date if the defendant was addressed outside any judicial district of the United States.* (Emphasis added.)

5. Failure to Answer Complaint

Failure by the defendant to file an answer to plaintiff's complaint can result in the entry of a default judgment. A default judgment is when the court allows the plaintiff to receive everything he or she is asking for in their complaint because the defendant has failed to answer the claims set forth by the plaintiff within the time period required by the law. *Blacks Law Dictionary,* Sixth Edition, defines default judgment as follows:

> Judgment entered against a party who has failed to defend against a claim that has been brought by another party. Under the Rules of Civil Procedure, *when a party against whom a judgment for affirmative relief is sought has failed to plead (i.e. answer) or otherwise defend,*

he is in default and a judgment by default may be entered either by the clerk or the court. (Emphasis added.)

Rule 55(a) allows for entry of a default judgment as follows:

(a) Entry. When a party against whom a judgment for affirmative relief is sought has failed to plead or otherwise defend as provided by these rules and that fact is made to appear by affidavit or otherwise, the clerk shall enter the party's default.

Rule 55(b)(1) and (2) explain in detail how default judgments can be entered by the clerk of court.

B. OTHER CLAIMS TO BE ASSERTED IN DEFENDING THE LAWSUIT

In addition to answering the complaint, the defendant has the option to assert against the plaintiff or a coparty claims are known as counterclaims and cross-claims. **Counterclaims** are any opposing claims presented by the defendant against plaintiff's claims. **Cross-claims** are any coparty claims generated from the transaction or occurrence pertaining to the original action or a counterclaim. **Permissive counterclaims** are opposing parties' claims generated outside of the transaction or occurrence that is the subject matter of the opposing party's claim. **Compulsory counterclaims** are any claims against an opposing party.

The decision whether to assert counterclaims or cross-claims is an important part of the defense strategy. Failing to assert a potential claim against the plaintiff or a coparty can result in your attorney's client being held 100 percent liable for the damage claimed by the plaintiff. There are times when the defendant has no counterclaims or cross-claims. Nonetheless, all possible claims should be discussed and evaluated with the attorney you work for at the time of drafting the answer to plaintiff's complaint. Failure to assert counterclaims or cross-claims at the time of answering the complaint results in the need for obtaining permission from the court to file subsequent amended pleadings.

PRACTICE TIP

At the time you are given the task of drafting the answer for your attorney, ask him or her what defense strategy he or she wishes to employ in this case. The answer should give you a good idea of the claims that will be made against the plaintiff or coparty.

---

1. Asserting Counterclaims

As stated above, the defendant has the option to assert claims against the plaintiff in answering the complaint. The claims that the defendant chooses to assert against the plaintiff are commonly referred to as counterclaims.

Rule 13 addresses the issue of asserting counterclaims and cross-claims. The counterclaims allowed by Rule 13 include the following:

> **(a) Compulsory Counterclaims.** A pleading shall state as a counterclaim any claim which at the time of serving the pleading, the pleader has against any opposing party, if it arises out of the transaction or occurrence that is the subject matter of the opposing party's claim and does not require for its adjudication the presence of third parties of whom the court cannot acquire jurisdiction. But the pleader need not state the claim if
>
> (1) at the time the action was commenced the claim was the subject of another pending action, or
>
> (2) the opposing party brought suit upon the claim by attachment or other process by which the court did not acquire jurisdiction to render a personal judgment on that claim, and the pleader is not stating any counterclaim under this Rule 13.
>
> **(b) Permissive Counterclaims.** A pleading may state as a counterclaim any claim against an opposing party not arising out of the transaction or occurrence that is the subject matter of the opposing party's claim.

The above referenced sections of Rule 13 allow the defendant to assert counterclaims if they do or do not arise from the event that is the subject of plaintiff's lawsuit and does not require the presence of third parties outside the court's jurisdiction. Compulsory counterclaims are claims required to be made. Permissive counterclaims are made at the option of the defendant.

Counterclaims are not limited by the recovery that is sought by the plaintiff. In fact, Rule 13(c) allows a party to file counterclaims that could or could not diminish or defeat the opposing party's recovery *and* could claim a recovery that *exceeds* that of the opposing party.

If counterclaims come about after pleading has occurred or claims are omitted, Rule 13(e) and (f) allow a party to amend the pleading and add additional counterclaims if permission is granted by the court.

> **(e) Counterclaim Maturing or Acquired After Pleading.** A claim which either matured or was acquired by the pleader after serving a pleading may, with the permission of the court, be presented as a counterclaim by supplemental pleading.
>
> **(f) Omitted Counterclaim.** When a pleader fails to set up a counterclaim through oversight, inadvertence, or excusable neglect, or when justice requires, the pleader may by leave of the court set up the counterclaim by amendment.

A good example of a counterclaim would include a claim for breach of contract. If you are assisting in the defense of a commercial lawsuit in which the plaintiff claims the defendant breached a contract, then a counterclaim could be asserted that states the plaintiff effectively breached the contract, not the defendant.

Once a counterclaim has been asserted by the defendant, the Federal Rules of Civil Procedure require a response by the plaintiff within a specific time period. Rule 12(a)(2) sets the counterclaim and cross-claim responsive pleading deadlines as follows:

> A party served with a pleading stating a cross-claim against that party shall serve an answer thereto within 20 days after being served. The plaintiff shall serve a reply to a counterclaim in the answer within 20 days after service of the answer, or, if a reply is

ordered by the court, within 20 days after service of the order, unless the order otherwise directs.

2. Asserting Cross-Claims

Another set of claims that can be asserted in defending a lawsuit are cross-claims. Cross-claims are normally asserted in lawsuits in which there are numerous defendants. Rule 13(g) indicates what cross-claims can be asserted against a coparty as follows:

> A pleading may state as a cross-claim any claim by one party against a coparty arising out of the transaction or occurrence that is the subject matter either of the original action or of a counterclaim therein or relating to any property that is the subject matter of the original action. Such cross-claim may include a claim that the party against whom it is asserted is or may be liable to the cross-claimant for all or part of a claim asserted against the cross-claimant. (Emphasis added.)

As previously stated, cross-claims can be asserted by a party against any coparty. A defendant could assert cross-claims against any other defendants named in the lawsuit. For example, if the case you are working on involves an automobile accident that includes several automobiles, cross-claims could be asserted against other defendant automobiles involved in the accident.

Once cross-claims are asserted, the party defending such claims has an obligation to respond to these claims. The cross-claim defendant must provide and answer to each cross-claim asserted within the time period allowed by the law. As previously stated above in Rule 12(a)(2), the deadline to respond to a claim is 20 days after service unless the court directs differently. This deadline should be calendared and placed within your tickler system.

C. THIRD-PARTY PRACTICE

Another possible defense strategy includes adding a third party to the lawsuit. For example, if the plaintiff has filed a complaint alleging that the distributor of a product failed to warn about potential risks associated with the product, then the distributor, in turn, could possibly add the manufacturer of this product as a third-party defendant. The ability to add a third party provides a defendant with the opportunity for shared responsibility regarding plaintiff's liability claims. The plaintiff is also allowed to assert third-party claims in specific instances. Through the third-party process, the legal system tries to ensure fairness so that no one defendant bares the responsibility for another defendant's liability, while still allowing the plaintiff an opportunity for full recovery against all liable parties.

Third-party claims are claims made against a third party not named in the lawsuit that involve the issues of that lawsuit. When the plaintiff files his or her complaint all of the liable parties may not be known, resulting in some specifically named defendants and numerous John Doe (or unknown) defendants. Frequently, the named defendants know of other parties who should be included in the lawsuit. The named defendants have the option to file a third-party complaint adding another party to the lawsuit. If the Defendants exercise this option, they become the third-party plaintiff with respect to any third-party claims.

Rule 14(a) explains in detail when a third party may be added to the lawsuit:

(a) When Defendant May Bring in Third Party. At any time after commencement of the action a defending party, as a third-party plaintiff, may cause a summons and complaint to be served upon a person not a party to the action who is or may be liable to the third-party plaintiff for all or part of the plaintiff's claim against the third-party plaintiff. *The third-party plaintiff need not obtain leave to make the service if the third-party plaintiff files the third-party complaint not later than 10 days after serving the original answer. Otherwise the third-party plaintiff must obtain leave on motion upon notice to all parties to the action.* . . . (Emphasis added.)

Rule 14 further indicates that the individual defending third-party claims shall assert any defenses pursuant to Rules 12 and 13. Rule 12 requires defenses to be asserted within 20 days after service.

In addition, Rule 14 allows a third-party defendant to assert against the plaintiff any of the third-party plaintiff's defenses and against the third-party plaintiff any of the plaintiff's claims. The plaintiff is also allowed to assert claims against the third-party defendant, and this third-party defendant can assert defenses pursuant to Rule 12 and 13. Any party may also make a motion to strike a third-party claim or separately try that claim (commonly referred to as *bifurcation*). Finally, under Rule 14, the third-party defendant is allowed to proceed against any nonparty who is or may be liable for all or part of the claim against the third-party defendant.

Plaintiffs normally are not allowed to bring third-party claims; however, Rule 14(b) of the Federal Rules of Civil Procedure allows the following:

(b) When Plaintiff May Bring in Third Party. *When a counterclaim is asserted against a plaintiff, the plaintiff may cause a third party to be brought in* under circumstances which under this rule would entitle a defendant to do so. (Emphasis added.)

D. RULE 26 DISCLOSURES

When you assist in defending a lawsuit in federal court, you most likely will be faced with the task of compiling case information for initial disclosures. The initial disclosure requirement was created primarily to facility the settlement of lawsuits early on before litigation became expensive. It was thought that if more information was disclosed in the early stages of a case, then case evaluation could be completed and the potential for settlement determined. The following four items should be considered when working on initial disclosures:

1. Time requirements
2. Information to be disclosed
3. Court clerk's local disclosure rules
4. Management and organization of disclosure documents

1. Time Requirements

In federal court, Rule 26(a)(1) sets the deadline for initial disclosures at no later than 10 days after the required meeting of the parties set forth in subdivision (f). Subdivision (f) requires that the parties meet and discuss the basis of their claims no later than 14 days before the scheduling conference or the deadline for a scheduling order. Normally, initial disclosures occur approximately 2 to 3 months after commencement of the lawsuit. At any rate, initial disclosures are completed early in the case and have to be completed without awaiting the submission of any discovery requests. It is important if you are working on a case in federal court that you be aware of the initial disclosure deadline, calendaring and tickling it at least four weeks before its due date.

2. Information to Be Disclosed

In federal court, the information to be provided during an initial disclosure is very specific. In most state court actions, information regarding witnesses, documents, damages, and insurance is not obtained until the discovery process commences. The discovery process cannot commence any earlier than 45 days after service of the summons and complaint. Rule 26(a)(1)(A)-(D) specifically state the information that must be provided during the initial disclosure process:

> . . . *[A] party shall, without awaiting a discovery request, provide to other parties:*
> (A) *the name and, if known, the address and telephone number of each individual likely to have discoverable information relevant to disputed facts* alleged with particularity in the pleadings, identifying the subjects of the information;
> (B) *a copy of, or a description by category and location of, all documents, data compilations, and tangible things in the possession, custody, or control of the party that are relevant to disputed facts* alleged with particularity in the pleadings;
> (C) *a computation of any category of damages claimed by the disclosing party, making available for inspection and copying as under Rule 34 the documents or other evidentiary material, not privileged or protected from disclosure, on which such computation is based,* including materials bearing on the nature and extent of injuries suffered; and
> (D) *for inspection and copying under Rule 34 any insurance agreement under which any person carrying on an insurance business may be liable to satisfy part or all of a judgment* which may be entered in the action or to indemnify or reimburse for payments made to satisfy the judgment. (Emphasis added.)

One of your duties as a paralegal will include obtaining the information listed in the above-cited rule. The majority of the information provided in the initial disclosure will come from the client and witnesses. Because obtaining this information will take some time, you should begin contacting the client and any witnesses at least one month before the disclosure deadline. Chapter 2 provides several helpful tips when initially interviewing the client. These tips are helpful during any interview and should be utilized when at all possible. You will soon discover in your work as a paralegal that rarely will you receive a complete listing of the information needed from the client initially. After the initial disclosure is filed, the client will inevitably remember some additional information. However, do not worry because Rule 26(e) allows the parties to amend and supplement the initial disclosure with any additional information obtained.

3. Court Clerk's Local Disclosure Rules

Prior to filing the initial disclosure, the paralegal should check the clerk of court's local rules for any additional filing procedures not included in the federal rules. Often the clerk's office will have additional local rules governing filing procedures. For instance, the clerk's office may require several copies of the disclosure to be filed along with the original, including extra copies for the clerk and judge. In addition, many clerks require that the extra copies filed be two-hole punched prior to filing. Although it sounds ridiculous, you will be denied the opportunity to file disclosures until you two-hole-punch the copies. Another local requirement may involve the clerk's refusal to accept any attached discoverable documents. The clerk office usually has limited filing space and will only accept the legal document being filed. Most federal courts do not allow for the filing of discovery because it is so voluminous.

PRACTICE TIP

In order to avoid any pitfalls when filing your initial disclosure, request from the clerk of court a copy of the local rules. Once you have obtained a copy of the local rules, review them thoroughly prior to any filing.

---

4. Management and Organization of Disclosure Documents

Chapter 5 addresses the management and organization of documents. The practices suggested there should be utilized when managing and organizing disclosure documents.

E. MOTIONS IN DEFENDING A LAWSUIT

Whenever parties need to request something that is not specifically provided for within the Federal Rules of Civil Procedure, they must do so through the filing of a motion with the court. **Motions** are requests made by a party to the court for specific action. *Black's Law Dictionary*, Sixth Edition, defines motion as follows:

> An application made to a court or judge for purpose of obtaining a rule or order directing some act to be done in favor of the applicant.

When the court receives a motion and proposed order, it can ask that the parties orally argue the legal issues prior to its rendering a decision, or it can render a decision based on the briefs supporting and opposing the motion. The court's decision on a motion is rendered through what is referred to as an order. An **order** is a document from the court or judge that is not included in a judgment. A court order states what action the court requires of the parties involved in the lawsuit.

An integral part of defending a lawsuit involves the filing of motions. There are numerous motions that can be filed to reduce, dismiss, or limit the claims made by a plaintiff. Each motion has certain legal requirements that must be met to render a successful decision. Developing a defensive case strategy regarding the filing of motions should be done as early as possible in the case. This section will focus on the various defensive motions that can be presented to the court, including their legal requirements.

1. Rule 12(b) Defenses to Be Made by Motion

Within Rule 12(b) of the Federal Rules of Civil Procedure there are several defenses that can be made by way of motion:

    a. Lack of jurisdiction over the subject matter
    b. Lack of jurisdiction over the person
    c. Improper venue
    d. Insufficiency of process
    e. Insufficiency of service of process
    f. Failure to state a claim upon which relief may be granted
    g. Failure to join a party under Rule 19

a. Motion for Lack of Jurisdiction over the Subject Matter

Subject matter jurisdiction is the power of a court to hear particular matters. If the plaintiff has commenced a lawsuit in a court not authorized to hear that matter, then the lawsuit can be dismissed for lack of subject matter jurisdiction. However, the defendant would need to request dismissal of this action from the court. Rule 12(b) allows the defendant to request a dismissal of the action for lack of subject matter jurisdiction by filing a motion.

Determining whether subject matter jurisdiction is proper should be done as soon as possible. As a paralegal you need to be thinking of all potential defenses when you are assisting the attorney you work for in drafting the answer to plaintiff's complaint. Part of this process includes checking that the court where the action was filed has the authority to hear the matter. If you discover that subject matter jurisdiction is improper, you should immediately inform the attorney you work for so it can be decided what the defensive strategy will be regarding this issue.

If it is decided that a motion to dismiss will be prepared, then it will most likely be your duty to compile the documentation and evidence that supports a motion for lack of subject matter jurisdiction. You may even be asked to draft the motion and proposed order.

When I first began work as a paralegal, the first motion I drafted included the following introductory language: "COMES NOW Plaintiff _____ and moves the Court for an Order . . . " The first question I was asked by the attorney I was working for was, "where are we moving the court?" Needless to say, I never started a motion with that language again. A better introduction would be "COMES NOW Plaintiff _____ and through this motion requests that the Court issue an Order . . . " When drafting legal documents, do not get so caught up in legalese that you forget to use proper grammar.

PRACTICE TIP

The primary categories used in motions to the court include introduction, facts, legal issues, argument, and conclusion. Further, any witness testimony or documents regarding the matter should be referred to in the motion and attached as exhibits (for example, affidavits and investigating reports).

---

b. Motion for Lack of Jurisdiction over the Person

Personal jurisdiction is the power a court has to make a party appear before it. Personal jurisdiction is focused on the state in which the parties reside or have minimum contacts. The argument usually made by the defendant filing a motion for lack of jurisdiction over the person involves a claim that (1) the defendant does not reside within the state where the suit has been filed, or (2) the defendant does not have the minimum contacts required within the state to be made a party to the suit. The plaintiff can sue a defendant only in the state where said defendant resides or has minimum contacts. The only exception to this legal requirement exists in a state's "long-arm statute." State long-arm statutes were created to further define what minimum contact is. Always refer to the applicable state long-arm statute when you are assessing the minimum contact requirement.

If no personal jurisdiction can be asserted to the defendant, then a motion to dismiss the suit for lack of personal jurisdiction can be filed by the defendant with the court. The decision regarding a motion such as this is made by the attorney you work for; however, you can assist your attorney by reviewing the long-arm statute in your state to determine what the minimum contact requirements are and whether they have been met. If you do not think the minimum contact or residency requirements have been met, you should let your attorney know this and provide him or her with the supporting statute or documentation. Once the attorney has this information, it can be easily determined whether or not a motion to dismiss for lack of personal jurisdiction would have merit.

c. Motion for Improper Venue

Venue is the geographic location where a case can be heard. In federal court, if jurisdiction is based only upon diversity of citizenship, then venue is proper:

1. in the defendant's resident district;
2. in the district where the event occurred or the property is located; or
3. in the district where the defendant is subject to personal jurisdiction during commencement of the action.

The federal statutes that address venue are 28 U.S.C. §§1391, 1394, and 1412. These statutes were previously discussed in Chapter 3 of this text. As you may also recall from Chapter 3, additional venue considerations exist if the defendant is a corporation.

To provide adequate assistance to your attorney, always review the specific statutes regarding venue requirements to determine if venue is proper. If you discover that venue is improper, you should inform your attorney. The attorney you work with may even have you obtain an affidavit from the client or a representative of the client proving improper venue. When obtaining such an affidavit remember the following: 1) this is a written sworn statement, 2) make sure the affiant reviews and certifies the accuracy of this sworn statement, and 3) keep the sworn statement simple and concise.

As previously discussed, a motion to dismiss the case based on improper venue can be filed with the court, as can a motion to change venue. There are numerous reasons for requesting a change of venue, but the one that most frequently occurs involves prejudicial publicity. If due to the publicity of a matter, there is no way that a party can obtain a fair trial, then a motion to change venue based on prejudicial publicity can be filed with the court. For example, I recently worked on a case filed in an extremely small town involving several city officials. There were numerous newspaper articles and other publicity regarding the dispute between the parties, and it was doubtful that our client could obtain an unbiased jury. A motion to change venue was requested due to prejudicial publicity.

Federal statute 28 U.S.C. §1412 allows for a change in venue in the interest of justice or for the parties' convenience. Any motion to change venue in federal court needs to satisfy the requirements of 28 U.S.C. §1412. The decision to file a motion requesting change in venue should not be done without forethought and discussion of defensive strategy, as it directly affects all aspects of the defensive strategy.

d. Motion for Insufficiency of Process

Another motion that can be filed with the court pursuant to Rule 12(b) is a motion to dismiss for insufficient process. Chapter 3 discussed the proper form and issuance of a summons for the lawsuit commenced in federal court. These requirements are listed in Rule 4:

> (a) Form. The summons shall be signed by the clerk, bear the seal of the court, identify the court and the parties, be directed to the defendant, and state the name and address of the plaintiff's attorney or, if unrepresented, of the plaintiff. It shall also state the time within which the defendant must appear and defend, and notify

the defendant that failure to do so will result in a judgment by default against the defendant for the relief demanded in the complaint. The court may allow a summons to be amended.

(b) Issuance. Upon or after filing the complaint, the plaintiff may present a summons to the clerk for signature and seal. If the summons is in proper form, the clerk shall sign, seal, and issue it to the plaintiff for service on the defendant. A summons, or a copy of the summons if addressed to multiple defendants, shall be issued for each defendant to be served.

If plaintiff does not comply with the above sections of Rule 4, then a motion for insufficient process can be filed by the defendant. If the case you are working on is filed in state court, you will need to review the state procedural rules and statutes governing what is sufficient process. As always, if you discover that process is insufficient, you need to inform the attorney you work with immediately.

e. Motion for Insufficient Service of Process

If the plaintiff fails to effect sufficient service of process, a motion to dismiss for insufficient service of process can be filed by the defendant. **Service of process** is the process that involves leaving documents with the appropriate party. Below is what Rule 4(c) generally requires for sufficient service of process regarding an action filed in federal court:

(c) Service with Complaint; by Whom Made.

(1) *A summons shall be served together with a copy of the complaint. The plaintiff is responsible for service of a summons and complaint within the time allowed under subdivision (m) and shall furnish the person effecting service with the necessary copies of the summons and complaint.*

(2) *Service may be effected by any person who is not a party and who is at least 18 years of age.* At the request of the plaintiff, however, the court may direct that service be effected by a United States marshal, deputy United States marshal, or other person or officer specially appointed by the court for that purpose. Such an appointment must be made when the plaintiff is authorized to proceed in forma pauperis pursuant to 28 U.S.C. §1915 or is authorized to proceed as a seaman under 28 U.S.C. §1916. (Emphasis added.)

Additional sections of Rule 4 also contain specific requirements for sufficient service upon different entities such as corporations or agencies.

There is a time limit for effecting sufficient service of process. Rule 4(m) outlines the time limit for sufficient service of process in federal court:

(m) Time Limit for Service. If service of the summons and complaint is not made upon a defendant within *120 days after the filing of the complaint,* the court, upon motion or on its own initiative after notice to the plaintiff, shall dismiss the action without prejudice as to that defendant or direct that service be effected within a specified time; provided that if the plaintiff shows good cause for the failure, the court shall extend the time for service for an appropriate period. This subdivision does not apply to service in a foreign country pursuant to subdivision (f) or (j)(1). (Emphasis added.)

As indicated within Rule 4(m) above, failure to effect service of process within 120 days after filing of the complaint will result in dismissal of the action without prejudice.

The appropriate state procedural rules and statutes regarding sufficient service should be reviewed if the case you are working on is filed in state court. If service has not been sufficient, a motion to dismiss should be discussed with your attorney.

f. Motion for Failure to State a Claim upon Which Relief May Be Granted

The defendant also has the option to file a motion for dismissal if the plaintiff has failed to state a claim upon which relief may be granted. To determine if a claim for relief is insufficient, one must know what a sufficient claim for relief includes. Rule 8(a) sets forth the requirements of a claim for relief as follows:

> (a) Claims for Relief. A pleading which sets forth a claim for relief, whether an original claim, counterclaim, cross-claim, or third-party claim, shall contain
> (1) *a short and plain statement of the grounds upon which the court's jurisdiction depends, unless the court already has jurisdiction and the claim needs no new grounds of jurisdiction to support it,*
> (2) *a short and plain statement of the claim showing that the pleader is entitled to relief, and*
> (3) *a demand for judgment for the relief the pleader seeks.*
> Relief in the alternative or of several different types may be demanded. (Emphasis added.)

If the plaintiff has failed to follow the requirements italicized above, then the claim for relief may be insufficient and your attorney should be notified.

This motion is frequently filed by the defendant, but in my experience rarely granted by the court. This motion is extremely difficult to prove and courts normally do not like to dismiss any claim for relief without substantial evidence supporting such a request. Nonetheless, you should keep this motion in mind when reviewing plaintiff's complaint listing the various claims for relief. If an insufficiency is discovered, the attorney needs to be notified immediately.

g. Motion for Failure to Join a Party under Rule 19

The final motion allowed pursuant to Rule 12(b) is a motion based on the plaintiff's failure to join a party under Rule 19. This motion would most likely request an order joining another party to the lawsuit. Rule 19 provides guidelines for the joinder of parties enabling adjudication of the matter. Specifically, Rule 19(a) states:

> (a) Persons to be Joined if Feasible. *A person who is subject to service of process and whose joinder will not deprive the court of jurisdiction over the subject matter of the action shall be joined as a party in the action if (1) in the person's absence complete relief cannot be accorded among those already parties, or (2) the person claims an interest relating to the subject of the action and is so situated that the disposition of the action in the person's absence may (i) as a practical matter impair or impede the person's ability to protect the interest or (ii) leave any of the persons already parties subject to a substantial risk of incurring double,*

multiple, or otherwise inconsistent obligations by reason of the claimed interest. If the person has not been so joined, the court shall order that the person be made a party. If the person should join as a plaintiff but refuses to do so, the person may be made a defendant, or, in a proper case, an involuntary plaintiff. If joined party objects to venue and joinder of the party would render the venue of the action improper, that party shall be dismissed from the action. (Emphasis added.)

The reason for this rule is to prevent one defendant from being assessed with 100 percent of the responsibility when another entity is partially responsible. It would not be fair to hold defendant ABC wholly responsible for an action that involved both ABC and John Doe. If a party is found liable for its actions, it should only be held financially responsible for the portion of damages it caused. The above-cited rule allows the court to order joinder of additional parties if they meet certain requirements; however, the court will not proceed with this act until a party requests such action by way of a motion.

Again, the decision to draft and file a motion for joinder of additional parties is one the attorney you are working for needs to make. Your responsibility includes being aware if an additional party needs to be joined to the lawsuit. You will most likely be reviewing the case documentation, which may contain evidence supporting the joinder of another party. You need to keep this in mind when you are reviewing documents, as it could be a key element in reducing a defendant's liability and damages.

If you are working on a case in state court, be sure to review the state procedural rules and statutes regarding the joining of additional parties.

2. Discovery Motions

During the discovery process, it may become necessary to file the following motions:

a. Motion for a protective Order: a request to the court for an order or decree protecting a person from further harassment, abusive service, or discovery
b. Motion to terminate or limit deposition examination: a request made to the court to limit deposition testimony or terminate it
c. Motion to compel discovery: a request to the court for an order or decree requiring an answer or supplement of discovery

Other discovery motions may need to be filed with the court; however, the three motions listed above are the most common.

a. Motion for Protective Order

A protective order is a court order that limits or excludes a party from the discovery of particular matters. Protective orders normally address the production of sensitive documentation, but can be entered to limit or exclude the testimony of a particular witness. Rule 26(c) sets forth guidelines for filing a **motion for protective order:**

(c) Protective Order. *Upon motion by a party or by the person from whom discovery is sought, accompanied by a certification that the movant has in good faith conferred or attempted to confer with other affected parties in an effort to resolve the dispute without court action, and for good cause shown the court in which the action is pending or alternatively, on matters relating to a deposition, the court in the district where the deposition is to be taken may make any order which justice requires to protect a party or person from annoyance, embarrassment, oppression, or undue burden or expense,* including one or more of the following:

(1) that the disclosure or discovery not be had;

(2) that the disclosure or discovery may be had only on specified terms and conditions, including a designation of the time or place;

(3) that the discovery may be had only by a method of discovery other than that selected by the party seeking discovery;

(4) that certain matters not be inquired into, or that the scope of the disclosure or discovery be limited to certain matters;

(5) that discovery be conducted with no one present except persons designated by the court;

(6) that a deposition, after being sealed, be opened only by order of the court;

(7) that a trade secret or other confidential research, development, or commercial information not be revealed or be revealed only in a designated way;

(8) that the parties simultaneously file specified documents or information enclosed in sealed envelopes to be opened as directed by the court.

If the motion for a protective order is denied in whole or in part, the court may, on such terms and conditions as are just, order that any party or other person provide or permit discovery. The provisions of Rule 37(a)(4) apply to the award of expenses incurred in relation to the motion. (Emphasis added.)

As the above rule indicates, before a motion for protective order is filed with the court the party requesting such an order must in good faith attempt a resolution of the matter with the other parties involved. Frequently, the parties involved will agree to execute a stipulation for protective order. Courts are very busy and should not be bothered with this matter unless the parties have diligently attempted resolution of the dispute without success.

Normally, evidence of a failed attempt at resolution exists in the form of correspondence among the parties. This correspondence will most likely be attached as an exhibit to the motion for protective order, as could an affidavit signed by the individual pursuing resolution of the matter.

It would not be wise to file a motion with the court prior to attempting good-faith resolution of the matter. Your duty as paralegal most likely will involve compiling the evidence supporting a good-faith attempt at resolution and possibly drafting the motion and proposed order.

When you are drafting the motion, refer back to your compliance with the rule and argue what allows you to make such a motion. Remember that Rule 26(c) allows the court to make any order protecting a party from annoyance, embarrassment, oppression, or undue burden or expense, and then lists eight items that limit or exclude discovery.

The court is also permitted to deny such a motion and order, allowing discovery to continue, so make your argument persuasive.

As for the proposed protective order, have an in-depth conference with the attorney you work for to determine what elements need to be included. This conference will ensure that the order you draft is useful and does not have to be completely rewritten by the attorney. Remember, it is your job to make the attorney's job easier, not more difficult.

b. Motion to Terminate or Limit Deposition Examination

The questions asked during a witness deposition are much less restrictive than those asked of the same witness during trial. The Rules of Evidence substantially limit witness questioning during trial. Deposition questioning is only slightly limited by Rule 30(d)(3) of the Federal Rules of Civil Procedure, which states:

> (3) At any time during a deposition, on motion of a party or of the deponent and upon a showing that the examination is being conducted in bad faith or in such manner as unreasonably to annoy, embarrass, or oppress the deponent or party, the court in which the action is pending or the court in the district where the deposition is being taken may order the officer conducting the examination to cease forthwith from taking the deposition or may limit the scope and manner of the taking of the deposition as provided in Rule 26(c). If the order made terminates the examination, it shall be resumed thereafter only upon the order of the court in which the action is pending. Upon demand of the objecting party or deponent, the taking of the deposition shall be suspended for the time necessary to make a motion for an order. The provisions of Rule 37(a)(4) apply to the award of expenses incurred in relation to the motion.

The above rule allows a party to move to terminate or limit the examination of a witness or party if such examination is conducted in bad faith or violates Rule 26(c). Normally the examination is suspended at the point an objection is made to allow for the filing of a **motion to limit or terminate deposition examination.**

Ideally, the attorney you are working with will allow you to attend depositions when you are first learning about the discovery process. Attending a deposition is a valuable learning experience that simply cannot be replaced by studying legal theory or procedures. Chances are that you will not attend very many depositions in which the deponent's examination is suspended, but it could happen. As with any motion, draft it citing the procedural violation that has occurred, while persuasively arguing the reasons for an order terminating or limiting the deposition.

c. Motion to Compel Discovery

Litigation is focused on meeting deadlines. Unfortunately, written discovery is an area of litigation that experiences constant abuse with regard to deadlines. In my experience, attorneys are annoyed by the constant paper pushing that occurs during written discovery, as most of it is unrelated to the specific issues of their case. A litigation attorney's job is focused on pulling needles *out* of haystacks, and written discovery increases the number of haystacks, making it more and more difficult to find the relevant needles. Combine this with the fact that most written discovery requests are due within 30 days after their receipt, and you end up with written discovery requests being answered late or not answered at all.

Filing a **motion to compel discovery** is the only action that can be taken when written discovery goes unanswered. However, such a motion can only be made if certain requirements have been met. Rule 37(a) sets forth the requirements for filing a motion to compel:

> (a) Motion for Order Compelling Disclosure or Discovery. A party, upon reasonable notice to other parties and all persons affected thereby, may apply for an order compelling disclosure or discovery as follows:
>
> (1) Appropriate Court. *An application for an order to a party shall be made to the court in which the action is pending. An application for an order to a person who is not a party shall be made to the court in the district where the discovery is being, or is to be taken.*
>
> (2) Motion.
>
> (A) If a party fails to make a disclosure required by Rule 26(a), any other party may move to compel disclosure and for appropriate sanctions. The motion must include a certification that the movant has in good faith conferred or attempted to confer with the party not making the disclosure in an effort to secure the disclosure without court action.
>
> (B) If a deponent fails to answer a question propounded or submitted under Rules 30 or 31, or a corporation or other entity fails to make a designation under Rule 30(b)(6) or 31(a), or *a party fails to answer an interrogatory submitted under Rule 33, or if a party, in response to a request for inspection submitted under Rule 34, fails to respond that inspection will be permitted as requested or fails to permit inspection as requested, the discovering party may move for an order compelling an answer, or a designation or an order compelling inspection in accordance with the request. The motion must include a certification that the movant has in good faith conferred or attempted to confer with the person or party failing to make the discovery in an effort to secure the information or material without court action.* When taking a deposition or oral examination, the proponent of the question may complete or adjourn the examination before applying for an order.
>
> (3) Evasive or Incomplete Disclosure, Answer, or Response. For purposes of this subdivision an evasive or incomplete disclosure, answer, or response is to be treated as a failure to disclose, answer, or respond. (Emphasis added.)

As indicated above, to make a motion to compel discovery there must be a certification confirming that a good-faith effort was made to resolve the matter. The rule further indicates that an evasive discovery response is treated as a failure to respond. Your role in preparing a motion to compel will most likely involve conducting a good-faith attempt at resolving the dispute without the court. Be sure you evidence your discussions with the opposing party through a confirming letter or some other documentation, as this will most likely be attached as an exhibit for the motion to compel.

My experience has been that the parties can normally work out discovery matters without court intervention. In order to maintain a good working relationship between the parties, it is always best to try and resolve discovery matters outside of the courtroom, but unfortunately this is not always possible. When I have assisted with a motion to compel, the response has been immediate by the opposing party, resulting in the receipt of discovery responses within a few days after the receipt of the motion. No attorney wants to go before a judge and explain why he or she is not complying with the deadlines set forth in the civil rules of procedure.

d. Motion for Summary Judgment

One common defense strategy includes filing a motion for summary judgment regarding all or part of the plaintiff's claims. A **motion for summary judgment** is a legal document used to dispose of a case when no issues of material facts exist. Summary judgment can be rendered by the court if the court determines there is no genuine issue of disputed fact and the dispute involves a legal question that should be decided by the court and not a jury. Judges are becoming more resistant to granting summary judgment motions because of the increased chances for reversals of their decisions.

Normally, it can be argued that there is some issue of disputed fact. However, if the court can be persuaded to render a judgment on some issues in a case, fewer issues are left to be presented to a jury during trial. A judgment reducing the disputed issues can also increase the chances of settlement between the parties. This type of motion, if granted, can save the parties a considerable amount of time and money.

Rule 56 discusses summary judgment. This rule indicates that a party may move for summary judgment with or without supporting affidavits as early as 20 days after commencement of the action or after receiving a motion for summary judgment from the opposing party. Rule 56(c) requires that a summary judgment motion be served 10 days before the time for hearing to allow the opposing party adequate time to respond. Further, Rule 56(c) discusses what is required for the motion for summary judgment to be granted by the court:

> (c) Motion and Proceedings Thereon. The motion shall be served at least 10 days before the time fixed for the hearing. The adverse party prior to the day of hearing may serve opposing affidavits. *The judgment sought shall be rendered forthwith if the pleadings, depositions, answers to interrogatories, and admissions on file, together with the affidavits, if any, show that there is no genuine issue as to any material fact and that the moving party is entitled to a judgment as a matter of law.* A summary judgment, interlocutory in character, may be reduced on the issue of liability alone although there is a genuine issue as to the amount of damages. (Emphasis added.)

As stated previously, the issue for which a party is requesting summary judgment must involve no genuine issue of material fact. Affidavits are frequently used to support a motion such as this, as well as deposition testimony and written discovery responses. Your duties most likely will include providing pertinent deposition testimony and discovery responses, as well as obtaining supporting affidavits.

Rule 56(e), (f), and (g) discuss the requirements of affidavits. Rule 56(e) indicates that affidavits need to be made based on the affiant's personal knowledge stating the facts as they would be admissible in evidence. This rule prevents the filing of affidavits that are considered hearsay. Other affidavit requirements under Rule 56(e) include competency of an affiant and certified or sworn-to referenced attachments. When affidavits are not available to adequately present the party's opposition to a motion for summary judgment, Rule 56(f) allows the court to order a continuance for obtaining affidavits, depositions, or discovery responses. If an affidavit is made in bad faith, Rule 56(g) provides for the following remedies:

> (g) Affidavits Made in Bad Faith. Should it appear to the satisfaction of the court at any time that any of the affidavits presented pursuant to this rule are presented in bad faith or solely for the purpose of delay, *the court shall forthwith order the party employing them to pay to the other party the amount of the reasonable expenses which the filing of the affidavits caused the other party to incur, including reasonable attorney's fees, and any offending party or attorney may be adjudged guilty of contempt.* (Emphasis added.)

When you are obtaining an affidavit from a witness, make sure you have an in-depth conversation with him or her to ensure the affidavit is accurate and true. Always make sure the witness knows that an affidavit is a sworn statement provided under oath and must be completely accurate. Have the witness read through the affidavit and make any changes necessary prior to signing the document.

Further, you should always make sure that the information contained within the affidavit is based on the witness' personal knowledge. The best way to ascertain if the witness has personal knowledge of a matter is to ask how he or she knows the information being sworn to. If the witness indicates he or she knows something because he or she was there and experienced it, then the information represents first-hand personal knowledge. If the witness indicates to you that he or she heard the information from someone else, the information cannot be used in an affidavit because it constitutes hearsay and is not admissible evidence.

As you can see, motions are an integral part of defending a lawsuit. They allow the court to simplify or dismiss the issues in a case, while ensuring that discovery proceeds appropriately and on schedule.

F. INDEPENDENT MEDICAL EXAMINATIONS

Another tool that can be utilized in defending a lawsuit is the **independent medical examination or IME**. Pursuant to Rule 35(a) of the Federal Rules of Civil Procedure, if a controversy exists regarding plaintiff's physical or mental condition, then it can be ordered by the court that plaintiff submit to a physical or mental examination, commonly referred to as an IME. An IME, when requested informally by the defendant, is rarely refused by the plaintiff because Rule 35(a) allows the court to order an examination if the plaintiff refuses.

A key decision in defending a lawsuit is whether an IME should be requested. Rule 35(b)(1) provides the following:

(b) Report of Examiner.

(1) If requested by the party against whom an order is made under Rule 35(a) or the person examined, *the party causing the examination to be made shall deliver to the requesting party a copy of the detailed written report of the examiner setting out the examiner's findings, including the results of all tests made, diagnoses and conclusions, together with like reports of all earlier examinations of the same condition.* After delivery the party causing the examination shall be entitled upon request to receive from the party against whom the order is made a like report of any examination, previously or thereafter made, of the same condition, unless, in the case of a report of examination of a person not a party, the party shows that the party is unable to obtain it. The court on motion may make an order against a party requiring delivery of a report on such terms as are just, and if an examiner fails or refuses to make a report the court may exclude the examiner's testimony if offered at trial. (Emphasis added.)

Because the above-cited rule requires that a copy of the examination report be provided to the plaintiff on request, the decision to request an examination is a complicated one. There are pros and cons to requesting an IME. During my career as a paralegal, I have seen IMEs that were invaluable to the defendant's case. Unfortunately, I have also seen IMEs that destroyed the defendant's case strategy because they confirmed in writing what the plaintiff was claiming. Essentially, an unnecessary IME could help increase the value of the plaintiff's claim.

One should always weigh the pros against the cons when determining if an IME should be requested. If the injury involved is substantial and the medical records support plaintiff's claims, then an IME is not normally necessary and could serve only to damage the defendant's arguments. I have found that attorneys only request an IME when the injury claimed is surrounded by strong causation and damage questions. Soft tissue injuries are normally the type of injury that I have seen IMEs requested on. When you are reviewing the medical records, keep the following questions in mind regarding an IME:

- Do the medical records support what the plaintiff is claiming?
- Was the condition preexisting and exacerbated by the current incident?
- What will an IME accomplish defensively?
- How sure are you that the IME will be favorable to the defense?

If you answer these questions and the responses support a request for an IME, then suggest the idea to your attorney. Remember, your job is to assist in addressing weaknesses in the plaintiff's lawsuit. not in strengthening it. Just because this tool exists does not mean it must be used.

G. EXPERT WITNESSES

Expert witnesses are individuals who have expertise in a particular area and can testify regarding such expertise. For example, in an automobile accident, someone working as an accident reconstructionist may be designated as an expert to testify regarding causation.

Expert witnesses can have a great deal of influence on a jury. The following six items must be considered when utilizing experts:

1. Determining what experts are needed
2. Selecting experts
3. Compiling documents for experts
4. Conversations with experts
5. Expert disclosures
6. Expert reports

1. Determining What Experts Are Needed

One of the main decisions made in defending a lawsuit involves determining what experts are needed. There are occasions when no expert will be necessary, but normally at least one expert will be designated to testify regarding either causation or damages. Defense experts are primarily used to point out weaknesses in the plaintiff's claims, while reinforcing the defendant's arguments.

The attorney you are working with will determine which experts are designated to defend the lawsuit. As you are reviewing the documents and performing the case investigation, remember to always provide the attorney with your opinion of any weaknesses in the plaintiff's case. This can help your attorney to determine what type of expert may be needed. If you have any ideas regarding the need for a particular type of expert, make sure you let the attorney you work for know. You may have noticed the need for an expert somewhere that the attorney has not; however, always remember your role. As a paralegal, you are there to assist the attorney by making suggestions and providing ideas; the final determination regarding experts is left to the attorney.

2. Selecting Experts

Once the attorney has determined what types of experts are needed, you probably will be asked to obtain them. For example, if the attorney is working on defending a medical negligence lawsuit and wants someone who specializes in neurology, you will need to determine how such an expert will be obtained. There are essentially two types of experts: local experts who testify occasionally, and national experts who testify frequently.

a. Local Experts

This type of expert normally works in his or her field of expertise and resides within the location of the lawsuit. Local experts do not make a living testifying, as they are usually employed in their area of expertise. A local expert usually will be obtained through a referral. Some believe that a local expert has more appeal to jury members because they can identify with the expert and the expert is not viewed as having an opinion just because he or she is paid to have that opinion. The disadvantage to a local expert is the lack of experience testifying. If the expert you select is a local expert and has never testified before, then he or she will have to be prepared for testifying prior to the deposition and trial.

b. National Experts

The national expert normally performs consulting work and offers his or her services testifying. National experts usually have very impressive credentials and are very knowledgeable regarding the topic of testimony. However, most national experts are not currently employed in their area of expertise. This type of expert usually testifies hundreds of times in a year. National experts are normally obtained through a national company.

Prior to selecting a national expert, you should run a search for past deposition and trial testimony through IDEX or another company. Such a search will help to ensure consistent expert testimony. The last thing you want is an expert who has testified with one opinion one time and then provided the opposite opinion on another occasion. This would be devastating during a deposition or trial. The opposing attorney could use past inconsistent testimony to destroy your expert's credibility on the witness stand through the impeachment process.

The expert selection process is not something to be taken lightly. One must consider all of the options and determine which type of expert will best fit the needs of the client. A conference with the attorney you work for would be advantageous to decide whether the expert will be located locally or nationally.

PRACTICE TIP

Keeping a database of experts by area of expertise is highly recommended as a time-saving and informational tool.

---

3. Compiling Documents for Experts

Once the experts have been selected, you will need to compile and send the documents for review. The expert's opinion will be based on his experience and the documents you provide him for review. The paralegal should always remember that any documentation sent to the expert that is not classified as privileged must be produced to opposing counsel pursuant to Rule 26 of the Federal Rules of Civil Procedure.

When you are compiling the documentation that is being sent to an expert, make sure to keep a copy for your expert file. If the documentation is voluminous, you can keep a produced documents list in the expert file. This practice will save a considerable amount of time when opposing counsel sends out a request for production asking for all documents the expert has reviewed. You should also make sure that any documents sent to the expert are bates numbered so that they can be easily identified. This practice alleviates confusion during the expert's deposition.

4. Conversations with Experts

As would be expected, several conversations will occur between you, the defense attorney, and the expert. During my years of experience as a paralegal, I have always preferred to talk with experts over the telephone or in person as opposed to communicating in writing. This reduces the number of problems regarding discovery, as written communications with an expert could potentially be discoverable to the opposing party. If I do correspond with an expert in writing, it is only to provide the expert with documentation, definitely not to discuss case strategy.

5. Expert Disclosures

Once the decision is made to use an expert at trial, he or she must be identified to the opposing party pursuant to Rule 26(a)(2)(A) of the Federal Rules of Procedure. The deadline for disclosing experts is provided in Rule 26(a)(2)(C), which indicates, "the disclosures shall be made at least 90 days before the trial date or the date the case is to be ready for trial." This same rule requires that rebuttal experts be designated within 30 days after the opposing party's disclosure of experts.

6. Expert Reports

The court requires that all experts provide a written report of their opinions. Pursuant to Rule 26(a)(2)(B), eight items must be contained within any expert's written report:

1. A statement of all opinions expressed
2. The basis for such opinions
3. Data and information considered in forming the opinions
4. Exhibits used to support the opinions
5. The qualifications of the expert
6. A list of publications authored by the expert
7. The compensation paid to the expert
8. A listing of the expert's past trial or deposition testimony

The Federal Rules of Civil Procedure have recently been amended to require the expert to generate and sign his or her expert report. When I am assisting with an expert witness report, I explain to the expert what elements are required and have him or her generate a draft report. Once the expert has provided me with a draft of the report, then I make changes only as to format and grammar not substance. If the attorney I am working with is not happy with the report, I have him or her work with the expert regarding any changes. On more than one occasion I have attended a deposition in which an expert's credibility was attacked because the opposing counsel made it appear as though the expert had little involvement in the drafting of his or her report. Not only does the attorney's drafting of an expert report currently violate the Federal Rules of Civil Procedure, it has been my experience that juries do not take kindly to this and will discard the expert's opinions because they believe it is not the expert's opinion, but the attorney's. Many juries view this behavior as manipulative and dishonest. Normally, by the time you designate an expert, you know what his or her opinion will be and therefore, you know what his report will say. You will need to find out how the attorney you are working for prefers to practice regarding expert witness reports and assist accordingly.

Another thing to keep in mind during the drafting of expert reports is the opposition's attempt to have the expert excluded from testifying. Recently, in the federal courts, several judges have been asserting a standard when evaluating whether an expert should be excluded from testifying. The standard focuses on the basis of an expert's opinion. The following questions are frequently asked:

- Does the expert have a basis for his or her opinion?
- What is the basis?
- Has the basis been tested for reliability?
- How has the basis for his or her opinion been tested?
- Is the basis for opinion reliable?

I have found that if the above-questions are addressed by the expert in his or her report, then opposing counsel is less likely to attempt a request for dismissal of expert testimony or a motion to exclude your expert. This approach also provides the expert with strong arguments supporting his or her methodology, preparing the expert for examination during deposition.

Experts can be an integral part of a case. Spending the time necessary to select, designate, and work with experts could assist in settlement of the case or a favorable verdict at trial.

PRACTICE TIP

Once you have discussed the type of expert needed and the type of testimony necessary to aid the average juror, start working immediately on locating potential experts, gathering resumes, fee information, prior testimony, and publications for the attorney's review. Always concentrate on ensuring that you have the necessary information readily available when the time comes for expert disclosure. Planning ahead is always the best practice.

H. CLASS ACTION LAWSUITS—HOW TO DEFEND AGAINST THEM

Class action lawsuits are lawsuits involving a group of persons, things, or activities. Class action lawsuits involve several members of a class filing a lawsuit as one collective group. To defend against class action lawsuits, you must first understand the requirements governing them. Any class action lawsuit that does not meet the court's requirements can be dismissed by the defending party for such insufficiencies.

1. Class Membership

Not everyone can be included as a member of a class. Certain requirements need to be met for class membership to apply. The individuals included within a class must have in common a similar set of legal issues or facts relating to their claims. If you have ever been notified of potential membership in a class action suit, then you most likely have been required to answer certain questions prior to obtaining such membership. These questions are asked to ensure that the legal issues or facts relating to your claims are common to the rest of the class.

2. Requirements for Obtaining and Maintaining Class Action Status

Not all lawsuits can be classified as class action lawsuits; the court has created several prerequisites that must be met before a lawsuit obtains class action status. Rule 23(a) and (b) provide a listing of the requirements for class action lawsuits. These requirements include:

(a) Prerequisites to a Class Action. One or more members of a class may sue or be sued as representative parties on behalf of all only if

(1) the class is so numerous that joinder of all members is impracticable,

(2) there are questions of law or fact common to the class,

(3) the claims or defenses of the representative parties are typical of the claims or defenses of the class, and

(4) the representative parties will fairly and adequately protect the interests of the class.

(b) Class Actions Maintainable. An action may be maintained as a class action if the prerequisites of subdivision (a) are satisfied, and in addition:

(1) the prosecution of separate actions by or against individual members of the class would create a risk of

(A) inconsistent or varying adjudications with respect to individual members of the class which would establish incompatible standards of conduct for the party opposing the class, or

(B) adjudications with respect to individual members of the class which would as a practical matter be dispositive of the interests of the other members not parties to the adjudications or substantially impair or impede their ability to protect their interests; or

(2) the party opposing the class has acted or refused to act on grounds generally applicable to the class, thereby making appropriate final injunctive relief or corresponding declaratory relief with respect to the class as a whole; or

(3) the court finds that the questions of law or fact common to the members of the class predominate over any questions affecting only individual members, and that a class action is superior to other available methods for the fair and efficient adjudication of the controversy. The matters pertinent to the findings include:

(A) the interest of members of the class in individually controlling the prosecution or defense of separate action;

(B) the extent and nature of any litigation concerning the controversy already commenced by or against members of the class;

(C) the desirability or undesirability of concentrating the litigation of the claims in the particular forum;

(D) the difficulties likely to be encountered in the management of a class action.

Each of the prerequisites listed above is focused on fairness and equitable adjudication. When you are assisting an attorney who is defending a class action lawsuit, you should check that the plaintiff has satisfied the required prerequisites. If the plaintiff has not fulfilled the requirements of obtaining and maintaining class action status, then be sure to inform your attorney. A motion supporting dismissal may need to be filed with the court prior to entry of an order maintaining the class action status.

Shortly after commencement of a class action, the court is required to issue an order determining if class action status is to be maintained. The court may decide to conditionally maintain the class action suit, requiring some amendments or alterations. As a defense paralegal, pay close attention to any amendments or alterations, ensuring that the plaintiff abides by them.

3. Notice to Class Members

Once the court has maintained a class action, a notice must be sent to all potential members of that class. It is the court's responsibility to determine what notice is practical under the circumstances. Rule 23(c)(2) requires that three items always be included in every class action notice to advise potential class members of their rights regarding the following:

1. A member will be excluded from the class if the member requests
2. Any judgment will include members who didn't request exclusion
3. Members who don't request exclusion can enter an appearance through counsel

4. Paralegal Role in the Class Action

If you are working with an attorney who is defending a class action lawsuit, you will be challenged. Class action lawsuits require a tremendous amount of investigation and discovery, not to mention meticulous organizational skills. You should meet with the attorney and create a clear investigation and discovery plan so there is no confusion as to the focus of your energies. Half of the battle is creating and adhering to a defense plan.

Usually class action lawsuits involve the production of voluminous documentation. Your document organization skills will definitely be challenged. Chapter 5 discusses methods on how to manage documents, including information on case indexing and database creation. In class action lawsuits, use a database program if at all possible. This could save you several hours when it comes to document searches.

Don't be intimidated by a class action lawsuit; it has some unique qualities, as discussed above, but essentially it is just another lawsuit. Your paralegal duties should be similar to those used with any lawsuit, only performed on a much larger scale.

ETHICS

The ethics section of this chapter focuses on ethical issues that arise when assisting with the defense of a lawsuit. Legal ethics are not confusing or mysterious. If in your gut you feel something could be dishonest, inappropriate, or unprofessional, there is most likely an ethical rule that prohibits such action.

This chapter has discussed several areas in defending a lawsuit. The areas most likely to create challenges ethically involve interaction with the client, witnesses, IME physicians, and experts.

Maintaining client confidentiality when having conversations with witnesses, IME physicians, and experts is of utmost importance. Never disclose verbally or in writing any discussions between yourself and the client to anyone other than your attorney.

Further, you must always be careful not to risk a waiver of any privilege afforded to the client. As discussed previously, you must never provide privileged documentation to witnesses, IME physicians, or experts as such production could result in a waiver of the asserted privilege.

The final area that must be considered ethically involves affidavits and expert witness reports. Affidavits and expert reports are sworn statements signed under oath and filed with the court. When you are assigned the task of obtaining affidavits and expert reports, it is your ethical responsibility to make sure that witnesses and experts realize these documents are sworn statements signed under oath. As would be expected, your duties will also include the task of ensuring that affidavits and expert reports are true and accurate to the best of your knowledge.

To avoid any ethical problems, always review available resources or consult with your attorney. For further information on ethics and professionalism, please refer to the following information on ethics and professionalism:

- The National Association of Legal Assistants Code of Ethics and Professional Responsibility
- The National Association of Legal Assistants Model Standards and Guidelines for Utilization of Legal Assistants

CONCLUSION

The defense of a lawsuit involves answering the complaint, arguing motions, requesting IMEs, and obtaining experts.

Drafting an answer to the complaint is extremely important because this sets the tone of the defendant's case. If the plaintiff's claims are not responded to within the time period required, in certain circumstances, the defendant can have a default judgment entered against it that awards the plaintiff everything asked for.

Arguing motions, requesting IMEs, and obtaining experts in the defense of a case is imperative to providing a sound defense. The paralegal's primary role regarding these three tasks involves tracking, maintaining, and compiling relevant information and documentation.

The paralegal must be aware of statutes and procedures to adequately assist the attorney during the defense of a lawsuit. As the paralegal reviews documents, performs interviews, and drafts defensive pleadings, consideration should be given to the applicable statutes and procedures entailed in defending the lawsuit.

USING TECHNOLOGY IN THE LAW OFFICE

The following section includes a detailed discussion of the technology tools and software applications commonly utilized in defending a lawsuit and arguing motions. The technology available today enables attorneys to defend a case visually in a way never imagined before. The focus of this chapter was on defending the lawsuit and utilizing motions. Presentation software such as Microsoft PowerPoint and Trial Director enables one to present exhibits in an extremely effective and influential manner. **Presentation software** are programs designed to present electronic image files.

Studies have proven that individuals retain 10 percent of the information presented when such information is solely auditory. If information is presented in both an auditory and visual format, individuals retain 65 percent of the information. PowerPoint and Trial Director provide attorneys with an opportunity to present information in a manner that can effectively increase audience retention by as much as five times the original rate. It stands to reason that when individuals can retain more of the information presented, they can reach decisions more quickly, setting forth less effort.

A. WHAT IS POWERPOINT?

PowerPoint is a software program that allows the user to create graphic presentations for speaking engagements. Slides are created and linked together to create a visually enhancing presentation regarding the topic of discussion. **Slides** are documents created in PowerPoint that can be added into a presentation. The user arranges text and graphics that appear when the slide is opened and effectively heighten the audience's interest. Outside files can be inserted within the slides and commented on throughout the presentation. For those who have limited experience with PowerPoint, template wizards exist to assist in slide creation. A single slide can be created, but more frequently slides are linked together in a particular order according to the topic being discussed. This software is extremely powerful and impressive when used during oral arguments of motions. In addition to its use in presentations, PowerPoint can be used to highlight or emphasize portions of scanned documents and play digital video.

As always, you will want to discuss any PowerPoint slide presentations or exhibits with your attorney prior to creation. This discussion should include slide content, color schemes, graphics, and animation.

B. POWERPOINT APPLICATIONS

PowerPoint's software applications are relatively simple to learn. To effectively use PowerPoint, you must be able to perform the following four general functions:

1. Create slide presentations
2. Insert and animate text
3. Insert and animate images
4. Run the slide presentation

1. Creating Slide Presentations

The process of creating slide presentations is as complex or simple as you want to make it. PowerPoint has several preformatted slide presentation templates that you can use. If you do not wish to use the templates, you can create a blank slide presentation, formatting it as you see fit. **Templates** are preformatted forms generated to assist in the creation of documents.

When you create a slide presentation, select New from the File menu. A screen will then appear with several tabs that can be selected. (See Figure 8.1.)

There are four tabs from which you can choose: General, Presentation Designs, Presentations, and Web Pages. The General tab allows you to create and format your own slides for a presentation. See Figure 8.2. The boxes shown in Figure 8.2 show the formats available for slides presentations. Once you find a format that works for your needs, you select it and begin adding text and graphics. For example, if you select the text and chart slide format you would be provided with a slide similar to Figure 8.3. You would then simply follow the instructions adding the title, text, and chart. At this point you will probably want to set up your color scheme. Your slide presentation color scheme is created by selecting Slide Color Scheme, and Background from the Format menu.

When you create your own slide presentations, you will need to use the Outline View tab (located in the lower left corner above the Draw tab) to add another slide to your Presentation. I accomplish this by creating one slide and then simply selecting Shift-Tab to create a second slide for entering text.

The other tabs available to you when creating slide presentations include presentation designs and presentations. These tabs include templates with preestablished formatting

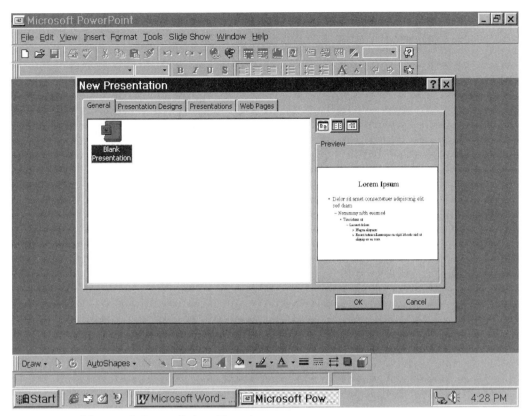

Figure 8.1. Microsoft PowerPoint—Templates

and color schemes. If you are just beginning your work with PowerPoint, it may be wise to utilize these templates.

2. Inserting and Animating Text

Inserting text into a slide is as simple as clicking the relevant box and typing the information desired. The text font and font size can be changed by selecting the font that is desired in the font style and size boxes within the formatting toolbar. Underlining and bolding of text can be accomplished by highlighting the text and selecting the bold and underline tools in the formatting toolbar.

Once the text has been entered into the slide, animation can be added to the separate text boxes. **Text boxes** are graphic boxes that allow for the entry of text. This is accomplished by selecting the desired text box, right-clicking and choosing Custom Animation from the drop-down menu. **Custom animations** are unique settings available in Power-Point, allowing the user to determine the type of animation. Figure 8.4 demonstrates how animation is selected.

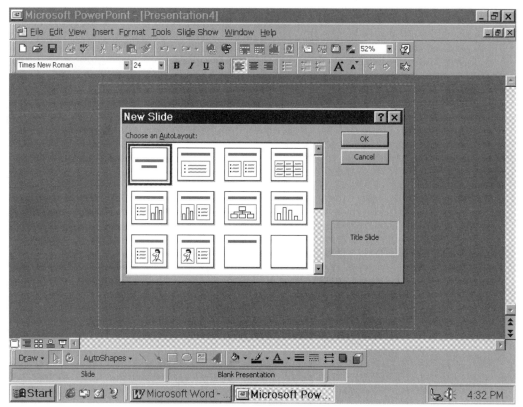

Figure 8.2. Microsoft PowerPoint—New Slides

As you can see above, the Effects tab provides you with several options for animation. There is also a Preview tab that allows you to select a type of animation and preview it before adding it to the slide.

The order that you want text boxes to appear can also be set through animation. An **animation order box** is a text box used to determine the sequence of each slide. Using the arrows located next to the animation order box, you can determine when each box appears. The Timing tab allows you to set the animation appearance by either a mouse click or after so many seconds. Usually the mouse click timing works best, as this allows for better control over animation. Once animation has been selected, you can specify how the text is introduced: all at once, by letter, by word, in reverse order, or grouped by paragraph levels.

3. Inserting and Animating Images

PowerPoint also allows you to insert images into slides, including but not limited to scanned documents, photograph, maps, and charts. **Images** are files generated from the

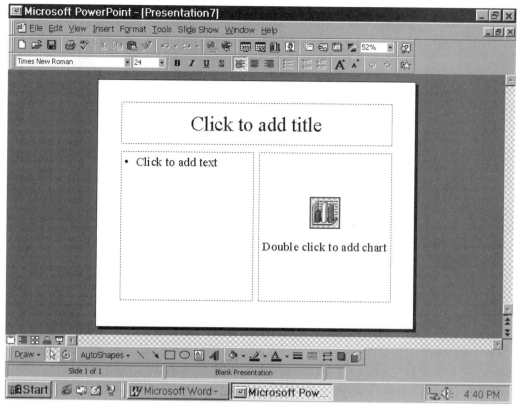

Figure 8.3. Microsoft PowerPoint–Slide Format

scanning of documents. Images can be inserted into a slide by selecting Picture From File from the Insert menu. Then you just highlight the file you want and select Insert. The image will probably be larger than you want, but you can reduce it by dragging the corner of the image with the mouse.

Other graphics can be added to an image after it is inserted, such as arrows, boxes, circles, and shading. **Graphics** are electronically animated pictures. Using the drawing toolbar at the bottom of the screen, you can use the graphic tool to insert a graphic on the image. Right-clicking when the graphic is selected on the slide can also animate the graphics inserted.

4. Running the Slide Presentation

Presentation mode—an option in PowerPoint used when presenting slide and slide presentations.

In my experience, I have found that it works well if the attorney has the paralegal run the slide presentation during oral argument or trial. This approach allows the attorney

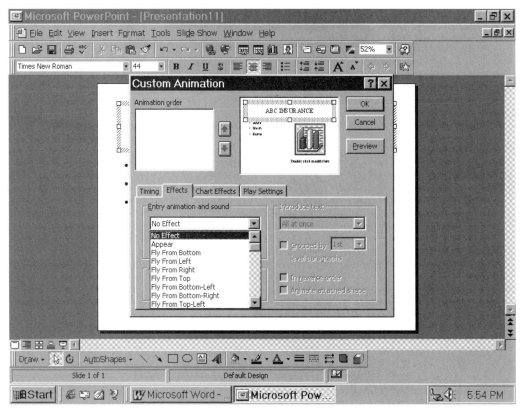

Figure 8.4. Microsoft PowerPoint—Animation

to present his or her argument and respond to questions without a delay while he or she is pulling up slides from the computer. However, this approach only works well if the attorney and paralegal work as a cohesive team, effectively communicating during the presentation. Running through the presentation several times before the hearing or trial will also help to ensure it is smooth and effective.

When you are running a PowerPoint presentation, keep in mind that the "n" key takes you to the next slide and the "p" key takes you back to the previous slide. Also, on every computer "Shift-F5 or monitor control function key" allows you to control what your audience views on the projected screen. The "Shift-F5 or monitor control function key" option has three modes when the computer is connected to a projection system. The first mode allows only you to see the image on your computer. The second mode allows the audience to view the computer image, but your screen remains blank. Finally, the third mode allows the image to appear on your screen and the projection screen. This function is useful if you are moving in and out of files and do not want the judge or jury to be distracted by your actions while the attorney is speaking.

PowerPoint presentations are usually most effective during structured arguments with limited interruptions, such as opening statements and closing arguments. Presentations are normally created with the slides placed in a particular order. If the attorney is forced to skip around during the presentation, you will have to pull slides out of their original order. Slides can be retrieved out of their original order, but it takes time and the presentation does not flow smoothly. If at all possible, it is always better to stay with the original slide presentation order.

C. CONCLUSION—POWERPOINT

The PowerPoint applications discussed above are fairly basic. There are numerous advanced applications that can be utilized when creating presentations. If you want an excellent resource, review *PowerPoint for Litigators,* published by NITA. This text is primarily written for those who have little experience with PowerPoint; however, the final chapters do discuss some advanced applications. The best way to become proficient in the use of PowerPoint is to use the program.

D. WHAT IS TRIAL DIRECTOR?

Trial Director is also presentation software; however, it was designed specifically for the legal field. Three programs combine to create the inData Director Suite:

1. Document Director: organizes and allows you to create exhibits from scanned documents
2. Deposition Director: organizes and allows you to generate clips from digital video transcripts (DVTs)
3. Trial Director: allows for the presentation of imaged documents or photographs and video/audio files.

The inData Director Suite contains several applications that PowerPoint currently does not possess. Document Director creates bar codes for scanned documents, allowing for immediate document retrieval through Trial Director. The inData Director Suite surpasses PowerPoint in the following areas: presenting linked video deposition testimony, graphically enhancing documents before or during trial, and allowing for the simultaneous presentation of exhibits.

This software was used during the Microsoft trial to present documents and the videotaped deposition testimony of Bill Gates. The inData Director Suite is compatible with the Summation database software, allowing for mass importation of database imaged files.

1. Document Director Applications

As indicated above, Document Director allows you to organize and create exhibits from scanned documents. The following applications must be learned if you are going to use Document Director effectively:

    a. Creation of a new case
    b. Adding items to a case
    c. Viewing items
    d. Using annotation tools

a. Creating a New Case

The first step in using Document Director is creating a case. This is done by selecting Create A New Case from the File menu or clicking on the New Case Button located on the toolbar. See Figure 8.5 Once you have done this, the Create A New Case window will appear and request that you type the name of the new case in the description field. There is also an option to add notes and information regarding the matter number. Once

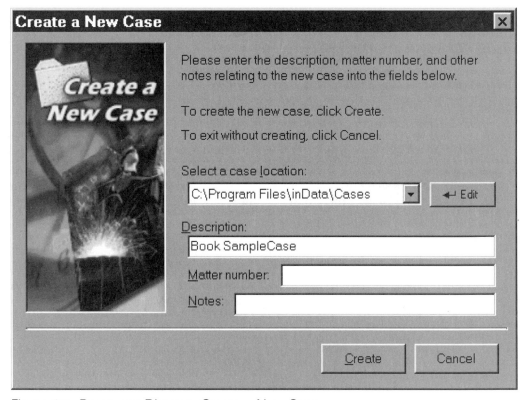

Figure 8.5. Document Director—Create a New Case

you have completed this window, select Create. Your case will be stored in the inData folder under cases (inData\Cases*New Case Name*).

b. Adding Items to a Case

Once a case has been created, you will need to add items to the case. This can be done manually, item by item, or through automated means. To add items manually, you select Items, Import New Items From and Manual Selection Dialog. You then need to decide what type of items you would like to add. Document Director can organize documents, photographs, audio/video, and OLE files. If you need to add documents you would right-mouse click on the documents folder on the right of the manual select drop-down box. Once you have done this, you will be provided with a window to Select Items. Then you simply highlight the files you want to add and click Open. Document Director will then copy these files into the created case.

If you have several items to add to a case, then the automated approach is more logical. You simply choose Items, Import New Items from and Batch Import File. Figure 8.6 displays the window that will appear. As Figure 8.6 demonstrates, there are two tab options—Add Selected Files and Batch Import. For automated importing of files, you

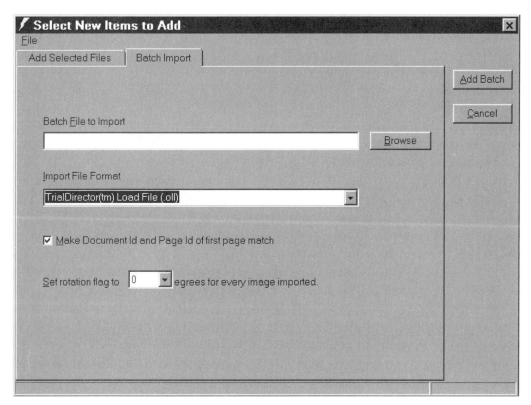

Figure 8.6. Document Director—Select New Items to Add

need to click on Batch Import, select the file you want imported, and choose Add Batch. The file will then be loaded into your case in a matter of seconds.

c. Viewing Items

There are tabs at the bottom of the screen when a case is open. These tabs allow you to select what type of item you want to view. There are tabs for documents, photographs, audio/video, and OLE files. OLE files are files created in another program that have been imported into Document Director (for example, PowerPoint, Adobe, Word, and Internet Explorer). Figure 8.7 provides a sample of the viewer screen that exists in Document Director. As Figure 8.7 demonstrates, if you want to view an item you simply highlight the item and it appears on the right-hand side of the screen. The arrows that appear on the far right of the screen allow you to page through the document.

A portion of any image can be copied onto the clipboard by holding the Shift key and dragging the mouse around the area you want to copy. When you release the mouse, the selected section will be copied to the clipboard. This information could then be pasted into another program or document. You can also rotate images with the Rotate Image

Figure 8.7. Document Director–Viewer Screen

button on the toolbar at the top of the screen (the arrow is shaped like a circle). Also, an image can be quickly enlarged by using your mouse to select an area to enlarge. This is done by holding down the left side of the mouse and dragging it across the area to enlarge. Upon your release of the mouse the area will appear enlarged. If you decide you want the enlarged area to return to its original size, then simply double-click the mouse. The magnifier tool (a magnifying glass) on the toolbar also will allow you to enlarge a specific section of an image.

d. Using Annotation Tools

There are several annotation tools available that allow you to add computer graphics to documents. The drawing tools available include arrows, lines, rectangle, ellipse, polygon, stamps, notes, text, redactions, polyline, highlighting, and freehand drawing. Figure 8.8 shows the annotation toolbar. As Figure 8.8 shows, in the upper left there is a selection tool (an arrow). When selected this tool allows you to select the area of an image and annotate it. This tool also allows you to delete, move, or edit/markup the area selected. The color for the background of text boxes and notes, as well as highlighting, can be

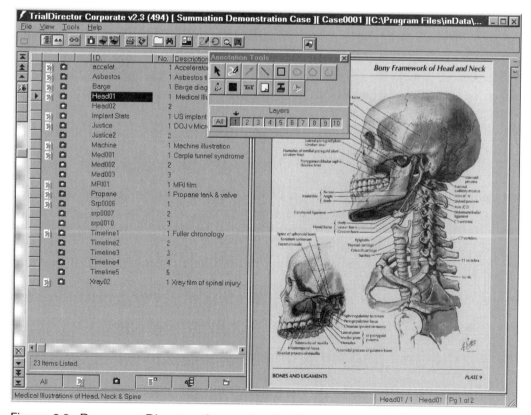

Figure 8.8. Document Director—Annotation Toolbar

selected by you through a drop-down menu. While in the viewer, you can tell an item is annotated when the document icon contains yellow highlighting on it.

Once an image has been annotated, you need to save the annotations by selecting the Save Revision button (a picture of a safe). A window will then come up that asks if you want to save, save as new revision, or cancel. If you select Save, the original document will be changed to include annotations. It is suggested that you select Save As A Revision so the original remains the same and the annotated image is created as a new image file.

2. Deposition Director Applications

Deposition Director allows you to organize and create video clips from digital video transcripts (DVT). As with Document Director, there are certain applications you must know to effectively use Deposition Director. The main applications are:

a. Opening a new case
b. Importing a DVT
c. Opening the DVT
d. Creating DVT clips
e. Attaching exhibits

a. Opening a New Case

If you have already created your case in Document Director, you will not need to create the case in Deposition Director because the two programs are linked. If you have not created the case yet, simply follow the same steps discussed in the Document Director applications section of this chapter.

b. Importing a DVT

Once the case is created, you will need to know how to import a DVT file. When a deposition is taken it can be videotaped. The video can then be put in digital format and linked with the written transcript. This results in scrolling written testimony as the digital video of the deponent plays.

To import DVT files you will need to select Import Digital Video Transcript(s) from the Transcript menu. You can then browse to the file you want and select Open. The digital video transcript window will then appear. From this window, you will need to decide which files you want to import and select Next. Figure 8.9 demonstrates the next window that will appear. Import will need to be selected to complete the import process. From the window pictured in Figure 8.9 if you select Next once the import is complete Deposition Director will provide you with a list of all the files imported.

c. Opening a DVT

Now that you have loaded the DVT files, you will need to open them. This application is relatively simple. In the Case Explorer, you will go into the Select A Digital Transcript

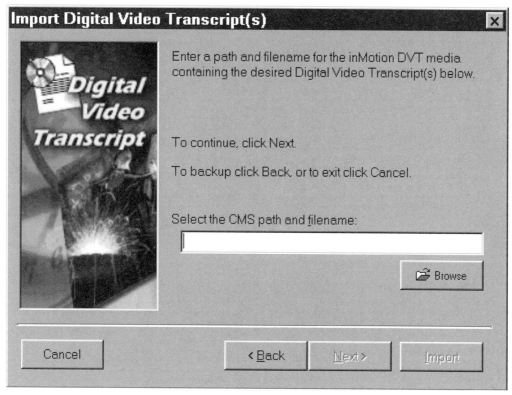

Figure 8.9. Document Director—Import Digital Video Transcripts

To Open window and select a transcript to open. Figure 8.10 provides you with an example of what will appear when a DVT file is opened. As Figure 8.10 illustrates, there are video buttons on the toolbar. These buttons are set up similarly to your VCR, making their use easy.

While you are viewing the DVT file, you probably want to move around in the transcript. This task can be accomplished three different ways. The first option is to select from the transcript window where you want to be in the transcript. The second option is to select the Find tool from the toolbar (the binoculars) or go to the Edit menu and select Find. This option requires you to request that a search be done for certain information. The final option is to use the slide bar on the audio/video controls.

d. Creating DVT Clips

From the DVT files you may want to create clips. Clips are normally used to impeach a witness's testimony at trial, but they can also be used to capture important testimony and objections.

You must use the Clip Wizard in Deposition Director to create a clip. The Clip Wizard needs to be selected from the clip menu. The Clip Wizard will then appear. See

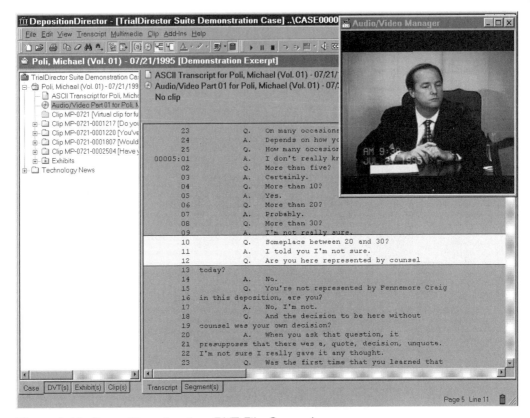

Figure 8.10. Deposition director—DVT File Opened

Figure 8.11. The easiest way to define the length of the video clip is by indicating the page and line range of the transcript. You can also define the video clip by using the time code of hours, minutes, and seconds. Once you have selected the range, you need to click the Next button to complete the clip creation process. At this time the program will allow you to choose if you want the page or line to be automatically or manually adjusted. Some adjustment to the starting and ending may need to be done after the clip is created, but this can be done through editing the clip.

Editing the clip requires that you first play the segment to determine what editing is needed. After you have played the clip, select the Record button below the digital video and adjust the starting and ending numbers according. You will then need to play the clip to ensure your editing was correct.

e. Attaching Exhibits

Attaching exhibits to the DVT files is usually done to provide further explanation of the testimony given. In the deposition presentation window the area below the video box is designated for exhibits. In order to attach an exhibit to an area of testimony, you need

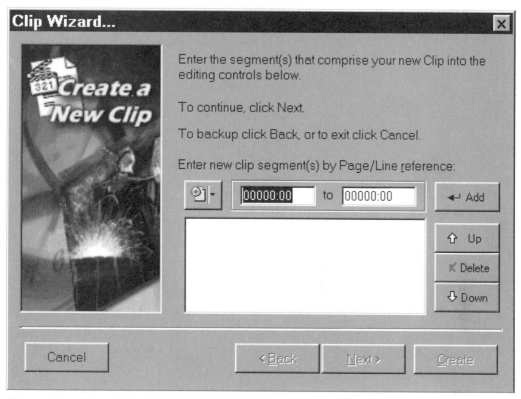

Figure 8.11. Deposition Director—Clip Wizard

to put the cursor on the desired area of testimony and select "Choose Synchronized Exhibit" from the Transcript menu. Figure 8.12 provides a visual showing what window will appear. You then need to select the exhibit you want to attach and click Next. Deposition Director will then ask you if you want to attach the exhibit by current transcript line or by current audio/video position. Once you have determined how to attach the exhibit, select Attach. Now the exhibit will appear at the precise position you have designated. If you want to turn off the exhibit synchronization, you need to disable the Exhibit Synchronization menu item or button.

3. Trial Director Applications

Trial Director is the final software program that is a part of the inData Director Suite. This program allows you to present exhibits and deposition testimony at trials or hearings. There are certain applications that you must learn in order to effectively utilize Trial Director. The primary applications needed are:

a. Opening Trial Director
b. Loading and displaying items

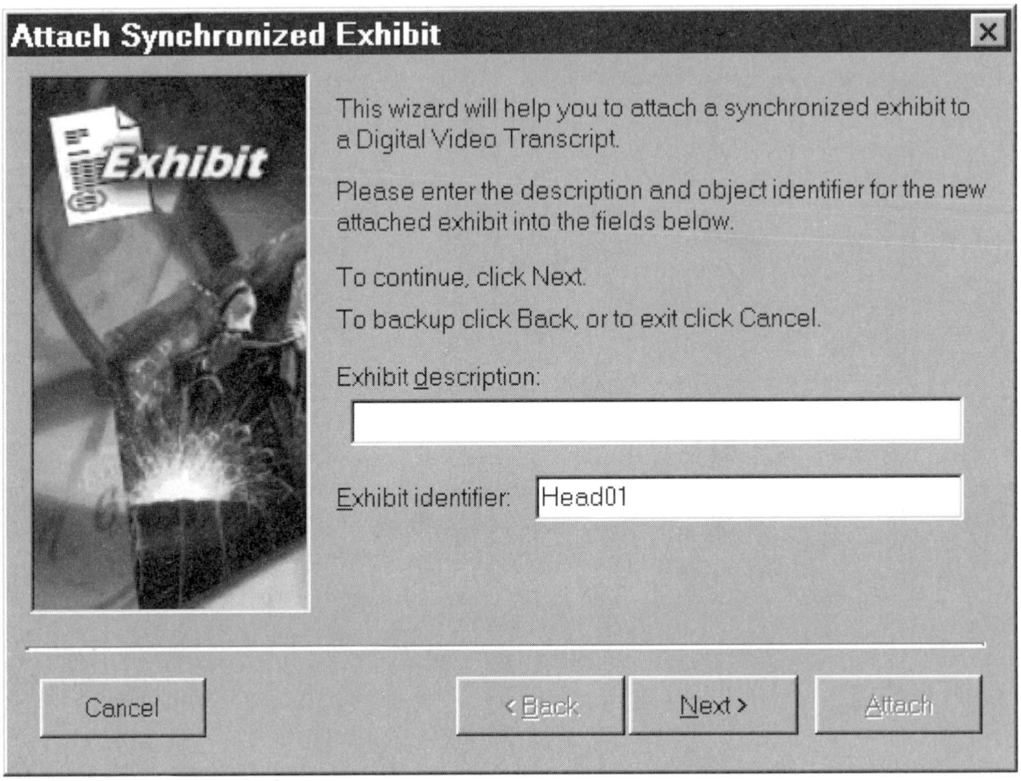

Figure 8.12. Deposition Director—Synchronized Exhibits
© inData Corporation. All rights reserved.

    c. Viewing items
    d. Determining the presentation of items

a. Opening Trial Director

Document Director must be installed if you want to run Trial Director. Trial Director is opened by opening Document Director and clicking the Presentation button or choosing Presentation Display from the View menu.

b. Loading and Displaying Items

Once you are in presentation mode, you need to enter an ID number or scan the barcode to load/display a desired item. Trial Director has nine zones available on the computer presentation screen. All items are automatically inserted into Zone nine which encompasses the entire screen. The final section of this application discussion will explain how to display more than one item on the screen simultaneously.

To display items you can type in the ID number, exhibit number, or trial exhibit number in and select Enter. Macros can also be used to set quick keys for pulling up

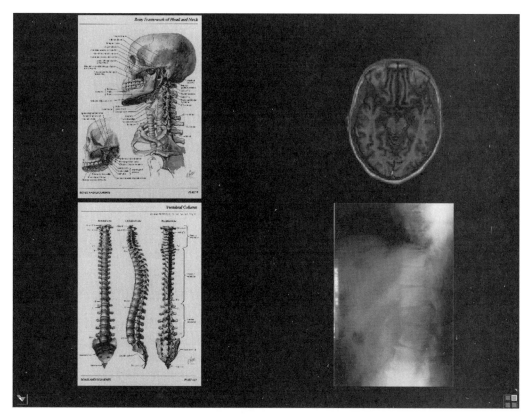

Figure 8.13. Trial Director—Viewing Exhibits

items. A macro is created by entering the letters wanted and then selecting the Control key with the function key you want the macro assigned to. Items can also be pulled up with a bar-code reader. The bar codes are printed out and read with a bar-code reader. Items can also be pulled up by using the presentation palette or a created script. The software user manual explains how to load items using these last two features.

c. Viewing Items

Once items have been loaded/displayed, they can be viewed. Keep in mind that you have available the rubber band zoom feature, as well as the annotations toolbar. These tools allow you to manipulate the view presented to the audience.

d. Determining the Presentation of Items

As indicated above, there are nine zones included within the Trial Director display. This means that up to four items can be displayed simultaneously on the presentation screen. Each zone has a function key: Zone 1 is F1 and so forth up to Zone 9 or F9.

The screen is divided as follows: Zones 1 and 2 split the screen in half vertically. Zones 3 and 4 split the screen in half horizontally. Zones 5 through 8 split the screen in equal fourths. Zone 9 takes up the entire screen.

Depending on how you want items displayed, you select the appropriate function keys. Figure 8.13 is an example of items presented in Zones 5 through 8. The F11 key allows you to add an item to a specific zone. The F10 key allows you to transfer an item into another zone. The F12 key allows you to replace an item in the active zone with a new item.

E. CONCLUSION—inData Director Suite

The inData Director Suite can enable your attorney to increase the amount of influence he or she has on the jury. Further, this type of presentation method increases a jury's retention rate. Unfortunately, not all software applications could be discussed, as the software is complex. You should take the time to become proficient in the use of this software. The best way to gain proficiently with this program is through use. As you are working with the software, experiment with the applications. If you get stumped and have a question, refer to the software user manual. Although most computer manuals are extremely confusing, this manual is fairly easy to follow.

KEY TERMS

Affirmative defense
Answer
Counterclaims
Cross-claims
Default judgment
Defense
Denial defense
Estoppel
Independent medical examination (IME)
Motion

Assumption of risk
Class action lawsuits
Motion for protective order
Motion for summary judgment
Motion to compel discovery
Motion to terminate or limit deposition examination

Compulsory counterclaims
Contributory negligence
Order
Permissive counterclaims
Personal jurisdiction
Service of process
Subject matter jurisdiction
Third-party claims
Tickler system
Venue

TECHNOLOGY TERMS

Animation order box
Custom animations
Graphics
Images

PowerPoint
Presentation mode
Presentation software
Slides

Templates
Text boxes

USEFUL WEBSITES

http://www.findlaw.com   Legal Web site
http://www.indatacorp.com   InData Corporation Web site
http://www.microsoft.com   Microsoft Corporation Web site
http://www.nita.org   National Institute for Trial Advocacy

chapter 9

Special Issues in Managing Complex Litigation

---

chapter objectives

In this chapter, we will discuss

- The issues involved in managing complex litigation
- The difference between multiple party lawsuits and class action lawsuits
- Common problems encountered in complex litigation and how to plan for these problems
- Joinder of additional parties and of additional claims and remedies
- Technology advances that can save time and money in complex litigation cases

For our discussion throughout this chapter, complex litigation includes class action lawsuits and multiple party lawsuits. These types of actions are truly challenging for both the attorney and the paralegal. The purpose of this chapter is to provide paralegals with some helpful hints when working on complex litigation cases.

A. WHAT ARE MULTIPLE PARTY AND CLASS ACTION LAWSUITS?

Multiple party lawsuits are actions involving multiple plaintiffs, multiple defendants, or both. **Class action lawsuits** are actions involving a group of persons, things, qualities or activities, having common characteristics or attributes from which there arises a common legal position against the opposing party. A class action lawsuit is a lawsuit in which several individuals become members of a specific class, filing a lawsuit as that collective class against a party. Recently, the most publicized class action lawsuits include lawsuits filed against the tobacco companies and breast implant manufacturers. Class action lawsuits make it possible for numerous individuals to consolidate their actions into one suit, pooling their resources to obtain a recovery for the entire class. The individuals included within a class must have in common a similar set of legal issues or facts relating to their claims. They also save the court system time and money by combining several similar claims into one lawsuit.

The issues involved in defending a class action lawsuit are discussed in Chapter 8.

B. WHAT CONSTITUTES A COMPLEX LITIGATION CASE?

You are probably wondering what types of cases evolve into what is considered "complex litigation." One good example is portrayed in the *Erin Brockovich* film. In the film, Brockovich worked as a paralegal on a case regarding water contamination. The attorney she worked for represented hundreds of plaintiffs in a civil lawsuit filed against PG&E, a California power company. Of course, this case did not start out huge; but it grew exponentially with time.

What makes complex litigation complex? It is usually the shear number of parties involved, which generates millions of details to investigate and organize. In the PG&E case, Brockovich was responsible for interviewing and obtaining medical information on each plaintiff. It was her job to manage all of the details, and there were plenty of details. A task like this can seem overwhelming, but it can be accomplished with a lot of hard work and a clear case strategy. Everyone has their own way of doing things. This chapter is not intended to tell you how to accomplish tasks as a paralegal, only to provide helpful suggestions.

C. COMMON PROBLEM AREAS IN COMPLEX LITIGATION

There are four main problem areas in complex litigation:

1. Case strategy: the formulation of a strategy to execute a case;
2. Time management: a strategy formulated to efficiently complete a task;
3. Organization: means of prioritizing and categorizing items; and
4. Expenses: costs involved in prosecuting or defending a lawsuit.

1. Case Strategy

Developing a **case strategy** is extremely important when you are dealing with numerous parties. Determining who will accomplish what is the first item that needs to be addressed. If you work for a small law firm, then the majority of the work will be done by you alone. Most small firms include only the attorney and the paralegal. There are pros and cons to working in this type of environment. Fewer employees and resources result in fewer miscommunications. In larger firms, the litigation team can consist of four or more individuals—the partner, the associate, the paralegal, and the secretary. In this case, determining what role each individual will play should be accomplished immediately. The responsible attorney, usually the partner, decides how to delegate all of the tasks necessary. An initial conference needs to be held including all members of the litigation team. This conference should be run by your attorney.

PRACTICE TIP

Offer to arrange the initial litigation team conference. It is always best to have the supervising attorney conduct this meeting. This reduces the number of problems that can occur among team members regarding task delegation and responsibility.

Having an initial case strategy conference accomplishes two things: It establishes a clear understanding of each individual's role in the case and it facilitates open communication between team members. Below is a listing of all the issues that should be addressed during the initial case strategy conference:

- What tasks need to be accomplished?
- Who should accomplish each task?
- What priorities should be assigned to each task?
- What responsibilities does each team member have regarding the case?
- What is the main theory of the case?
- How will the case strategy incorporate this theory?

This is by no means meant to be a complete listing of the items to be addressed at the initial conference, just a suggested topic outline. During the initial conference, if the attorney fails to address any of the items listed above, ask him or her about them.

It is crucial that the litigation team clearly understands the case strategy during complex litigation. The numerous legal and factual issues involved in complex litigation demands a clear case strategy that is stringently adhered to by all members of the litigation team.

2. Time Management

Another problem encountered in complex litigation involves **time management**. Complex litigation is extremely time intensive. Developing and maintaining effective time management skills is crucial to successful case management. As the paralegal, you will have responsibility for more tasks than you believe can be accomplished. Complex litigation involves seemingly impossible deadlines.

Effective time management is not an accident. By adhering to consistent guidelines, you will find that you become a more efficient paralegal while at the same time minimizing stress that is bound to result from poor time management. When it comes to effective time management, always try to adhere to the following guidelines:

a. Plan each day
b. Prioritize tasks by completion date and time
c. Attempt to control distractions and interruptions
d. Allow time to deal with unforeseen events
e. Know your limitations—don't overcommit

a. Plan Each Day

To manage your time efficiently, you must establish a clear plan for each day. One way to accomplish this by creating a to-do list. Be careful not to overspecify items on this to-do list, because this can lead to a lack of flexibility. Instead, create a general outline that affords you the flexibility to add unforeseen tasks as needed.

b. Prioritize Tasks by Completion Date and Time

While you are creating your to-do list for the day, prioritize items by their completion date and time. Obviously, the tasks with the earliest completion dates and time should be placed at the beginning of your list. You should always discuss the priority of tasks with your attorney, as he or she may want certain tasks to take precedence over other tasks. If several attorneys are working on the case, make sure that you let each attorney know the tasks you have been asked to accomplish. If there is a priority conflict regarding various tasks, let the attorneys determine which task takes priority. Communication is always the key to being an effective and efficient paralegal. If the attorneys don't know there is a conflict, they can't address the problem.

c. Attempt to Control Distractions and Interruptions

Distractions and interruptions are something that everyone in the work force must learn to deal with. As a litigation professional, these are daily and sometimes numerous. Open communication with the attorneys and staff you work with is the single best tool to avoid distractions that will disrupt your productivity. By articulating your schedule and pertinent deadlines to coworkers, you can avoid costly interruptions that will prevent you from adhering to your daily plan. Developing skills to control or minimize distractions and interruptions is a necessity to effectively managing your time during complex litigation.

d. Allow Time to Deal with Unforeseen Events

You should never expect that your day will always proceed as planned. There are going to be things that come up that have to be addressed immediately. Realizing this is the key to minimizing your frustration and reducing your stress level. When you plan your day, you should always allow for at least an hour of unforeseen events.

This time allowance will help to prevent missing a deadline or being forced to request an extension.

e. Know Your Limitations—Don't Overcommit

Most dedicated paralegals at one time or another make the mistake of overcommitting themselves. They try to be "super" paralegals and ultimately end up stressed out, producing compromised results, and more often than not missing deadlines.

3. Organization

Another problem encountered in working on complex litigation involves keeping the case organized. As you can imagine, multiple party and class action lawsuits generate a tremendous amount of paper during investigation and discovery. As the paralegal, it will be your responsibility to organize all of the paperwork and ensure that it remains organized. This section of the chapter will provide you with the following suggested tools to facilitate complex case organization:

1. Work rooms: a room created to house all of the case documents
2. Databases: a software application that includes fields, forms, queries, and reports

a. Work Rooms

In larger cases, it is strongly recommended that a work room be created to house all of the documentation. The work room accomplishes two things: It provides one central location for all case documents, and it prevents any litigation team member's office from becoming the store room for case documents.

The paralegal is normally responsible for creating and organizing a work room. When you are creating your work room you need to organize case documents by their document type. For instance all of the pleadings should be stored together, as should all of the discovery documents. You also need to develop and adhere to a document management system. Chapter 5 provides a guide for managing case documents, including a discussion on creating case indexes. A case index should be created and provided to each litigation team member.

The work room must also have an open area for individuals to search for and review documentation. When you set up work rooms, try to arrange the documents around the walls of the room in a "U." This approach leaves the middle of the room open for locating documents.

Case documents should be plainly marked to allow for easy identification. There should also be a case document log kept in the work room. This log allows for the quick location of case documents that have been removed from the work room. All of the litigation team members must utilize this log to prevent documents from turning up in a team member's office where others can't find them.

A good work room can provide the litigation team with quick and easy access to volumes of documents. Establishing and maintaining case document organization reduces the considerable amount of stress that can occur during complex litigation.

b. Databases

Another tool that can be used to assist you in case organization is a database. Creating a database takes several hours; however, it is definitely worth the time when you are working on complex litigation. In complex litigation, one can end up spending hours searching for documents. This time is substantially reduced if you develop and use a database. Thousands of documents can be searched in minutes by date, document type, author, or other criteria. Chapter 5 discusses how to set up a database. Placing a summary of each document in the database is referred to as coding. The paralegal can code the case documents by dictating summaries or typing them in manually. If you are pressed for time to create a searchable database, then you might want to consider hiring a vendor to code the case documents. If a vendor is hired to code documents, make sure he or she knows exactly how you want things done. The vendor should also quality check the coding so that it is error free. A database is useless if it is filled with errors.

4. Expenses

Expenses can elevate out of control in complex litigation, but there are ways to control the expenses incurred. Discovery documents can be scanned onto a CD-ROM. The CD-ROM can then be copied and produced to opposing counsel instead of hardcopies, which can end up costing a small fortune. Also, when documents are being produced by the other side, instead of simply having them copy everything suggest a document inspection date. Document inspection allows for the copying of only the relevant case documents. The only drawback to document inspection is that as the case progresses documents that were not copied could become relevant to the case.

Interviews and depositions can be conducted over the telephone or via videoconferencing, thus eliminating traveling expenses. Keep in mind that opposing counsel needs to consent to an appearance via telephone or videoconference. There may be interviews and depositions that are too important for an appearance by phone or videoconference. These interviews and depositions might require an appearance in person. One drawback of telephone interviews and depositions includes the fact that you or your attorney will not be able to easily assess the witness's credibility.

The cost of hearing and deposition transcripts can potentially be reduced if you choose to simply order a disc copy of the transcript instead of a hardcopy. Many court reporting firms will e-mail you copies of the transcripts, negating any shipping costs. Of course, requesting a transcript in electronic format will be a decision that only your attorney needs to make.

The above suggestions are just some of the ways expenses in complex litigation can be reduced.

D. THINGS TO CONSIDER REGARDING THE JOINDER OF ADDITIONAL PARTIES AND CLAIMS

As complex litigation progresses, there will likely be the need to join claims and remedies and additional parties. Rule 18 of the Federal Rules of Civil Procedure addresses adding claims and remedies. Rule 19 of the Federal Rules of Civil Procedure governs the process involved in joining additional persons.

Rule 19 provides for the joinder of persons as follows:

(a) **Persons to be Joined if Feasible.** *A person who is subject to service of process and whose joinder will not deprive the court of jurisdiction over the subject matter of the action shall be joined as a party in the action if (1) in the person's absence complete relief cannot be accorded among those already parties, or (2) the person claims an interest relating to the subject of the action and is so situated that the disposition of the action in the person's absence may (i) as a practical matter impair or impede the person's ability to protect that interest or (ii) leave any of the persons already parties subject to a substantial risk of incurring double, multiple, or otherwise inconsistent obligations by reason of the claimed interest.* If the person has not been so joined, the court shall order that the person be made a party. If the person should join as a plaintiff but refuses to do so, the person may be made a defendant, or, in a proper case, an involuntary plaintiff. If the joined party objects to venue and joinder of that party would render the venue of the action improper, that party shall be dismissed from the action. (Emphasis added.)

As this rule indicates, a person can be joined as a party when without this person complete relief cannot be afforded among the current parties or when that person's absence impairs his or her ability to protect his or her interest. It further allows for the joinder of a person as a party to reduce the chance that other parties will bear responsibility for that person's interest. However, such a joinder cannot result in the court having lack of jurisdiction or improper venue. Any joinder that violates the stipulations included in Rule 19 can result in a dismissal of the joined party from the action. As a paralegal working on complex litigation, you will likely be the one performing investigative work and reviewing documents. As you are performing your duties, you need to consider if people need to be added to the action. You should then inform your attorney so that he or she can make a decision regarding a possible joinder motion.

Rule 19(b) provides the court with full discretion when joinder of a person is not feasible. Rule 19(c) requires that the pleader of a claim for relief identify all persons known who are not joined as parties but could be under Rule 19(a)(1) and (2). Finally, Rule 19(d) indicates that any joinder under this rule is subject to Rule 23 of the Federal Rules of Civil Procedure, which deals with class action lawsuits.

As indicated above, Rule 18 governs joinder of additional claims and remedies. Rule 18(a) provides for the joinder of as many claims as the party has against an opposing party. Rule 18(b) allows for the joining of two claims if one of the claims can only be understood after the prosecution of the other claim.

The other procedural rules that address joining parties to the lawsuit include Rules 20, 21, and 22. Rule 20 provides for the joining of additional parties if the individuals assert their rights to relief jointly or their rights arise out of the same occurrences. This same rule permits the court to order separate trials, prevent delay, or prevent prejudice. Rule 21 indicates that any misjoinder of a party is not grounds for an action's dismissal.

ETHICS

The same ethical rules apply to complex litigation as to simple litigation. Since complex litigation deals with multiple parties, one ethical concern that may arise involves the identification of all represented parties versus nonparties. The ethical rules of professional conduct do not allow for direct contact with individuals represented by counsel, most commonly referred to as ex parte contact.

As the paralegal assisting with complex litigation, you must clearly identify all parties and nonparties and confirm which of the individuals are represented by counsel to ensure you are not having ex parte contact with anyone. Creating an index that contains each party's name, contact information, attorney name, and contact information can be invaluable. Remember, anything you do as a paralegal reflects on the attorney you are working for, and ultimately your attorney is responsible for your actions. Your job as a paralegal is to make your attorney's job easier, not more difficult.

CONCLUSION

Complex litigation can be overwhelming, but it can also be very rewarding. The complex litigation discussed during the film *Erin Brockovich* resulted in the largest direct action dollar award in U.S. history.

As a paralegal, your role can be vital to the success or failure of the case. To adequately perform your paralegal duties while working on complex litigation, you will need to work with your attorney to establish a clear plan regarding case strategy, time management, organization, and expenses. This approach will definitely increase the odds of obtaining positive results, while decreasing everyone's stress level.

USING TECHNOLOGY IN THE LAW OFFICE

As this chapter discusses, there are several expense-reducing suggestions that involve the use of technology. These suggestions include scanning and writing to CD-ROM all discovery documents, using videoconferencing to reduce travel, and obtaining electronic copies of transcripts.

A. SCANNING FILES ONTO CD-ROM

A **scanner,** a machine developed to take electronic photocopies of documents and photographs, enables you to take a digital picture of whatever documents you run through the scanner. The picture is saved as an **image file,** an electronic file consisting of a photocopy of the original document scanned. Image files are available in a variety of formats: for example, JPG, TIF, and bitmap. JPG files are one of the smallest image files available and TIF files are one of the largest. The TIF files take up more disc space because they save the image at a higher resolution. The JPG files are considerably smaller because they save the image at a much lower resolution. Figure 9.1 demonstrates an example of a scanned document saved as an image file.

Once the images are scanned, named, and saved, they can be transferred onto a CD-ROM with a CD writer. **CD burning** is the process that involves saving information onto a CD-ROM. **CD writers** are hardware developed to electronically place information onto a CD-ROM. If you plan on using image files, then you would be wise to invest in a CD writer, as most image files are too large to be saved on disk. CD writers are relatively inexpensive. Writing the scanned files onto CD-ROM is relatively simple. The CD writer will most likely come with software that walks the individual through a set of wizards when saving the information. Once the CD-ROM has been created, it can only be rewritten if the CD-ROM used is rewritable.

You can also have the scanner "OCR" a document. **OCR** stands for optical character recognition. With this type of scanning, documents can be easily manipulated, changed, or rewritten.

B. VIDEOCONFERENCING

Another technology tool available to save on expenses includes videoconferencing. **Videoconferencing** is a method for facilitating conferences via satellite or land lines. Some businesses have the advanced software for videoconferencing. For example, in Billings, Montana, one of the medical facilities allows people to use its videoconferencing system. Many federal courtrooms include the equipment for videoconferencing. In fact, federal courts will conduct hearings using videoconferencing. Attorneys who normally would have to travel miles for a hearing can now appear before the court through videoconferencing, incurring virtually no expenses.

C. OBTAINING ELECTRONIC COPIES OF TRANSCRIPTS

A final way to reduce expenses in complex litigation is by using electronic copies of the depositions and hearings. Most court reporters have the capability to generate electronic copies of transcripts. Normally these electronic transcripts are less expensive than ordering

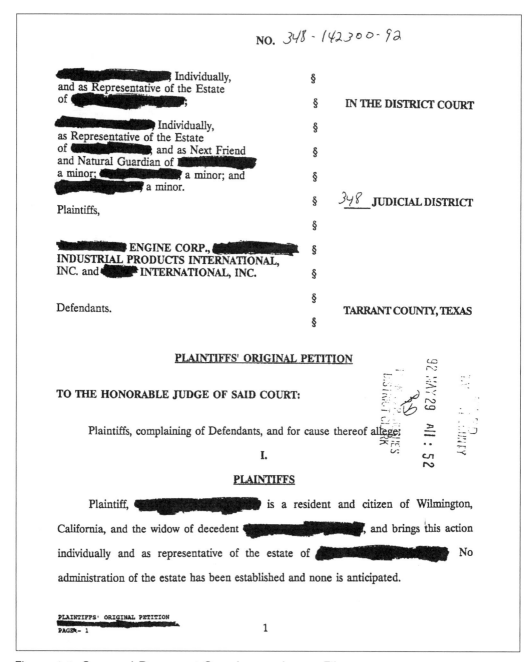

Figure 9.1. Scanned Document Saved as an Image File

hardcopies. Electronic transcripts can be opened in Notepad, Wordpad, Word, and various other programs. Another advantage to electronic transcripts is that they can be word searched.

KEY TERMS

Case strategy	Database	Time management
Class action lawsuits	Multiple party lawsuits	Work rooms

TECHNOLOGY TERMS

CD burning	Image file	Scanner
CD writers	OCR	Videoconferencing

USEFUL WEBSITES

http://www.balancetime.com/   Time Management Tips and Seminars Site
http://www.getmoredone.com/   Time Management Tips and Products
http://www.daytimer.com/content/welcome.asp   Organizer and Time Manager
http://www.palm.com/   Organizer and Time Manager
http://www.handspring.com/   Organizer and Time Manager

chapter 10

Evidence

chapter objectives

In this chapter, we will discuss

- The definition of evidence
- The various types of evidence and the differences between those types
- The Federal Rules of Evidence

This chapter focuses on the topic of evidence. Everything that is done in civil litigation focuses on obtaining and maintaining evidence. In civil litigation, the **burden of proof** requires a party to prove the validity of claimed facts by presenting conclusive evidence. A **burden of proof** is the duty of proving a fact in dispute regarding an issue between the parties. The standard of proof required in most civil lawsuits is a **preponderance of the evidence** where the evidence demonstrates the facts sought to be proven are more probable than not, otherwise known as 51 percent. A case cannot be proven or defended without the admission of evidence.

Assisting your attorney in compiling evidence will definitely be one of your most important duties. To assist your attorney in obtaining evidence, you must first know what materials encompass evidence. Once you know what the court considers to be evidence, then you must learn the limits or rules placed on such evidence. The Federal Rules of Evidence are cited throughout this chapter, affording the paralegal an opportunity to interpret these rules.

Evidence is one of the most complex areas in civil litigation. It is extremely important that you work with your attorney regarding evidentiary questions. You must not only consider all evidentiary rules, but also incorporate statutes, case law, and trial procedures. Normally, when you have answered one evidentiary question, another question will need to be considered. A good paralegal recognizes evidentiary problems and suggests possible solutions.

A. WHAT IS EVIDENCE?

Evidence is any item or fact that can be used to prove or disprove a case. It is any type of proof presented at the trial for the purpose of inducing belief in the minds of the court or jury. Examples of evidence are witnesses, records, documents, exhibits, and concrete objects.

B. TYPES OF EVIDENCE

There are several types of evidence that can be used in the trial of a lawsuit. The following is a listing of the four main types of evidence:

1. **Tangible or physical evidence**—physical evidence which can be touched or seen, for example, documents or weapons.
2. **Demonstrative evidence**—evidence directed to the senses without testimony.
3. **Testimonial evidence**—evidence obtained from a witness;
4. **Character evidence**—evidence describing a person's character.

Each of the above-listed types of evidence have certain limitations placed on them by the court. To perform your duties as paralegal, you must be able to define the different types of evidence and understand their limits. Please keep in mind that all of the types of evidence discussed below will need to adhere to the Hearsay Rule, as well as to accepted trial practices regarding the establishment of foundation for such evidence. Foundation and the hearsay rule are discussed at the end of this chapter.

1. Tangible or Physical Evidence

Tangible or **physical evidence** is evidence that you can see or touch, such as weapons or documents.

In civil litigation, the tangible or physical evidence that you most likely will be working with includes records, documents, and photographs. Rules 1001 to 1008 of the Federal Rules of Evidence govern physical evidence in the form of records. Rule 1002 requires that the original record be provided to the court in order to be admitted as evidence. This rule is commonly referred to as **the best evidence rule.**

> To prove the content of a writing, recording, or photograph, the original writing, recording, or photograph is required, except as otherwise provided in these rules or by Act of Congress.

Rules of Evidence 1004, 1005, and 1007 provide for exceptions to the original record requirement. Rule 1004 provides specific exceptions to the original record requirement:

> The original is not required, and other evidence of the contents of a writing, recording, or photograph is admissible if—

(1) Originals lost or destroyed. All originals are lost or have been destroyed, unless the proponent lost or destroyed them in bad faith; or

(2) Original not obtainable. No original can be obtained by any available judicial process or procedure; or

(3) Original in possession of opponent. At a time when an original was under the control of the party against whom offered, that party was put on notice, by the pleadings or otherwise, that the contents would be a subject of proof at the hearing, and that party does not produce the original at the hearing; or

(4) Collateral matters. The writing, recording, or photograph is not closely related to a controlling issue.

Public records are another exception to Rule 1002. Normally, the original of a public record cannot leave the agency in which it has been filed. The reason for this is fairly obvious: It prevents the originally filed document from being lost, stolen, or altered in any way. Specifically, Rule 1005 provides:

The contents of *an official record,* or of a document authorized to be recorded or filed and actually recorded or filed, including data compilations in any form, if otherwise admissible, *may be proven by copy, certified as correct in accordance with rule 902 or testified to be correct by a witness who has compared it with the original.* If a copy which complies with the foregoing cannot be obtained by the exercise of reasonable diligence, then other evidence of the contents may be given. (Emphasis added.)

a. Certified Copies

As required by Rule 1005, the process to obtain copies of public records involves requesting certified copies from that agency. This task will most likely be yours when it comes time to obtain exhibits for trial. You will need to know what records are considered public record. Any records readily accessible to the public are public records. Public records include those records filed with a court or governmental agency.

PRACTICE TIP

When you request certified copies of public records, it is suggested that you do so in writing. The written request should be sent to the records custodian of the appropriate court or agency. Prior to sending any written request, contact the court or agency custodian by phone to confirm fees for copying and certification. The written request should explain to the custodian the format and content required for the certification statement.

Rule 902 regarding self-authentication requires that certified documents include the following:

(1) **Domestic public documents under seal.** *A document bearing a seal* purporting to be that of the United States, or of any State, district, Commonwealth, territory, or insular possession thereof, or the Panama Canal Zone, or the Trust Territory of the Pacific

Islands, or of a political subdivision, department, officer, or agency thereof, *and a signature purporting to be an attestation or execution.*

(2) Domestic public documents not under seal. *A document purporting to bear the signature in the official capacity of an officer or employee of any entity included in paragraph (1) hereof, having no seal, if a public officer having a seal and having official duties in the district or political subdivision of the officer or employee certifies under seal that the signer has the official capacity and that the signature is genuine. . . .*

(5) Certified copies of public records. *A copy of an official record or report or entry therein, or of a document authorized by law to be recorded or filed and actually recorded or filed in a public office, including data compilations in any form, certified as correct by the custodian or other person authorized to make the certification,* by certificate complying with paragraph (1), (2) or (3) of this rule or complying with any Act of Congress or rule prescribed by the Supreme Court pursuant to statutory authority. (Emphasis added.)

Certified copies, as described in the rules, must be certified by an individual who has the authority to do so. The individual certifying documents must indicate in the certification statement that the copy is a true and correct copy of the original document on file with the agency or court from which you are requesting document certification.

Another exception to Rule 1002 is Rule 1007, which discusses testimony as a means of getting copied records, documents, or photographs admitted as evidence. Rule 1007 states:

Contents of writings, recordings, or photographs may be proved by the testimony or deposition of the party against whom offered or by that party's written admission, without accounting for the nonproduction of the original. (Emphasis added.)

As indicated above, a witness can testify either at trial or during deposition regarding the authenticity of a copied record. Rule 1005 also provides for the admissibility of a copied public record if a witness who has compared the copy with the original testifies regarding the copy's authenticity.

b. Authentication

Tangible or physical evidence is also governed by the rules that encompass authentication and identification. Rule 902 has already been discussed regarding certification. This rule also indicates that evidence of authentication is *not* required for the following documents to be admissible:

- Certified copies of public records
- Official publications
- Newspapers and periodicals
- Trade inscriptions and the like
- Acknowledged documents
- Commercial paper and related documents
- Presumptions under acts of Congress

c. Relevancy

The Rules of Evidence that focus on relevancy (Rules 401 to 415) also must be considered when you have tangible or physical evidence in the form of records, documents, and photographs. Specifically, Rules 402, 403, 407, 408, 409, and 411 could need to be considered when you are dealing with tangible or physical evidence. The court defines **relevant evidence** as evidence that tends to make the existence of any fact more or less probable than it would be without the evidence.

Rule 402 generally states that all relevant evidence is admissible and all irrelevant evidence is inadmissible. Therefore, the paralegal should also make sure that any physical or tangible evidence being used tends to prove or disprove the issues of the case on a more-probable-than-not basis. If the evidence cannot support this test, then it most likely will be objected to by the opposing party and could be deemed inadmissible by a judge.

Rule 403 serves to exclude relevant evidence if it is determined that the proving value of the evidence is outweighed by the possibility of unfair prejudice, confusion of the issues, or misleading of a jury. Proving unfair prejudice, confusion of the issues, or misleading of the jury is a very difficult task not frequently undertaken by an attorney unless absolutely necessary.

Rule 407 governs the admissibility of remedial measures, items that afford a remedy. This rule does not allow evidence regarding remedial measures to be admitted to prove negligence, culpable conduct, a product defect, a product design defect, or a need for a warning or instruction. However, remedial measures are admissible to prove ownership, control, or feasibility of precautionary measures. In other words, if someone slipped and fell on stairs, and after the incident, the owner added handrails to the stairs, the photographs of this change (or remedial measure) would not be admissible to prove negligence, culpable conduct, defective product, defective design, or a need for a warning or instruction. The photographs could be used as evidence to prove ownership, control, or feasible precautions.

This evidentiary rule primarily came about to encourage remedial measures. If remedial measures could be used to prove liability or damages of a party, parties might never correct anything for fear of admitting liability if sued. This rule considers what is in the public's best interest and promotes public safety through the encouragement of continued remedial measures while a party is faced with litigation.

Rule 408 deals with the inadmissibility of evidence regarding compromise and offers to compromise. **Compromise evidence** is evidence pertaining to offers of compromise. This rule states as follows:

> Evidence of (1) furnishing or offering or promising to furnish, or (2) accepting or offering or promising to accept, a valuable consideration in compromising or attempting to compromise a claim which was disputed as to either validity or amount, is not admissible to prove liability for or invalidity of the claim or its amount. Evidence of conduct or statements made in compromise negotiations is likewise not admissible. This rule does not require the exclusion of any evidence otherwise discoverable merely because it is presented in the course of compromise negotiations. This rule also does not require exclusion when the evidence is offered for another purpose, such as proving bias or prejudice of a witness, negativing a contention of undue delay, or proving an effort to obstruct a criminal investigation or prosecution.

Normally, this rule pertains to settlement negotiation between parties. A situation comparable to this involves the client and his or her attorney. If the client is assured that the information disclosed to his lawyer will remain confidential, then the client is more likely to be open and honest with the attorney. If the parties involved in litigation cannot openly negotiate for fear of admitting claim liability, invalidity, or damages, then the chances of resolving the matter decrease substantially. If possible, it is usually in the best interest of both parties to settle their dispute prior to trial.

Rule 408 does not exclude discoverable evidence simply because it was presented during negotiations. Further, Rule 408 does not exclude evidence offered to prove witness bias, negating an undue delay contention, or proving efforts to obstruct prosecution or criminal investigation. These are the exceptions to the inadmissibility of compromise evidence.

The next rule may need to be considered when getting tangible or physical evidence admitted is Rule 409. Rule 409 deals with the payment of medical and other expenses. According to this rule, if you have several medical bills or other expenses that you want admitted into evidence which show payment made by the defendant for plaintiff's injury; then these records cannot be admitted if you intend to use such records to prove the defendant's liability regarding the injury. Normally, medical bills are not used to prove liability. The more common use for getting medical records admitted into evidence involves proving or disproving damages.

Certain types of documents are dealt with specifically by the rules of evidence; these documents include insurance records and written agreements.

i. Insurance Records

Rule 411 specifically addresses the admission of records regarding liability insurance. This rule states:

> Evidence that a person was or was not insured against liability is not admissible upon the issue whether the person acted negligently or otherwise wrongfully.
>
> If liability insurance records are offered for any reason other than proving liability, then they are admissible by the court. This rule is understandable. If liability could be proven simply by the existence of liability insurance, then people may not carry such insurance to protect from an admission of liability.

ii. Written Agreements

Frequently, written agreements are the focus of civil litigation. The parol evidence rule deals specifically with the limitations placed on evidence admitted regarding written agreements. The parol evidence rule can be defined as follows:

> Preservation of written agreements by refusing to permit contracting parties to alter their contract through use of additional oral declarations. This rule does not forbid a resort to parol evidence consistent with matters stated in the writing.

The parol evidence rule generally does not allow the admission of oral agreements that contradict a written agreement between the parties. Preserving the integrity of written agreements is a valid pursuit, especially since most commercial litigation focuses on contract breaches. If oral agreements can invalidate written agreements, then what would be the reason for having written agreements? Not to mention the fact that oral agreements are difficult to authenticate, being merely one party's word against the other.

Tangible or physical evidence is extremely important to proving or disproving a case.

When you are reviewing records or documents in a case, keep in mind the evidentiary rules that govern such records or documents.

There are three areas pertaining to tangible or physical evidence that are not discussed above: establishing foundation, the hearsay rule, and evidentiary privilege. These three topics are discussed later in the chapter. Because foundation, hearsay, and privilege establish limits for all the types of evidence, they are crucial to the admissibility of tangible or physical evidence. A good paralegal will always consider these issues, as well as other pertinent evidentiary rules, while reviewing tangible or physical evidence.

PRACTICE TIP

It can be helpful to keep an internal memorandum for your paralegal file, listing the evidence that influenced you most while reviewing the file documents. This same memorandum includes a column that indicates if the evidence was positive or negative and lists what evidence problems could be faced. This internal memorandum is especially helpful when it comes time to discuss exhibits with the attorney. If the attorney asks you to review case documents, you should be able to identify important case documents and point out potential evidence problems encompassing these documents.

---

2. Demonstrative Evidence

The next type of evidence that you will be working with is demonstrative evidence. **Demonstrative evidence** is evidence directed to the senses without intervention of testimony. In civil litigation, this type of evidence is used to further explain an issue to the jury. Demonstrative exhibits usually involve more than one of the human senses. For example, in a case in which a medical condition is the primary focus, models, diagrams, illustrations, xrays and photographs are used to explain the condition further to a jury. If models are used, then the senses of touch, sound, and sight are employed to teach the jury. If photographs, diagrams, charts, maps, illustrations, and xrays are used, then the senses of sound and sight are employed.

Demonstrative exhibits are very important to the trial of a case because they help to clarify the issues to a jury. The paralegal can be very involved in suggesting what type of demonstrative exhibits should be used at trial. For example, he or she could be provided with a rough idea regarding what the attorney wants to explain and then asked to create a demonstrative exhibit that will adequately explain the topic. It is for this reason that a paralegal must know the limitations of demonstrative exhibits.

One of the attorney's I work with, Bruce Fredrickson, always says "Any admissible evidence can be used to create a demonstrative exhibit." If you keep that general rule of practice in mind, you should not have problems with admissibility. However, there are several evidence rules that need to be considered when creating a demonstrative exhibit. They include but are not limited to the following: 402, 403, 1002, 1003, 1004, and 1006.

Rules 402 and 403 have been previously discussed in this chapter. Both of these rules deal with the issue of relevance. Any demonstrative exhibit created must be based on relevant issues or it could be deemed inadmissible based on Rule 402. Further, pursuant to Rule 403, demonstrative exhibits cannot unfairly prejudice, confuse the issues, or mislead the jury.

Evidentiary Rules 1002, 1003, and 1004 govern the admissibility of records and should be considered when you are pondering the use of photographs as demonstrative exhibits. Rule 1002, as previously discussed, requires that the original photograph be provided to the court for admission into evidence. Rules 1003 and 1004 allow for duplicates or copies of photographs to be admitted into evidence if certain requirements are met regarding the original photograph.

Finally, Rule 1006, which also falls under the records section of the Federal Rules of Evidence, provides admissibility guidelines with regard to summaries. Rule 1006 states the following:

> The *contents of voluminous writings, recordings, or photographs which cannot conveniently be examined in court may be presented in the form of a chart, summary or calculation. The originals or duplicates shall be made available for examination or copying,* or both, by other parties at reasonable time and place. The court may order that they be produced in court. (Emphasis added.)

If you are creating a demonstrative exhibit based on information located in voluminous writings, recordings, or photographs, make sure you have the records readily available for examination. An example of this would include a graph of expenditures generated from Microsoft Excel. Normally such monetary information would be pulled from bank statements and entered into Excel to generate a graph. Rule 1006 provides opposing counsel and the court with the opportunity to examine such bank statements if necessary.

Demonstrative exhibits are one area in which you can utilize both your analytical and creative thinking skills. Ask yourself the following questions when you are creating demonstrative exhibits.

- What are we trying to show the jury?
- What human senses should we employ?
- How do we explain the topic simply?
- What Rules of Evidence will apply?
- How will foundation be established for this exhibit?
- Are there any violations of the hearsay rule or other evidentiary rules?
- How do we deal with any evidentiary violations?

Finally, remember to always keep the demonstrative exhibits simple. If the exhibit gets too busy, it will confuse the jury and distract from the primary issue. The individual who coined the phrase "keep it simple stupid" was very insightful. Human beings too often feel the need to needlessly complicate issues. A demonstrative exhibit that confuses your audience defeats the purpose for its creation.

3. Testimonial Evidence

Another type of evidence you will work with in civil litigation is testimonial evidence. **Testimonial evidence** is evidence obtained from a witness. Testimony is evidence coming from the speaking of a live witness under oath or affirmation in the presence of a tribunal. Testimonial evidence includes recorded interviews, sworn statements, affidavits, declarations, depositions, and trial testimony. Several different types of individuals provide the court with testimonial evidence. The following is a list of the types of testimony that exist:

a. Witness testimony —evidence which comes from an individual who has personal knowledge of the facts and details regarding a particular incident;
b. Lay witness opinion testimony —evidence of what the witness thinks, believes, or infers in regard to facts in dispute, as distinguished from his person knowledge of the facts themselves; and
c. Expert testimony —opinion evidence of some person who possesses special skills or knowledge in some science, profession, or business which is not common to the average man.

a. Witness Testimony

Witness testimony is evidence that comes from an individual who has personal knowledge of the facts and details regarding a particular incident. Rules 601 through 615 of the Federal Rules of Evidence pertain to witnesses. Some of the main items discussed in the witness evidence rules include personal knowledge, witness impeachment, and witness interrogation.

i. Witness Personal Knowledge

Rule 602 requires witnesses to have personal knowledge of the subject matter they are testifying about in order to testify. As a paralegal, it is important to recognize this when you are obtaining statements, declarations, interviews, and affidavits from witnesses. If the witness does not have personal knowledge of the matter, he or she cannot testify. Any statements, declarations, interviews, or affidavits obtained from a witness without personal knowledge are normally inadmissible as evidence.

Witness testimony that adheres to the personal knowledge requirement of Rule 602 is frequently referred to as **direct evidence**, defined as follows:

> Testimonial evidence from a witness who actually saw, heard, or touched the subject of questioning.
> Evidence which establishes and/or proves a fact.

Evidence that fails to comply with the personal knowledge requirement is referred to as **circumstantial evidence,** evidence that does not provide for personal knowledge.

ii. Witness Impeachment

An item that may occur during witness testimony is that of impeachment. **Impeachment** regarding a witness is defined as follows:

> Questioning the integrity and/or credibility of a witness, based upon prior inconsistent statements, bias, character, or contradicting facts.

As indicated above, impeachment of a witness normally occurs as a result of contradicting or inconsistent statements made by the witness. Once the witness contradicts his or her testimony, the witness's credibility can be questioned. Impeachment of a witness stems from the following questions.

- What is the accurate testimony?
- Is the witness being honest?
- How trustworthy is the witness?
- How can you believe anything the witness says if his or her story changes each time he or she testifies?

These are questions a jury will want answers to when listening to witness impeachment evidence. As one would expect, the impeachment process normally results in a jury who has little to no faith in the witness because they view him or her as dishonest.

Rules 607 to 609 pertain specifically to impeachment evidence. Rule 607 indicates who may impeach a witness:

> The credibility of a witness may be attacked by any party, including the party calling the witness.

Rule 608 also deals with impeachment of a witness, discussing evidence regarding a witness's character and conduct. The rule indicates the following:

> **(a) Opinion and reputation evidence of character.** *The credibility of a witness may be attacked or supported by evidence in the form of opinion or reputation,* but subject to these limitations:
> (1) the evidence may refer only to character for truthfulness or untruthfulness, and
> (2) evidence of truthful character is admissible only after the character of the witness for truthfulness has been attacked by opinion or reputation evidence or otherwise.
> **(b) Specific instances of conduct.** *Specific instances of the conduct of a witness, for the purposes of attacking or supporting the witness' credibility, other than conviction of crime as provided in rule 609, may not be proved by extrinsic evidence. They may, however, in the discretion of the court, if probative of truthfulness or untruthfulness, be inquired into on cross-examination of the witness*
> (1) concerning the witness' character for truthfulness or untruthfulness, or
> (2) concerning the character for truthfulness or untruthfulness of another witness as to which character the witness being cross-examined has testified.
> The giving of testimony, whether by an accused or by any other witness, does not operate as a waiver of the accused's or the witness' privilege against self-incrimination when examined with respect to matters which relate only to credibility. (Emphasis added.)

As indicated above, a witness's credibility can be attacked regarding character or conduct. However, this impeachment evidence is limited to a discussion regarding the truthfulness or untruthfulness of such conduct or character.

Rule 608 also indicates that witness character impeachment evidence cannot be obtained through the use of extrinsic evidence, otherwise known as external evidence. For example, extrinsic evidence regarding a contract agreement would include oral statements made by the parties not listed within the written agreement. Normally, extrinsic evidence is considered unreliable because it cannot be placed before the court the way a document or agreement can be. (See the prior discussion regarding the parol evidence rule.) However, as with most evidentiary rules, there is an exception to this exclusion of evidence located within Rule 613.

Rule 613(b) states as follows:

(b) Extrinsic evidence of prior inconsistent statement of witness. Extrinsic evidence of a prior inconsistent statement by a witness is not admissible *unless the witness is afforded an opportunity to explain or deny the same and the opposite party is afforded an opportunity to interrogate the witness thereon, or the interests of justice otherwise require.* This provision does not apply to admissions of a party-opponent as defined in rule 801(d)(2). (Emphasis added.)

Rule 609 discusses the issue of impeachment evidence regarding the witness's conviction of a crime, indicating that if the proving value of admitting conviction evidence outweighs its potential prejudicial effect, then the court shall admit the evidence. Further, if the conviction involved dishonesty or a false statement, it is admissible as impeachment evidence. This rule also provides for a ten-year time limit on the admission of a witness's conviction.

The evidentiary rules discussed above govern impeachment evidence; however, case law and statutes must also be considered. Any decision regarding whether to obtain impeachment evidence from a witness is one that will be made by your attorney. You can always assist your attorney in this area by pointing out any contradictions or inconsistencies you notice in the witness's testimony.

Another paralegal duty that can assist the attorney during witness impeachment involves deposition summaries. Deposition summaries can assist the attorney tremendously because they allow for the quick location of any inconsistencies or contradictions during a witness's direct or cross-examination.

iii. Witness Interrogation

The final main item discussed in the witness portion of the Federal Rules of Evidence includes limitations regarding witness interrogation. Rule 611 provides the court with mode and control over the questioning of a witness. This rule requires that attorneys adhere to the following guidelines when questioning a witness: obtain the truth, avoid unnecessary wasting of time, and protect the witness from harassment or embarrassment. This rule also limits an attorney's cross-examination of a witness to the subject matter discussed during direct examination or to the issue of witness credibility. The attorney is only allowed to inquire into additional matters during cross-examination if the court permits it. The last item this rule limits is the use of leading questions. Primarily, leading questions are only permitted during cross-examination or if the witness is hostile or an adverse party.

The next rule pertaining to witness interrogation is Rule 612, which governs the witness's use of writing to refresh his or her memory during interrogation. Specifically, Rule 612 states:

> Except as otherwise provided in criminal proceedings by Section 3500 of title18, United States Code, *if a witness uses a writing to refresh memory for the purpose of testifying, either—*
> > *(1) while testifying, or*
> > *(2) before testifying, if the court in its discretion determines it is necessary in the interests of justice,*
> > *and adverse party is entitled to have the writing produced at the hearing, to inspect it, to cross-examine the witness thereon, and to introduce in evidence those portions which relate to the testimony of the witness.* If it is claimed that the writing contains matters not related to the subject matter of the testimony the court shall examine the writing in camera, excise any portions not so related, and order delivery of the remainder to the party entitled thereto. Any portion withheld over objections shall be preserved and made available to the appellate court in the event of an appeal. If a writing is not produced or delivered pursuant to order under this rule, the court shall make any order justice requires, except that in criminal cases when the prosecution elects not to comply, the order shall be on striking the testimony or, if the court in its discretion determines that the interests of justice so require, declaring a mistrial. (Emphasis added.)

If your attorney intends to allow a witness to use writings to refresh his or her memory, make sure that prior to the witness's testimony such writings are reviewed by yourself and your attorney. If you recognize some problems with the writings, inform your attorney immediately so that he or she has ample time to deal with any potential problems.

The final set of evidence rules pertaining to witness interrogation includes Rules 614 and 615. Rule 614 allows the court to call, interrogate, and object to any witness. Rule 615 allows the court to exclude witnesses so they cannot hear the testimony of other witnesses. The only exception to this exclusion rule include the following individuals:

> This rule does not authorize exclusion of (1) a party who is a natural person, or (2) an officer or employee of a party which is not a natural person designated as its representative by its attorney, or (3) a person whose presence is shown by a party to be essential to the presentation of the party's cause, or (4) a person authorized by statute to be present.

You will need to check with your attorney those witnesses he or she wants to exclude prior to trial. You will also want to discuss which witnesses will serve as the party representative and which witnesses will be essential to presenting the case, especially since the opposing party may seek to exclude the witnesses that your attorney prefers watch testimony.

b. Lay Witness—Opinion Testimony

Lay witness opinion testimony is another type of testimonial evidence.

Normally, lay witnesses are not permitted to testify regarding opinions or conclusions. The ability to provide opinion testimony usually is provided only to experts. However,

Rule 701 of the Federal Rules of Evidence provides for lay witness opinion testimony as follows:

> If the witness is not testifying as an expert, the witness' testimony in the form of opinions or inferences is limited to those *opinions or inferences which are (a) rationally based on the perception of the witness and (b) helpful to a clear understanding of the witness' testimony or the determination of a fact in issue, and (c) not based on scientific, technical, or other specialized knowledge within the scope of Rule 702.* (Emphasis added.)

One example of a lay witness providing opinion testimony would include the testimony of a investigative police officer (not designated as an expert) providing an opinion as to the cause of a motor vehicle accident. This type of testimony would be allowed under subdivision (a) of Rule 701. This rule attempts to encourage the receipt of accurate information regarding the event being disputed. Recently, subdivision (c) of this rule was added to substantially limit lay witness testimony. Several corporations began using employees to provide expert testimony, referring to it as lay witness testimony. This subdivision narrows the spectrum of testimony a lay witness can provide.

Rule 704(a) provides limits on the objections that can be asserted regarding opinion testimony. Essentially, this rule indicates that opinion testimony is not objectionable because it "embraces an ultimate issue to be decided by the trier of fact." This rule focuses on providing the trier of fact with all opinion testimony that is helpful.

In addition to the specific rules discussed above, lay witness opinion testimony must adhere to the rules of evidence pertaining to witnesses, relevancy, privilege, hearsay, and foundation. If you have referred to these rules and still have questions, you should discuss such questions with your attorney. Keep in mind that statutes and case law may place additional limitations on lay witnesses providing opinion testimony.

c. Expert Testimony

Expert testimony is the final type of witness testimony to be discussed in this chapter.

Rules 701 through 706 discuss the limitations placed on opinion and expert testimony. Rule 701 was previously discussed in connection to lay witness opinion testimony. Testimony by experts is provided for in Rule 702 as follows:

> If scientific, technical, or other specialized knowledge will assist the trier of fact to understand the evidence or to determine a fact in issue, a witness qualified as an expert by knowledge, skill, experience, training, or education may testify thereto in the form of an opinion or otherwise.

As indicated above, expert testimony is allowed if it serves to assist a jury or judge in understanding the evidence or determining a disputed fact. Expert testimony is crucial to most civil litigation, and the rules of evidence governing it should be carefully considered.

Rule 703 provides three ways for an expert to base his or her opinion. The first is through the expert's personal observations. For example, a treating physician could base an opinion on observing the patient and his or her chart. The second acceptable basis for an expert's opinion is through observing testimony at the hearing or trial. The third basis accepted is if the expert's opinion is based on facts or data reasonably relied on by experts in the field. For instance, an expert physician who did not treat the plaintiff can review the medical records and xrays to determine his or her medical opinions based on these records. Rule 703 further indicates that when an expert relies on facts or data, this data do not need to be admitted into evidence; the expert's direct testimony subject to cross-examination should be sufficient. However, you should keep in mind that production of such facts or data can be requested during cross-examination.

The pertinent section of Rule 704 was previously discussed in the lay witness opinion testimony section. This rule is also applicable to expert witness testimony.

Rule 705 allows the expert to testify regarding his or her opinion prior to any testimony about underlying facts or data. Any exception to this would require the court's intervention. As mentioned above, Rule 705 provides for the production of facts and data on request during cross-examination.

The final evidence rule pertaining to expert testimony is Rule 706. Rule 706 allows for court appointment of an expert, reasonable compensation for the expert, disclosure to the jury regarding any court appointment, and parties' selection of their own expert.

Once again, the additional evidence rules governing witnesses, relevancy, privilege, hearsay, and foundation must be considered regarding expert testimony.

4. Character Evidence

The final type of evidence we are going to discuss in this chapter is character evidence. This type of evidence is

Evidence describing a person's character.

Rule 404 discusses the admissibility of character evidence. Pursuant to this rule, character evidence is not admissible; however, there is the following pertinent exception regarding evidence of the character of a witness:

(a) **Character evidence generally.** Evidence of a person's character or a trait of character is not admissible for the purpose of providing action in conformity therewith on a particular occasion, *except:* . . .
(3) **Character of witness.** *Evidence of character of a witness, as provided in rules 607, 608, and 609.* (Emphasis added.)

Rules 607 through 609 are the rules of evidence pertaining to impeachment. These rules were previously discussed above in the section regarding testimonial evidence. If your attorney is considering presenting character evidence, the impeachment rules should be thoroughly reviewed.

The other rule that discusses character evidence is Rule 405, which provides the methods for proving character evidence. This rule states as follows:

(a) **Reputation or opinion.** In all cases in which evidence of character or a trait of character of a person is admissible, *proof may be made by testimony as to reputation or by testimony in the form of an opinion.* On cross-examination, inquiry is allowable into relevant specific instances of conduct.
(b) **Specific instances of conduct.** *In cases in which character or a trait of character of*

a person is an essential element of a charge, claim, or defense, proof may also be made of specific instances of that person's conduct. (Emphasis added.)

As the rules indicates, you must keep in mind that character evidence is proven by opinion testimony; therefore, any opinion testimony must adhere to the evidentiary rules regarding opinion-expert testimony and witnesses. Also, if the attorney you are working with wants to present character evidence involving a specific instance, such evidence must be an essential element of the case.

Most character evidence is inadmissible and will be strongly objected to by the opposing party. A strong argument will need to be made to get character evidence admitted regarding a witness. If you are going to suggest the admission of character evidence to your attorney, make sure you are able to adhere to the above-referenced evidentiary rules.

C. OTHER RULES OF EVIDENCE

There are certain rules of evidence and issues that must always be considered in getting the types of evidence discussed above admitted into evidence. Three evidentiary considerations that always must be evaluated are:
1. The hearsay rule
2. establishing foundation
3. Privilege

> **The Hearsay Rule** is rule making most hearsay evidence in admissible.
> **Foundation** is the identification of evidence sought to be admitted and connecting this evidence with case issues.
> **Privilege** is a particular benefit or advantage enjoyed by a person, company, or class.

1. Hearsay Rule

To discuss the Hearsay Rule, we must understand what evidence constitutes hearsay. Hearsay is a statement made by someone besides the declarant offered into evidence to prove the truth of the matter. Rule 801(c) of the Federal Rules of Evidence defines hearsay as follows:

> "Hearsay" is a statement, other than one made by the declarant while testifying at the trial or hearing, offered in evidence to prove the truth of the matter asserted.

The main weakness of any hearsay evidence is that it is not derived from personal knowledge. Such evidence is based on secondhand information that cannot be proven reliable. Gossip is an example of hearsay. Documentary evidence can be considered hearsay if the witness testifying about the document is not the author of such document. Handwriting on a document can also be considered hearsay if the author is not present to testify about it.

When I was in school, one of my professors had us perform an exercise during class.

He whispered a statement to one of the students and then asked that student to provide the information to the next student until the information had been circulated to everyone in the room. The professor then asked us to write down the information and provide it to him. This resulted in the professor's receipt of several different versions of the information, none of which exactly matched the original information provided. The professor then looked at all of us and said, "Now you understand the reason for the hearsay rule."

Rule 802 is the **hearsay rule** and it states the following:

> *Hearsay is not admissible except as provided by these rules or by other rules prescribed by the Supreme Court* pursuant to statutory authority or by Act of Congress. (Emphasis added.)

As with most evidentiary rules, the hearsay rule has several exceptions. We will only discuss the exceptions provided in the Federal Rules of Evidence. You will need to consult with the attorney you work with for any additional exceptions.

Rule 801(d)(1) provides a description of which statements are *not* hearsay:

> **(d) Statements which are not hearsay.** A statement is not hearsay if—
>
> **(1) Prior statement by witness.** The declarant testifies at the trial or hearing and is subject to cross-examination concerning the statement, and the statement is (A) inconsistent with the declarant's testimony, and was given under oath subject to the penalty of perjury at a trial, hearing, or other proceeding, or in a deposition, or (B) consistent with the declarant's testimony and if offered to rebut an express or implied charge against the declarant of recent fabrication or improper influence or motive, *or (C)* one of identification or a person made after perceiving the person; or
>
> **(2) Admission by party-opponent.** The statement is offered against a party and is (A) the party's own statement, in either an individual or a representative capacity or (B) a statement of which the party has manifested an adoption or belief in the truth, *or (C)* a statement by a person authorized by the party to make a statement concerning the subject, *or (D)* a statement by the party's agent or servant concerning a matter within the scope of the agency or employment, made during the existence of the relationship, *or (E)* a statement by a coconspirator of a party during the course and in futherance of the conspiracy. The contents of the statement shall be considered but are not alone sufficient to establish the declarant's authority under subdivision (C), the agency or employment relationship and scope thereof under subdivision (D), or the existence of the conspiracy and the participation therein of the declarant and the party against whom the statement is offered under subdivision (E). (Emphasis added.)

If you are considering presenting a statement at trial, but the individual who gave the statement cannot be present to testify, you should review Rule 801(d)(2) and consult with your attorney regarding any admissibility problems.

Rules 803 and 804 provide the additional exceptions to the hearsay rule. If the hearsay evidence you are proposing for admission is included within the following list, you should refer to Rules 803 and 804 for the hearsay exception:

1. Statement of declarant's present sense impression
2. Statement relating to a startling event or condition
3. Statement of declarant's existing state of mind, emotion, sensation, or physical condition
4. Statements for purposes of medical diagnosis or treatment
5. Recorded recollection
6. Records of regularly conducted activity
7. Absence of entry in records
8. Public records and reports
9. Records of vital statistics
10. Absence of public record or entry
11. Records of religious organizations
12. Marriage, baptismal, and similar certificates
13. Family records
14. Records of documents affecting an interest in property
15. Statements in documents affecting an interest in property
16. Statements in ancient documents
17. Market reports, commercial publications
18. Learned treatises
19. Reputation concerning personal or family history
20. Reputation concerning boundaries or general history
21. Reputation as to character
22. Judgment of previous conviction
23. Judgment as to personal, family, or general history, or boundaries
24. Former testimony
25. Statement under belief of impending death
26. Statement against interest
27. Statement of personal or family history
28. Forfeiture by wrongdoing

Rule 805 provides for the admission of hearsay included within hearsay as long as each part of the statement conforms to an exception of the hearsay rule.

Rule 806 pertains to attacks on the declarant's credibility, stating:

> *When a hearsay statement,* or a statement defined in Rule 801(d)(2)(C), (D), or (E), *has been admitted in evidence, the credibility of the declarant may be attacked, and if attacked may be supported, by any evidence which would be admissible for those purposes if declarant had testified as a witness.* Evidence of a statement or conduct by the declarant at any time, inconsistent with the declarant's hearsay statement is not subject to any requirement that the declarant may have been afforded an opportunity to deny or explain. If the party against whom a hearsay statement has been admitted calls the declarant as a witness, the party is entitled to examine the declarant on the statement as if under cross-examination. (Emphasis added.)

This rule provides the opposing party with an opportunity to question the credibility of a declarant, when that declarant provides a hearsay statement that is admitted into evidence.

The final evidence rule pertaining to hearsay is Rule 807. This rule indicates that a statement with equal circumstance to Rules 803 and 804 but not covered in these rules, will not be excluded by the hearsay rule if:

1. The statement is offered as a material fact
2. The statement more proves its point than any other evidence that can be reasonably obtained
3. The purpose of the rules and the interests of justice are served by admitting such evidence

The hearsay rule is complicated. Remember, any evidence that fails to satisfy the personal knowledge requirement could fall into the category of hearsay. Hearsay issues are not limited to testimonial evidence. Documentary evidence can be considered hearsay if the author is not present to testify. A paralegal needs to always consider this evidentiary rule when talking with witnesses and reviewing documents.

2. Establishing Foundation

Another primary consideration regarding evidence is establishing **foundation** for the evidence's admission. Whenever you are evaluating potential evidence for trial, you should consider how the attorney will establish foundation for such evidence. The attorney is required by the court to ask questions that lay the foundation for getting evidence admitted. These questions are discussed in Rule 104:

(a) **Questions of admissibility generally.** Preliminary questions concerning the qualification of a person to be a witness, the existence of a privilege, or the admissibility of evidence shall be determined by the court, subject to the provisions of subdivision (b). *In making its determination it is not bound by the rules of evidence except those with respect to privileges.*

(b) **Relevancy conditioned on fact.** *When the relevancy of evidence depends upon the fulfillment of a condition of fact, the court shall admit it upon, or subject to, the introduction of evidence sufficient to support a finding of fulfillment of the condition.* (Emphasis added.)

As the above rule indicates, the court is responsible for determining the admissibility of evidence. Further, the court is not bound by the rules of evidence (except the rules regarding privilege) in making its admissibility determination. It is for this reason that the attorney places so much importance on the establishment of foundation. The attorney has to be able to persuade the court that appropriate foundation exists to admit the evidence presented. All questions regarding the completeness, authenticity, reliability, and accuracy of the proposed evidence need to be addressed by the attorney presenting such evidence.

Your role as a paralegal is to consider how foundation will be established for any evidence you feel should be presented at trial or hearing. If you believe that a document is critical to the case, before you suggest that it be used as an exhibit you should consider ways to establish its foundation.

PRACTICE TIP

Ask yourself the following questions with regard to foundation.

1. Is the information authentic, complete, reliable, and accurate?
2. If yes, then who can testify to such authenticity, reliability, and accuracy?
3. What authority does this person have? What qualifies them to provide such testimony?
4. If the exhibit is demonstrative, is the information used in generating it based on evidence previously admitted?
5. Will opposing counsel stipulate to the evidence's admission prior to trial?

These questions will help you to provide your attorney with suggestions on laying foundation.

Evidence that fails to establish foundation most likely will be rendered inadmissible by the court. You are not assisting your attorney if you continually suggest evidence that has no foundation to support it.

One example of a foundation issue could occur during the admission of a medical chart. Frequently, a physician's medical chart is obtained informally through the use of a release. The paralegal submits a written request for a complete copy of the medical chart, providing the signed release. The records are then copied and mailed to the paralegal. Unfortunately, this approach can be questioned by opposing counsel because it is unknown if the medical chart obtained is complete. One way to avoid this foundation problem is to obtain medical records through a records deposition. During this process, the medical records custodian is required to swear under oath that the copied records provided constitute a complete copy of the medical chart. Further, at the records deposition the copied chart can be compared with the original for completeness. Records obtained in this manner cannot be questioned as to completeness by opposing counsel. Foundation has been established for the medical chart during the discovery process and will not need to be addressed at trial.

Foundation issues are numerous and not every possible scenario can be addressed in this textbook. The technology section of this chapter will discuss additional foundation questions that need to be addressed when utilizing computer presentations and animations, as well as digitized documents, photographs, and video.

3. Privilege

The final evidence issue that must be considered when getting all types of evidence admitted is that of **privilege**. Rule 501 provides as follows:

> Except as otherwise required by the Constitution of the United States or provided by Act of Congress or in rules prescribed by the Supreme Court pursuant to statutory authority, *the privilege of a witness, person, government, State, or political subdivision thereof shall be governed by the principles of the common law as they may be interpreted by the courts of*

the United States in the light of reason and experience. However, in civil actions and proceedings, with respect to an element of a claim or defense as to which State law supplies the rule of decision, the privilege of a witness, person, government, State, or political subdivision thereof shall be determined in accordance with State law. (Emphasis added.)

As indicated above, the evidentiary privileges afforded are governed by either statute or case law. This rule provides states with the authority to determine privilege. Some examples of privileged evidence include governmental secrets or records, informant identity, grand jury proceedings, specific accident reports, and attorney's work product. Statements made by people in a protected relationship, including but not limited to, husband-wife, attorney-client, and physician-patient, are considered privileged. If the witness has information regarding statements that occurred within a privileged relationship, the law provides that witness protection from any forced disclosure. For additional privileges available, consult with your attorney and review state statutes and case law. The paralegal should always consider any potential privilege when evaluating evidence.

ETHICS

In this section we will discuss two main ethical considerations with regard to evidence: accurately portraying evidence and obtaining all the necessary evidence.

A. ACCURATELY PORTRAYING EVIDENCE

As we have discussed above, you will work with several different types of evidence. One of your duties will include determining how to present such evidence. Ethically you must always remember that you can only present what you have. You must never alter the evidence you are presenting. Remember: "The case is what it is." Presenting evidence in a way that misleads the jury or judge is unethical and likely will result in sanctions against your attorney. Always make sure that the evidence you are presenting is true and accurate to the best of your knowledge.

Further, if you find out that evidence you originally believed to be true and accurate is not, then you must notify your attorney immediately.

I received a lesson about the ethical use of evidence early on in my career. I was working on a medical malpractice trial with Attorney Ron Mullin. Ron represented the plaintiff regarding his claimed drug-induced aggravation of a disease. The plaintiff claimed that he had never been prescribed the drug in question prior to this incident. On the third day of trial, the defense showed a chart listing all of the medications the plaintiff had taken during the time period in question. Their argument was, "How do you know this particular drug caused plaintiff's injuries? Look at all of the other medications he was already taking." Understandably, this argument upset the plaintiff. He informed Ron that he would bring in all of his prescription bottles for the last several years to demonstrate that the defendant's chart was inaccurate. The next morning plaintiff provided us with a bag of prescription bottles. When Ron and I went through them, we discovered that the plaintiff had in fact received a prescription for the drug in question over a year prior to the date claimed in the complaint. The plaintiff had been prescribed this drug previously with no adverse side effects. This evidence destroyed any causation claims we were making. At this time, Ron had a decision to make.

The trial was going well for us, and we were to receive a favorable ruling. As you would expect, the client was opposed to revealing this newly discovered evidence. Should Ron reveal this evidence? Well, this decision didn't take Ron long to make. Ron knew what to do. Being the Christian that he is, he immediately requested a meeting with opposing counsel and the judge, providing them with the prescription bottle. Needless to say, we lost the case. Afterwards Ron said to me, "I may have lost the case, but I can sleep with myself at night."

When you compromise your values and ethics, you lose yourself. The objective in any legal proceeding should be to find the truth, even if the truth may not be what you want to hear.

B. OBTAINING ALL THE NECESSARY EVIDENCE

The other ethical issue that can spring up occurs when you are obtaining evidence. You must always conduct yourself in a professional and ethical manner. There are occasions when identifying yourself will prevent you from obtaining the evidence you need. Most people will avoid talking with anyone from a law office. However, there is almost always a formal method for obtaining this information if the individuals you are dealing with refuse to cooperate. Always identify yourself to individuals you are interviewing. Never be deceptive to obtain information.

CONCLUSION

Evidence is one of the most important elements to any civil lawsuit. A good paralegal should know the types of evidence and understand the rules governing this evidence, so as to provide adequate assistance to the attorney. The paralegal has an opportunity early on to review all pertinent documents and interview witnesses. The tasks he or she performs require that she understand how to obtain admissible evidence. Many times evidentiary problems can be avoided if you understand the rules of evidence. This is an area of civil litigation that is extremely complicated, but it can be learned. A paralegal with a strong grasp of evidentiary concepts is invaluable to his or her attorney.

USING TECHNOLOGY IN THE LAW OFFICE

The technology available in today's world affords attorneys and paralegals the tools to present evidence in new and exciting ways. There are software programs that allow the presentation and graphic enhancement of exhibits electronically. Chapter 8 discusses two software programs that can be used during hearings and trials — Microsoft PowerPoint and Trial Director. These programs allow scanned documents, audio/video files, and graphic exhibits to be presented in digital format on the computer. This new way of presenting exhibits is exciting, but it is also a source of evidentiary worry for the attorney. A good paralegal will consider the evidentiary pitfalls of *digital evidence* and suggest approaches to obtaining admissibility.

The main concern most attorneys have when it comes to using digital evidence is **foundation** and **authenticity.** How do they convince the court that the evidence presented is accurate and has not been tampered with? How do they assure the court that the scanned images are identical to the original? The paralegal needs to assist in addressing these issues before trial to avoid any admissibility problems.

One way to deal with admissibility problems regarding digital evidence is to stipulate with opposing counsel prior to trial. Objections to exhibits are normally submitted several weeks prior to trial. Oftentimes opposing counsel will not object to the admissibility of digital evidence, especially if they plan to utilize similar evidence. If an agreement can be reached prior to trial regarding digital evidence, then you know beforehand that admissibility is not a problem.

If opposing counsel objects to your digital evidence, you will need to establish **foundation** and **authenticity** of this evidence. When it comes to scanned images, the best way to address this issue is through testimony. If you have an outside vendor provide scanning services for your office, this vendor can testify as to the authenticity of the scanned documents and photographs. This same individual should be able to testify regarding the scanning program used, explaining how the software functions and professing to its reliability. An outside vendor's testimony during trial is much more persuasive than a law office employee's. Another option when providing proof of authenticity would be through the witness who authored the document or took the photograph. This individual could testify that the digital version of a document or photograph is an accurate representation of the original.

Another example of digital evidence includes **digital video transcript,** a videotaped transcript placed in digital format, and digital video. A digital video transcript is a deponent's videotaped deposition that has been linked with the written deposition transcript. This evidence is normally fairly easy to get admitted into evidence, as the court reporter certifies the written transcript and the videographer certifies the video. As you saw in Chapter 8, the deposition transcript is shown next to the video, scrolling while the person speaks. Any inaccuracy in this testimony should appear during the presentation of such linked testimony. Nonetheless, opposing counsel could question the accuracy of the software program and the synchronization process. **Synchronizing video deposition,** video transcripts that have been electronically synchronized to tract with the written transcript, is normally done through an outside vendor, as the equipment is extremely expensive. If necessary, you could always call this vendor to testify regarding authenticity and foundation.

Any evidentiary questions regarding digital video can be addressed through the above-mentioned methods. The person who recorded the video could also be called to testify to establish authenticity and foundation.

The final digital evidence that may be presented includes digital charts and graphs and **computer animations,** computer-generated video illustrations of an activity or an event. These exhibits are considered demonstrative and will require witness testimony to establish authenticity and foundation. The individual creating the chart, graph, or computer animation will need to be present to testify. This individual must be able to explain how the exhibit was created. He or she may also need to explain how the software functions and provide evidence supporting its reliability. Currently, computer animations are not used frequently because they are expensive and difficult to get admitted into evidence. However, if you can get a computer animation admitted into evidence, it potentially could influence a jury to your client's benefit.

When you are creating digital exhibits, make sure to always consider the foundation and authenticity issues so that such exhibits are not deemed inadmissible by the court. You should not be afraid to present digital evidence at trial. Technology is simply another tool that can be used to influence a jury at trial.

KEY TERMS

Best evidence rule
Burden of proof
Character evidence
Circumstantial evidence
Compromise evidence
Demonstrative evidence
Direct evidence

Evidence
Foundation
Hearsay rule
Impeachment
Parol evidence rule
Preponderance of the evidence

Privilege
Relevant evidence
Tangible or physical evidence
Testimonial evidence

TECHNOLOGY TERMS

Computer animations
Digital evidence
Digital video transcript

Synchronizing video deposition

USEFUL WEB SITES

http://www.access.gpo.gov/nara/cfr/cfr-table-search.html   Code of Federal Regulations
http://www.law.cornell.edu/rules/fre/overview.html   Federal Rules of Evidence
http://www.ilrg.com   Internet Legal Resources Guide

chapter **11**

Settlement, ADR, and Mediation

chapter objectives

In this chapter, we will discuss

- The purposes of litigation
- Alternative dispute resolution
- Different methods of alternative dispute resolution, including settlement and negotiation, arbitration, medication, minitrials, and summary judgment/jury trials
- Ethical issues in alternative dispute resolution situations
- How software can help prepare effective settlement brochures

A. OVERVIEW AND PURPOSE OF LITIGATION

> *Discourage Litigation. Persuade your neighbors to compromise whenever you can. Point out to them how the nominal winner is often a real loser in fees, expenses and waste of time.* —*Abraham Lincoln, 1850*

The purpose of litigation is to resolve disputes, the disputes that arise when there is a perceived difference in the interests of the parties involved. If one person, individual, or company (traditionally referred to as the "parties") believes that his or her interests are not identical to those of the others, there will be a dispute. Certainly this perceived difference in interest can arise in any situation and oftentimes stems from a misunderstanding. The best way to prevent disputes from arising is to make sure that each party knows what the other party wants and to obtain in writing any agreements between the parties. Practically speaking, written agreements are not always obtained, and many parties do not take the time to understand the wants and needs of the opposing party. Therefore, raising each party's knowledge about the other lowers the chance of a dispute arising because of a misunderstanding. Also, when common business practices universally accepted are utilized, the potential for misunderstanding and disputes are reduced dramatically.

There are many reasons for disputes to arise. They can happen when the parties don't know each other well, don't understand the facts, are engaging in new forms of business, or come from different cultures. Disputes that do arise can be resolved in any number of ways:

1. The parties can agree to a compromise.
2. The parties can submit the dispute to an impartial person or panel.
3. The perceptions of one or more parties can change, so that there is no longer a perceived difference in interests.
4. The interests of one or more parties can change, so that there is no longer a difference in interests.

There are three *independent* fundamental factors that affect the resolution of disputes: the interests of the parties, the power they have, and the rights they have. Interests are defined by a party in a situation and are the things that party is concerned over, for example, money, recognition, or physical goods. Power is given by a combination of external circumstances and perceived position. Rights are given by an external circumstances such as rules, regulations, or statutes. Either rights or power may be given up to satisfy an interest; conversely, to satisfy an interest may require giving up rights or power: For example, authors whose interests are financial rewards typically give up their copyright rights to a publisher. Thus there are connections between interests, power, and rights, and in real life there are usually trade-offs between them.

B. METHODS OF ALTERNATIVE DISPUTE RESOLUTION

Alternative dispute resolution(ADR) is a means of settling disputes outside of a courtroom. The various types of ADR are explained in the following paragraphs.

1. Settlement and negotiation: Settlement conferences are simple evaluative meetings in which a neutral third party reviews the case with the parties, enters into discussion of the issues, and suggests a settlement number or range. Settlement conferences can also be informal between attorneys with or without the parties present.

Negotiation is the process of submitting and considering offers until an acceptable offer is proposed and agreed to. Negotiation is a process of reviewing the strengths and weaknesses of both sides and is a method of dispute resolution based on perceptions of advantages or disadvantages.

2. Arbitration: Arbitration is the process of dispute resolution where a neutral third party renders a decision after a hearing in which both parties have presented their case. Arbitration can be binding or nonbinding.

3. Mediation: Mediation is an informal dispute resolution process where a neutral third party helps the disputing parties reach an agreement. A mediator helps settle the dispute. The mediator looks for some common ground to bring the parties to a understanding.

4. Minitrials: A minitrial is a nonbinding trial wherein counsel present a summary of the issues and evidence to a jury. Minitrials are a structured process in which the parties voluntarily submit their case to an expert in the area at issue, not a judge.

5. Summary judgment/jury trial: A summary judgment trial is also a nonbinding trial wherein counsel present a summary of the issues and evidence to a jury. Summary judgment trials are highly structured processes in which a private jury pool is assembled to hear the case. A neutral party sets up and presides over the process and oversees a mediation/negotiation period following the proceedings to obtain agreement.

Let's take a look at those various broad categories of ADR more closely. Obviously, the process of resolving a dispute through litigation can be a long, stressful, draining, and costly experience. There are, fortunately, these other methods available for resolving disputes, as seen above. Very often, the best alternative to any lawsuit is negotiation. When you think about it, each of us negotiates every day, whether we negotiate the terms of a business contract, haggle over the price paid for a product, or decide which movie to see with friends. When a dispute arises, direct negotiation between parties either with or without a neutral third party more often than not leads to a resolution. In negotiation or settlement, each side perceives that they retain control over the process and the outcome.

But what if the dispute cannot be resolved by direct negotiation? What alternatives are available? The primary forms of ADR used today are the following:

- Arbitration
- Mediation
- Summary judgment trial
- Abbreviated or minitrials

In today's legal arena, only a very small percentage of lawsuits are decided by jury trial (1.2 percent according to the National Center for State Courts), and more and more individuals, companies and corporations now turn to ADR methodologies to settle their differences. ADR is experiencing rapid growth because it offers numerous key benefits over litigation. ADR is universally applicable, resolves case quickly, is economical, less adversarial, private, less disruptive, and can be binding or nonbinding. Taking each benefit separately, we see:

1. Universal applicability. ADR can be used for any type of case from the multimillion dollar dispute to the smallest employment claim. It can be applicable in any area—employment, labor, contracts, business, or a variety of other areas.
2. Cases resolve more quickly. ADR resolves cases faster than the litigation process does. There are no delays due to overburdened court systems. Almost as soon as the dispute arises, the ADR process can commence. In the litigation process, it can take years to get the dispute to the courtroom.
3. Economical. The lengthy, expensive, and time-consuming process of discovery is curtailed or eliminated; there is no need for pretrial motion practice; there is little or no expert witness expenses; and, attorneys' fees and related costs are reduced.
4. Less adversarial atmosphere. ADR creates a less adversarial atmosphere than the litigation process. This less adversarial process oftentimes allows companies to maintain equitable relationships with each other into the future.

5. Private proceedings. ADR is a private proceeding as opposed to the highly public courtroom drama. Issues won't be publicized or blown up in the media. (However, remember that some arbitration awards are made public.)
6. Less disruptive. ADR is certainly less disruptive of the lives of the parties involved. There is no need for depositions, file searches, interrogatories, and other legal discovery.
7. May be nonbinding. With the use of mediation, nonbinding arbitration, summary jury trials, and related ADR mechanisms, the parties involved do not have to accept the results.

Far less formal than trial, ADR does not depend on elaborate courtroom procedures. Although parties can and do represent themselves in ADR proceedings, more likely than not, they will hire an attorney. Attorneys and paralegals have a significant ADR role to play, directly assisting clients when, for example, complex legal issues are involved or a substantial amount of money or property are at stake. The lawyer can help the client when the latter lacks self-assurance or presentation skills, or may be intimidated by the other party. The lawyer can render a professional opinion about the dispute's legal strengths and weaknesses, how a judge or jury would decide it, and can advise the client about the legal and related consequences of settlement options. Outside counsel can also help the client to select the most appropriate type of ADR, be it mediation, arbitration, or some other ADR procedure. It is the paralegal who assists the lawyers in performing these functions.

As with litigation, ADR requires comprehensive planning and preparation. Unlike litigation, however, most types of ADR present disputants with only one chance to get it right. This is ironic, considering the nonbinding nature of many ADR methods. ADR must be carefully considered when facing the finality of the decisions if using binding arbitration or when all sides agree to abide by the final decision.

There are, of course, other variations of ADR aside from arbitration, mediation, summary trials, or abbreviated trials that are commonly used. We will simply look at the most common ones in order to understand the scope and nature of ADR. Before we explore these areas more fully, let's take a look at the overall process of ADR and exactly what it is.

C. PROCESS OF ALTERNATIVE DISPUTE RESOLUTION

As stated, ADR refers to the means of settling disputes outside of the courtroom. ADR typically includes arbitration, mediation, summary jury trial, abbreviated trial, and conciliation. As burgeoning court calendars, rising costs of litigation, and time delays continue to plague litigants, more states have begun experimenting with ADR programs. Some of these programs are voluntary; others are mandatory. The two most common forms of ADR are arbitration and mediation.

Arbitration is the ADR process by which disputes are submitted to a neutral decision maker or a panel of neutral decision makers. It is an abbreviated version of a trial involving relaxed rules of evidence. Either both sides agree on one arbitrator, or each side selects one arbitrator and the two arbitrators elect the third to comprise a panel. Arbitration hearings can last a few hours to a few days, and the opinions are generally not public record. Arbitration has long been used in labor, construction, and securities regulation, but is now gaining popularity in other business disputes such as contractual disputes, family law, and workers' compensation.

Title 9 of the U.S. Code establishes federal law supporting arbitration. It is based on Congress's power over interstate commerce. Where it applies, its terms prevail over state law. There are, however, numerous state laws on ADR. Thirty-five states have adopted the Uniform Arbitration Act as state law. Thus, the arbitration agreement and decision of the arbiter may be enforceable under state and federal law.

Mediation is an even less formal alternative to litigation. Mediators are individuals trained in negotiations (oftentimes retired judges) who bring opposing parties together in an attempt to work out a settlement or agreement that both parties accept or reject. Mediation is used for a wide variety of cases, ranging from juvenile felonies to federal government negotiations with Native American Indian tribes, but any case can be voluntarily mediated.

Before making a determination as to which method of ADR is most appropriate for the dispute at hand, consideration must be given to the extent the party or parties are willing to: have the final outcome determined by the process, allow third parties to make decisions for them, surrender control of the process to others, and play a direct role in the resolution of the dispute.

Let's now look at mediation and arbitration more closely.

1. Mediation

Mediation is an informal dispute resolution process where a neutral third party helps parties in dispute reach an agreement. Mediation is an increasingly common and meaningful alternative to formal adjudication. In mediation, as opposed to arbitration, a neutral third party listens to the disputing parties and attempts to guide them toward compromise. The mediator's role is to help the parties understand the problem, the position of the other side, and the options that may satisfy both parties. The third party does not decide the dispute, but helps in the negotiation process. It is important that the mediator take a back seat to the parties, allowing the parties themselves to derive a solution. The mediator's job is to facilitate the negotiations and to ensure that all interested parties will be satisfied that the result is a fair one. Mediation is nonbinding unless otherwise determined by a court of law. Mediation, however, differs from arbitration in the following two ways.

1. The third party is not empowered to enter a binding decision.
2. The disputing parties fully control the process and the results.

Mediation is an informal process. There is no swearing of oaths, no cross-examination or formal testimony, no objections, and no rules of evidence. Furthermore, mediation can be "cheaper, faster, and potentially more hospitable to unique solutions that take more fully into account nonmaterial interests of the disputants"[1] (as opposed to the trial process or arbitration).

Mediation is advantageous over traditional methods of dispute resolution because it enables the parties to "expand traditional settlement discussions and broaden resolution options, often by going beyond the legal issues in controversy."[2] Therefore, mediation is often selected because it

- Enables the disputing parties to reach an agreement with which both parties are willing to comply
- Promotes judicial economy outside of the adversarial process, which avoids an unnecessary determination of liability

Because a mediated decision is nonbinding, participants can walk away from the process whenever they like. Ironically, this seemingly positive attribute can sometimes prove a negative one. Failed mediation sessions sometimes mean that disputants are reluctant to go back. Another problem is that participants who do not come across strongly during mediation signal that they may also perform poorly as witnesses or advocates in court, thus increasing the likelihood of costly litigation.

Some mediation arrangements provide that, if unsuccessful, it will be followed by binding arbitration. Failure to perform well during mediation will almost certainly negatively affect the pending arbitral award.

As stated, mediation is a process through which the parties to the dispute engage a third party to assist them in coming to a mutual resolution. Mediation can improve stalled negotiations because it is assisted and guided by the mediator. The mediator is neutral with respect to outcome; however, he or she does have control over the process and pace of the negotiations. The mediator's duty and expertise lies in assisting the parties in exploring the range of settlement options and coming to a mutually acceptable outcome. The mediator cannot compel either party to resolve the dispute in any given way, because the parties retain absolute control over the outcome. Mediators meet jointly and privately with all parties to gain a thorough understanding of the parties' needs and interests. Because the process is confidential, parties are able to test their perception of the facts and the law with the assistance of an unbiased third party. Even in those cases where resolution is not achieved, mediation is still beneficial because it serves to streamline the issues in dispute. Ultimately, if a mutually acceptable resolution cannot be achieved, resolution by some other process will be required.

Mediation is most appropriate when an ongoing business or personal relationship is involved. It is in no one's best interest to subject a business or personal relationship to the adversarial and divisive system of litigation if the parties wish to conduct business together in the future. Mediation enjoys a very high rate of success (approximately 85 percent), especially when the parties have mutual interests that can be satisfied by a resolution of the dispute. It is best entered into early in the life of a dispute before parties have committed to hard and fast positions, and before anger, hostility, and the expenditure of large sums of time and money have poisoned the atmosphere. There is the point in

---

[1]Goldberg, Sander & Rodgers, *Dispute Resolution: Negotiation, Mediation and Other Processes* (1999).

[2]*ADR and Settlement in the Federal District Courts: A Sourcebook for Judges & Lawyers* 65 (Federal Judicial Center and the CPR Institute for Dispute Resolution 1996).

time when a neutral, objective, and impartial third party may assist the parties in achieving results that, experience has shown, can be imaginative, inventive, and not necessarily based on a monetary settlement. It is this ability to craft results that meet the parties' underlying interests and overall objectives that is unique to mediation and one of its many significant benefits.

Mediation can be done quickly and in a cost-effective manner. The process can be started within days or weeks, and, because it is a somewhat informal process, preparation time can be kept to a minimum. The fees for mediation generally run between $150 and $250 per hour (reaching $3,000 a session) and the parties split the costs equally (although low-cost alternatives are available in the community). Unlike litigation, the process of mediation is one that allows the direct participation of those actually involved in the dispute (as well as their lawyers), thus creating the likelihood of more satisfactory and durable settlements.

a. The Process of Mediation

The process of mediation varies greatly depending on the style of the mediator. Typically, however, the mediator will take an active approach and suggest resolutions to the dispute. Usually, when the parties are represented by an attorney, both parties will provide a list of possible mediators to the opposing side. From that list a mutually agreeable mediator will be chosen. The chosen mediator then may request a confidential position paper or brochure from all parties that provides a background of the dispute at issue. He or she will review the paper prior to the mediation. The mediator will take a very active role in talking to all parties and trying to come up with some settlement or resolution. Remember, however, that the resolution of the mediator is not binding on the parties. Often mediations are conducted very similarly to settlement conferences. Sometimes mediators will request to meet with the parties prior to the mediation to better understand their positions and issues. Furthermore, there are mediators who do not require or even want anything prior to the mediation. They simply want to start the process fresh, with both parties stating their positions directly.

There is no set order as to how a mediation is conducted or carried out. It is up to the mediator. Typically, though, both parties are afforded the opportunity to present their sides. From there the mediator will attempt to foster an environment in which the parties can review their options, focus on the issues, and determine the best possible resolution to the disputes. If any agreement is reached, the mediator will clearly set forth the terms of that agreement. The agreement is then reduced to writing and signed by all parties involved.

b. Paralegal Responsibilities

In mediation the paralegal has the opportunity to utilize communication and interpersonal skills to a great extent when dealing with the party that his or her attorney represents. The process is similar to the settlement process. The paralegal would

- Assist with obtaining documentation and organizing it
- Assist with preparing any brochures or papers requested by the mediator

- Assist with preparing documents required for the mediation process
- Assist with preparing any settlement documents and preparing the client

---

PRACTICE TIP

Make sure you or your secretary calendars all important dates. Some mediators prefer to have the necessary documents 30 days prior to the mediation, some mediators like the documents 2 weeks prior. Be sure you know how your particular mediator likes to have the paperwork prepared and that you know his or her deadlines. If a document is due on the 15th of the month, calendar it on the 7th so you have a week to prepare.

A typical Mediation Confidentiality Agreement is shown in Figure 11.1.

2. Arbitration

If the dispute is not amenable to mediation, the other alternative, short of litigation, is arbitration. **Arbitration** is the process of dispute resolution where a neutral third party renders a binding decision after a hearing where both parties have presented their case. It is a contractual process between parties in dispute who agree to present to the arbitrator the issues in dispute for decision. It can be binding or nonbinding.

In arbitration parties submit their evidence to an impartial, neutral arbitrator (or panel of three arbitrators) whose decision is final and enforceable in court. Arbitration is swift (generally concludes three to four months from inception), private, and informal with relaxed rules of evidence. The process is chaired by a party-selected neutral person, assuring that the decision maker has experience, knowledge, and understanding of the issues. Like mediators, arbitrators are well-trained, highly skilled neutrals who bring their own experience and expertise to the service of the parties.

Surprisingly, arbitration has been around for many centuries and is not a product of modern society. English merchants, for example, utilized arbitration as early as the thirteenth century to resolve their disputes so that they could rely on their own customs instead of the common law. In the United States, arbitration has been a widely utilized tool for most of this century. According to a timeline published by the American Arbitration Society,[3] the development of arbitration in this country in part looked like this:

1920 Enactment of the New York State Arbitration Statute, the first modern arbitration statute in the United States.

1925 Enactment of the United States Arbitration Act (Federal Arbitration Act).

1926 American Arbitration Association founded through the consolidation of the Arbitration Society of America, the Arbitration Foundation, and the Arbitration Conference.

1936 Membership in AAA's National Panel of Arbitrators totaled 7,000.

1938 First course ever in arbitration law given by New York University Law School.

---

[3]This timeline is accessed on the Internet at http://www.adr.org/timeline.html.

MEDIATION CONFIDENTIALITY AGREEMENT

To promote communication among the parties and the mediator and to facilitate settlement of the dispute, all parties agree that the mediator has no liability for any act or omission in connection with this mediation, and further agree as follows:

1. All statements made during the course of the mediation are privileged, are made without prejudiced to any party's legal position, and are nondiscoverable and inadmissible for any purpose in any legal proceeding.
2. The privileged character of any information is not altered by disclosure to the mediator. Disclosure of any records, reports, or other documents received or prepared by the mediator cannot be compelled. The mediator shall not be compelled to disclose or to testify in any proceeding about (a) any records, reports, other documents received or prepared by the mediator, or (b) information disclosed or representations made in the course of the mediation or otherwise communicated to the mediator in confidence.
3. No aspect of the mediation shall be relied upon or introduced as evidence in any judicial or other proceeding.
4. Since the parties are disclosing sensitive information in reliance upon this agreement of confidentiality, any breach of this agreement would cause irreparable injury for which monetary damages would be inadequate. Consequently, any party to this agreement may obtain an injunction to prevent disclosure of any such confidential information in violation of this agreement.
5. Any party breaching this agreement shall be liable for indemnifying the non-breaching parties and the mediator for all costs, expenses, liabilities, and fees, including attorneys' fees, which may be incurred as a result of such breach.

Signed before commencement of the mediation by each of the persons whose signatures appear below.

Figure 11.1. Mediation Confidentiality Agreement

1944 Bureau of Labor Statistics reports that 75 percent of collective bargaining agreements in leading industries in the country provide for arbitration as the terminal point in grievance machinery.
1946 Membership in AAA's National Panel of Arbitrators reached 10,821.
1960 In a series of three landmark decisions known as the Steelworkers Trilogy, the Supreme Court ruled that doubts about arbitrability of labor-management grievances should be resolved in favor of arbitration and that courts should permit arbitrators to exercise flexibility in awarding remedies for violations of collective bargaining agreements.
1982 Chief Justice Warren E. Berger issued a nationwide call for greater use of private arbitration as an alternative to litigation.
1994 Martindale-Hubbell publishers introduced the new Martindale-Hubbell Dispute Resolution Directory, which lists approximately 70,000 arbitrators, mediators, judges, attorneys, law firms, and other neutral professionals who specialize in ADR.

A common benefit to both mediation and arbitration is that each is a private process. If the dispute involves competitive bidding practices, trade secrets, critical employment information, long-term corporate strategies, or other sensitive information, that information can be kept in strict confidence and free from public scrutiny. One of the biggest distinguishing characteristics between arbitration and mediation is that arbitration is more formal than mediation.

Since arbitration normally does not include a right to appeal (unless there is fraud, corruption, or an abuse of the process), arbitration awards—which in most cases are binding—are virtually impossible to overturn. The Federal Arbitration Act and state arbitration statutes severely limit the grounds for judicial review of arbitral awards. This stark finality of outcome differs sharply from full-blown litigation, which offers litigants varied appeal options. Do poorly in arbitration, however, and there's usually no chance to turn things around later.

Arbitration is a very popular form of dispute resolution and can be an excellent alternative to the court system. Arbitration can go through the court system or through a private agency. When it goes through the court system, it is referred to as a judicial arbitration, and unless agreed to by the parties, it is nonbinding. The most used private agency is the American Arbitration Association (AAA), and when this agency is used, the arbitration is binding.

Traditionally, arbitration is classified as follows:

- **Domestic arbitration:** the process of dispute resolution involving the settlement of disputes where the disputing parties all come from the same legal jurisdiction and the law application to the dispute is that of the jurisdiction.
- **Commercial arbitration:** the process of dispute resolution involving the settlement of a dispute between two commercial enterprises.
- **Consumer arbitration:** the process of dispute resolution involving the resolution of disputes between a consumer and a supplier of goods or services.
- **Labor arbitration:** the process of dispute resolution involving the resolution of employment-related disputes.
- **International arbitration:** the process of dispute resolution involving the resolution of disputes between parties of different legal jurisdictions and involving international law issues.

As states vary in their approaches and rules governing judicial arbitration, this chapter will look at the process of arbitration through the AAA.

a. The Process of Arbitration

Under the rules of AAA, arbitration is commenced through the use of a demand for arbitration and submitting the appropriate fee to the AAA. The party filing the demand, the claimant, must serve a copy of the demand on all opposing parties. The party responding to the demand is the respondent.

Once the demand form has been filed and received, a case administrator will be assigned to the case. At that time the administrator will submit a list of names to both sides. After review of the list, each party may strike any names they object to. From a compilation of both lists, the administrator picks a name that has not been objected to by both sides. From there, a hearing is set usually to start within a few months. The hearing will proceed similar to a trial.

The paralegal can assist in this process, as he or she would in the process of trial preparation. The paralegal usually drafts the demand and responds to any motions filed. Also, paralegals typically assist with conducting background checks on the possible arbitrators and researching to determine if any conflicts of interest exist between the arbitrators and the parties involved. Similar to preparing for trial, the paralegal would continue to assist the attorney by

- Identifying and locating all pertinent documentation
- Determining documents not available and obtaining subpoenas directed to the appropriate party or parties
- Determining witnesses to be called
- Assisting with preparation of questions and examination of witnesses
- Conducting research and assisting in preparing the written brief

As arbitration can be binding, it is necessary to pay very close attention to the details of the case and to adequately and fully prepare for the arbitration. The paralegal also must be cognizant of the current rules governing arbitration and ensure that they are being followed.

Paralegals from all areas of the law are typically involved in the arbitration process. A paralegal who enjoys working in this area and who develops a particular expertise in the process may want to consider becoming an arbitrator or mediator. There are a number of programs to attend to assist in that endeavor. Once a paralegal has garnered a reputation for efficiency, thoroughness, fairness, and a complete understanding for the process, he or she will gain the respect of the legal community and will become successful as an arbitrator or mediator.

b. Paralegal Responsibilities

As with mediation, in arbitration the paralegal has the opportunity to utilize communication and interpersonal skills to a great extent when dealing with the party his or her attorney represents. The paralegal would assist with obtaining documentation and organizing it, assist with preparing documents required for the arbitration process, and assist with preparing the client.

PRACTICE TIP

It is advisable to help your attorney keep the client advised of the entire arbitration process. Calendaring periodic status reports every 30 to 60 days can eliminate unnecessary phone calls from the client wondering what is going on. It can also foster trust and an appreciative attitude from your client.

---

3. **Summary Judgment Trials and Abbreviated Trials**

Summary judgment and abbreviated or minitrials are nonbinding trials wherein counsel present a summary of the issues and evidence to a jury. To use the summary judgment trial approach to ADR, the parties must be ready for trial and have completed discovery. A jury is selected from the jury pool through voir dire. Then the attorneys present a summary of the issues and evidence to be presented. The jury is next allowed to deliberate and hopefully deliver a verdict. Although the jury's verdict is nonbinding (something the jury does not know), the attorneys are allowed to sit down with the jury and discuss their deliberations, thoughts, feelings, and impressions.

Although the primary benefit of using this approach is the reduction in trial costs, the costs can actually increase when the parties do not agree to the verdict and insist on going to trial. Many feel that another problem with this approach is that the jurors are not provided the complete picture as all evidence is presented in abbreviated form. Also, as actual witnesses do not testify, many feel that the jury makes a decision based on the attorney, not on their possible impressions of live witnesses.

Many states have adopted rules that encourage the use of summary jury trials, and on the federal level many proponents of the idea point to Federal Rule of Civil Procedure 16, which gives the judge the right to order litigants to attend pretrial conferences. However, there is considerable controversy surrounding this issue as to whether litigants can be mandated to attend summary jury trials. Rule 16 states in pertinent part:

> (a) Pretrial Conferences; Objectives. In any action, the court may in its discretion direct the attorneys for the parties and any unrepresented parties to appear before it for a conference or conferences before trial for such purposes as
> (1) expediting the disposition of the action;
> (2) establishing early and continuing control so that the case will not be protracted because of lack of management;
> (3) discouraging wasteful pretrial activities;
> (4) improving the quality of the trial through more thorough preparation;
> and
> (5) facilitating the settlement of the case.

Rule 16 therefore not only provides judges with the power to require attendance, it is also a vehicle for case management.

Abbreviated trials are very similar to summary jury trials accept that the case is not presented to a jury, but to party representatives who have the authority to settle the case. The abbreviated trial is voluntary, not mandatory, and the mediator is usually an expert in the area at issue, not a judge. There is no set format for the abbreviated trial. The parties are simply encouraged to focus on the issues. Attorneys feel this type of ADR is very helpful when their client has unreal expectations or overestimates the value or strength of the case. It can also satisfy the clients' need to "have their day in court" and have the ability to verbalize their position.

While it is true that findings in a summary jury trial are nonbinding, it is also true that these decisions—predictive of how actual jurors in a full trial will decide a lawsuit—are meant to provide the primary basis of settlement. A negative verdict will therefore prove extremely costly for the losing side during settlement negotiations. This is why it is critical that the attorney and the paralegal present the most winning case possible during the summary jury trial.

The paralegal is invaluable in summary jury trial and abbreviated trial settings. Preparation is similar to trial preparation. It is extremely important in both procedures to be intimately familiar with the documents, exhibits, and witnesses to effectively assist the attorney. Since abbreviated trials have no set format, the paralegal needs to anticipate the unexpected. He or she needs to be flexible and to be able to think quickly. The summary jury trial is more formal, but again, since the evidence presented is abbreviated, the paralegal needs to carefully think through the most important evidence, the shortest and most concise way to present it, and what evidence is essential to telling the story.

PRACTICE TIP

Since the trial is abbreviated, carefully think through the most important evidence, the shortest, and most concise way to present it, and what evidence is essential to telling the story. Oftentimes it is helpful to sit down with a coworker and outline your case along with the evidence you will use. When someone not intimately familiar with the details and facts of a case hears it for the first time, he or she can point out the gaps in your story and indicate additional evidence helpful to the jury.

---

4. Settlement

Settlement is an agreed outcome between disputing parties regarding their dispute. The vast majority of legal disputes are settled in one form or another without the need for trial. In fact, the moment a case is initiated, the opposing attorneys are usually thinking about the possibilities of settlement, and the strengths and weaknesses of both cases. There are substantial incentives for the parties to settle, such as the tremendous costs of a trial, the length of time needed to complete the litigation process, and the public exposure.

Judges prefer settlement as opposed to trial and during pretrial conferences, settlement is one of the subjects listed for consideration, as is summary adjudication (motion for summary judgment). Rule 16 of the Federal Rules of Civil Procedure states in pertinent part:

> (c) Subjects for Consideration at Pretrial Conferences. At any conference under this rule consideration may be given, and the court may take appropriate action, with respect to . . .
>
> (5) the appropriateness and timing of summary adjudication under Rule 56; . . .
>
> (9) settlement and the use of special procedures to assist in resolving the dispute when authorized by statute or local rule.

Settlements are certainly encouraged and can be considered at any stage in the litigation process. However, oftentimes settlement discussions may not take place until after the discovery process is complete and the parties are near the pretrial conference stage of the proceedings. Remember that settlement can occur at any time in the litigation process, before a complaint is file, before trial, at trial, and after verdict. It is at that time the paralegal can be of primary importance. So how do settlement negotiations commence?

More and more lawyers like to present **settlement brochures,** an outline of the case, to opposing counsel and to the insurance company given in an effort to settle the case. They rely heavily on the paralegal to draft the brochure. The primary purpose of a settlement brochure is to present the claim in as persuasive a fashion as possible. The preparation of such a brochure has two secondary advantages.

1. It disciplines the lawyer and the paralegal to analyze liability, marshal evidence, and appraise the case.
2. It provides a dress rehearsal for trial in the event efforts at settlement are fruitless.

There are a number of reasons why the brochure will enhance the likelihood of a satisfactory settlement. The brochure presents the case in an orderly, dramatic, and persuasive manner. The typical claim is presented by the plaintiff's lawyer to the claims representative as an oral argument, more emotional than logical, more conclusionary than factual. Too often the settlement negotiation descends to a shouting match with each party becoming more partisan as the exchange continues with a lessening of a chance of settlement. The oral, face-to-face confrontation is not the most effective vehicle for settlement negotiations. Each side feigns an air of confidence in his or her case. The plaintiff's lawyer claims that there is "good" liability; the defendant insists it's "question-able."

A settlement brochure eliminates these problems. The plaintiff's case is presented in a written documentary form. It is based on facts—statements, reports, exhibits. There is no oratorical flourish or emotional argument. The claims representative receives the information factually and can appraise the case rationally.

There are some additional benefits as well. A well-ordered, carefully planned brochure carries with it an aura of importance. The bulk alone suggests value. The preparation of a brochure demonstrates that the plaintiff has sufficient confidence in the magnitude of his or her case to warrant a detailed presentation. It immediately creates an impression of great import.

The following are factors to be considered and elements found in a typical settlement brochure (plaintiff's case):

- A preface, setting out the conditions under which the brochure is being submitted
- Personal history of plaintiff
- Medical history of plaintiff—summary
- Medical history and physical report by initial attending physician
- Operative record of initial attending physician
- Consultation reports
- Additional operative records
- X-ray interpretations

- Discharge summary
- Additional medical reports
- Medical expenses
- Effects of injuries
- Evaluation of claims
- Conclusion

Other factors to consider for a settlement brochure might be the amount of damages, the ability of the defendant to pay, insurance coverage, proof or evidence discovered, the nature of the injury, similar verdicts, and whether this is a sympathetic plaintiff. Of course, the form varies to meet the particulars of the case and what side your firm represents, but this is the basic format used.

Another basic type of a settlement brochure might include:

- Preface, setting out the conditions under which the brochure is being submitted
- Summary of liability facts
- Summary of injuries
- Compilation of special damages
- Projected future damages and losses
- Legal authorities, together with a discussion of any novel issues of law
- A demand, setting out how it was arrived at

Also, a settlement brochure should include as exhibits some or all of the following:

- Photographs of injured victims
- Photographs of the scene of the accident if liability is an issue
- Hospital records, excerpts, or summaries
- Reports of experts such as an economist, doctor, or liability expert
- Any official reports of the accident such as a police report
- The curriculum vitae of any special doctor or expert whose testimony is critical to the case

A "settlement demand" or settlement letter, much like a settlement brochure, is just as effective and can be prepared in letter format for a small case to a multimillion dollar case. It should follow the same general outline so far as setting out a summary of the facts, both liability and damages, and have attached to it the appropriate photographs and documents.

How do you decide the appropriate vehicle to use? Discuss it with your supervising attorney. Talk about the case, the facts and strategy, and from there decide what you want the settlement letter or brochure to accomplish. How much do you want to say? How much do you want to keep to yourself for the time being. There will be times when you do not want to "tip your hand" and alert the opposing party or parties to your strategy. Let the attorney you work for decide with you the way to handle this aspect of the case.

Figure 11.2 is an example of a settlement brochure outline for a personal injury case. Study it carefully.

Date:

Re: Settlement Brochure—Doe v. Johnson

Gentlemen:

This brochure is submitted upon the following conditions (cannot be used at trial, etc.): (state terms)

SUMMARY

On January 2, 2002, at approximately 9:00 A.M. in clear, dry weather . . .

Liability is clear.

INJURIES AND DAMAGES

Mary Doe, born January 8, 1971, sustained a severe, closed-head injury, pelvic fractures, broken ribs, and a broken arm in the collision of January 2, 2002. Her medical condition is described in summary form in the Admission and History and Physical Notes made at ABC Hospital (Exhibit 1). . . .

All of the written words and evidence found in the medical records of Ms. Doe cannot adequately describe her injuries and the catastrophic nature of the effect those injuries have had on her life. Therefore, we have prepared a 15-minute day-in-the-life video for your consideration. See Exhibit 2. . . .

Figure 11.2. Settlement Brochure Outline

See previous chapters for further discussion on how to investigate and collect information on the medical condition of the plaintiff, investigate the finances of the defendant, collect damage documentation, and prepare settlement demands.

As stated, settlement is perfectly proper during any phase of the case. Settlement is even appropriate during trial and even after trial if the decision seems on shaky intellectual and legal grounds and appeal costs would be prohibitive. In the past, some defense attorneys believed that settlement delay worked to their advantage. However, this well-accepted thought is largely dispelled with the evidence of the high cost of litigation. Compromise is now the key word.

The tactical decision of when to settle is up to the attorney. Oftentimes settlement early in a dispute can be advantageous. As a case drags on, personalities, counsel, and the parties involved may become set in their positions and less willing to compromise.

PAST MEDICAL COSTS

As of March 30, 2002, the following list summarizes the reasonable and necessary charges made by the various health care providers and hospitals for the care and treatment of Ms. Doe. All supporting documents and bills are attached as Exhibit 3.

ABC Hospital $
Surgeon
Physicians
Lab work
Clinic of the Valley
TOTAL $ _____

FUTURE MEDICAL COSTS

We have retained Dr. Charles Rickman of XYZ Health Services Institute who is a specialist in health care costs to determine future medical costs of Ms. Doe. Dr. Rickman's report, including his curriculum vitae, is contained here as Exhibit 4.

The cost of Ms. Doe's future medical care, reduced to present value as reflected in Dr. Rickman's report, is $325,822.00.

EDUCATIONAL BACKGROUND AND POTENTIAL OF MARY DOE

Mary Doe was a normal, healthy individual prior to the collision of January 2, 2002. She attended . . .

LOSS OF EARNING CAPACITY

Had Ms. Doe not had these injuries inflicted upon her, she could have expected to live a normal life expectancy of _____ years from the date of occurrence. Based on her education attainments, and work history, Ms. Doe . . .

LOSS OF ENJOYMENT OF LIFE, PAIN, AND SUFFERING

In evaluating this case for settlement purposes, we have looked to the prospective damage issues that would be submitted to the jury at trial. . . .

Past medical expenses
Future medical expenses
Loss of earning capacity
Past pain and suffering
Future pain and suffering

Figure 11.2. (Continued)

MARY DOE'S PRESENT CONDITION

At this time, Ms. Doe . . .

DEMAND

Our evaluation and research show the jury verdict range is from _____ to _____, calculated as set forth above.

We are authorized to settle this claim . . .

Respectfully submitted,

Attorney

APPENDIX

Exhibits and photographs.

Figure 11.2. (Continued)

At the earlier stages of litigation, there tends to be a more amenable view of issues and facts, and less exposure in the public eye. In this respect, early settlement may be appropriate. On a different and practical front, one must also gauge the negative impact that certain delays will have on both litigants.

Structured settlements have become very common in recent years. A **structured settlement** simply provides the plaintiff with periodic payments rather than one lump sum. The benefit is that the plaintiff has a guaranteed income over a specified period of time. The benefit to the defendant is that the actual cost of settlement is reduced since paying the sum over a period of years reduces its cost. Usually, a large initial lump sum is provided and then the subsequent periodic payments start. The lump sum is designed to pay any unpaid bills of the plaintiff, the plaintiff's costs, and attorneys' fees. Periodic payments are spread over a specified period of time and ensure that the plaintiff will not become indigent and a drain on society. The periodic payments are funded by the defendant's insurer through the purchase of an annuity. A structured settlement/release is a document that formalizes two parties' agreement to resolve their disputes. Figure 11.3 is an example of the outline of a settlement agreement and release.

In settlement, the paralegal has the opportunity to utilize communication and interpersonal skills to a great extent when dealing with the party his or her attorney represents. The process involves obtaining and organizing documentation, preparing settlement brochures, and assisting with preparation of the client.

RELEASORS:

RELEASEES:

DESCRIPTION OF CLAIM:

CIVIL CAUSE:

SUM OF SETTLEMENT:

     1. Release.

     2. Present and Future Injuries and Damages.

     3. Release of Insurer.

     4. No Admission of Liability.

     5. Apportionment of Payment to Lienholders.

     6. No Additional Claims.

     7. Consent/Warranty.

     8. Stipulation for Dismissal with Prejudice.

     9. Confidentiality.

    10. Drafting of Documents and Reliance by Releasors.

    11. Future Cooperation.

    12. Entire Agreement.

    13. Controlling Law.

This Settlement Agreement and Release shall be construed and interpreted in accordance with the laws of _____.

DATED this _____ day of _____, 2002.

                        CAUTION: READ BEFORE SIGNING

                       _____

Figure 11.3. Settlement Agreement and Release

5. Releases, Agreements, Stipulations for Dismissal, and Offers of Judgment

Releases are documents that formalize the agreement between the parties to resolve the dispute. Releases are documents executed by a plaintiff/claimant that frees the defendant from future obligation or liability in exchange for monetary consideration. The release when signed completely discharges all claims of a party against another party in an action. For example, a plaintiff can release one defendant in an action and not the other defendants when there are multiple defendants involved. Certainly, a plaintiff can also release all defendants. Various forms of releases can be drafted and authored by the paralegal under the attorney's guidance. However, paralegals must be extremely cautious in drafting releases, especially in cases of multiple defendants or in causes of action for other legal theories not yet determined. The paralegal must include language that specifically exempts and excludes those issues yet to be resolved from the release document. This type of release language is generally used in cases that have yet to reach any stage of formal litigation. See an example of a general release in Figure 11.4.

Drafting the settlement agreement can be a time-consuming process, but devoting the appropriate time to details to ensure the agreement is specific to the case involved is well worth the investment. Many paralegals are entrusted with the job of drafting such agreements. As such, the paralegal must ensure that the agreement clearly sets forth

- The parties involved
- The issues and claims
- A description of the case
- How the pending court case will be terminated
- The monetary sum involved
- Choice-of-law clause
- Type of settlement document
- Enforcement provisions for any breach

Once a settlement agreement has been reached and any applicable releases signed, the lawsuit must be terminated in the form agreed to. The standard is to file a stipulation and proposed order for dismissal with the clerk of court, signed by the attorneys for all parties. The stipulation should be with prejudice (which bars the plaintiff from refiling the claim later) or without prejudice (which does not so bar the plaintiff). A **stipulation for dismissal with prejudice** is a legal document filed with the clerk of court dismissing the case and barring the plaintiff from refiling the claim later.

In certain cases there must be court approval for settlement. Under Rule 23(e) of the Federal Rules of Civil Procedure, settlements of class actions must have court approval. A petition is presented to the court having jurisdiction over the parties, a hearing is then held, and an appropriate court order entered.

Rule 68 of the Federal Rules of Civil Procedure provides that either party can serve an offer of judgment on the opposing party more than ten days before the trial. Rule 68 states:

> At any time more than 10 days before the trial begins, a party defending against a claim may serve upon the adverse party an offer to allow judgment to be taken against the defending party for the money or property or to the effect specified in the offer, with

RELEASE OF ALL CLAIMS

FOR AND IN CONSIDERATION of the payment to _____ at this time of the sum of _____ Dollars, ($_____), the receipt of which is hereby acknowledged,_____ (hereinafter referred to as releasors) being of lawful age, do/does hereby release, acquit and forever discharge _____ and his/her/their/its agents, directors, employees, administrators, successors, assigns, representatives, parent companies, owners, subsidiaries, insurance companies, and attorneys and any and all other persons, entities, corporations, associations and partnerships (the foregoing released persons and entities referred to as "releasees" of and from any and all actions, causes of action, claims, demands, damages, costs, loss of services, expenses and compensation, on account of, or in any way growing out of, any and all known and unknown personal injuries, potential wrongful death claims, property damages claims, and any and all other types of claims and/or damages referred to in the Complaint filed in civil action _____ in the _____ Judicial Disctrict Court, _____ County, Montana. Releasees is/are also released from any and all known and unknown damages and any and all other types of claims, including claims for attorneys' fees and punitive damages and including any claims arising directly or indirectly from any claims, adjusting or settlement practices by releasees, which are in any way related to the incidents referred to in said Complaint.

Releasors shall hold releasees harmless from any further costs, attorneys' fees or claims by any third party which relate in any way to health care or other services or products provided by any third parties to releasors or his/her/its/their agents, directors, employees, administrators, successors, assigns, representatives, parent companies, owners, subsidiaries, insurance companies and attorneys at any time from _____ [DATE OF INCIDENT] to the present.

In the event releasors settles his/her/its/their claims against _____, or any other individuals or entities, such settlement shall by its terms conclude and release releasees and his/her/its/their agents, directors, employees, administrators, successors, assigns, representatives, parent companies, owners, subsidiaries, insurance companies and attorneys from any claims for contribution or indemnity to such other parties.

The provisions of this agreement shall apply to any claims releasors may make against any person or entity now or in the future arising out of the facts or circumstances upon which this claim and/or lawsuit arises. The undersigned releasors agree that his/her/its/their attorneys of record shall stipulate to the dismissal with prejudice, as fully settled upon the merits, the above-described Civil Cause. Each party shall pay their respective costs and attorneys' fees.

Should releasors proceed in litigation against _____ [non-dismissed party], or any other individuals or entities, releasors will not pursue or execute any judgment against releasees in any amount or manner which would exceed the causative fault actually apportioned against releasees or the actual dollar amount of the settlement paid by releasees, whichever is less. In all events releasors will pursue or collect such judgment against such third parties in a way that will preclude such parties from acquiring or advancing any claim for contribution or indemnity against releasees.

Figure 11.4. General Release of All Claims

Releasors hereby declares and represents that the injuries and damages sustained are permanent and progressive and that recovery therefrom is uncertain and indefinite, and in making this release and agreement it is understood and agreed that releasors rely wholly upon his/her/its/their own judgment, belief and knowledge of the nature, extent and duration of said injuries and damages, and that he/she/it/they has/have not been influenced to any extent whatever in making this release by any representations or statements regarding said injuries or damages, or regarding any other matters, made by the persons, firms, entities or corporations who are hereby released, or by any person or persons representing them.

It is further understood and agreed that this settlement is the compromise of a doubtful and disputed claim, and that the payment is not to be construed as an admission of liability on the part of releasees, by whom liability is expressly denied.

Releasors agrees to pay all liens, presently asserted or which may be asserted, in connection with medical care and treatment or other services provided to releasors from _____ [DATE OF INCIDENT] through the present.

Releasors represents that _____, is the only counsel employed by him/her/it/them to represent him/her/it/them as to the aforementioned lawsuit, and that no other lawyer, law firm or representative has been retained or can claim any lien for attorneys' fees or settlement proceeds in connection with this litigation. In the event any lawyer, law firm or other representative makes a claim pursuant to a lien for attorneys' fees or settlement proceeds against releasees, releasors agrees to indemnify and hold harmless releasees and their insurers and atorneys from and against any such claims, including costs and attorneys' fees.

It is understood and agreed that each party to this release shall pay their own costs and attorneys' fees.

Releasees makes no warranty, representation, or promise, in any respect, with respect to the taxability of the sums which have been received by releasors. It is hereby expressly understood and agreed that releasors is/are fully and exclusively responsible for complying with the tax laws of the United States or any state and that releasors shall make no claim or demand in the future upon releasees in any respect, including claims related to the issue of taxability of the benefits to be paid hereunder.

This release contains the ENTIRE AGREEMENT between the parties hereto, and the terms of this release are contractual and not a mere recital.

Releasors further states that his/her/its/their attorney has carefully read the foregoing release and knows the contents therof, that his/her/its/their attorney has explained to him/her/it/them the contents thereof, and he/she/it/they signs the same as his/her/its/their own free act and it is his/her/its/their intention to be legally bound hereby.

Figure 11.4. (Continued)

In light of the possibility of adverse publicity to the releasees and potential harm to the releasees' professional and business reputation if this settlement were to be publicized, releasors, as an express condition of the settlement of these claims, agrees that the amount, terms, conditions of settlement, and identity of parties are to remain strictly confidential and that they will not be publicized or directly or indirectly disclosed or revealed in any fashion to the electronic or printed media or any professional business publication or to any professional business organization, or anyone else, except to releasors' attorneys or tax advisors, or except pursuant to Court Order.

CAUTION! READ BEFORE SIGNING

_____

STATE OF MONTANA   )
                    :ss
County of Yellowstone   )

On this _____ day of _____, 1999, before me, the undersigned, a Notary Public for the State of Montana, personally appeared _____, known to me to be the person whose name is subscribed to the within instrument and acknowledged to me that he/she/it/they executed the same.

IN WITNESS WHEREOF, I have hereunto set my hand and affixed my official seal the day and year first above written.

(NOTARIAL SEAL)
Notary Public for the State of Montana
Residing at Billings, Montana
My Commission Expires: _____

Figure 11.4. (Continued)

costs then accrued. If within 10 days after the service of the offer the adverse party serves written notice that the offer is accepted, either party may then file the offer and notice of acceptance together with proof of service thereof and thereupon the clerk shall enter judgment. An offer not accepted shall be deemed withdrawn and evidence thereof is not admissible except in a proceeding to determine costs. If the judgment finally obtained by the offeree is not more favorable than the offer, the offeree must pay the costs incurred after the making of the offer. The fact that an offer is made but not accepted does not preclude a subsequent offer. When the liability of one party to another has been determined by verdict or order or judgment, but the amount or extent of the liability remains to be determined by further proceedings, the party adjudged liable may make an offer of judgment, which shall have the same effect as an offer made before trial if it is served within a reasonable time not less then 10 days prior to the commencement of hearings to determine the amount or extent of liability.

An offer of judgment is an offer by a party defending a claim to have judgment entered in a specific amount. The purpose of Rule 68 is to encourage settlements when reasonable offers of settlement have been made. If the offer is refused and a judgment following trial is the same or less favorable to the refusing party than the pretrial offer of judgment, the refusing party becomes responsible for the offering party's "costs" incurred from the time of the offer. Rule 68 is an important weapon in the arsenal of the attorney during the settlement phase of the litigation process. Parties use Rule 68 offers when settlement negotiations have broken down and trial is about to commence. The offer can be made in a letter or can be made more formally with an attached copy of service. It is a better practice to formally prepare the offer in the form of a pleading so that record of the offer can be documented in the court file and docketed. If the plaintiff elects to accept the offer of judgment, notice is sent to the defendant. Figure 11.5 is an example of an offer of judgment.

The paralegal has a responsibility to not only assist with preparing releases, agreements, stipulations for dismissal, and offers of judgment, but with ensuring that all information on those documents is complete and accurate. Paralegals are also charged with the responsibility of ensuring that the necessary paperwork is filed with the court, that all parties are provided conformed copies, and that the firm's client is informed.

PRACTICE TIP

Before providing a release or agreement to your supervising attorney, it can be helpful to have another paralegal review the document to make sure there are no errors or inconsistencies.

[Court Caption]

OFFER OF JUDGMENT

TO: Plaintiff and Plaintiff's Attorney

    Defendant ABC Corporation, pursuant to Rule 68 Federal Rules of Civil Procedure, offers to allow judgment to be entered against, in favor of plaintiff John Doe, in the amount of Seventy Five Thousand ($75,000) dollars, and costs of suit incurred to the date of this offer.

    This offer is made as a settlement offer and is not to be taken as an admission or indication of liability on the part of this defendant.

    Dated this _____ day of _____, 2002.

    [Attorney signature]

Figure 11.5. Offer of Judgment

ETHICS

Do ethics play a role in ADR methodologies? Certainly, ethics play a strong role in this process. If everyone did not adhere to high ethical standards, the process simply would not work. Ethical rules for mediators are found in the set of standards used as guidelines through the American Arbitration Association and the Society of Professionals in Dispute Resolution.

What about the paralegal? What areas of ethics must the paralegal be aware of? First and foremost, the paralegal must at all times be an advocate for the client and protect the client's interests, as in any other process or stage of the case. The paralegal must be keenly aware of protecting the parties' confidentiality. Also, the paralegal must conduct due diligence in conducting background checks on possible mediators or arbitrators to uncover and expose possible conflicts of interest. This means that the paralegal must be competent and thorough in conducting the background searches. Not only should the paralegal watch for conflicts of interest, but also for potential biases that would impede the impartiality required of a mediator or arbitrator. No ex parte communications should be held with the settlement master, mediator, or arbitrator. To make the process work well, the parties must have confidence in the players and confidence that all proceedings will be honest, forthright, and conducted in good faith. Last, the paralegal must put every effort forward in preparing for any ADR. Just because it is not a full-blown formal trial does not mean that the same time, effort, and expense should not be invested if necessary.

CONCLUSION

In summary, there are numerous benefits achieved through the use of ADR. Those benefits include

- Reduced costs
- Reduced time
- Preservation of relationships
- Greater control over the process
- Flexibility
- Enhanced ability to manage resources
- Confidentiality
- Experts serving as neutrals

It is becoming increasingly clear that ADR options are producing dramatic cost savings not only for individuals, but for private companies and governmental agencies. According to a recent survey of the litigation system in the United States, the average lawsuit takes over 30 months to reach resolution. For anyone who is personally or economically impacted by a problem or conflict that is being resolved via litigation, 3 years is much too long to wait for resolution. In courts that promote the early application of ADR techniques, most cases reach trial in approximately 20 months. That same survey also suggests that only about 4 percent of cases filed in court actually ever reach trial. The other 96 percent ultimately are settled usually after the expenditure of tremendous amounts of time, energy, and money.

On the other hand, mediation enjoys a settlement rate of nearly 85 percent and can usually be scheduled and completed very quickly. A 1994 survey of corporate law departments by Price Waterhouse indicates that 45 responding companies enjoyed an annual cost savings of $100,000 through the use of ADR, and 10 percent of those surveyed reported saving over $1 million per year.

There have been many recent surveys conducted about experience with ADR. Sixty-seven percent of those who had used ADR reported saving typically 15 to 50 percent of the cost of litigation. The CPR Institute for Dispute Resolution resolved business disputes involving over 440 companies with over $6.8 billion in controversy using ADR. This resulted in substantial savings to the parties involved.

As court calendars become clogged, costs continue to soar, and time investments continue to expand, we must explore every means possible to preserve business relationships, maintain profits, and cut costs. As ADR has clearly demonstrated, all of these benefits can be achieved through the sensible and consistent use of alternatives to litigation. It is well worth the time to include ADR mechanisms in written agreements and to explore ADR as a means of resolving controversies so as to avoid the pitfalls of litigation and enjoy the benefits of ADR.

USING TECHNOLOGY IN THE LAW OFFICE

Effective settlement brochures are short, concise, to the point, and carry visual examples of the issues and specific events of a case. All kinds of software today offers assistance in the process. However, CaseSoft, a division of DecisionQuest, offers some of the best products on the market: CaseMap, TimeMap, and NoteMap.

For many years, law firms have been using document database programs to organize case documents and transcripts. Most of the document database programs allow the user to enter and retrieve information through keyword searches and customizable databases. **Document databases** are a group of fields created to organize and search for documents based on document summaries or abstracts. However, a document database program doesn't provide the user with a mechanism to analyze strengths and weaknesses of a given case.

As the name implies, CaseSoft's CaseMap 3 is an analytical tool, designed to make it easy to organize and explore case facts, the parties involved, and the issues in any case. By using CaseMap 3 at the beginning of a case, information that comes from the client and your initial impressions of the case are put into a relational database. This database creates a central repository available to others who work on the case. As a central repository, the program allows for the identification of tasks to be completed by individuals, including completion dates.

Once the information is entered, the user can build case chronologies, including witness lists, create document indexes, and issue specific reports. CaseMap 3 works in conjunction with informational database programs to allow importing of transcripts and other document databases. The program also links with document viewer systems, which allow the user to attach images of the items referenced in the program.

The first step in using CaseMap usually falls to the paralegal. The paralegal creates a case file in the program when a new matter is assigned. Here is where the information storage process will begin. The program has four default tabs: Object, Fact, Issue, and Question. See Figures 11.6, 11.7, 11.8, and 11.9 for examples of these four tabs. After discussion with the client and the supervising attorney, the paralegal will select the Object field and input the case of characters, locations, and documents. Names, addresses, and phone numbers of the parties involved can be entered.

Once the objects are listed, you can enter individual facts as they become available. There are many data fields available under the Fact tab, including date and time, fact text, information source, and issues linked to the fact.

After the preliminary facts have been entered, the next step would be to switch to the Issue tab. The Issue tab is used to summarize the initial analysis of the issues and to revise the facts as the case develops.

The last step is to use the Question tab, which enables you to outline questions that need answers. This tab is basically a to-do list for trial preparation, discovery, and strategy.

Once all the information is entered you have the ability to sort and analyze in many different ways. You can then run reports on objects, facts, issues, and questions and use that information to develop strategy, keep clients and other team members informed, prepare for depositions, prepare settlement brochures, and prepare for settlement conferences, mediation and trial.

CaseMap 3 works in conjunction with another CaseSoft program called TimeMap. TimeMap takes information from CaseMap 3 and creates a timeline for demonstrative purposes. This timeline is a visual chart of when events occurred over a period of time. When creating a chart, the program automatically generates a proportional time scale

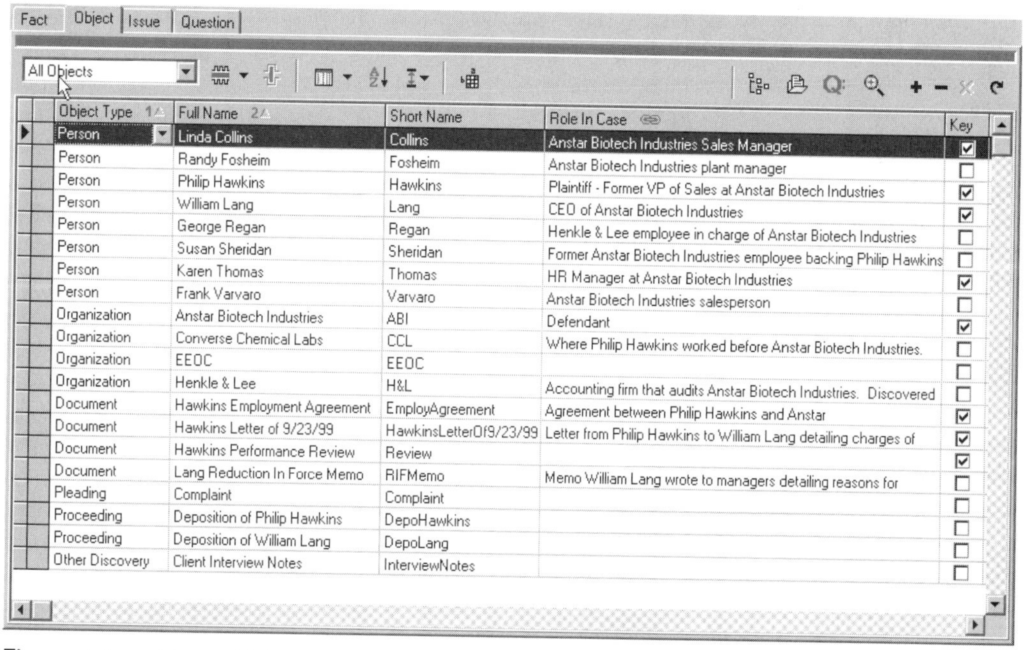

Object Type	Full Name	Short Name	Role In Case	Key
Person	Linda Collins	Collins	Anstar Biotech Industries Sales Manager	☑
Person	Randy Fosheim	Fosheim	Anstar Biotech Industries plant manager	☐
Person	Philip Hawkins	Hawkins	Plaintiff - Former VP of Sales at Anstar Biotech Industries	☑
Person	William Lang	Lang	CEO of Anstar Biotech Industries	☑
Person	George Regan	Regan	Henkle & Lee employee in charge of Anstar Biotech Industries	☐
Person	Susan Sheridan	Sheridan	Former Anstar Biotech Industries employee backing Philip Hawkins	☐
Person	Karen Thomas	Thomas	HR Manager at Anstar Biotech Industries	☑
Person	Frank Varvaro	Varvaro	Anstar Biotech Industries salesperson	☐
Organization	Anstar Biotech Industries	ABI	Defendant	☑
Organization	Converse Chemical Labs	CCL	Where Philip Hawkins worked before Anstar Biotech Industries.	☐
Organization	EEOC	EEOC		☐
Organization	Henkle & Lee	H&L	Accounting firm that audits Anstar Biotech Industries. Discovered	☐
Document	Hawkins Employment Agreement	EmployAgreement	Agreement between Philip Hawkins and Anstar	☑
Document	Hawkins Letter of 9/23/99	HawkinsLetterOf9/23/99	Letter from Philip Hawkins to William Lang detailing charges of	☑
Document	Hawkins Performance Review	Review		☑
Document	Lang Reduction In Force Memo	RIFMemo	Memo William Lang wrote to managers detailing reasons for	☐
Pleading	Complaint	Complaint		☐
Proceeding	Deposition of Philip Hawkins	DepoHawkins		☐
Proceeding	Deposition of William Lang	DepoLang		☐
Other Discovery	Client Interview Notes	InterviewNotes		☐

Figure 11.6. Object Tab

	Date & Time △	Fact Text ⊕	Source(s) ⊕	Key	Status +	Linked Issues ⊕
▶	??/??/1996	William Lang meets Philip Hawkins while touring Converse Chemical Labs plant in Bakersfield.	Deposition of William Lang, 25:14; Client Interview	☐	Undisputed	Demotion, Hawkins Deserved
	12/??/1996	William Lang invites Philip Hawkins to visit Anstar Biotech Industries facilities in Irvine.	Client Interview Notes	☐	Prospective	Pattern & Practice
	01/??/1997	William Lang offers Philip Hawkins sales manager position at Anstar Biotech Industries.	Client Interview Notes	☐	Undisputed	
	Mon 01/13/1997	Philip Hawkins begins working at Anstar Biotech Industries as a sales manager.	Anstar Employment Records	☐	Undisputed	
	Mon 12/01/1997	Philip Hawkins promoted to Anstar Biotech Industries VP of Sales.	Client Interview Notes	☐	Undisputed	
	Sat 01/10/1998 to Wed 01/21/1998	Philip Hawkins negotiates draft Hawkins Employment Agreement with William Lang.	Hawkins Employment Agreement	☑	Undisputed	Wrongful Termination
	02/??/1998	William Lang tells Philip Hawkins that he has changed his mind regarding the Hawkins Employment Agreement	Philip Hawkins, Deposition of William Lang, p. 19, l.3.	☑	Disputed by: Opposition	Wrongful Termination
	Fri 01/15/1999	Philip Hawkins turns 51.	Deposition of Philip Hawkins, 5:11	☐	Undisputed	Age Discrim Against Hawkins
	Tue 05/11/1999	Philip Hawkins receives performance Hawkins Performance Review from William Lang. Is rated a 1	Hawkins Performance Review	☑	Undisputed	Wrongful Termination,
	06/??/1999	William Lang makes decision to reduce size of staff.	Deposition of William Lang, 43:19	☐	Undisputed	Age Discrim Against Hawkins
	07/??/1999	Susan Sheridan is terminated.	Deposition of Philip Hawkins	☐	Undisputed	Pattern & Practice
	Sun 07/04/1999	Philip Hawkins allegedly makes lewd remarks to Karen Thomas during Anstar Biotech Industries Fourth of July	Client Interview Notes	☑	Disputed by: Opposition	Hawkins Deserved Termination

Figure 11.7. Fact Tab

	Full Name △	Short Name	Description ⊕	Eval by CA	LS: Facts	LS: Documents	LS: Persons
▶	Wrongful Termination	WrongfulTermination		↘	5	3	7
	2 Age Discrimination	AgeDiscrimination		↘	8	2	5
	2.1 Age Discrim Against Hawkins	AgeDiscrimAgainstHawkins		↘	5	0	2
	2.2 Pattern & Practice	Pattern&Practice		↘	3	2	4
	3 Retaliation	Retaliation		↓	6	1	6
	3.1 Transfer	Transfer		↘	1	1	5
	3.2 Demotion	Demotion		↓	5	1	4
	4 Hawkins Deserved Termination	HawkinsDeservedTermination	Even though Philip	↗	5	1	7
	5 Damages	Damages		↗	2	1	3
	5.1 Failure to Mitigate	FailureToMitigate		↗	1	0	2
	5.2 Lost Wages	LostWages		↗	0	1	1
	5.3 Mental Anguish	MentalAnguish		↑	1	0	2

Figure 11.8. Issue Tab

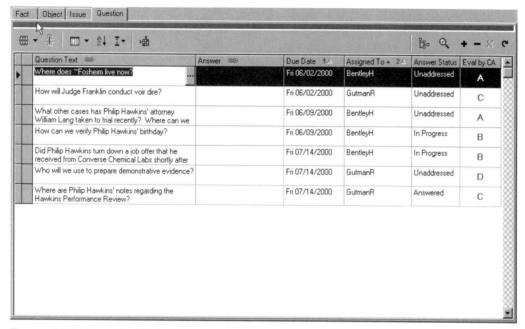

Figure 11.9. Question Tab

and positions fact boxes above the dates on which the facts occurred. TimeMap walks the paralegal or attorney through user-friendly steps to create chronologies and timelines.

Combined with an informational database, both programs are essential knowledge management software products.

KEY TERMS

Alternative dispute resolu-
  tion
Arbitration
Commercial arbitration
Consumer arbitration
Domestic arbitration

International arbitration
Labor arbitration
Mediation
Minitrial
Negotiation
Nonbinding arbitration

Releases
Settlement
Settlement brochures
Stipulation for dismissal
  with prejudice
Structured settlements

TECHNOLOGY TERMS

Document database

USEFUL WEB SITES

http://www.adr.org   American Arbitration Association
http://expertpages.com/   Find an expert or mediator

chapter 12

Trial Preparation

chapter objectives

In this chapter, we will discuss

- Briefs, motions, and pleadings drafted when preparing for trial
- Trial notebooks
- Preparing the witness list and the exhibits list before trial
- Preparing witnesses for trial
- Understanding jury instructions and evaluating a jury
- How to use technology to assist in preparing depositions and deposition summaries, trial notebooks, and trial exhibits

Preparing for trial is one of the hardest but most rewarding processes you will go through. Most likely you will work 12- to 14-hour days to get everything done. There are several items that must be addressed prior to trial:

1. Trial brief
2. Motions in limine
3. Final pretrial memorandum, order, and conference
4. Trial
5. Witnesses
6. Exhibits
7. Jury instructions
8. Pattern jury instructions

A. TRIAL BRIEF

A **trial brief** is a legal pleading drafted by both parties separately for the court setting forth their cases before trial. Before the trial begins, each side is required to submit a trial brief supporting their case. The primary purpose for this legal document is to provide the presiding judge with a concise summary of each party's case.

You will need to review the court's order to ensure that the trial brief contains all of the information requested by the court. Normally, a trial brief is formatted as follows: introduction, factual background, legal arguments, and conclusion. As a paralegal, you will most likely be responsible for drafting the introduction and factual background information, including references to exhibits and deposition transcripts throughout these sections of the legal document. The reason for this is relatively simple: The paralegal is normally the individual reviewing and organizing case information. This role provides you with a good grasp of the facts and events.

Usually, the legal arguments section of the trial brief will be drafted by your attorney since he or she will perform most of the legal research during trial preparation.

PRACTICE TIP

Before you begin drafting any portion of the trial brief, be sure to arrange a conference with your attorney to discuss the "theory" of the case. You need to know where the attorney's focus is to draft good introduction and factual background sections for the trial brief. Communication is always the key when you are asked to draft a document for your attorney. If you don't know what the attorney is thinking, then you can't customize your work for him or her.

Remember, as with any legal writing, always consider your audience. The judge is not going to want to read a trial brief that goes on and on and includes details with little or no relevance. Be sure you make each relevant point quickly and then proceed to the next item. Remember you don't want to get so caught up in the details that you lose the case focus.

Another task that you may be asked to perform with regard to the trial brief involves Shepardizing the case law cited throughout the document to ensure all the cases mentioned are "good law." To **Shepardize** is a process whereby case law is checked for validity. The attorney does not want to be citing to case law that has been reversed or negatively referenced, because he or she could lose credibility with the judge before trial even begins.

You can use Westlaw's cite check application for Shepardizing the case law in the trial brief. This application allows you to import the trial brief into cite check and run a search for all negative history on each case cited. This application is very efficient, taking only two to five minutes. The process can also be performed manually by entering each case cite, but this approach takes substantially more time.

Once you have completed cite checks on the trial brief, request a printout of all the cases that indicate a negative opinion or reference. Review the negative opinions and references to identify in what context these statements are referenced in relation to the trial brief. Sometimes there may be negative case history that is not relevant to the issue your attorney is citing to in the trial brief. If you are not sure in what context the case is being cited to, you should confer with your attorney. If the attorney you are working with wants to review the negative case history, do not take the time to review the negative history printouts, as your efforts would be duplicative.

The trial brief is an extremely important document in that it affords your attorney an opportunity to set the tone of the case with the presiding judge prior to trial. Any work you perform on this document should be done with the utmost of care and attention to detail.

B. MOTIONS IN LIMINE

Motions in limine are motions drafted by each trial attorney to exclude evidence at trial, for example, a proposed exhibit or the testimony of a witness. These motions are drafted before trial and are usually decided by the judge at the final pretrial conference. The Federal Rules of Evidence and case law govern what evidence your attorney can move to exclude.

One example of a motion in limine would involve a motion to exclude the testimony of an expert witness. As with any motion, a legal brief would need to be included that provides legal research supporting an argument for exclusion. Currently, the controlling case law regarding expert witness testimony is *Daubert v. Merrell Dow Pharmaceutical, Inc., Kumo Tire*. Daubert resulted in a 1993 U.S. Supreme Court decision regarding the admissibility of expert testimony. The Court found that expert testimony must pertain to "scientific knowledge" and that this "scientific knowledge" must be supported by appropriate validation. The primary purpose for the Court's ruling was to provide some kind of evidentiary reliability with regard to expert testimony. When preparing an expert witness for trial testimony, his or her exposure to a *Daubert* motion in limine should be considered.

Another example of a motion in limine is an argument to exclude the opposing side's presentation of documents pertaining to insurance coverage. In Montana, evidentiary Rule 411 prohibits the admission of liability insurance to prove negligence. There is even case law in Montana that will support a request for a mistrial, as the Montana Supreme Court has held that just the introduction of a party's lack of insurance can carry with it enough prejudice to constitute reversible error. Your attorney will need to research the appropriate case law in your state to determine the admissibility of insurance coverage.

Normally, you will not be asked to draft motions in limine; however, when you are compiling exhibits or reviewing the opposing party's exhibits, it helps to know what types of evidence could result in a motion in limine. Always remember, the best way for you to assist your attorney is to think like he or she does. If you consider the concerns the attorney may have while you are performing your paralegal duties, then you can present these concerns and assist in addressing them as the case progresses.

Figure 12.1 is an example of the general language and format normally used in a motion in limine.

If you are asked to draft a motion in limine, you first will need to find case law that supports your argument to exclude evidence. If you are charged with doing the legal

---

Attorneys for _____

        UNITED STATES DISTRICT COURT, DISTRICT OF _____,

_____,	) Civil No.
Plaintiff,	) **MOTION IN LIMINE**
vs.	) _____,
	) Judge
_____,	)
Defendants.	)

        COMES NOW, _____, and files this Motion in Limine with respect to the use of the following matters at trial. _____ should be prohibited from _____ and should be precluded from introducing any evidence of the same at trial. A Brief letter explaining and in support of this Motion in Limine will be filed separately.

        Dated this _____ day of _____, 2002.

                By _____
                P.O. Box 555
                Billings, MT 59101
                Attorneys for _____

                CERTIFICATE OF SERVICE

        I, _____, hereby certify that on the _____ day of _____, 2002, I mailed a true and correct copy of the foregoing document, postage prepaid, to the following:

                _____

Figure 12.1. Motion in Limine

research, research cases regarding the subject and draft a legal memorandum to your attorney so that you can discuss the results with him or her. After you have discussed the case law with your attorney, find out where he or she wants the focus of the motion in limine to be. As always, make sure the case law cited is current and has not been reversed or negatively referenced. Further, you need to consider your audience (the judge) when drafting such a motion, making sure your arguments are concise and to the point.

C. FINAL PRETRIAL MEMORANDUM, ORDER, AND CONFERENCE

A **final Pretrial Memorandum** is a legal pleading drafted by both parties separately for the court setting forth their cases before trial. Before trial, the presiding judge will usually require that a jointly drafted final pretrial order be submitted. The court usually requires that the final pretrial order be submitted by both parties prior to the pretrial conference so that the judge can review the document before he or she meets the parties. This document is drafted for the judge to provide him or her with a statement regarding the agreed facts and legal issues prior to trial. The final pretrial order also supercedes all prior pleadings and represents the final road map for trial. Remember, preparing for trial involves the organization and filtering of information.

If the judge knows which issues are agreed on and disputed, he or she can focus energy on addressing the disputed areas during the final pretrial conference.

Figure 12.2 is a form pretrial memorandum and order located in the Federal Rules of Civil Procedure.

MONTANA _____ JUDICIAL DISTRICT COURT, _____ COUNTY

_____,   )   Cause No.: _____
)
        Plaintiff,   )   Judge's Name _____
)
  vs.   )   **FINAL PRETRIAL ORDER**
)
_____,   )
)
        Defendants.   )

Pursuant to Rule _____ of the _____ Rules of Civil Procedure, a pretrial conference was held in the above-entitled cause on the _____ day of _____, 2000 at _____ o'clock, A.M.

_____, of the firm of _____ represented the _____.
_____, of the firm of _____ represented the _____.

I.   AGREED FACTS

The following facts are true and require no proof:

1. _____

Figure 12.2. Pretrial Memorandum and Order

II.   PLAINTIFF'S CONTENTIONS

Plaintiff's contentions are as follows:

1. _____

III.   DEFENDANTS' CONTENTIONS

Defendants' contentions are as follows:

1. _____

IV.   ISSUES OF FACT TO BE DECIDED AT TRIAL

Plaintiff's Issues of Fact

1. _____

Defendants' Issues of Fact

1. _____

V.   ISSUES OF LAW TO BE DECIDED BEFORE TRIAL

Plaintiff's Issues of Law

1. _____

Defendants' Issues of Law

1. _____

VI.   ISSUES OF LAW TO BE DECIDED AT TRIAL

Plaintiff's Issues of Law

1. _____

Figure 12.2. (Continued)

Defendants' Issues of Law

     1. _____

VII. <u>ADDITIONAL ISSUES</u>

_____

VIII. <u>WITNESSES</u>

Plaintiff's Witnesses

NAME, ADDRESS AND PHONE NUMBER—INDICATE WILL/MAY TESTIFY.

Defendants' Witnesses

NAME, ADDRESS AND PHONE NUMBER—INDICATE WILL/MAY TESTIFY.

IX. <u>EXHIBITS</u>

Attached to the Pretrial Order are exhibit lists identifying by number and brief description each exhibit and stating any objections to the exhibits. Objections to other exhibits are preserved to the time of trial and are dependent on the issues to be tried.

Defendants may present their exhibits in numerical, rather than alphabetical order, starting with Exhibit No. _____.

Plaintiff's Exhibits

See Plaintiff's Exhibit List attached to this Final Pretrial Order.

Defendants' Exhibits

See Defendants' Exhibit List attached to this Final Pretrial Order.

Figure 12.2. (Continued)

X.   FRUITS OF DISCOVERY

Plaintiff's Discovery

  1. The following depositions may be used in whole or in part:

  2. Defendants' Answers to Plaintiff's First Set of Discovery Requests, or excerpts therefrom.

Defendants' Discovery

  1. Defendants may offer depositions listed in Paragraph 1 of Plaintiff's Discovery, above.

  2. Defendants may offer any exhibits or writings produced during the depositions of any of the witnesses listed in Paragraph 1 of Plaintiff's Discovery, above.

Stipulations

_____

XI.   ADDITIONAL PRETRIAL DISCOVERY

_____

XII.   PRETRIAL RULINGS OF THE COURT

_____

XIII.   TRIAL MEMORANDA

Trial memoranda shall be exchanged by the parties and submitted to the court no later than _____.

XIV.   JURY SELECTION AND PROCESS

  1. The Court shall preselect the jurors and may call them in their order of selection.

  2. The Plaintiff shall have four peremptory challenges and the Defendants shall have a combined total of four peremptory challenges.

Figure 12.2. (Continued)

3. Initial jury instructions shall be exchanged simultaneously by both parties and made available to the Court on the _____ day of _____, 2000.

XV. LENGTH OF TRIAL

The Plaintiff estimates that the trial will last _____ trial days. Defendants estimate that the trial will last _____ days. The case will be tried before the Court with a jury.

XVI. APPROVAL

This Pretrial Order having been formulated after a conference at which counsel for the respective parties appeared, and reasonable opportunity having been afforded counsel of corrections or additions prior to signing,

IT IS HEREBY ORDERED that this Pretrial Order shall supersede the pleadings and govern the course of the trial of this cause, unless modified by the court to prevent manifest injustice.

IT IS FURTHER ORDERED that all pleadings herein shall be amended to conform to this Pretrial Order.

Done and dated this _____ day of _____, 2000.

_____
Court Judge

Approved:

_____
Attorney for Plaintiff

_____
Attorney for Defendants

Figure 12.2. (Continued)

As you can see, this form document provides the attorneys with guidelines regarding the format and general content of the final pretrial memorandum and order. You should always check the court's local rules and the presiding judge's rules, if any, to ensure you are drafting this document in a format specified by your court.

There will be a lot of negotiation between your office and the opposing party regarding agreed facts and current contentions. This task is normally performed by the attorneys;

however, if you get asked to perform this task make sure you discuss every agreed fact with your attorney before committing him or her to an agreement that may adversely affect the case. Always remember your role is to assist the attorney and make his or her job easier, not more difficult.

Finally, the pretrial memorandum and order normally contains both parties' witness and exhibit lists. The drafting of witness and exhibit lists is discussed during subsequent sections of this chapter. A **witness list** is a document attached to the Final Pretrial Memorandum and Order which contains all relevant information regarding witnesses. An **exhibits list** is a document attached to the Final Pretrial Memorandum and Order which contains all relevant information regarding exhibits.

After the pretrial memorandum and order is drafted and submitted to the court, a pretrial conference will be held between the presiding judge and the representative attorneys. This conference affords the judge an opportunity to meet with the attorneys and discuss the trial procedures that will be employed during trial. At this conference the judge may decide to rule on pending motions, for example, motions in limine and motions for summary judgment. If the judge chooses to rule on these motions at the pretrial conference, the issues discussed during trial could be substantially limited. Certain exhibits may be prohibited from being offered into evidence at trial and certain witnesses may be excluded from testifying. If your attorney allows you to attend the pretrial conference, you should take very detailed notes regarding any rulings or opinions provided by the court. These notes should then be summarized into a memo and circulated to every member of the litigation team.

Rule 16 of the Federal Rules of Civil Procedure contains a listing of specific subjects that can be considered during the final pretrial conference:

1. Simplifying all claims and eliminating frivolous claims
2. The need or desire to amend the pleadings
3. The chance of obtaining admissions of fact and documents, including advance court rulings regarding the admission of evidence
4. Avoiding unnecessary proof and cumulative evidence, including limits on using testimony under Rule 702 of the Federal Rules of Evidence
5. Timing and forum of summary adjudication under Rule 56
6. Control and scheduling of discovery
7. Identification of witnesses and documents, as well as the need and schedule for pretrial briefs and additional conferences/trial
8. Possibility of referring the matter to a magistrate or settlement master
9. Consideration of settlement or settlement procedures
10. Form and content of the pretrial order
11. Outcome of pending motions
12. Special procedures needed for complex issues, multiple parties, difficult legal questions, or unusual proof problems
13. Orders for separate trials regarding counterclaims
14. Order requiring that evidence that could result in judgment as a matter of law be presented early on during the trial
15. Order setting a reasonable limit on the presentation of evidence
16. Any other matters that will encourage a fair, speedy, and inexpensive trial

As previously stated, the witness and exhibit lists for both parties should be contained within the final pretrial order. It is normally required that the trial exhibits be available for review by the opposing party at the time of the final pretrial conference. When you compile trial exhibits, you should generate copies for opposing counsel and the judge, as well as your attorney. You should then keep the original trial exhibits in a box in your office so that they remain in order until they are presented for admission into evidence at trial. Some courts require that the original trial exhibits be sent to them prior to the trial. If this is the case, then keep a copy of the trial exhibits for your reference. At first this method may seem expensive and overdone, but this is the best way to maintain the organization of exhibits at trial. The attorney has a "working" set of exhibits, and you have control over the originals or your copy. If exhibits get out of order, you can always refer to your set.

D. TRIAL NOTEBOOK

A **trial notebook** is a binder created for the attorney, containing all relevant trial information in some type of organized fashion. Compiling and organizing a trial notebook for your attorney and yourself is essential to maintaining order and organization at trial. A trial notebook should contain at a minimum the following information:

- Witness and exhibit lists from both parties
- Names, addresses, and phone numbers for all witnesses
- Names, addresses, and phone numbers for all other individuals and resources
- Final pretrial order
- Deposition transcripts and summaries for each witness
- Jury questionnaires with jury box diagram
- Jury instructions

You should include labeled tabs for each of the above-listed items and place the appropriate documentation behind each tab in a three-ring binder. You should also have your own copy of the trial notebook so that you can access the necessary information as quickly as possible without having to borrow the attorney's notebook to perform your paralegal tasks. You can use your trial notebook to contact witnesses during trial regarding their expected testimony date. Further, as exhibits are admitted or refused, you can keep track in your trial notebook.

PRACTICE TIP

You should compile and organize a trial supply box, enclosing pens, pencils, highlighters, staples, stapler, sticky-notes, three-hole punch, two-hole punch, paper (notebook, printer, and computer), paper clips, cough drops, aspirin, and any other items that might be needed at trial. This supply box makes rushed trips back to the office unnecessary.

E. WITNESSES

Witnesses are individuals who testify to what they have seen, heard, or observed. Witnesses are a key element in every trial. These individuals provide the jury with the "story of the case." The paralegal is normally responsible for coordinating the witnesses at trial. The five primary duties you will most likely be asked to perform before trial regarding witnesses involve the following:

1. Subpoenas
2. Interviews
3. Witness preparation
4. Deposition summaries
5. Exhibits

1. Trial Subpoenas

A **trial subpoena** is a document commanding an individual's appearance in court at a certain time and place to give testimony in the matter before it. Before trial begins, witnesses need to be served with subpoenas. A **subpoena** is a document commanding an individual's appearance at a certain time and place to give testimony on a certain matter. Rule 45 of the Federal Rules of Civil Procedure governs the format required for trial subpoenas. Rule 45(a)(2) states as follows:

> (2) A subpoena commanding attendance at a trial or hearing shall issue from the court for the district in which the hearing or trial is to be held. A subpoena for attendance at a deposition shall issue from the court for the district designated by the notice of deposition as the district in which the deposition is to be taken. If separate from a subpoena commanding the attendance of a person, a subpoena for production or inspection shall issue from the court for the district in which the production or inspection is to be made.

In federal court, an authorized attorney can issue the trial subpoena pursuant to Rule 45(a)(3):

> (3) The clerk shall issue a subpoena, signed but otherwise in blank, to a party requesting it, who shall complete it before service. *An attorney as officer of the court may also issue and sign a subpoena on behalf of*
> (A) *a court in which the attorney is authorized to practice; or*
> (B) a court for a district in which a deposition or production is compelled by the subpoena, if the deposition or production pertains to an action pending in a court in which the attorney is authorized to practice. (Emphasis added.)

The above-referenced section of the federal subpoena rule provides that you no longer have to send your trial subpoenas to the clerk of court for issuance. Some state courts have adopted a similar practice. This practice is a special advantage when your attorney is practicing in another county because subpoenas can be issued immediately by the attorney with little to no time delays for mailing and issuance. You will want to review the procedural rules regarding trial subpoenas prior to issuance or service, to ensure you are complying with the appropriate court rules.

A federal subpoena is depicted in Figure 12.3. As you can see from Exhibit 12.3, the federal subpoena form is set up to require appearance at deposition, production of documents, inspection of property, and trial.

If your attorney is concerned about whether a witness will appear at trial voluntarily, a trial subpoena should be issued and served to ensure trial attendance. The last thing you want to happen is to not issue and serve a trial subpoena on a witness, only to find out at trial that the witness has no intention of appearing to testify voluntarily. This would be very embarrassing for your attorney and most likely adversely affect the presentation of his or her case. At least one month before trial, you should meet with the attorney you are assisting and determine which witnesses are going to be called and who will need to be served with trial subpoenas.

A trial subpoena must allow reasonable time for compliance pursuant to Rule 45(c)(3)(A). If a trial subpoena does not allow enough time for compliance, the court can quash or modify the subpoena. You should always try to serve trial subpoenas at least two to three weeks prior to trial. If you wait until a week before trial to serve subpoenas you may not be able to get the witness served and have the subpoena modified or quashed by the court.

Once your attorney has determined which witnesses need to be subpoenaed, you will need to arrange for service of the subpoenas. Rule 45(b)(1) governs the service of subpoenas and states as follows:

United States District Court

_____DISTRICT OF_____

SUBPOENA IN A CIVIL CASE

CASE NUMBER:

V.

To:

☐   YOU ARE COMMANDED to appear in the United States District Court at the place, date, and time specified below to testify in the above case.

PLACE OF TESTIMONY	COURTROOM
	DATE AND TIME

Figure 12.3. Federal Subpoena

☐   YOU ARE COMMANDED to appear at the place, date, and time specified below to testify at the taking of a deposition in the above case.

PLACE OF DEPOSITION	DATE AND TIME

☐   YOU ARE COMMANDED to produce and permit inspection and copying of the following documents or objects at the place, date, and time specified below (list documents or objects):

PLACE	DATE AND TIME

☐   YOU ARE COMMANDED to permit inspection of the following premises at the date and time specified below.

PREMISES	DATE AND TIME

Any organization not a party to this suit that is subpoenaed for the taking of a deposition shall designate one or more officers, directors, or managing agents, or other persons to consent to testify on its behalf, and may set forth, for each person designated, the matters on which the person will testify, Federal Rules of Civil Procedure, 30(b)(6).

ISSUING OFFICER SIGNATURE AND TITLE (INDICATE IF ATTORNEY FOR PLAINTIFF OR DEFENDANT	DATE

ISSUING OFFICER'S NAME, ADDRESS AND PHONE NUMBER

(See Rule 45, Federal Rules of Civil Procedure, Parts C& D on Reverse)

PROOF OF SERVICE

SERVED	DATE	PLACE
SERVED ON	(PRINT NAME)	MANNER OF SERVICE
SERVED BY	(PRINT NAME)	TITLE

DECLARATION OF SERVER

I declare under penalty of perjury under the laws of the United States of America that the foregoing information contained in the Proof of Service is true and correct.

Executed on _____

_____
Date   SIGNATURE OF SERVER

_____
                                                ADDRESS OF SERVER

_____

Figure 12.3. (Continued)

Rule 45, Fed.R.Civ.P. Parts (C) & (C:

(c) PROTECTION OF PERSONS SUBJECT TO SUBPOENAS.

(1) A party or attorney responsible for the issuance and service of a subpoena shall take reasonable steps to avoid imposing undue burden or expense on a person subject to that subpoena. The court on behalf of which the subpoena was issued shall enforce this duty and impose upon the party or attorney in breach of this duty an appropriate sanction, which may include, but is not limited to, lost earnings and a reasonable attorney's fees.

(2)(A) A person commanded to produce and permit inspection and copying of designated books, papers, documents or tangible things, or inspection of premises need not appear in person at the place of production or inspection unless commanded to appear for deposition, hearing or trial.

(B) Subject to paragraph (d)(2) of this rule, a person commanded to produce and permit inspection and copying may, within 14 days after service of the subpoena or before the time specified for compliance if such time is less than 14 days after service, serve upon the party or attorney designated in the subpoena written objection to inspection or copying of any or all of the designated materials or of the premises. If objection is made, the party serving the subpoena shall not be entitled to inspect and copy the materials or inspect the premises except pursuant to an order of the court by which the subpoena was issued. If objection has been made, the party serving the subpoena may, upon notice to the person commanded to produce, move at any time for an order to compel the production. Such an order to compel production shall protect any person who is not a party or an officer of a party from significant expense resulting from the inspection and copying commanded.

(3)(a) On timely motion, the court by which a subpoena was issued shall quash or modify the subpoena if it:

(i) fails to allow reasonable time for compliance;
(ii) requires a person who is not a party or an officer of a party to travel to a place more than 100 miles from the place where that person resides, is employed or regularly transacts business in person, except that, subject to the provisions of clause (c)(3)(B)(iii) of this rule, such a person may in order to attend trial be commanded to travel from any such place within the state in which the trial is held, or

(iii) requires disclosure of privileged or other protected matter and no exception or waiver applies, or
(iv) subjects a person to undue burden.

(B) If a subpoena

(i) requires disclosure of a trade secret or other confidential research, development, or commercial information, or
(ii) requires disclosure of an unretained expert's opinion or information not describing specific events or occurrences in dispute and resulting from the expert's study made not at the request of any party, or
(iii) requires a person who is not a party or an officer of a party to incur substantial expense to travel more than 100 miles to attend trial, the court may, to protect a person subject to or affected by the subpoena, quash or modify the subpoena or, if the party in whose behalf the subpoena is issued shows a substantial need for the testimony or material that cannot be otherwise met without undue hardship and assures that the person to whom the subpoena is addressed will be reasonably compensated, the court may order appearance or production only upon specified conditions.

(d) DUTIES IN RESPONDING TO SUBPOENA.

(1) A person responding to a subpoena to produce documents shall produce them as they are kept in the usual course of business or shall organize and label them to correspond with the categories in the demand.

(2) When information subject to a subpoena is withheld on a claim that it is privileged or subject to protection as trial preparation materials, the claim shall be made expressly and shall be supported by a description of the nature of the documents, communications, or things not produced that is sufficient to enable the demanding party to contest the claim.

Figure 12.3. (Continued)

A subpoena may be served by any person who is not a party and is not less than 18 years of age. Service of a subpoena upon a person named therein shall be made by delivering a copy thereof to such a person and, if the person's attendance is commanded, by tendering to that person the fees for one day's attendance and the mileage allowed by law. . . .

Normally service is effected through the utilization of a process server. A **praecipe** is a legal document that provides instruction to the process server regarding the proper service of documents. Some small towns with only the sheriff's office available for serving subpoenas still require praecipes. This document provides the process server with the information needed to effect service, along with relevant service instructions. If a praecipe is not required, you may include service information and instructions in a letter.

As the above-referenced rule states, proper service of a trial subpoena must include a copy of the subpoena and appropriate attendance and mileage fees. Currently in federal court the attendance fee is $40 per day with mileage at $0.365 per mile. Failure to provide these fees can result in inadequate service of process.

A subpoena issued in federal court has jurisdiction and authority in the states throughout the United States. The only limitation to federally issued subpoenas is Rule 45(b)(2), which states:

> Subject to the provisions of clause (ii) of subparagraph (c)(3)(A) of this rule, a subpoena may be served at any place within the district of the court by which it is issued, *or at any place without the district that is within 100 miles of the place of the deposition, hearing, trial, production, or inspection specified in the subpoena or at any place within the state where a state statute or rule of court permits service of a subpoena issued by a state court of general jurisdiction sitting in the place of the deposition, hearing, trial, production, or inspection specified in the subpoena.* When a statute of the United States provides therefor, the court upon proper application and cause shown may authorize the service of a subpoena at any other place. A subpoena directed to a witness in a foreign country who is a national or resident of the United States shall issue under the circumstances and in the manner and be served as provided in Title 28, U.S.C. 1783. (Emphasis added.)

Rule 45(b)(2) does not allow for service of a trial subpoena on anyone outside the district who resides more than 100 miles from the trial; even subpoenas have a jurisdictional limit.

2. Interviews

An **interview** is the process of questioning someone to obtain facts and information. Inevitably, there will be witnesses listed that your attorney will want you to interview before trial. Mainly, the interviews will be done just to verify the witness's knowledge regarding the litigated matter. If the witness is a third party and not designated as an expert by opposing counsel, you may interview him or her. Please refer to and utilize the interviewing techniques discussed in Chapter 2.

Be careful not to speak directly with anyone represented by an attorney or anyone designated as an expert by opposing counsel. This type of contact is considered **Ex parte**, which is contact outside of the presence of a representing attorney. **Ex parte contact** is considered an ethical violation. Also be cautious interviewing witnesses who are former employees of an opposing party, particularly if they had managerial or executive duties while they were employed. Their knowledge may be protected by the attorney-client privilege, even though they are no longer an employee. Consult with the attorney with whom you are working before conducting former employee interviews.

Remember to always identify yourself to the witness. After you interview witnesses before trial, draft a memo to your attorney regarding your discussions with the witnesses. This ensures accurate documentation of your conversation with witnesses.

3. Witness Preparation

As the paralegal working on a case, you will have the majority of witness contact. For this reason, you will most likely be the individual who works with the witnesses before and during trial. The attorney may even ask you to do some of the trial preparation work with the witnesses.

Most people have never testified in a formal legal process. They will have a lot of questions and will want reassurance. The process is very intimidating, and the witnesses will most likely be extremely nervous. Any preparation that you do with the witness must not involve providing legal advice. If a witness has a legal question, always refer those questions to your attorney. A lot of times the paralegal becomes the person that "holds the witness's hand" and reassures him or her. It is very important that you help to make your witnesses feel as comfortable as possible.

Ideally, the witnesses you are working with will have already had their depositions taken. The deposition process provides the witness with an idea of what he or she can expect during trial. However, the witness must be made aware of the fact that deposition testimony is much more encompassing than trial testimony. They need to be informed that questions asked during trial are restricted by the Federal Rules of Evidence. The witness needs to be aware of objections made by the attorney during testimony. Once an objection has been made, the witness needs to delay his or her answer until the judge has ruled on the objection.

The witness should also be asked to thoroughly review prior deposition testimony. It should be explained to the witness that any deviation from this prior deposition testimony at trial can result in the witness's impeachment. The witness should always be reminded to honestly answer all of the questions posed during trial.

Another item you should address with the witnesses is appropriate attire at trial. Most people wonder what clothing is appropriate for a trial setting. You should tell a witness that this is a very formal legal proceeding and formal attire is necessary. If you have a key witness who appears "rough looking," then you should discuss how his or her appearance can be altered to present a "clean-cut" look. Discussions regarding attire will have to be done with the utmost tact. The last thing you want to do is insult or upset a key witness before trial during discussions regarding attire.

Witnesses are essential to any trial and need to be worked with extensively prior to trial. Your work with the witnesses is crucial to your attorney presenting a good case at trial. Most likely, your attorney will work with each of the witnesses for several hours before trial. If you can assist with witness preparation regarding attire, past testimony, and trial expectations, this will help your attorney tremendously. The attorney already has to go over all exhibits pertaining to each witness in detail. Your attorney probably will not have the time to go over attire and expectations at trial with each witness. Any assistance you can provide your attorney in this area will be very much appreciated.

4. Deposition Summaries

Another pretrial duty you will be asked to perform by your attorney is summarizing witness depositions. A **deposition summary** is a digest or synopsis of the testimony provided by a deponent. You will need to talk with your attorney to determine the format of these deposition summaries, but most summaries contain information on the Page/Line and Summary of the contents of each page and line in the deposition. Some attorneys like you to include a Topic column so they can quickly locate a particular topic. The most important thing to remember when summarizing depositions is to be completely accurate and never insert personal assumptions from the testimony. The attorney will rely on your deposition summaries during direct and cross-examination of a witness, as well as for impeachment of testimony. If the summary is not completely accurate, it could be disastrous. Another item to keep in mind when summarizing depositions is that the summary should be just that, a summary. You should not regenerate the deposition word for word. Remember that the attorney was at the deposition. A general rule to use comes from attorney Ron Mullin: "For every 10 pages of testimony, you should have 1 page of summary."

Summarizing depositions allows you to obtain a strong grasp of the facts and legal issues surrounding the case. Deposition summaries are extremely helpful to your attorney, especially if he or she has numerous lengthy depositions to use during trial.

> **PRACTICE TIP**
>
> Another method for summarizing depositions involves generating the witness's story in paragraph format chronologically. After each summary sentence in parenthesis the page and line should be inserted as a reference. This method creates a deposition summary which reads like a book or story, which is how the case will be presented at trial.

5. Filing of Original Depositions

If your attorney plans to use deposition testimony at trial, the original deposition transcript will need to be filed. You will need to ensure that the appropriate original sealed deposition transcripts get filed with the court.

6. Witness Exhibits

If it is possible, try to obtain from your attorney a listing of exhibits to be used with each witness. You may be able to begin drafting this list based on your knowledge of the case. Once you have a rough draft list, have your attorney review and add to it. Having these lists done before trial will allow you to compile the trial exhibits according to each witness.

While you are working with the witnesses, be considering what demonstrative exhibits would help to further explain each witness's testimony. Computer software has made creating demonstrative exhibits relatively simple and inexpensive. A more detailed discussion of computer generated demonstrative exhibits occurs in the technology section of this chapter.

Your paralegal duties with regard to witnesses are very important, as witnesses develop the "story of the case." How a witness presents at trial is crucial to the case. The impression each witness has on the jury can determine if your attorney wins or loses the case. If your attorney gives you duties regarding witness preparation, be sure to put forth your best effort, because these individuals may determine whether the outcome of the case is positive or negative.

F. EXHIBITS

Exhibits encompass all documentary evidence presented by each party at a trial. Prior to trial, you will most likely be asked to organize and compile the trial exhibits your attorney plans to submit into evidence. You will be working from a document referred to as an **exhibit list**. In fact, you may even be responsible for drafting the initial exhibit list. Every court has special formatting requirements for the exhibit list.

> ### PRACTICE TIP
> Check with the judge's clerk for any local rules created by that judge regarding the required format of the exhibit list.

See Figure 12.4 for an example of an exhibit list form.

As you can see in Figure 12.4, the exhibit list should include a very detailed description of exhibits, cross-referencing deposition exhibit numbers and bates identifying numbers. The exhibit list is a perfect place for cross-references, as both you and your attorney will have quick access to this list in your trial notebooks. In addition, the judge and opposing counsel have copies of this list and can locate documents by deposition exhibit number and bates number if necessary.

Before you begin organizing and labeling trial exhibits, you should contact the clerk of court to find out how these exhibits should be numbered. Normally, the clerk of court asks that one party utilize numbers while the other utilizes letters. Some courts simply ask that each party utilize a range of numbers (for example, plaintiffs from 1 to 200, defendants from 201 to 400). The court establishes these number systems to prevent parties from utilizing the same trial exhibit number. If your attorney has been assigned letters, make sure that you number trial exhibits with A1 to Z1, A2 to Z2 and so forth. This process will ensure that you have clear, concisely lettered exhibits.

> ### PRACTICE TIP
> Another reason for numbering and lettering trial exhibits A1 to Z1, etc., is that if your exhibits exceed A to Z and you have not utilized a numbering system, then you would be forced to number additional exhibits AA to ZZ, which could be redundant and confusing.

Attorney and Firm Name
Firm Location
Firm Phone Number
Attorneys for _____

UNITED STATES DISTRICT COURT, DISTRICT OF

_____,	Civil No. _____
Plaintiff,	
	_____,
	Judge
vs.	
	RECORD OF EXHIBITS
_____,	
Defendants.	

EXHIBIT NUMBER	OBJECTIONS AND RULINGS					EXHIBIT DESCRIPTION
	YES	NO	ADM	REF	RES	
1						Letter, July 6, 1998, John Smith to Jeff Robins re: inventory. Deposition Exhibit #5. (15 pages) JS 00001-00015
2						
3						
4						
5						
6						
7						
8						

Figure 12.4. Exhibit List

Once you have contacted the clerk of court regarding trial exhibit numbers, you can begin compiling, organizing, labeling, and numbering the exhibits. The rules of evidence do not require authentication of public records, as long as the public records submitted are certified copies. **Certified copies** are copies of documents that have been deemed to be true and correct copies of the originals on file in the appropriate public office. Federal Rule of Evidence 902 instructs:

Extrinsic evidence of authenticity as a condition precedent to admissibility is not required with respect to the following: . . . .

(4) Certified copies of public records. A copy of an official record or report or entry therein, or of a document authorized by law to be recorded or filed and actually recorded or filed in a public office, including data compilations in any form, certified as correct by the custodian or other person authorized to make the certification, by certificate complying with paragraph (1), (2), or (3) of this rule or complying with any Act of Congress or rule prescribed by the Supreme Court pursuant to statutory authority.

Certification of documents must be done by someone who has the authority to attest that the original document is on file. Normally, the sworn statement includes the following language: "I certify that this document is a true and correct copy of the original which is on file in the _____ office."

Once you have established whether you use numbers or letters for your exhibits and you have reviewed and finalized the exhibit list with your attorney, you can begin compiling and labeling exhibits. Most exhibits consist of more than one page. For multiple page exhibits, you should label the first page with the exhibit sticker, and any page after this should be labeled "Exhibit ____ Page ____." There are stamps you can use to label multiple page exhibits. Once each page has been stamped, you complete by hand the exhibit number and page number for each page of the exhibit. This process is very time-consuming but becomes a lifesaver when you are at trial. Your attorney can simply refer to the page number of an exhibit by glancing at the labeled lower right-hand corner. If you have any exhibits that are 20 pages or more, this method of labeling increases your attorney's efficiency and effectiveness. Figure 12.5 demonstrates the multiple page trial exhibit labeling.

Another item that must be considered when you are compiling exhibits involves the number of copies needed. Once you have compiled and labeled all of the trial exhibits, determine how many copies you will need to have made for your attorney, opposing counsel, and the court. You should then insert the copies in three-ring binders with labels indicating the exhibits included in each notebook. You should also insert numbered or lettered tabs in front of each trial exhibit consistent with the exhibit number or letter. This approach may seem tedious and mundane, but during trial it is the only way to go. The judge has a copy of the exhibits, as does opposing counsel and your attorney. Your attorney can work with the copies for direct and cross-examinations, while you maintain the originals. The originals will not end up out of order or missing. In fact, you may want to keep the originals loose and in a box with numbered or letter tabs separating the original trial exhibits. This will allow you to quickly pull any exhibit needed. As previously stated, you will also need to keep track of which exhibits are admitted, withdrawn, and objected to at trial by completing the exhibit lists located in your trial notebook. You may also want to indicate on your copy of the exhibit lists which witness testified about each exhibit.

The technology section of this chapter discusses ways to digitally compile, organize, label, and copy trial exhibits. This approach will most likely be the wave of the future, simply because more and more courtrooms are requiring that evidence be presented digitally to save time in the courtroom.

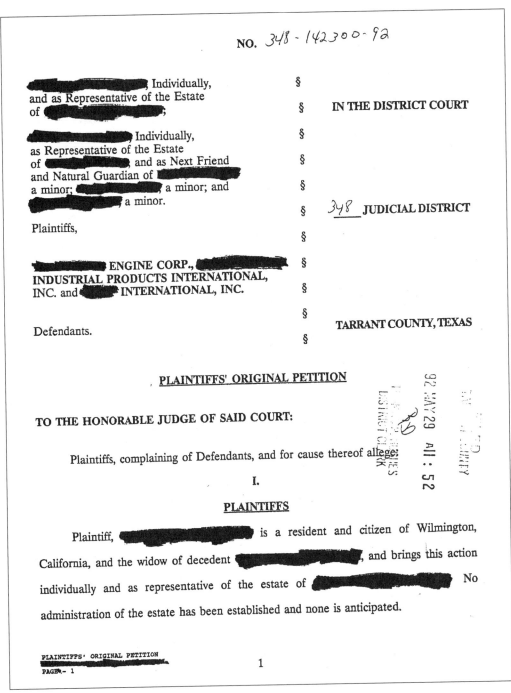

NO. 348 - 142300 - 92

▆▆▆▆▆▆▆▆▆ Individually, and as Representative of the Estate of ▆▆▆▆▆▆▆ ;	§ §	IN THE DISTRICT COURT
▆▆▆▆▆▆▆ Individually, as Representative of the Estate of ▆▆▆▆▆ , and as Next Friend and Natural Guardian of ▆▆▆▆▆ a minor; ▆▆▆▆▆ a minor; and ▆▆▆▆▆ a minor.	§ § §	
Plaintiffs,	§ §	348 JUDICIAL DISTRICT
▆▆▆▆▆ ENGINE CORP., ▆▆▆▆▆ INDUSTRIAL PRODUCTS INTERNATIONAL, INC. and ▆▆▆ INTERNATIONAL, INC.	§ § §	
Defendants.	§ §	TARRANT COUNTY, TEXAS

PLAINTIFFS' ORIGINAL PETITION

TO THE HONORABLE JUDGE OF SAID COURT:

Plaintiffs, complaining of Defendants, and for cause thereof allege:

I.

PLAINTIFFS

Plaintiff, ▆▆▆▆▆▆▆ is a resident and citizen of Wilmington, California, and the widow of decedent ▆▆▆▆▆▆ , and brings this action individually and as representative of the estate of ▆▆▆▆▆▆ No administration of the estate has been established and none is anticipated.

PLAINTIFFS' ORIGINAL PETITION
▆▆▆▆▆▆▆
PAGE - 1

1

Figure 12.5. Multiple Page Trial Exhibit

Plaintiff, ██████████, is a resident and citizen of Claremont, California, the widow of decedent ██████████, the mother of ██████████ and ██████████, the natural minor children of ██████████ and brings this action individually, as next friend and natural guardian of minors ██████████ and ██████████ and as representative of the estate of ██████████. No administration of the estate has been established and none is anticipated.

II.

DEFENDANTS

Defendant ██████████ ENGINE CORP. (Defendant ██████████) is a privately-owned Delaware corporation, having its principal place of business in the State of Texas, which at all times relevant hereto had an agency or representative doing business in Tarrant County, Texas, at ██████████ Texas 78051. Defendant ██████████ may be served by serving its registered agent for service of process:

U.S. Corporation Company
807 Brazos, Suite 102
Austin, Texas 78701

Defendant ██████████ NDUSTRIAL PRODUCTS, INC. (Defendant ██████████) is a privately-owned Delaware corporation, having its principal place of business in California, which at all times relevant hereto had an agency or representative doing business in Texas, and which may be served by serving its registered agent for service of process:

Figure 12.5. (Continued)

G. JURY INSTRUCTIONS AND JURY EVALUATION

1. Jury Instructions

Jury instructions are directions given by the judge to the jury pertaining to the law of the case. Before the trial begins the proposed jury instructions must be submitted. Normally, each state has established a set of pattern instructions that can be included in your attorney's set of instructions. **Pattern instructions** are forms that provide the judge with directions to the jury pertaining to the law of the case. The court is not required to admit these pattern instructions, but it is more likely that the court would admit these instructions as opposed to instructions drafted by you or your attorney. Most attorneys will submit a combination of pattern instructions along with attorney-drafted instructions. Some attorneys are very aggressive when it comes to drafting jury instructions, while others choose to be more conservative. You will need to discuss what approach your attorney wishes to employ regarding jury instructions.

The formatting of jury instructions is normally one copy of numbered instructions with citations and one copy of unnumbered instructions without citations. You will need to check the court's rules regarding the format of jury instructions, as well as the judge's order pertaining to jury instructions.

Once the instructions have been drafted and formatted, opposing counsel and the judge should be provided with one copy of each type of formatted instructions. An internal copy should be placed in both your trial notebook and your attorney's trial notebook. One way the paralegal can assist during jury instruction negotiation is by having a laptop computer and portable printer available. This will allow your attorney to provide immediate revised jury instructions and possibly prevent the refusal of some instructions.

2. Jury Evaluation

Every potential juror fills out a questionnaire. These questionnaires usually provide you with at least the following information regarding jurors:

- Names and addresses
- Ages
- Description of employment backgrounds
- Information regarding past lawsuits
- Affirmities or illnesses that may impact their ability to serve

You will want to review in their entirety the jury questionnaires to initially assess prospective jurors. You should review the questionnaires and draft a memo regarding your thoughts and impressions of each prospective juror for your attorney. This is only the initial phase of jury evaluation; no one has met the prospective jurors at this point.

A lot of jury evaluation occurs during jury selection (voir dire). At this time, the jurors' personalities are somewhat revealed through their mannerisms and vocalizations.

Another pretrial duty that your attorney may ask you to perform involves limited surveillance of the jurors. You cannot have contact with any juror before or during the trial, but you can observe jurors from a distance. In fact, you may learn something about a juror just by watching him or her or observing where he or she lives that you never would through a questionnaire or during voir dire. However, if doing surveillance makes you feel uncomfortable, then you should inform your attorney that you do not wish to perform this task.

H. PREPARING FOR TRIAL—SUMMARY

Become familiar with the rules of civil procedure and any specific court rules for the court in which the trial will occur. Approximately 100 days prior to trial, scrutinize that discovery plan and see what has been accomplished and what remains. Determine witnesses not yet deposed, review written discovery responses, send out requests to update information, send out requests to supplement discovery, and consider drafting requests for admissions to allow the opposing party to admit to any issues that are not truly in dispute so they don't have to be proven at trial. Review, review, review to see if there is anything missing.

Think about any dispositive motions that might be appropriate such as motions for summary judgment. Summary judgment requires presentation of evidentiary facts much as they would be presented at trial. Demonstrating the facts that justify summary judgment generally falls to the paralegal, either by locating pertinent deposition testimony or discovery responses to support particular facts, or by drafting and following up to obtain signatures on sworn declarations. A paralegal might also be involved in researching the applicable law or preparing exhibits.

The first contact with trial witnesses should be made at this time. Send out a reminder letter setting forth the trial date and requesting that the witness contact you if there might be a problem with the date. This will allow time for a motion to move the court for a postponement if necessary.

At 60 days you need to file any motions to compel discovery, or any other necessary motion.

At 30 days it is time to focus in on the evidence. Set aside some time to meet with the attorney and discuss evidence issues. What does your side need to prove and what documents support that? What witnesses will be used to authenticate those documents and testify to their significance?

Witnesses must be recorded and tracked through the trial notebook. A common way to organize the trial notebook is with tabs for each witness. All contact information, notes, and documents pertaining to that witness can be placed behind the appropriate tab and placed alphabetically in the trial notebook. A settlement conference might take place within this time frame. Be aware of what the court requires for the conference such as certain required attendance by individuals with authority to settle.

With 10 days left you need to ensure all documents are ready and prepared, copies are made, jury instructions have been completed, trial briefs are done, motions in limine prepared, and witnesses contacted again. Within the last few days prior to trial, you need to finalize all briefs, motions and jury instructions, maintain order, and update your to-do lists.

On the day of trial, pack everything the attorney needs and be on time.

ETHICS

As a paralegal, your ethical considerations during trial preparations will be primarily focused on trial exhibits. You must ensure that all demonstrative exhibits are a true and accurate representation of the evidence. Demonstrative exhibits should not mislead or confuse the jury. Demonstrative exhibits exist to accurately explain evidence to the jurors.

CONCLUSION

As indicated earlier, preparing for trial is one of the hardest but most rewarding processes you will experience as a litigation paralegal. This is also one of the most important paralegal processes because the information and materials you organize, compile, and prepare will be relied on by your attorney and used by him or her during trial. Every duty you perform during trial preparation will need to be checked and rechecked to ensure the utmost attention to detail and accuracy. For example, if you have summarized a deposition inaccurately and your attorney uses this summary to locate an area for impeachment of the witness at trial, any error in your summary could result in your attorney's credibility with the jury being questioned.

Trials are expensive, and you may not get the opportunity to prepare for a trial for several years into your career. This chapter provides practical guidance and helpful practice tips that will allow you to prepare for a trial as if you have been doing it for years. The best way to refine your pretrial preparation skills is through practice.

USING TECHNOLOGY IN THE LAW OFFICE

Technology is simply another tool that can be utilized when you are preparing for trial. The following are just some of the areas in which you can use technology to assist you before and during trial:

- Depositions
- Deposition summaries
- Trial notebook
- Trial exhibits

A. DEPOSITIONS

Depositions can be requested in electronic format on disc or e-mail. This digital format allows for quick searching by issue or topic.

B. DEPOSITION SUMMARIES

The traditional approach to summarizing depositions involves dictating them for transcription into a word processing table. Currently, technology does exist that could change the way you summarize depositions. Other technology tools available to digest depositions include

- Databases
- Applications in Summation
- Applications in Microsoft Word

1. Databases

Deposition summaries entered into a database allow for multiple term or full Boolean searches. **Full Boolean Searches** are database searches that allow for multiple information and field searching in a database simultaneously. Further, every occurrence of a search term can be generated into a queried report and printed out for the attorney.

All of your deposition summaries could be stored in one database if you add a witness field so you know who testified to what. The database searching capability is substantially increased when all of your deposition summaries are located in one database. For example, you could search every witnesses deposition summary for the testimony on a particular topic. You could then print out a report indicating what every witness testified to regarding that subject.

Setting up a deposition summary database is the same as creating a document database (see Chapter 5) except for the fields you use. A deposition summary database should contain the following fields: Page/Line, Summary, Topic, and Witness. Of course, you do not have to use all of these fields; you may decide you want some different fields. The database software programs previously discussed in this textbook include Access and Summation, but another database software program could be utilized if you do not have these software programs in your office.

2. Applications in Summation

The software program Summation also contains an application referred to as "notes." **Summation notes** are electronic sticky notes attached to a transcript that allow for searching and issues establishment, as well as attachment of image and audio files. The notes application not only attaches to each individual transcript, but also serves as a mini-database that is fully searchable and can generate queried reports. Essentially, your notes could contain your deposition summary for each transcript. To summarize depositions in this manner, you highlight the pertinent testimony by positioning the mouse pointer, holding down the left mouse key, and dragging the mouse to the end of the section of testimony. Once the testimony is highlighted, you double-click outside the far left margin of the transcript. A drop-down notes window should appear, as shown in Figure 12.6.

As you can see in Figure 12.6, there is a section for you to type your notes, which in this case would contain your summary of the testimony. Below this text box are boxes for issue, date, and author. The issues box can be used to create a searchable mini-database for your testimony topic. The date box can be used to create a timeline as you summarize the deposition. The author box informs anyone using the notes application who has created this note. This feature allows different individuals to create notes while providing the option to separate these notes by author. The attorney can generate notes and you, as the paralegal, can generate notes, both of which are searchable in one database but separated by author.

There are also buttons located in the lower-right corner of notes that allows for (1) a quick jump back to the transcript, (2) the attachment of an image file, (3) the attachment

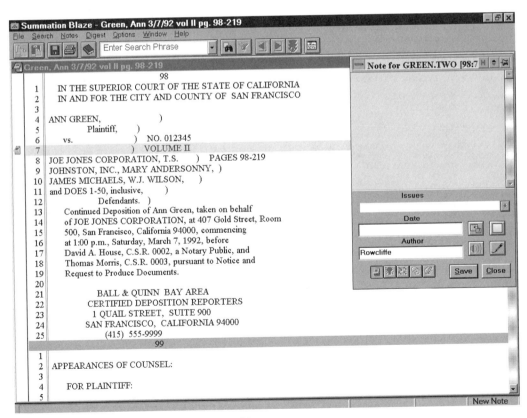

Figure 12.6. Summation–Drop-Down Notes

of an audio file, and (4) the attachment of a voice annotation. A good example of a use for the image button would be if the summarized deposition testimony discusses a deposition exhibit; you could then attach the scanned document for viewing.

At the very bottom of the notes box are several buttons that can be selected for classifying the note you are creating. The note classifications are as follows:

- Standard Note
- Thought Note
- Rebuttal Note
- Revised Testimony Note
- Follow-up Question Note

Once you have classified your notes, you can search for one type only.

Summation also allows you to create a deposition digest file that can be opened or inserted into word processors such as Microsoft Word and Corel WordPerfect. Figure 12.7 provides an example of the deposition digest text file that can be created through Summation's notes application. A digest is created by simply right-clicking on highlighted testimony and selecting "Write to Digest Digest.txt" or by placing the information on the clipboard and pasting it into your word processor. Using the digest application, you

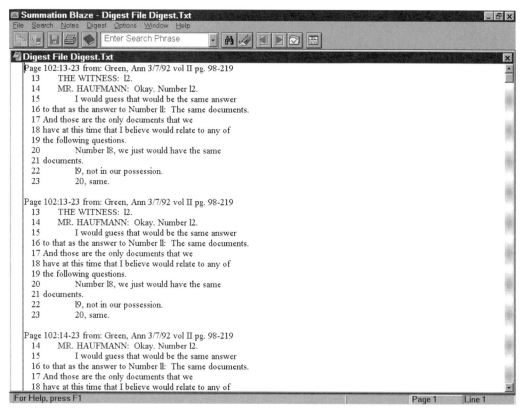

Figure 12.7. Summation—Deposition Digest Text Files

can create a digest file for current transcripts, selected transcripts, or all transcripts, as well as just for the current note, for specific issues, or all issues.

Summation also has an option referred to as **rapid fire digesting**, which allows for the simultaneous copying of highlighted testimony into a note while it is being created. This is accomplished through selecting the rapid fire button on the toolbar. **Rapid fire digesting** is the simultaneous copying of highlighted testimony into a note while it is being created.

Once you become familiar with the notes application, this method of deposition digesting has some distinct advantages when compared with the traditional method simply because several things can be accomplished while you are digesting (for example, image attaching, issues designating, timeline creation, and notes classification). Further, the notes application has a relatively small learning curve and the time it takes to become proficient is minimal.

3. Applications in Microsoft Word

If all you have at your office is word processing software, then there are some software applications available that will provide you with more options regarding your deposition summaries.

Word comments are electronic notes attached to Word text indicating the author and the thought. The comments function can be used to summarize depositions. You simply highlight the pertinent text and mouse-click on the Insert Comments option on the main toolbar. The text selected will then be highlighted, and when your mouse is positioned on this text, your comments will be visible through a pop-up text box. These comments can be sorted, printed out, and searched.

D. TRIAL NOTEBOOK

A trial notebook must be created for every trial; however, this notebook does not necessarily need to be a bound hardcopied compilation of information. It could be created in digital format and stored in your litigation computer laptop. As discussed previously, the following information would need to be contained within this digital trial notebook:

- Witness and exhibit lists from both parties
- Names, addresses, and phone numbers for all witnesses
- Names, addresses, and phone numbers for all other individuals and resources
- Final pretrial order
- Deposition transcripts and summaries for each witness
- Jury questionnaires with jury box diagram
- Jury instructions

Your trial notebook can be created similarly to a Web page with the above-listed primary title tabs linking to the pertinent scanned document images referenced by these tabs. See Figure 12.8.

As previously discussed in Chapter 3, a **hyperlink** can be created by highlighting the text you want linked and selecting Ctrl-K. The hyperlink menu box will then be activated and you will be asked to tell the computer what file you want to link to the text. Once you select the image file link, the process is complete and the link has been created.

For example, in Figure 12.8, your "Opposing Side's Witness and Exhibit List" text would be linked to the scanned image file. That way when you clicked on the "Opposing Side's Witness and Exhibit List," it would jump to the actual scanned document for your review. The scanned image file is a read-only file; it cannot be edited once it has been scanned and saved as an image file.

You can link to text that sends you to another text document and then links you to the image file (that is, layering each level). For instance, the "Deposition Transcripts and Summaries" tab can be linked to another Word file that has each witness listed. Then the witness name can be linked to the imaged deposition summary with this document linked to the imaged transcript. Court reporters will provide you with an ASCII or disk copy of the transcript that you can load into your computer and use for linking.

Once you have created this digital trial notebook, you can drag the files out to your desktop for easy access. Instead of shuffling through documents in a notebook you will simply need to open the trial notebook on your desktop and double-click your mouse.

TRIAL NOTEBOOK
Witness and Exhibit List
Opposing Side's Witness and Exhibit List
Witness Information
Information on Other Individuals (Vendors, etc.)
Pretrial Memo and Order
Deposition Transcripts and Summaries
Jury Questionnaires
Proposed Jury Instructions from Both Sides

Figure 12.8. Primary Title Tabs

Other technology tools available to organize deposition testimony include deposition databases and deposition summary tables. A **deposition database** is a group of fields created to organize and search deposition testimony based on a summary of this testimony. A **deposition summary table** is a group of columns and rows created to organize and search deposition testimony based on a summary of this testimony. These tools allow for searching of testimony and provide an abbreviated version of witness testimony.

E. TRIAL EXHIBITS

Technology can also be utilized in the creation, organization, and retrieval of trial exhibits. Traditionally, trial exhibits are admitted into evidence as hardcopied original documents marked by exhibit labels and page numbers. However, the legal field is beginning to recognize the waste of time and money that occurs when you present your evidence in this manner. In Montana, all of the federal courthouses have been modified to facilitate what is referred to as the paperless trial.

Federal Chief Justice Donald Molloy has been one of the individuals responsible for bringing Montana's courtrooms into the new millennium. Judge Molloy supports using technology in the courtroom primarily because it speeds up the trial process and evidence presented in this manner is more readily understood by the jury.[1] For your reference, his specific comments regarding the use of technology in the courtroom are contained in *Reflections and Thoughts about Litigation in an Electronic Court, Mont. Trial Law.,* (Summer 1998).

The Montana federal courtrooms have been created so that you can either continue preparing hardcopied exhibits or you can have all of your exhibits scanned onto your laptop and present the evidence electronically. Even if your attorney chooses to prepare exhibits the old fashioned way, most electronic courtrooms have a projector that allows hardcopies of exhibits to be placed on it and projected onto computer monitors throughout the courtroom. This projector's primary purpose is to level the playing field for those attorneys who do not have the trial presentation software to create digital trial exhibits.

1. Making Trial Exhibits Digital

As indicated above, trial exhibits can be put into digital format for presentation at trial. Electronic image files are created from the documents when they are run through a scanner. A **scanner** is a machine that reproduces documents in digital format, saving them as **image files**. There are several different types of image files: for example, **TIF, JPEG,** and **bitmap** files.

Although most scanners have an **OCR (optical character recognition)** feature, using it is not recommended because it allows the computer to determine what certain letters

---

[1]No specific page number. The entire article contains this info.

and words are. Because the OCR feature does not always accurately interpret each character, substantial authentication problems are created.

Image files are fairly large and normally have to be stored on a computer hard drive or written onto a CD-ROM. Floppy disks can usually only store one or two image files before they reach capacity. When the image files are scanned, they should be saved by trial exhibit number for easy identification. Bar codes can also be created as the images are scanned to allow for easy retrieval during trial. **Bar codes** are electronic symbols attached to an image file that are searchable.

Imaged trial exhibits can also be loaded into the following software:

- Microsoft PowerPoint
- Summation
- Trial Director

a. PowerPoint

Imaged exhibits can be inserted into PowerPoint using the Insert Picture From File function on the main menu. The size of document images can then be adjusted by dragging the mouse until the image fits on the page. A text box indicating what exhibit number the image is can be inserted in the lower right corner for reference. Figure 12.9

Figure 12.9. Image in PowerPoint with Text Box

is an example of an image that has been inserted into PowerPoint and text box labeled with a trial exhibit number.

b. Summation

The software program Summation has a Case Scan application that allows you to scan documents into an image format readable by Summation software. Using Case Scan is most feasible if the number of exhibits to be scanned is minimal. If you have a substantial number of trial exhibits to image—several hundred, for instance—you should consider a reputable documents imaging vendor. If you decide to have an outside vender perform your scanning, be sure that they are familiar with Summation's imaging requirements. To automatically load and link all of the image files with your document summaries in Summation, a **dii load file**, a file created specifically to link Summation database entries with their related image files, must be created by the outside vendors. If the load file is written incorrectly, then the images will not link to your document summaries.

c. Trial Director

Trial Director is another software program that allows you to load your imaged trial exhibits for viewing. An oll file is a file created specifcally to load image files into Trial Director. If you want your exhibits loaded automatically an oll file must be created to tell the computer where to load the image files. If you use a vendor, you will want to make sure that this vendor has enough expertise with Trial Director to properly draft the oll load file.

If you prefer to load the imaged trial exhibits manually, then you will need to select Add Document Images. The program will then ask you if you are adding a single page document/photo/graphic or a multiple page document/photo/graphic. You will then need to highlight and right-click on the image type and manually select your file. You will then have to select each item manually going through this process over and over. If you have several images, it is definitely worthwhile to utilize the automated image loading application, as it only takes a few minutes to load hundreds of images.

F. USING TECHNOLOGY TO CREATE POWERFUL DEMONSTRATIVE EXHIBITS

The computer software available today allows for the creation of incredible demonstrative exhibits. Remember when you are creating your demonstrative exhibits to make sure they accurately reflect the evidence of the case.

You can use computer software to generate charts, graphs, timelines, or chronologies, as well as to combine and emphasize exhibits. There are several software programs available that can be used to generate demonstrative exhibits. We will discuss the applications available in the following software programs:

1. Microsoft Excel
2. PowerPoint
3. Time Map

1. Excel

Excel is Microsoft's spreadsheet software. This software can not only calculate numerical values, but also be used to generate explanatory charts and graphs. The charts and graphs generated by Excel are created on an x and y axis and show a comparison of the values input into the spreadsheet.

Your chart or graph can be generated by entering the appropriate values into an Excel spreadsheet, highlighting the spreadsheet, and selecting the Chart button on the Excel toolbar. Once the Chart button is selected, Excel will go through a chart wizard application, allowing you to generate the type of chart desired.

An Excel chart or graph can be created to explain a claim of lost wages, both past and future. For example, if your attorney represents the defendant and the plaintiff is claiming future lost wages that are beyond any documented past earnings, the most effective way to show this discrepancy to a jury is through the use of a chart or graph. Figure 12.10 provides an example of a chart created in Excel to demonstrate a discrepancy in plaintiff's past lost wages. As you can see, this visual depiction could be extremely persuasive to a jury. Visually, it emphasizes the fact that the plaintiff had very little wages before the incident and now wants to claim substantial future lost wages after the incident.

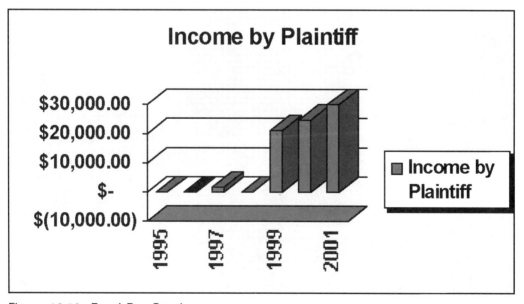

Figure 12.10. Excel Bar Graph

The coloring and format of the chart or graph used is your choice. Figure 12.11 gives you an example of the same information from Figure 12.10 placed in a pie chart.

As you can see, some types of charts demonstrate your point better than others. You will have to experiment with different chart types to determine which one demonstrates your point the best.

Any chart created can be copied and pasted into another file (for example, Word or PowerPoint) through the use of Ctrl-C and Ctrl-V functions. This is very useful when you are drafting settlement brochures, mediation statements, or arbitration statements because you can insert explanatory charts into the word processing document.

2. PowerPoint

PowerPoint is another software program that can be used to create demonstrative exhibits presented digitally at trial. A few examples of demonstrative exhibits that can be created through the use of PowerPoint are as follows: timelines, accident diagrams, multiple demonstrative exhibits, and emphasized exhibits. Timelines and accident diagrams are created through utilization of the drawing tools and text boxes. Multiple demonstrative exhibits are created by using the cut-and-paste application and resizing each image to fit on the page. Emphasized exhibits are created by using the art highlighting tool at the bottom of the PowerPoint screen and selecting Transparent from the Color Formatting

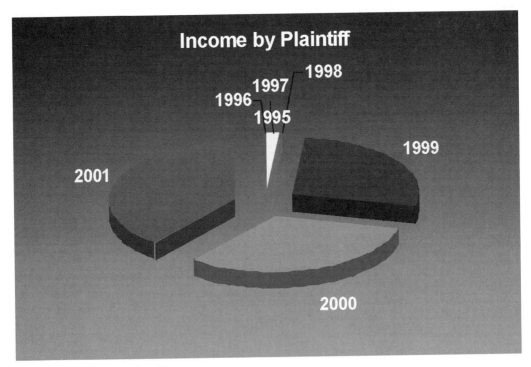

Figure 12.11. Excel Pie Chart

menu. Using the drawing tools, you can circle information and create rekeyed callouts, as well as callouts pulled directly from the scanned image.

Figure 12.12 has just a few examples of demonstrative exhibits created in PowerPoint. You are really only limited by the evidence available and your imagination.

3. TimeMap

Every case contains two primary elements, witnesses and events. Litigation requires an explanation of the events through witnesses. The best way to explain numerous events in chronological order is through the use of a timeline. Cognitive neuropsychology studies have shown that when information is presented through the use of a timeline, people recall more of the information presented.

Timelines can be generated through Word using text boxes; however, TimeMap is a relatively inexpensive program that makes generating timelines simpler and less time-consuming. In TimeMap you simple click on File and select New. At this time you are provided with a blank document with a time scale. The next step involves selecting Insert. At this point you have the option to insert a fact that provides you with a date entry and

Figure 12.12. PowerPoint Demonstrative Exhibits

a fact box entry. Once you have entered the fact you can simply select from the available tabs what color the fact box is and what type of font you would like to utilize.

The other option once Insert is selected is Text Box. This type of entry does not provide you with the opportunity to enter a date. You select the area on the new document where you want the text box and then drag it in the desired area. Formatting of the font and the text box color and shape can be done through the tabs. Several TimeMap screens have been inserted to show you examples of what the software can do. See Figures 12.13, 12.14, and 12.15.

G. USING TECHNOLOGY TO ORGANIZE YOUR TRIAL EXHIBITS

There are several presentation software programs that can be used to organize your trial exhibits. We will discuss use of the following software programs for organizing exhibits:

1. PowerPoint
2. Document Director/Deposition Director

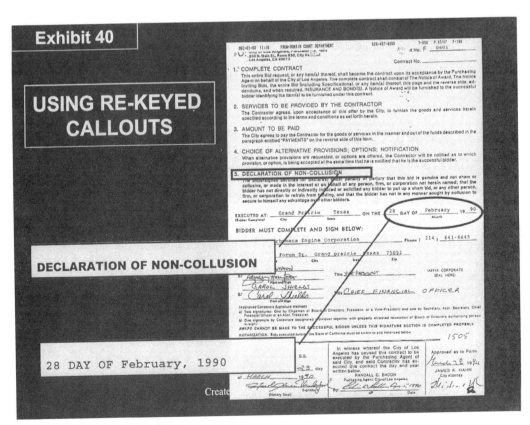

Figure 12.13. TimeMap Timeline

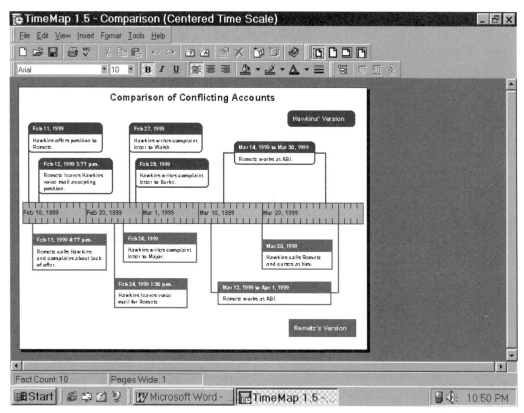

Figure 12.14. TimeMap Features

1. PowerPoint

PowerPoint is a powerful technology tool that can be used to influence the jury. Each trial exhibit can be placed upon a slide and labeled with a text box in the lower right-hand corner indicating the exhibit number. You can organize your trial exhibits according to exhibit number. The slide sorter view allows you to print out small versions of each PowerPoint slide to insert in the trial notebook so you can keep each slide organized. Figure 12.16 provides an example of how slides can be used to organize trial exhibits in PowerPoint.

2. Document Director/Deposition Director

To organize trial exhibits and digital video transcript (DVT) clips, InData created two software applications, one located in Document Director—exhibit outline—and the other located in Deposition Director—case clip reports. Further, the printing options in these programs allow for thumbnail outlines, which are very similar to exhibit outlines.

Each of these applications will be explained below for use in organizing trial exhibits.

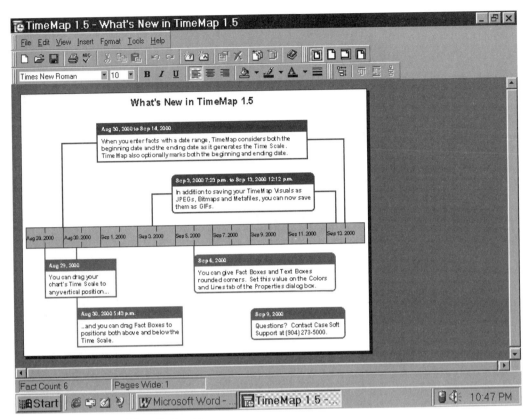

Figure 12.15. TimeMap Color Usage

a. Exhibit Outline

The exhibit outline application in Document Director is entered by selecting the Show Folder button on the toolbar. You then need to choose the folder containing your exhibits. You can then create an exhibit outline in one of two ways: right-click on Send To Exhibit Outline or select Exhibit Outline from the Tools menu and then select Create Outline From Current Folder.

Figure 12.17 provides a depiction of an exhibit outline page.

b. Case Clip Report

The case clip reports application in Deposition Director allows the user to organize DVT clips. This report contains a summary of all video clips within a case.

To generate a case report you need to open the case, click on the Print button, and select the type of case clip report you want to print. See Figure 12.18 for an example of how to print the clip report.

As you can see from Figure 12.18, you can select either a summary report of clips or a detailed report of clips. Figures 12.19 and 12.20 demonstrate the differences in clip reports.

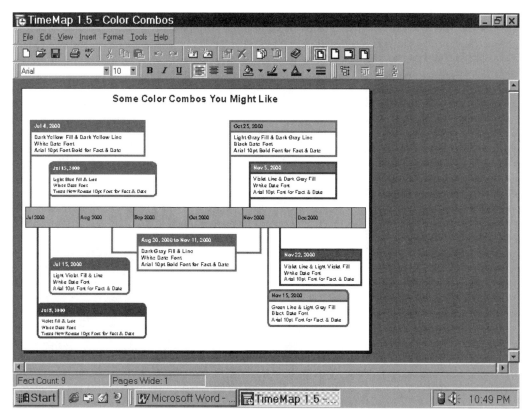

Figure 12.16. PowerPoint–Organizing Trial Exhibits

As you can see from Figure 12.20, the detailed clip report contains the transcript text related to the clip segments. Both reports provide the user with the clip segments and bar codes. These reports can be inserted into the trial notebook for quick retrieval during trial by using the bar code assigned to each clip.

H. RETRIEVAL OF DIGITAL TRIAL EXHIBITS

As discussed briefly above, trial exhibits can be retrieved in two different ways:

1. Manually through the use of a courtroom projector
2. Electronically through the use of a laptop computer

1. Manual Retrieval

Trial exhibits can be retrieved manually by providing the courtroom clerk with the original trial exhibit. In an electronic courtroom, the clerk simply places the first page of the

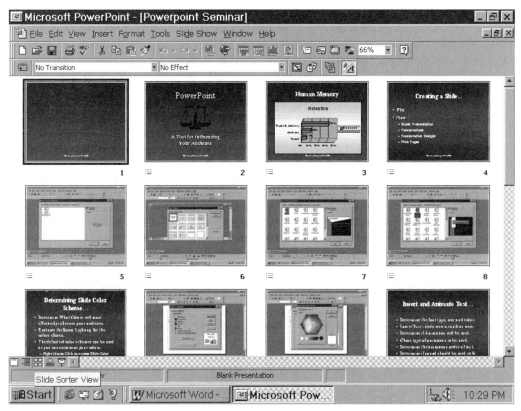

Figure 12.17. Document Director Exhibit Outline

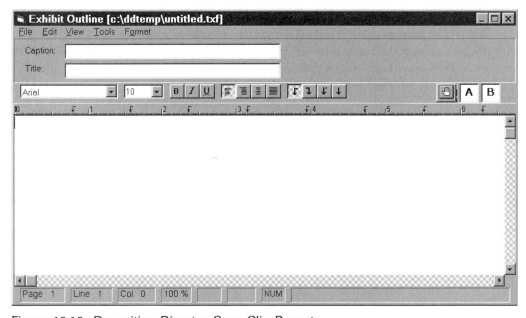

Figure 12.18. Deposition Director Case Clip Reports

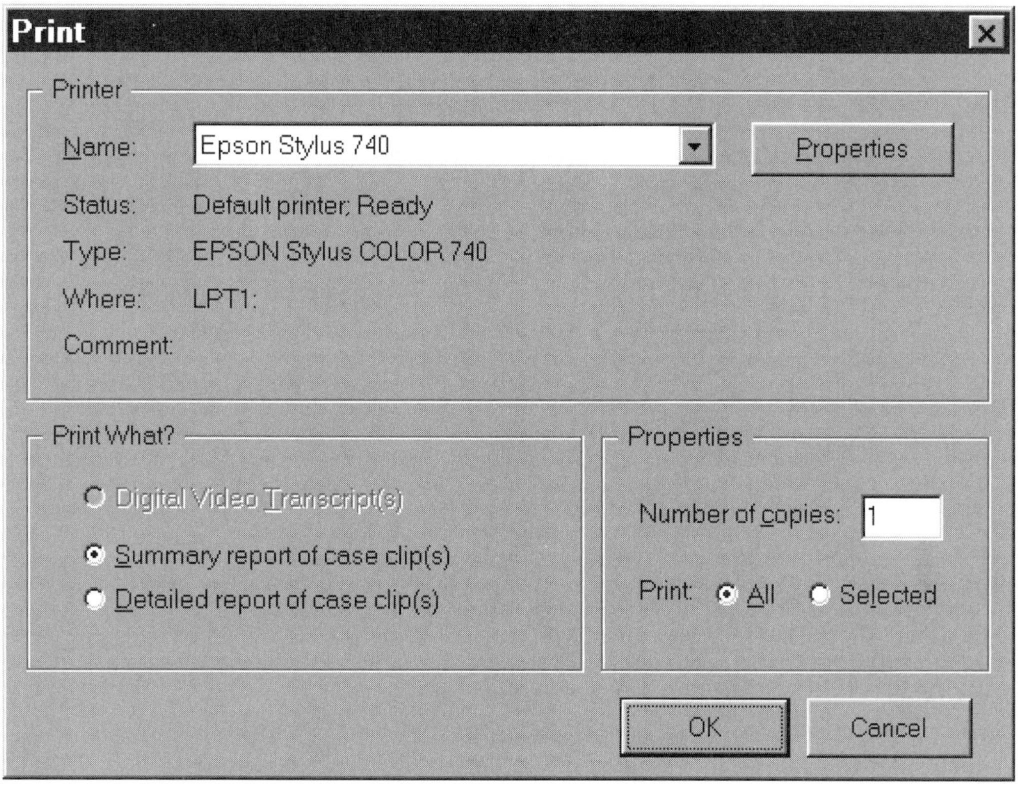

Figure 12.19. Case Clip Reports—Summary

hardcopied exhibit onto the projection system. Once the exhibit has been admitted into evidence by the judge, the document is projected to the jurors.

Manual retrieval is slower than digital retrieval in that each page of the trial exhibit must be hand placed on the projector. Further, trial exhibits in this format have a distinct disadvantage to that of digital exhibits in that they cannot be emphasized electronically and used as additional demonstrative exhibits. However, if your office does not have the equipment required to retrieve exhibits electronically, the projector system allows for a similar trial exhibit presentation.

2. Electronic Retrieval

If your office decides to electronically retrieve digital trial exhibits, you most likely will be the person in charge of pulling these images. The images can be retrieved by using file names or bar codes. If you choose to retrieve your exhibits by file name, you should keep a detailed list of the file names along with a brief exhibit description. The other option for digital trial exhibit retrieval is through the use of bar codes. This retrieval method is quick and accurate. In utilizing this method, you also don't have to worry about accidentally pulling up the wrong digital trial exhibit because using a bar code reader makes this practically impossible.

TrialDirector Suite Demonstration Case

📁 Poli, Michael (Vol. 01) - 07/21/1995 [Demonstration Excerpt]

🎬 Do you understand that you're here to give a deposition...

MP-0721-0001217	1 SEGMENTS / 00:00:05:13 DURATION	‖‖‖‖‖‖‖‖‖

1. Page 12:17 - 12:19 / Duration 00:00:05:13

```
17              Q.   Mike, do you understand that you're here
18    to give a deposition in this case?
19              A.   I do.
```

🎬 You've been called as an adverse...

MP-0721-0001220	6 SEGMENTS / 00:01:23:05 DURATION	‖‖‖‖‖‖‖‖‖

1. Page 12:20 - 13:02 / Duration 00:00:20:09

```
20              Q.   And do you understand that you've been
21    called as an adverse party for this deposition by
22    Halliburton?  As an adverse witness for this deposition
23    by Halliburton?
24              A.   I have no idea what is in your mind or
25    Halliburton's mind.  I just know that you called me as a
00013:01    witness.  Whether you think I'm adverse or not, I don't
02    know.
```

2. Page 13:07 - 13:13 / Duration 00:00:16:08

```
07              A.   I'm not going to agree to anything.
08    Quite to the contrary, during the phone conversations
09    that we had a couple weeks ago, I had the distinct
10    impression that you were attempting to foster kind of a
11    divide-and-conquer strategy.  So I don't know that you
12    thought I was adverse.  I don't really know what you
13    thought, to be honest with you.
```

3. Page 13:15 - 13:16 / Duration 00:00:04:02

```
15              A.   If you want me to tell you what you
16    thought about whether I'm adverse, I don't know.
```

4. Page 13:22 - 13:24 / Duration 00:00:07:12

```
22              A.   That wasn't the question you asked.  You
23    asked whether I knew that you thought I was adverse, and
24    the answer is, I don't know what you thought, Preston.
```

5. Page 14:04 - 14:06 / Duration 00:00:07:21

```
04              A.   I'm not a party to this case and I'm no
05    longer an attorney.  So I don't know if I'm adverse or
06    not.  I mean, I've really never given it any thought.
```

6. Page 14:11 - 14:21 / Duration 00:00:27:13

```
11              A.   I'm not adverse to anybody at this point
12    and -- nor would my testimony be affected in any way.
13    My job is to come here, as any witness should, and
```

page 1

Figure 12.20. Case Clip Reports—Detailed

TrialDirector Suite Demonstration Case

```
14   respond to the questions that are posed in a truthful
15   and forthright fashion.
16              You know, I don't know what overlay you
17   want to put on it, adverse, not adverse, whatever.  I'm
18   just here to answer your questions.  You didn't serve a
19   subpoena on me, but nonetheless I voluntarily appeared.
20   And let's get to your questions, and I'll try and answer
21   them as best as I can.
```

 Would you hand the witness Exhibit 417...

MP-0721-0001807	2 SEGMENTS / 00:00:34:13 DURATION

1. Page 18:07 - 18:08 / Duration 00:00:03:18

```
@        07              MR. LONGINO:  Would you hand the witness
         08   Exhibit 417, please.
```

2. Page 18:16 - 18:25 / Duration 00:00:30:25

```
16              THE WITNESS:  Okay.  I've got it.
17         Q.   BY MR. LONGINO:  417 is the document
18   that's been produced to us by Greyhound as the Greyhound
19   phone log with respect to the Chem-Lig transaction.
20              Reviewing that document, does it refresh
21   your recollection as to whether you had seen it prior to
22   filing the First Amended Complaint in this case?
23         A.   I don't really know.  I mean, I might
24   have seen it, and if so, exactly when, I'm just not
25   sure.
```

 Have you gone back and reviewed...

MP-0721-0002504	2 SEGMENTS / 00:00:48:28 DURATION

1. Page 25:04 - 25:15 / Duration 00:00:40:14

```
04         Q.   Since Mr. Ball's testimony, have you gone
05   back and reviewed any of the financial statements of
06   Chem-Lig that were submitted to Hal -- I mean that were
07   submitted to GFC?
08         A.   No, except that a couple minutes ago --
09   while I was sitting in this chair before the deposition
10   started, I was glancing through this statement of facts
11   that I looked at this morning, and one of the financial
12   statements is in here and I looked at the front page.
13   That's all I looked at.  In other words -- and it's
14   Exhibit 293 to the depo.  And I looked at just the title
15   page.  That's the only financial statement.
```

2. Page 25:19 - 25:23 / Duration 00:00:08:14

```
19         Q.   Since Mr. Ball's deposition was taken,
20   have you gone back and reviewed any of the monthly
21   financial statements from Chem-Lig that were submitted
22   to GFC?
23         A.   No.
```

page 2

Figure 12.20. (Continued)

TrialDirector Suite Demonstration Case

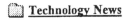 **Technology News**

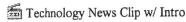 Technology News Clip w/ Intro

CH12-0002   **2 SEGMENTS / 00:00:29:07 DURATION**

1. **Time 00:00:01:00 - 00:00:07:07 / Duration 00:00:06:07**
2. **Page 1:10 - 1:16 / Duration 00:00:23:00**

```
10  Good morning everyone.  Jurors in Microsoft's anti-trust
11  trial finally heard from Bill Gates, albeit on video
12  tape.  The government claims at a key meeting in 1995,
13  the Microsoft chief purposed carving up the browser
14  software market with rival Netscape.  The government says
15  it shows that Microsoft used predatory behavior against its
16  competitors.  The trial is now in its third week.
```

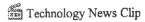 Technology News Clip

CH12-0001   **1 SEGMENTS / 00:00:23:00 DURATION**

1. **Page 1:10 - 1:16 / Duration 00:00:23:00**

```
10  Good morning everyone.  Jurors in Microsoft's anti-trust
11  trial finally heard from Bill Gates, albeit on video
12  tape.  The government claims at a key meeting in 1995,
13  the Microsoft chief purposed carving up the browser
14  software market with rival Netscape.  The government says
15  it shows that Microsoft used predatory behavior against its
16  competitors.  The trial is now in its third week.
```

Figure 12.20. (Continued)

TrialDirector Suite Demonstration Case

📁 <u>**Poli, Michael (Vol. 01) - 07/21/1995 [Demonstration Excerpt]**</u>

🎬 Do you understand that you're here to give a deposition...

MP-0721-0001217	1 SEGMENTS / 00:00:05:13 DURATION

1. Page 12:17 - 12:19

🎬 You've been called as an adverse...

MP-0721-0001220	6 SEGMENTS / 00:01:23:05 DURATION

1. Page 12:20 - 13:02
2. Page 13:07 - 13:13
3. Page 13:15 - 13:16
4. Page 13:22 - 13:24
5. Page 14:04 - 14:06
6. Page 14:11 - 14:21

🎬 Would you hand the witness Exhibit 417...

MP-0721-0001807	2 SEGMENTS / 00:00:34:13 DURATION

1. Page 18:07 - 18:08
2. Page 18:16 - 18:25

🎬 Have you gone back and reviewed...

MP-0721-0002504	2 SEGMENTS / 00:00:48:28 DURATION

1. Page 25:04 - 25:15
2. Page 25:19 - 25:23

📁 Technology News

🎬 Technology News Clip w/ Intro

CH12-0002	2 SEGMENTS / 00:00:29:07 DURATION

1. Time 00:00:01:00 - 00:00:07:07
2. Page 1:10 - 1:16

page 1

Figure 12.20. (Continued)

TrialDirector Suite Demonstration Case

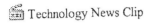 Technology News Clip

CH12-0001   1 SEGMENTS / 00:00:23:00 DURATION

1. **Page 1:10 - 1:16**

page 2

Figure 12.20. (Continued)

Summation and Trial Director can generate bar codes for each exhibit. Also, PowerPoint presentations can be imported into Trial Director and assigned bar code numbers.

One important item to consider when printing bar coded thumbnails of trial exhibits is the quality of the printer. Sometimes lower-end printers will generate bar codes that are unreadable by the bar code reader or wand.

Different bar code readers and wands can be purchased. Spending the extra money to obtain a reliable bar code reader is recommended. The last thing you want to have problems with at trial is your retrieval of electronic exhibits.

If you choose to use the bar code method, you should print out bar code labels and attach them to your exhibit list or utilize the bar code labels listed below your exhibit outline. This will prevent confusion for you at trial.

It is easy to see that the technology available today can be overwhelming. Time spent mastering an understanding of technological applications and integration of some of these tools will become increasingly critical to the legal professional in the new millennium. The courts are beginning to require greater degrees of technical persentation during trial. Those who embrace this shift and aquaint themselves with the prevailant hardware and software available to assist in case preparation and presentation are sure to enjoy a distinct advantage over those who do not! The student study guide contains exercises to assist you in taking the first steps towards mastering some of the available legal technology tools. As always, please use the information provided in this chapter to practically apply your gained knowledge in the student study guide excercises.

KEY TERMS

Certified copies
Deposition summary
Exhibit lists
Exhibits
Ex parte
Final pretrial
   memorandum and
   order

Interview
Jury instructions
Motions in limine
Pattern jury instructions
Praecipe
Shepardize
Subpoenas
Trial brief

Trial notebook
Witnesses
Witness list

TECHNOLOGY TERMS

Bar codes
Bitmap
Deposition database
Deposition summary tables

Dii load file
Full Boolean searches
GIF
Hyperlink
Image file
JPEG

OCR
Rapid fire digesting
Scanner
Summation notes
TIF
Word comments

USEFUL WEB SITES

http://www.tasanet.com   Expert witness/consultants
http://www.expertwitness.com
http://www.pacer.psc.uscourts.gov   Federal judiciary

chapter 13

Trial

chapter objectives

In this chapter, we will discuss

- An overview of the trial process, including the main parts of the trial
- How a paralegal might be involved during trial
- Ethical issues for paralegals to be aware of during trial
- How to use technology to create more effective trial presentations

In this day and age, very few cases go to trial. Trial is expensive, and very few individuals or entities can afford to follow their disputes through to trial. You may work as a paralegal for several years before you get to assist with a trial. Take every opportunity you have to observe trials to help prepare you for assisting with a trial.

Through the course of a trial, several tasks will be performed by your attorney. Your job, as always, is to make your attorney's job easier throughout the trial process. The following is a listing of the main events that occur during a trial:

- Voir dire
- Opening statements
- Presentation of cases in chief
- Closing arguments
- Selection of jury instructions
- Jury deliberations
- Jury decision

There are certain tasks you can perform during each of these events that can help in assisting your trial attorney. We will discuss these paralegal tasks below. As always, this discussion includes suggested tasks and is in no way meant to be a comprehensive listing. If you discover additional tasks that assist your attorney at trial, definitely employ them.

A. VOIR DIRE

Voir dire ("to speak the truth") is the preliminary examination made by the court and attorney of prospective jurors to determine their qualifications and suitability as jurors. Voir dire is the jury selection process. The attorney for each party is afforded the opportunity to question each prospective juror. Some courts, including most federal courts, have shifted the primary responsibility for voir dire to the trial judge. At any time during voir dire, the judge can dismiss a prospective juror for cause. Cause is defined by statute. Further, based on the prospective jurors' responses, the attorneys then decide which individuals they wish to dismiss from the jury pool. In a civil trial, each side has several peremptory challenges (the number will vary depending on jurisdiction) allowing them to dismiss an individual from the jury pool for no specific reason. Specifically, 28 U.S.C.A. §1870 states as follows:

> In civil cases, each party shall be entitled to three peremptory challenges. Several defendants or several plaintiffs may be considered as a single party for the purposes of making challenges, or the court may allow additional peremptory challenges and permit them to be exercised separately or jointly.
>   All challenges for cause or favor, whether to the array or panel or to individual jurors, shall be determined by the court.

Any additional requests for dismissals of prospective jurors can only occur if a substantial reason exists and the judge dismisses the juror for cause.

Your role during the voir dire process can be extensive or minimal depending on what your attorney wants. You may be asked to assist in the drafting of jury questions. Before you draft these questions, be sure to thoroughly review the jury questionnaires so that you know a little about the prospective jurors. The purpose of voir dire is to get to know the prospective jurors better. This is never an easy task. Some prospective jurors will say what they think your attorney wants to hear in order to get selected as a juror. There will also be prospective jurors who, for a variety of reasons, will not want to serve. Normally, a juror is not excused from jury duty unless there is a medical or other compelling reason. Usually, one or two alternate jurors will be selected to sit through trial and fill in if any juror is dismissed from service. Alternate jurors have a difficult but important job, as they have to be present during the entire trial but cannot participate in jury deliberations unless they replace a juror who has been dismissed from jury service before the trial concludes.

Another important task for which you provide assistance involves the creation of a seating diagram of the prospective jurors. This is normally done a few minutes prior to voir dire. The additional questionnaire information is helpful to the attorney during his or her questioning of prospective jurors.

PRACTICE TIP

Use sticky notes including each prospective juror's name and questionnaire information. This way, when the prospective jurors are called by the court to be questioned, you can place appropriate sticky notes in their seat location on the jury box diagram. This allows your attorney to address each prospective juror by name, which helps facilitate open communication early in their voir dire process.

The final task you should perform during voir dire is to take notes during the questioning. These notes provide the attorney with your impressions of the prospective juror, whether negative or positive. Since the attorney is performing the questioning, he or she probably will not be able to keep detailed notes of the prospective jurors' responses. Note each juror's nonverbal communication since this often tells you more about a person than verbal responses to voir dire questioning. Further, you should make note of prospective jurors who demonstrate strong opinions and personality traits.

B. OPENING STATEMENTS

Once the jury has been selected, each attorney will be given the opportunity to present opening statements. **An opening statement** is an outline or summary of the case and of anticipated evidence to be presented by the attorney to the jury. There has been much debate about how much argument can be inserted in an opening statement. Most discussions regarding opening statements are focused on the belief that an opening statement should contain just that—statements not arguments. However, since trial is an adverse proceeding most attorneys will be very aggressive in presenting their opening statements, inserting arguments throughout their statements. If you are assisting your attorney with opening statements, remember that they are statements. Do not draft an opening statement that could result in reprimand from the judge. Let your attorney make the decision to insert more aggressive statements that lean towards an argument.

The other duty you may perform during opening statements involves note taking. During opening statements, your attorney will make several promises to the jury regarding what he or she is going to prove on behalf of his client. You should keep track of these promises because the jury will remember them and expect them to be kept during the course of the trial. A similar situation occurs when a politician makes promises throughout a campaign and then fails to keep all of them after he or she wins the election. People usually only remember the promises that the policitian fails to keep. If you keep track of the promises made during opening statements, you can remind your attorney what he or she needs to address prior to closing arguments.

PRACTICE TIP

Draft a memo that lists the promises made by your attorney and opposing counsel so that your attorney has a record of what was said. If you are using real-time reporting during the trial, you can simply mark portions of the closing arguments for your attorney.

C. PRESENTATION OF CASES IN CHIEF

After opening statements have been made, the attorneys present their case in chief. **Case** in chief is that part of a trial in which the party with the burden of proof presents its evidence. If you are working for the plaintiff's attorney, your case will be presented first. If you are working for the defendant's attorney, your case will be presented last. Some believe that if the case in chief is presented last it will be remembered better by the jury. Others feel that when the case in chief is presented first, there is a distinct advantage because you set the stage and create the story of the case for the jury.

PRACTICE TIP

Trials are as much about image and perception as they are about facts. It is not the facts alone, but how they are delivered and presented to the jurors that determine the outcome. Litigators must educate, motivate, and persuade to prevail at trial. Engage the jury with a story by developing a clear theme. The use of metaphors and analogies are important elements of persuasion. A metaphor is an idea that organizes complex issues into something easily understood and visualized by the jury. Analogies translate an abstract concept into an everyday occurrence to foster understanding and identification. Remember to chose your analogies wisely, as an inappropriate analogy can be used against you by a worthy opponent.

Use demonstrative aids such as charts, maps, photographs, images, and videotapes. Graphics help a story come alive for a jury. Show, don't tell. Opening statements are primarily for teaching. They should be clear and logical. Closing statements connect the dots for the jury and fill in the blanks. Arm the jurors with the information and tools they need to argue the case during deliberations.

Whenever your attorney presents his or her case, you will need to perform certain tasks to assist. For each witness you should have an index of the trial exhibits that your attorney plans to use during direct examination. Some attorneys will provide you with a copy of their examination listing the exhibits as they will be addressed. If you have an index you can pull these exhibits prior to each witness's direct examination. If you do not have an index or a copy of the attorney's examination, you will have to pull exhibits as the attorney asks for them, which substantially slows down the process. You should also have these original trial exhibits readily available in a box loose and separated by numbered exhibit tabs. The above practices should reduce any delays that may occur when you are retrieving trial exhibits for admission into evidence. The technology section of this chapter discusses the technology tools available to assist you in retrieving trial exhibits that are in digital format. Using technology to retrieve exhibits is the most efficient approach and likely will, in the near future, become the standard in courtrooms throughout the country.

In your trial notebook you should keep a copy of both parties' trial exhibit lists so that you can keep a log of the trial exhibits admitted, refused, and objected to during trial. When you are logging in an admitted trial exhibit, indicate which witness testified about the exhibit. This may seem like a trivial task, but it becomes extremely important after the trial is over because it is the only record you have of what exhibits were presented during trial and who testified about them. If the case is ever appealed, this log is imperative to determining what information was admitted into evidence. It is very easy to get behind on this log, especially when you are retrieving the exhibits for your attorney. Meet with the clerk of court at the end of each trial day to check your log for accuracy. This process only takes a few minutes but it provides you with the peace of mind to confidently tell the attorney which exhibits have been admitted into evidence. It also reduces any possible errors that can occur during trial.

Another procedure that helps tremendously during trial involves providing the attorney with trial exhibit binders. These binders contain copies of the trial exhibits, which he or she can use as working copies during direct and cross-examinations of witnesses. This way you have possession of the original trial exhibits for retrieval and organizational purposes.

The final tasks performed during the presentation of a case in chief involve note taking, scheduling of witnesses, and the reading of testimony into the record. Keep detailed notes of the testimony presented. A discussion of the technology tools available to assist you in note taking will be discussed in the technology section below. Scheduling witnesses also becomes an important task since the presentation order of witnesses may change as the trial progresses.

There are occasions when witnesses cannot appear in person to testify. Their testimony can be entered into evidence two different ways. First, your attorney can elect to have a videotaped trial deposition taken of the witness for playback to the jury at trial. Second, your attorney can have the testimony read into the record similar to a script. Of course, the most effective testimony is live, but this is not always possible. You may have to read testimony into the record for your attorney at trial. This can be extremely boring for jurors. If you have to read testimony into the record, be concise and animated so you do not bore your audience. If testimony is going to be read into the record, you will need to provide the opposing counsel and the judge with a highlighted copy of the deposition testimony to be read into the record. This highlighting can be done manually with hardcopied exhibits and color copied for the opposing counsel and judge. The technology section of this chapter discusses how digital deposition testimony can be highlighted for presentation to opposing counsel and the judge.

D. CLOSING ARGUMENTS

The final event that will be presented to the jury is closing arguments. **Closing arguments** are the final statements to the jury or court that summarize the evidence established and the evidence the other side has failed to establish. This is the attorney's final opportunity to summarize the evidence presented and to reinforce his or her case arguments. You may have to retrieve some exhibits during your attorney's closing arguments. The technology section of this chapter will discuss tools that can be used during closing arguments. If computer software is used during closing, you probably will run the equipment for your attorney.

> PRACTICE TIP
>
> Displaying and explaining jury instructions to the jury during closing arguments is crucial to increasing the jury's understanding of how to apply the law to the evidence presented.

E. SELECTION OF JURY INSTRUCTIONS

Jury instructions are the directions given by the court to the jury pertaining to the law. Jury instructions are extremely important because they explain your case to the jury. Your attorney's case can be won or lost during the jury instruction negotiations. If the jury does not understand an instruction or is not allowed to review certain instructions, then its decision-making process is modified.

Normally, your attorney will draft the jury instructions. Your involvement in drafting jury instructions will be minimal, with you possibly performing some legal research. The primary area you can assist with occurs during the negotiations on jury instructions. Jury instruction negotiations normally occur in the judge's chambers or the courtroom behind closed doors with the attorneys and the judge present. However, when I work with my attorneys, they prefer that I be present during these negotiations for organizational purposes.

In my trial notebook, I keep a copy of the proposed instructions. As each instruction is submitted, I number those that are accepted and note those that are denied. If any instructions are revised prior to being accepted or denied, I make the revision on my copy. It is also wise to have a laptop computer with a printer so that revisions can be quickly made and submitted to the judge.

At the end of jury instruction negotiations, I separate the accepted and denied instructions for each party by tabs in my trial notebook. Document organization is imperative when it comes to jury instructions, as this is the record you will need to preserve if the case is appealed. If the case is appealed, jury instructions are almost always one of the issues appealed.

F. JURY DELIBERATIONS

Once closing arguments have been made, the judge will dismiss the jurors for deliberations in the jury room. **Jury deliberations** are the discussions held by jurors after the trial presentations in order to render a decision. The alternate jurors are dismissed at this time because they do not have any decision-making power.

The jury is allowed to see any trial exhibit admitted into evidence. Demonstrative exhibits usually cannot be provided to the jury during deliberations. The technology section of this chapter will discuss the software available to electronically generate demonstrative exhibits from admitted trial exhibits.

While the jury deliberates, your attorney will probably want to wait at the office or, if you are out of town, somewhere away from the courthouse. You should keep a cell phone with you so that the court can contact your attorney when the jury has made a decision. Jury deliberations can occur within a few hours or a few days depending on the evidence and the case.

G. JURY DECISION

Jury decision is the final decision made by a jury regarding a case. Once the jury has made a decision the judge will contact the representative attorneys and announce that the court is in session. At this time the judge will ask the jury foreperson to provide him or her with the verdict form indicating the decision rendered. After the verdict is read by the judge, either party can request that the jury be polled. Polling consists of asking each juror how they voted on the issues listed in the verdict form. In your trial notebook you should have a copy of the verdict form on which you can note what the decision was. If the jury is polled, make a record of the polling on the jury questionnaires. This provides you with a record of how each juror voted. At this point the trial is concluded and the jurors are dismissed.

The follow-up work performed regarding the jury, if allowed by the court, is to interview them regarding the case and their verdict. Not all jurors will want to talk to you regarding the case. Before interviewing the jurors, meet with your attorney to see what areas the interview should focus on. After the interviews of the jurors, draft a memo for the attorney setting forth the information obtained during these interviews. These interviews primarily provide the attorney with insight into the jury's understanding of the case. When you conduct these interviews, you will be amazed to discover what information the jury did or did not retain. The attorney can use this information to work on his or her trial techniques for the future and determine if there are any issues for appeal. As with any interview, make sure to identify yourself at the beginning of the conversation and ask open-ended questions to obtain the greatest amount of information regarding trial, jury deliberations, and the verdict.

ETHICS

During a trial, certain behavior is expected of the judges and attorneys, as well as the paralegal. If you are carrying a cell phone be sure to have the cell phone turned off whenever you are in the courtroom. You should also be sure not to make unnecessary noise in the courtroom. Cell phones and unnecessary noise will only serve to distract the jury and disrupt the flow of the trial. Most judges will have you removed from the courtroom if you fail to respect the proceedings by leaving your cell phone turned on or making unnecessary noise.

The other ethical practice that should be employed by the paralegal during trial involves the location of case and case strategy discussions. Any discussions regarding the case or case strategy should be performed in a secure room or outside area, not in the courtroom hallways. The best practice to employ as a paralegal is not to discuss the case with anyone unless your attorney has instructed you to do so. You never know who might be listening to your conversation.

> **PRACTICE TIP**
>
> During trial, remember everything you do or say is being observed by the jurors. Attire should be formal, and you should refrain from any reactions you may have regarding testimony. You should always stand for the jury when they enter the courtroom, respecting the fact that they are taking time out of their busy lives to participate in this process.

CONCLUSION

This chapter has discussed the ways in which the paralegal can make the attorney's job easier during trial. The items discussed included voir dire, opening statements, presentation of cases in chief, closing arguments, selection of jury instructions, jury deliberations, and the jury decision. The practice tips and suggestions provided throughout this chapter will allow you to assist your attorney in presenting a well-polished case. Your job is to make him or her look good, and trial is the ultimate test of your effectiveness and skill as a paralegal.

There are various ways in which the paralegal can assist in a smooth trial presentation by the attorney. Technology tools available today provide for a smooth, polished presentation. A litigation paralegal assisting in today's courtrooms must learn and become proficient in presenting evidence electronically. This presentation method is quickly becoming the preferred method by judges, attorneys, and juries. Trials that would normally take two weeks can be finished in half the time if the evidence is presented digitally. Juries retain more information during a well-crafted digital presentation. Some of the tools available, will be discussed below in the technology section.

USING TECHNOLOGY IN THE LAW OFFICE

The advances in technology hardware and software have made trial presentation easier and more effective. Technology can be used to assist during the following areas of a trial:

- Opening statements
- Presentation of cases in chief
- Selection of jury instructions
- Closing arguments

A. OPENING STATEMENTS

There are numerous software packages available that will enable you to emphasize key points during opening statements. Studies have shown that human memory retention is increased to 60 percent when both verbal and visual stimulus are utilized. Opening statements can be set forth graphically in conjunction with demonstrative images using Microsoft PowerPoint. **PowerPoint** is a software program that allows the user to create graphic presentations. Timelines, graphs, and charts can be inserted throughout your PowerPoint presentation to emphasis important points and promises made to the jury. A **Timeline** is a graphic that depicts facts in chronological order. A graph or chart is a graphic that illustrates a point using lines, bars, or pies. Creation of timelines, graphs, and charts was discussed in Chapters 11 and 12.

Once you have created your graphics, they can be inserted into your "Opening Statements" slide presentation by using the copy-and-paste function.

You will want to meet with your attorney to determine what information will be inserted into the "Opening Statements" slide presentation. Some attorneys will simply give you their opening statements outline to insert into a PowerPoint presentation. Any text inserted into PowerPoint can be formatted and animated. Text can be animated by highlighting the desired text, right-clicking, and selecting Animation from the drop-down menu. See Figure 13.1.

Remember to be consistent if you decide to use animation, so that the jury is not constantly searching for each animated point. Animation controls how the text or graphics appear in PowerPoint. Animation is normally controlled by the mouse click so that the attorney can move through the slides as quickly or slowly as desired. **Slides** are simply pages within a PowerPoint presentation, documents created in PowerPoint that can be added into a presentation. You can draft the opening statement slides based on your attorney's outline, adding some graphics to emphasize important statements. Once you have drafted the "Opening Statements" slide presentation, it can be presented to the attorney for review and revision. Several modifications will be made before the final presentation is complete.

B. PRESENTATION OF CASES IN CHIEF

During your attorney's case the presentation of digital exhibits can be accomplished through the use of litigation software and bar codes. The software program Trial Director allows for the retrieval of digital exhibits either by name or through the use of bar codes and a bar code wand. **Bar code wands** are hardware created to read bar codes. Once you are in presentation mode, you simply type in the exhibit name and select Enter or you swipe the bar code for the desired exhibit with a wand. To allow for quick retrieval of digital trial exhibits, it is suggested that you have thumbnail printouts made of the exhibits, indicating their names and bar codes referenced. **Thumbnails** are miniature graphics of image files containing descriptive text and bar codes identifying the files. This printout

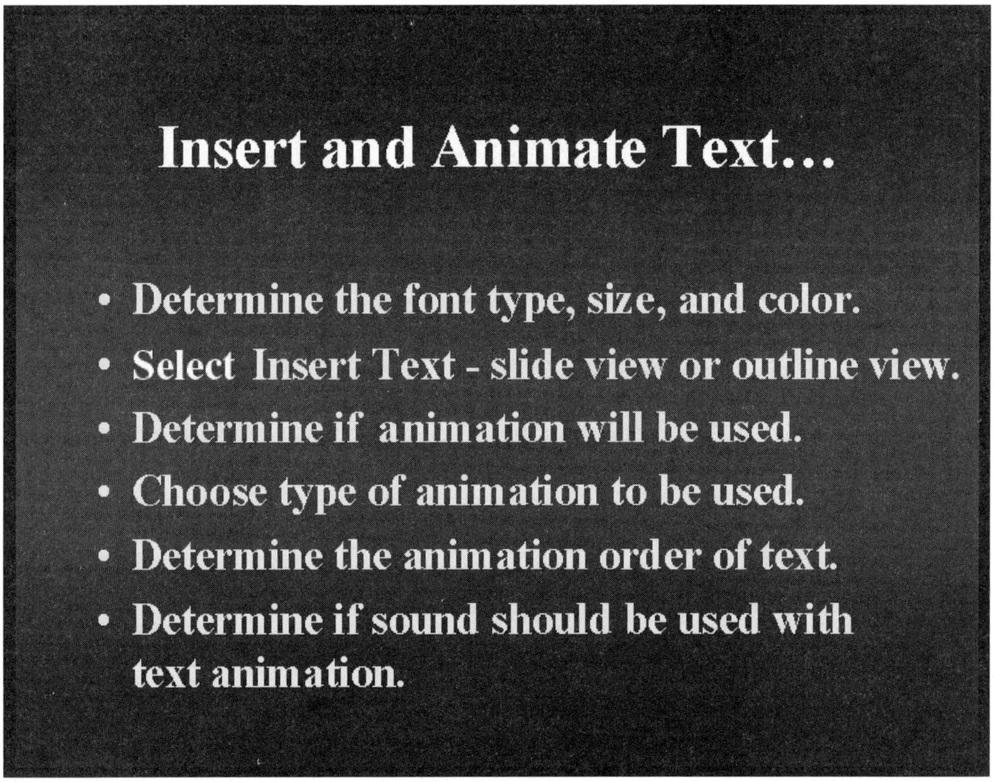

Figure 13.1. Animating Text in PowerPoint

should then be inserted in your trial exhibit notebook. The bar codes for your digital exhibits can also be printed out onto labels and affixed to the exhibit lists.

The **bar code label** (a label that has a printed bar code on it for digital exhibit retrieval) method for digital trial exhibit retrieval can also be used; it is helpful when your attorney wants to refer to trial exhibit numbers. Figure 13.2 provides an example of an exhibit list that accommodates bar code labels. As you can see from Figure 13.2, if you use the bar code labels, you can simply swipe the appropriate label with your bar code wand. This method is especially advantageous when you have hundreds of trial exhibits. Thumbnails can take up a lot of space in your trial notebook and result in substantial delays during exhibit retrieval.

One distinct advantage in using digital exhibits involves the ability to electronically emphasize such exhibits. **Digital exhibits** are exhibits that are scanned into electronic image file formats. Document Director allows you to highlight, underline, and circle exhibits, either prior to or during exhibit presentation. The drawing toolbar and the mouse can be used to emphasize these digital exhibits. If you add emphasis before presenting the exhibit, Document Director will ask if you want to save this exhibit as a new exhibit. You will want to save any preemphasized trial exhibits as new exhibits. Document Director will place these newly emphasized exhibits directly below the original

EXHIBIT LIST

Barcode	Exhibit Number	Date Offered	Date Admitted	Date Refused	Description
TEXT0001	001	/ /	/ /	/ /	Trauma: Pathophysiologic Effects, Diagnosis and Emergency Treatment by Kennedy, M.D. & Caswell, Medical Editor
+GEXH04	002	/ /	/ /	/ /	Rotary Wing
+GEXH18	003	/ /	/ /	/ /	Wing Reinforcement
+GEXH36	004	/ /	/ /	/ /	Wing Spar Cap
+GEXH41	005	/ /	/ /	/ /	Air Worthiness Directive Tag
+GEXH42	006	/ /	/ /	/ /	Enlarged Air Worthiness Directive Tag
PURSUIT	007	/ /	/ /	/ /	Car Chase and Crash Video
+XRAY	008	/ /	/ /	/ /	Hip Gunshot X-Ray
	009	/ /	/ /	/ /	
	010	/ /	/ /	/ /	
	011	/ /	/ /	/ /	

Figure 13.2. Trial Director—Exhibit List with Bar Code Labels

exhibit. Remember, if you emphasize the digital trial exhibits during their presentation, the emphasis will not be saved.

Another technology tool that can be used by the paralegal throughout the trial presentation is real-time transcript reporting by the court reporter. **Real-time transcript reporting** is a method of court reporting which involves receipt of the transcript immediately, as the testimony is being given. If you bring your laptop to the trial, you can arrange to obtain a real-time trial transcript for each trial day. This allows you to obtain and search trial testimony throughout the day. Further, your attorney can use this draft trial transcript to prepare for the next day of testimony. Real-time transcript reporting can be utilized if your laptop has software to accommodate such an application. The software Summation and Cheetah have the ability to perform real-time transcript reporting. These programs will also allow you to mark important testimony as it occurs by striking the space bar. You can also preset certain keywords to automatically be marked by these programs. You simply enter the real-time setup and create keywords or issues for marking. You will need to link your laptop with the court reporter's computer to receive the transcript feed. If you have problems with the real-time application, it is most likely the baud rate setting, the court reporter's cords or connection, or your cords or connection. You should run a real-time transcript test with the court reporter several days prior to the trial so that time is not wasted during the trial. Further, testing allows you to work through any bugs that may occur when using the real-time transcript application

The final technology tools that you will most likely utilize during the presentation of your attorney's case in chief is your database and the Internet. Your database can assist in quickly locating a document that was not anticipated to be used as a trial exhibit. Searching and printing reports in a database is discussed in Chapter 5 regarding document management. The Internet can also be a very valuable tool during trial presentation. It's like having an electronic investigator there in the courtroom with you. You have immediate access to any information discovered. For further information on using the Internet, please review Chapter 4.

Currently there are several courtrooms throughout the United States that are wired to present evidence electronically. Figures 13.3 through 13.8 are photographs of the digital federal courtroom located in Billings, Montana. Special thanks go out to Cecil Chandler and Judge Richard Cebull for allowing these photographs to be taken.

As you can see from Figures 13.3 to 13.8, there are computer monitors for each juror, the judge, the attorneys, the witnesses, and the clerk, as well as two monitors for those sitting in the courtroom observing. This courtroom also has a projector that accommodates those attorneys using hardcopied trial exhibits (Figure 13.5). The hardcopies can simply be placed upon the projector and digitally presented to the entire courtroom.

Electronic trial presentation is more efficient and effective than manual trial presentation. Learning to use the technology tools for electronic trial presentation is a worthwhile endeavor. As technology becomes more and more common, courtrooms will expect that evidence be presented digitally and not manually. Jurors are becoming more technology savvy, with most owning a personal home computer.

C. CLOSING ARGUMENTS

PowerPoint allows you to heighten the emphasis placed on your attorney's closing arguments just as it does with opening statements. The only difference during closing arguments is that throughout the PowerPoint slide presentation, you can use any trial exhibits that have been admitted into evidence. This potentially increases the jurors' memory retention

Figure 13.3. Front View of Courtroom

Figure 13.4. The Attorney Presentation Podium

Figure 13.5. The Projection Machine

Figure 13.6. The Witness Chair with Digital Monitor

Figure 13.7. The Jury Box with Digital Monitors

Figure 13.8. The Observers' Area with Digital Monitor

rates regarding your attorney's closing arguments. As would be expected, studies have shown that when individuals recall more information, they reach a consensus quicker.

D. SELECTION OF JURY INSTRUCTIONS

During jury instruction negotiations, it becomes extremely helpful to have the proposed instructions on a laptop. A portable printer is also a necessity during jury instruction negotiations. If any instructions need to be revised, you can perform this task for your attorney within a few minutes. Having the ability to immediately revise a jury instruction affords your attorney a second opportunity to get a proposed instruction accepted by the court.

KEY TERMS

Case in chief	Jury deliberations	Voir dire
Closing argument	Jury instructions	
Jury decision	Opening statements	

TECHNOLOGY TERMS

Bar code labels	PowerPoint	Slides
Bar code wands	Real-time transcript	Thumbnails
Digital exhibits	reporting	Timelines

USEFUL WEB SITES

http://www.lawyers.martindale.com   Martindale-Hubbell Lawyer Locator
http://www.atlanet.org   The Association of Trial Lawyers of America
http://www.experts.com   Directory of Experts

chapter 14

Posttrial Considerations

chapter objectives

In this chapter, we will discuss

- An overview of posttrial motions
- Judgments and collections
- The appellate process
- Rules governing the appellate process

There are various procedures that occur after a verdict is rendered: making posttrial motions, filing for judgment, enforcing a judgment, and appealing the verdict. The losing party may appeal the decision rendered. During the appeal process the paralegal can provide much needed support. Organizational skills become extremely important.

A. POSTTRIAL MOTIONS

There are motions that can be filed posttrial. A few of those possible motions include

Motion for new trial: a request that the judge order a new trial based on the fact that the trial was improper or unfair due to specified prejudicial errors that occurred or because of newly discovered evidence

Motion for reconsideration: a request filed by a party who is not satisfied with the results of a judicial finding

Motion for judgment N.O.V.: a request to have judgment entered in a party's favor notwithstanding the jury's verdict against the party

Motion to amend findings and judgment: a request made after trial and entry of judgment asking the court to amend findings and judgment

> ***Motion to set aside the judgment:*** a request that the judge order judgment set aside
> based on mistake, fraud, or newly discovered evidence

Therefore, victory at the end of trial is not necessarily complete, nor does it ensure that the winning party will receive the judgment entered. To the distress of winning plaintiffs, defendants either intentionally choose not to pay or lack the finances to meet the mandated obligation. From a defendant's perspective, the judgment may be based on bad law or fact finding. Often defendant's counsel may opt for numerous challenges to the finding of the court. Under Federal Rule of Civil Procedure 62, the judgment defendant can seek a stay.

According to Rule 59 of the Federal Rules of Civil Procedure, a motion for new trial may be granted "to all or any of the parties and on all or part of the issues," shall be served no later than 10 days after entry of judgment, and, if the motion is based on affidavits, they shall be served with the motion.

At the end of the plaintiff's case, a motion for a directed verdict is usually made. The defendant is entitled to a directed verdict on any cause of action if the plaintiff has failed to prove the allegations. The motion will fail if the plaintiff has not made out a prima facie case. Motions for directed verdict can be made by either party and are made at the end of the trial phase, following rebuttals. The judge is always free to bypass the jury and render an immediate verdict. However, most judges are very cautious in the use of that power to grant a directed verdict and do so only in circumstances where the correct outcome is clear. Federal Rule of Civil Procedure 50 states in pertinent part:

> (a) Judgment as a Matter of Law in Jury Trials
> (1) If during a trial by jury a party has been fully heard on an issue and there is no legally sufficient evidentiary basis for a reasonable jury to find for that party on that issue, the court may determine the issue against the party and may grant a motion for judgment as a matter of law against that party with respect to a claim or defense that cannot under the controlling law be maintained or defeated without a favorable finding on that issue.
> (2) Motions for judgment as matter of law may be made at any time before submission of the case to the jury. Such a motion shall specify the judgment sought and the law and the facts on which the moving party is entitled to the judgment.

A defendant or plaintiff who is not satisfied with the results of a judicial finding or verdict may file a motion for reconsideration. A party may also file a motion to set aside the judgment, which asks the court to set aside the judgment entered. The motion may be based on a number of grounds such as mistake, fraud, or newly discovered evidence. A motion to amend the findings and judgment is a motion made after the trial and entry of judgment to have the court amend the findings and to amend the judgment in conformity with the amended findings. A motion for judgment n.o.v. is a motion to have judgment entered in a party's favor notwithstanding the jury's verdict against the party. A motion for new trial after a judgment n.o.v. is a motion made by a party for a new trial after that party's verdict has been set aside because the judge has granted a motion for judgment n.o.v.

Motions for a new trial and motions for a judgment notwithstanding the verdict are used in very different situations. Motions for a new trial are used when the judge has made some mistake during the trial itself, such as allowing evidence that should have been excluded, procedural error, or allowing improper argument. Motions for judgment n.o.v. are used when the claim is that the jury reached the wrong decision. Refer to Federal Rule of Civil Procedure 50.

A Motion for directed verdict requests the judge to instruct the jury to issue a verdict based on the fact that the defendant has not presented any credible evidence to rebut any elements of plaintiff's cause of action. Figure 14.1 is an example of a Motion for directed verdict.

A Motion for reconsideration is a request by a party who is not satisified with the results of a judicial finding to have that finding reconsidered. The motion must state the grounds for the request. Figure 14.2 shows a motion for reconsideration.

A Motion for new trial is a request that the judge order a new trial based on the fact that the trial was improper or unfair due to specified prejudicial errors that occurred or because of newly discovered evidence. Again, the motion must state the grounds for the request of a new trial. See Figure 14.3 for an example of a motion for a new trial.

Attorneys for _____

UNITED STATES DISTRICT COURT, DISTRICT OF _____

_____,   )   Civil No. _____

    Plaintiff,   )   **MOTION FOR DIRECTED VERDICT**

vs.   )

)   _____,

_____,   )   Judge

    Defendants.   )

_____, Plaintiff above-named, moves the Court to instruct the jury to return a verdict against _____ and in favor of _____. The grounds for this motion are: _____.

    Dated this ____ day of _____, 2002.

            By _____
            P.O. Box 555
            Billings, MT 59101
            Attorneys for _____

Figure 14.1. Motion for Directed Verdict

Attorneys for _____

UNITED STATES DISTRICT COURT, DISTRICT OF _____

_____,)
) Civil No. _____
Plaintiff,)
) **MOTION FOR RECONSIDERATION**
vs.)
) _____,
) Judge
_____,)
)
Defendants.)
)

TO: _____ and his attorney, _____

    Please take notice that _____ (party) will move the court to reconsider the previous ruling made in Order dated _____, Order No. _____, at _____ (time) and at _____ (location). Such motion is based on the ground _____.

    Dated this _____ day of _____, 2002.

                     By _____
                     P.O. Box 555
                     Billings, MT 59101
                     Attorneys for _____

Figure 14.2. Motion for Reconsideration

    A Motion for judgment N.O.V. is a request to have judgment entered in a party's favor notwithstanding the jury's verdict against the party. Again, grounds for the motion must be stated in the motion. See Figure 14.4 for an example of a motion for judgment N.O.V.

    A Motion to set aside the judgment is a request that the judge order judgment set aside based on mistake, fraud, or newly discovered evidence. See Figure 14.5 for an example of a motion to set aside the judgment.

B. JUDGMENTS AND COLLECTIONS

The event that formally ends the trial phase of the litigation is the entry of judgment. The judgment evidences the party who won the lawsuit. However, winning at trial does

Attorneys for _____

UNITED STATES DISTRICT COURT, DISTRICT OF _____

_____,   )
)   Civil No. _____
)
        Plaintiff,   )   **MOTION FOR NEW TRIAL**
)
    vs.   )   _____,
)
)   Judge
_____,   )
)
)
        Defendants.   )
)

TO THE HONORABLE JUDGE OF SAID COURT:

        COMES NOW, _____ plaintiff in the above-referenced cause of action, and moves this Court to set aside the judgment heretofore rendered against it on _____ and grant it a new trial this cause, for the following good and sufficient reasons:

        This motion is presented within the time limits prescribed by Rule _____, Rules of Civil Procedure for a Motion for New Trial.

        The judgment of the Court is contrary to the law [state basis].

        [In the alternative] There was insufficient evidence to support the judgment as delivered. [State the facts supporting the above].

        WHEREFORE, _____ prays that after notice and hearing the judgment rendered in this case be set aside and movant be granted a new trial.

        Dated this _____ day of _____, 2002.

                        By _____
                        P.O. Box 555
                        Billings, MT 59101
                        Attorneys for _____

Figure 14.3. Motion for New Trial

Attorneys for _____

UNITED STATES DISTRICT COURT, DISTRICT OF _____

_____,)
) Civil No. _____
)
Plaintiff,   ) **MOTION FOR JUDGMENT**
) **NOTWITHSTANDING THE VERDICT**
vs.   )
) _____,
_____,   )
) Judge
)
Defendants.   )
)

TO THE HONORABLE JUDGE OF SAID COURT:

Defendant, _____, respectfully moves this court to enter Judgment Notwithstanding the Verdict and to enter judgment for the defendant and that plaintiff take nothing in this case, and for its motion would respectfully show the court as follows:

The evidence presented in this proceedings conclusively establishes the opposite of this jury finding and there is no evidence of probative value to support the jury's finding of _____ in this issue. [Make specific statements here to allude to testimony that support your allegation that the jury finding is incorrect; repeat for each and every issue for which you maintain an incorrect jury finding.]

WHEREFORE, defendant respectfully requests that the court disregard the above jury findings and enter a Judgment Notwithstanding the Verdict in favor of defendant and against plaintiff.

Dated this _____ day of _____, 2002.

By _____
P.O. Box 555
Billings, MT 59101
Attorneys for _____

Figure 14.4. Motion for Judgment Notwithstanding the Verdict

not automatically put any money in the plaintiff's pocket. There are, therefore, certain procedures to enforce that judgment. But to enforce the judgment we must establish that we are entitled to do so.

Subsequent to the trial the winning party may be entitled to have judgment against the loser for taxable court costs. Taxable costs do not relate to all expenses incurred, but

Attorneys for _____

UNITED STATES DISTRICT COURT, DISTRICT OF _____

_____,   )
)   Civil No. _____
)
          Plaintiff,   )   **MOTION TO SET ASIDE JUDGMENT**
)
     vs.   )   _____,
)   Judge
_____,   )
)
          Defendants.   )
)

TO THE HONORABLE JUDGE OF SAID COURT:

   Defendant, _____, respectfully moves this court to set aside the judgment entered herein for the following reasons: [state reasons]. Note: Granted only in situations in which it would be grossly unfair or unjust to let the judgment stand.

   WHEREFORE, defendant respectfully requests that the court amend the findings and judgment entered herein.

   Dated this _____ day of _____, 2002.

       By _____
       P.O. Box 555
       Billings, MT 59101
       Attorneys for _____

Figure 14.5. Motion to Set Aside the Judgment

may include filing fees, printing fees, pleadings, witness fees, and so on. Rule 54 of the Federal Rules of Civil Procedure outlines judgments and costs and sets forth required deadlines and filing periods, unless otherwise directed by the court. The procedure for determining the amount of costs to assess is through filing a statement or bill of costs. The losing party can then file any written objections to any items felt to be improper. Although not generally recoverable, proceedings to determine the amount of attorneys' fees to award can become quite complex and can require evidentiary hearings as the parties argue the reasonableness of various charges. Refer to Rules 54(d)(1) and (2).

  State laws govern the enforcement of money judgments where the property or money of the judgment debtor is located. Therefore, the paralegal must carefully review the statutes in his or her state and become intimately familiar with those statutes.

  The four most common procedures for enforcing money judgments are

1. Writ of execution
2. Writ of garnishment
3. Prejudgment attachments
4. Specific state remedies provided by state statutes and court rules

A **writ of execution** is a document asking the sheriff to take the judgment debtor's property into custody. It is normally prepared by the clerk of the court where the judgment was entered on receipt of an application for writ of execution. The application is filed with the clerk of court along with the appropriate fee. There are specific court rules for filing and requesting writs, so be sure to check your local rules. Normally, once issued, the writ is delivered to the sheriff or some other levying officer. The writ directs the sheriff to levy, in other words, to take the judgment debtor's property into custody pursuant to the writ of execution.

A **writ of garnishment** is a document that attaches an individual's wages. In most states, a writ of garnishment must be requested from the court. Papers are served on the judgment debtor's bank and employer providing notice. When the judgment debtor's wages are attached, they are attached by very specific percentage formulas until the judgment amount is satisfied. The specific procedures are outlined in state statutes and should be carefully reviewed and followed. In some states, it is considered a violation of law or contempt of court for failure to comply with a garnishment.

Prejudgment attachments secure possession of property in controversy or of creating a security for the debt in controversy before the final judgment of the court on the merits of the case.

The Uniform Reciprocal Enforcement of Support Act provides a method to enforce duties of support where the petitioning party and the respondent are in different but reciprocating jurisdictions. If your state has adopted that act, read the statute as accepted. All fifty states and the District of Columbia are reciprocating states. There is also a Uniform Enforcement of Foreign Judgments Act, which is not reciprocal. Any state that adopts it can allow a judgment of a sister state to be registered and executed on under the latest revision of that act (1964). The act, when adopted by a state in its revised form, allows a sister-state judgment enforcement similar to the interdistrict enforcement of the judgment of the federal district courts (28 U.S.C. §1963). Check your own state statutes governing judgments and execution to find out which version, if any, your state has adopted.

C. APPEALS

1. The Appeals Process

An **appeal** is a request made after a trial by a party who has lost on one or more issues that a higher court review the trial court's decision to determine if it was correct. The losing party in a decision by a trial court in the federal system normally is entitled to move to have the judgment set aside or to appeal the decision to a federal court of appeals. Similarly, a litigant who is dissatisfied with a decision made by a federal administrative agency usually may file a petition for review of the agency decision by a court of appeals. Judicial review in cases involving certain federal agencies or programs—for example, disputes over Social Security benefits—may be obtained first in a district court rather than directly to a court of appeals.

In a civil case, either side may appeal the verdict. In a criminal case, the defendant may appeal a guilty verdict, but the government may not appeal if a defendant is found not guilty. Either side in a criminal case may appeal with respect to the sentence that is imposed after a guilty verdict.

A litigant who files an appeal, known as an **appellant,** must show that the trial court or administrative agency made a legal error that affected the decision in the case. The court of appeals makes its decision based on the record of the case established by the trial court or agency. It does not receive additional evidence or hear witnesses. The court of appeals also may review the factual findings of the trial court or agency, but typically may only overturn a decision on factual grounds if the findings were clearly erroneous.

Appeals are decided by panels of three judges working together. The appellant presents legal arguments to the panel, in writing, in a document called a brief. **A brief** is formal argument citing reasons why a trial court decision was or was not in error. In the brief, the appellant tries to persuade the judges that the trial court made an error and that its decision should be reversed. On the other hand, the party defending against the appeal, known as the **appellee,** tries in its brief to show why the trial court decision was correct or why any error made by the trial court was not significant enough to affect the outcome of the case.

Although some cases are decided on the basis of written briefs alone, many cases are selected for an oral argument before the court. **Oral argument** in the court of appeals is structured discussion between the appellate lawyers and the panel of judges focusing on the legal principles in dispute. Each side is given a short time—usually about 15 minutes—to present arguments to the court.

The court of appeals decision usually will be the final word in the case, unless it sends the case back to the trial court for additional proceedings or the parties ask the U.S. Supreme Court to review the case. In some cases the decision may be reviewed **en banc,** that is, by a larger group of judges (usually all) of the court of appeals for the circuit.

A litigant who loses in a federal court of appeals or in the highest court of a state may file a petition for a **writ of certiorari,** which is a document asking the U.S. Supreme Court to review the case. The Supreme Court, however, does not have to grant the review. The Court typically will agree to hear a case only when it involves an unusually important legal principle or when two or more federal appellate courts have interpreted a law differently. There are also a small number of special circumstances in which the Supreme Court is required by law to hear an appeal. When the Supreme Court hears a case, the parties are required to file written briefs and the Court may hear oral argument.

2. Rules Governing the Appellate Process

The rules governing the appellate process in federal courts are found in the Federal Rules of Appellate Procedure. These rules are similar to rules that have been adopted in state courts and must be carefully followed to avoid forfeiture of the client's rights. The whole appellate process is governed by very detailed court rules.

Every party has as a matter of right the opportunity to appeal a decision from a district court to a court of appeals. This means that the losing party is permitted to appeal the trial court's judgment, and the court of appeals must hear the appeal. An appellate court has the power to review the judgment of a lower court (trial court) or tribunal. For example, the U.S. circuit courts of appeals review the decisions of the U.S. district courts. If a party loses in the court of appeals, however, that party must petition the Supreme Court to hear the appeal; the appeal will be heard by the Supreme Court only if the petition is granted. Since petitions to the Supreme Court are rare, we will not focus on those types of appeals.

Federal Rule of Appellate Procedure 3 discusses appeal as of right and how that appeal is taken. Rule 3 covers filing the appeal, contents of the notice of appeal, serving the notice of appeal, and payment of fees. **A notice of appeal** is a legal document that initiates the appeal process in federal court. Figure 14.6 shows a notice of appeal.

It is extremely important to not only be aware of the rules governing appeals, but to be intimately familiar with them to protect the client's interest. It is the paralegal who is usually requested to handle the scheduling of the appeal process.

Attorneys for _____

UNITED STATES DISTRICT COURT, DISTRICT OF _____

_____,	)	Civil
	)	No. _____
Plaintiff,	)	
	)	**NOTICE OF APPEAL**
vs.	)	
	)	_____,
_____,	)	Judge
	)	
Defendants.	)	

Notice is hereby given that Plaintiff, _____, hereby appeals to the United States Court of Appeals for the Ninth Circuit from that portion of the final judgment entered on January 24, 2002, awarding the plaintiff only $15,000 in damages.

Dated this _____ day of _____, 2002.

By _____
P.O. Box 555
Billings, MT 59101
Attorneys for _____

Figure 14.6. Notice of Appeal

Let's look quickly at some parts of Rule 3:

(a) Filing the Notice of Appeal. An appeal permitted by law as of right from a district court to a court of appeals must be taken by filing a notice of appeal with the clerk of the district court within the time allowed by Rule 4. At the time of filing, the appellant must furnish the clerk with sufficient copies of the notice of appeal to enable the clerk to comply promptly with the requirements of subdivision (d) of this Rule 3. Failure of an appellant to take any step other than the timely filing of a notice of appeal does not affect the validity of the appeal, but is ground only for such action as the court of appeals deems appropriate, which may include dismissal of the appeal. Appeals by permission under 28 U.S.C. §1292(b) and appeals in bankruptcy must be taken in the manner prescribed by Rule 5 and Rule 6 respectively. . . .

   (c) Content of the Notice of Appeal. A notice of appeal must specify the party or parties taking the appeal by naming each appellant in either the caption or the body of the notice of appeal. An attorney representing more than one party may fulfill this requirement by describing those parties with such terms as "all plaintiffs," "the defendants," "the plaintiffs A, B, et al.," or "all defendants except X." A notice of appeal filed pro se is filed on behalf of the party signing the notice and the signer's spouse and minor children, if they are parties, unless the notice of appeal clearly indicates a contrary intent. In a class action, whether or not the class has been certified, it is sufficient for the notice to name one person qualified to bring the appeal as representative of the class. A notice of appeal also must designate the judgment, order, or part thereof appealed from, and must name the court to which the appeal is taken. An appeal will not be dismissed for informality of form or title of the notice of appeal, or for failure to name a party whose intent to appeal is otherwise clear from the notice. Form 1 in the Appendix of Forms is a suggested form for a notice of appeal.

   (d) Serving the Notice of Appeal. The clerk of the district court shall serve notice of the filing of a notice of appeal by mailing a copy to each party's counsel of record (apart from the appellant's), or, if a party is not represented by counsel, to the party's last known address. The clerk of the district court shall forthwith send a copy of the notice and of the docket entries to the clerk of the court of appeals named in the notice. The clerk of the district court shall likewise send a copy of any later docket entry in the case to the clerk of the court of appeals. When a defendant appeals in a criminal case, the clerk of the district court shall also serve a copy of the notice of appeal upon the defendant, either by personal service or by mail addressed to the defendant. The clerk shall note on each copy served the date when the notice of appeal was filed and, if the notice of appeal was filed in the manner provided in Rule 4(c) by an inmate confined in an institution, the date when the clerk received the notice of appeal. The clerk's failure to serve notice does not affect the validity of the appeal. Service is sufficient notwithstanding the death of a party or the party's counsel. The clerk shall note in the docket the names of the parties to whom the clerk mails copies, with the date of mailing.

   (e) Payment of Fees. Upon the filing of any separate or joint notice of appeal from the district court, the appellant shall pay to the clerk of the district court such fees as are established by statute, and also the docket fee prescribed by the Judicial Conference of the United States, the latter to be received by the clerk of the district court on behalf of the court of appeals.

The losing party in the trial court may file an appeal by filing a document called a notice of appeal. This notice must contain the name of the party or parties making the appeal and state the judgment or part of the judgment the party is appealing from. Note that the defendant usually would appeal the entire judgment. The appeal must also contain the name of the court to which the appeal is taken. Federal Rule of Appellate Procedure 4 covers appeal as a right and when appeals can be taken. It states:

> (a) Appeal in a Civil Case.
>
>   (1) Except as provided in paragraph (a)(4) of this Rule, in a civil case in which an appeal is permitted by law as of right from a district court to a court of appeals the notice of appeal required by Rule 3 must be filed with the clerk of the district court within 30 days after the date of entry of the judgment or order appealed from; but if the United States or an officer or agency thereof is a party, the notice of appeal may be filed by any party within 60 days after such entry. If a notice of appeal is mistakenly filed in the court of appeals, the clerk of the court of appeals shall note thereon the date when the clerk received the notice and send it to the clerk of the district court and the notice will be treated as filed in the district court on the date so noted.
>
>   (2) A notice of appeal filed after the court announces a decision or order but before the entry of the judgment or order is treated as filed on the date of and after the entry.
>
>   (3) If one party timely files a notice of appeal, any other party may file a notice of appeal within 14 days after the date when the first notice was filed, or within the time otherwise prescribed by this Rule 4(a), whichever period last expires.
>
>   (4) If any party files a timely motion of a type specified immediately below, the time for appeal for all parties runs from the entry of the order disposing of the last such motion outstanding.
>
>   This provision applies to a timely motion under the Federal Rules of Civil Procedure:
>
>   (A) for judgment under Rule 50(b);
>
>   (B) to amend or make additional findings of fact under Rule 52(b), whether or not granting the motion would alter the judgment;
>
>   (C) to alter or amend the judgment under Rule 59;
>
>   (D) for attorney's fees under Rule 54 if a district court under Rule 58 extends the time for appeal;
>
>   (E) for a new trial under Rule 59; or
>
>   (F) for relief under Rule 60 if the motion is filed no later than 10 days after the entry of judgment.
>
>   A notice of appeal filed after announcement or entry of the judgment but before disposition of any of the above motions is ineffective to appeal from the judgment or order, or part thereof, specified in the notice of appeal, until the entry of the order disposing of the last such motion outstanding. Appellate review of an order disposing of any of the above motions requires the party, in compliance with Appellate Rule 3(c), to amend a previously filed notice of appeal. A party intending to challenge an alteration or amendment of the judgment shall file a notice, or amended notice, of appeal within the time prescribed by this Rule 4 measured from the entry of the order disposing of the last such motion outstanding. No additional fees will be required for filing an amended notice.
>
>   (5) The district court, upon a showing of excusable neglect or good cause, may extend the time for filing a notice of appeal upon motion filed not later

than 30 days after the expiration of the time prescribed by this Rule 4(a). Any such motion which is filed before expiration of the prescribed time may be ex parte unless the court otherwise requires. Notice of any such motion which is filed after expiration of the prescribed time shall be given to the other parties in accordance with local rules. No such extension shall exceed 30 days past such prescribed time or 10 days from the date of entry of the order granting the motion, whichever occurs later.

(6) The district court, if it finds (a) that a party entitled to notice of the entry of a judgment or order did not receive such notice from the clerk or any party within 21 days of its entry and (b) that no party would be prejudiced, may, upon motion filed within 180 days of entry of the judgment or order or within 7 days of receipt of such notice, whichever is earlier, reopen the time for appeal for a period of 14 days from the date of entry of the order reopening the time for appeal.

(7) A judgment or order is entered within the meaning of this Rule 4(a) when it is entered in compliance with Rules 58 and 79(a) of the Federal Rules of Civil Procedure.

In federal court it is permissible to identify the parties in the notice of appeal by their status in the trial court, that is, plaintiff and defendant. However, subsequent to the filing of the notice of appeal, the parties will be identified based on who is making the appeal, either the appellant or the appellee.

The notice of appeal is filed with the trial court. The clerk of the court will then mail out a notice of appeal to each party or each party's counsel of record. The fee for filing a notice of appeal varies from state to state and between districts. Be sure to check with the court to determine the amount of filing fee before filing the notice of appeal.

The notice of appeal must be filed within 30 days after entering of the judgment. In cases where the United States or one of its officers or agencies is a party, the appeal may be filed within 60 days after entry of the judgment. Accordingly, you must keep very careful track of the dates so that an appeal may be timely taken. It can be very helpful to draft an appellate checklist. Such a checklist might include the following information:

- Date judgment entered
- Deadline for filing appeal
- Appeal filed
- Deadline for filing cross-appeal
- Cross-appeal filed
- Opening brief due
- Responsive brief due
- Reply brief due

Remember, an appellate court is limited to reviewing the record of the court below. Therefore, there are no witnesses called and no new evidence presented. The parties must submit to the appellate court the transcript of the trial court proceedings and any documents and exhibits that were filed in the trial court. The transcript, original documents, exhibits, and a copy of the docket sheet that lists all the documents that were filed in the trial court are collectively referred to as the record on appeal.

Under Rule 10 of the Federal Rules of Appellate Procedure, the appellant has ten days from the filing of the notice of appeal to order the written transcript of the trial court proceedings from the court reporter. Rule 10 also governs situations when there is no transcript. If there is no transcript of the proceedings available, the appellant may provide a statement of the evidence and proceedings from the best available means. This includes the attorney's notes and the attorney's own recollection. The appellee will have ten days in which to serve objections or amendments to the statement filed by the appellant.

Rule 28 of the Federal Rules of Appellate Procedure governs the content and format of the written briefs. The appellant's brief must contain the following items:

- Table of contents
- Table of authorities
- Statement of the issues
- Statement of the case
- Statement of the facts
- Summary of the argument
- Short conclusion
- Certificate of compliance (if required)

Let's take a closer look at Rule 28, Federal Rules of Appellate Procedure to see how specific the rules are:

(a) Appellant's Brief. The appellant's brief must contain, under appropriate headings and in the order indicated:

(1) a corporate disclosure statement is required by Rule 26.1;

(2) a table of contents, with page references;

(3) a table of authorities—cases (alphabetically arranged), statutes, and other authorities—with references to the pages of the brief where they are cited;

(4) a jurisdictional statement, including:

(A) the basis for the district court's or agency's subject-matter jurisdiction, with citations to applicable statutory provisions and stating relevant facts establishing jurisdiction;

(B) the basis for the court of appeals' jurisdiction, with citations to applicable statutory provisions and stating relevant facts establishing jurisdiction;

(C) the filing dates establishing the timeliness of the appeal or petition for review; and

(D) an assertion that the appeal is from a final order or judgment that disposes of all parties' claims, or information establishing the court of appeals' jurisdiction on some other basis;

(5) a statement of the issues presented for review;

(6) a statement of the case briefly indicating the nature of the case, the course of proceedings, and the disposition below;

(7) a statement of facts relevant to the issues submitted for review with appropriate references to the record;

(8) a summary of the argument, which must contain a succinct, clear, and accurate statement of the arguments made in the body of the brief, and which must not merely repeat the argument hearings;

(9) the argument, which must contain:

(A) appellant's contentions and the reasons for them, with citations to the authorities and parts of the record on which the appellant relies; and

(B) for such issue, a concise statement of the applicable standard of review (which may appear in the discussion of the issue or under a separate heading placed before the discussion of the issued);

(10) a short conclusion stating the precise relief sought; and

(11) the certificate of compliance, if required by Rule 32(a)(7).

After the appellant files and serves a written brief, the appellee has 30 days to serve and file a response to the appellant's brief. The appellee's brief should contain the following:

- Jurisdictional statement
- Statement of the issues
- Statement of the case
- Statement of the facts
- Statement of the standard of review

Rule 32 provides specific rules on the type size that may be used in briefs and the covers that must appear on each brief submitted. It also covers reproduction of the brief, number of copies, the cover and binding of the brief, paper size, line spacing and margins, length, and form of an Appendix. In federal court the cover of the appellant's brief must be blue, and the cover of the appellee's brief must be red. In state court the color of the briefs may be different. Therefore, you should always check the state rules before filing an appellate brief in state court.

Federal Rule of Civil Procedure 26 covers filing, proof of filing, service, and proof of service. It requires a thorough review.

(a) Filing.

(1) Filing with the Clerk. A paper required or permitted to be filed in a court of appeals shall be filed with the clerk.

(2) Filing: Method and Timeliness.

(A) In General. Filing may be accomplished by mail addressed to the clerk, but filing is not timely unless the clerk receives the papers within the time fixed for filing.

(B) A Brief or Appendix. A brief or appendix is timely filed, however, if on or before the last day for filing, it is:

(i) mailed to the clerk by First-Class Mail, or other class of mail that is at least as expeditious, postage prepaid; or

(ii) dispatched to the clerk for delivery within 3 calendar days by a third-party commercial carrier.

(D) Electronic Filing. A court of appeals may by local rule permit papers to be filed, signed, or verified by electronic means that are consistent with technical standards, if any, that the Judicial Conference of the United States establishes. A paper filed by electronic means in compliance with a local rule constitutes a written paper for the purpose of applying these rules.

(3) Filing a Motion with a Judge. If a motion requests relief that may be granted by a single judge, the judge may permit the motion to be filed with the judge; the judge shall note the filing date on the motion and give it to the clerk.

(b) Service of All Papers Required. Copies of all papers filed by any party and not required by these rules to be served by the clerk shall, at or before the time of filing, be served by a party or person acting for that party on all other parties to the appeal or review. Service on a party represented by counsel shall be made on counsel.

(c) Manner of Service. Service may be personal, by mail, or by third-party commercial carrier for delivery within 3 calendar days. When reasonable considering such factors as the immediacy of the relief sought, distance, and cost, service on a party shall be by a manner at least as expeditious as the manner used to file the paper with the court. Personal service includes delivery of the copy to a responsible person at the office of counsel. Service by mail or by commercial carrier is complete on mailing or delivery to the carrier.

(d) Proof of Service; Filing. A paper presented for filing shall contain an acknowledgment of service by the person served or proof of service in the form of a statement of the date and manner of service, of the name of the person served, and of the addresses to which the papers were mailed or at which they were delivered, certified by the person who made service. Proof of service may appear on or be affixed to the papers filed. When a brief or appendix is filed by mailing or dispatch in accordance with Rule 25(a)(2)(B), the proof of service shall also state the date and manner by which the document was mailed or dispatched to the clerk.

(e) Number of Copies. Whenever these rules require the filing or furnishing of a number of copies, a court may require a different number by local rule or by order in a particular case.

3. Role of the Paralegal

If your firm is defending against the appeal, your analysis of the trial transcript will focus on locating trial excerpts that show that there were no errors or, at a minimum, the error claimed by the opposing side did not affect the trial outcome. If your firm is appealing the judgment, you can assist in analyzing the trial transcript to locate any prejudicial errors. The prejudicial errors that may justify grounds for appeal include objections that were improperly ruled on by the judge, evidence that was improperly denied or admitted, or jury instructions improperly given or denied. The paralegal can also assist with writing and research as well as identifying pertinent excerpts from the record.

According to Federal Rule of Appellate Procedure 10, the record on appeal consists of the original papers and exhibits filed in the district court, the transcript of proceedings, if any, and a certified copy of the docket entries prepared by the clerk of the district court. It is the duly of the appellant to order the transcript of proceedings within ten days after filing the notice of appeal or entry of an order disposing of the last timely motion outstanding of a type specified in Rule 4(a)(4), whichever is later. The appellant shall order from the reporter a transcript of such parts of the proceedings not already on file as the appellant deems necessary, subject to local rules of the courts of appeals. The order shall be in writing and within the same period a copy shall be filed with the clerk of the district court. Furthermore, unless the entire transcript is to be included, the appellant shall, within the ten-day time provided, file a statement of the issues the appellant intends to present on the appeal, and shall serve on the appellee a copy of the order or certificate and of the statement. An appellee who believes that a transcript of other parts of the proceedings is necessary shall, within ten days after the service of the order or certificate and the statement of the appellant, file and serve on the appellant a designation of additional parts to be included. Rule 10(4) states that at the time of ordering, a party must make satisfactory arrangements with the reporter for payment of the cost of the transcript.

ETHICS

Is it ethical for a paralegal who has worked on a particular case and gone through the entire litigation process to discuss the proceedings with other paralegals? Things that are of public record certainly may be discussed with others. However, the paralegal should take care to not discuss posttrial strategy or the basis for appeal.

There are a number of other ethical considerations posttrial such as preserving the evidence and filing timely appeals, motions, or other necessary paperwork.

CONCLUSION

Appellate procedure consists of the rules and practices by which appellate courts review trial court judgments. Appellate review performs several functions, including the correction of errors committed by the trial court, development of the law, a uniform approach across courts, and the pursuit of justice, more generally. Appellate procedure focuses on several main themes: what judgments are appealable, how appeals are brought before the court, what will be required for a reversal of the lower court (for example, a showing of abuse of discretion, clear error, and so on), and what procedures parties must follow. Appealable issues are commonly limited to final judgments. See, for example, the federal "final judgment rule" at 28 U.S.C. §1291. There are, however, exceptions to the "final judgment rule." They include instances of plain or fundamental error by the trial court, questions of subject-matter jurisdiction of the trial court, or constitutional questions. See, for example, the federal statute on appealable interlocutory (nonfinal) decisions at 28 U.S.C. §1292.

Argument in appellate court centers around written briefs prepared by the parties. These state the questions on appeal and enumerate the legal authorities and arguments in support of each party's position. Only a few jurisdictions allow for oral argument as a matter of course. Where allowed, oral argument is intended to clarify legal issues presented in the briefs. Ordinarily, oral arguments are subjected to a time limit extended only on the discretion of the court. Federal appellate courts are governed by the Federal Rules of Appellate Procedure. State appellate courts are governed by their own state rules of appellate procedure.

Paralegals should develop data files in motion practice, since it is such a regular and consistent part of their professional lives. Numerous software companies offer comprehensive packages in the area of litigation and posttrial motions. However, the best way to maintain a motion data file is to keep examples of previous motions filed and update the file every time the firm files a new motion. That way the current research and forms are there and easily accessible. However, a word of caution when using such a data file. The paralegal should always be sure the cases cited and the research provided are current and up-to-date.

Paralegals can be very valuable in assisting the attorney to enforce judgments. The paralegal should be familiar with the state statutes and local rules governing enforcement of judgments. Also, the paralegal should keep careful and accurate records concerning any appropriate deadlines or statutory time periods. If you work in the area of judgment collections, you will find the use of electronic systems to be invaluable. See the technology section that follows.

USING TECHNOLOGY IN THE LAW OFFICE

Oftentimes is it very helpful to prepare timelines for use in keeping track of various deadlines. Timelines provide visual reminders of what needs to be accomplished when. They can be very useful. With the use of such software as **TimeMap** (a software program designed to generate timelines) the paralegal can quickly and easily prepare such a timeline as shown in Figure 14.7.

Evidence and documents can be preserved on **CD-ROM.** If a number of documents are put into evidence, it is very helpful to keep copies of those documents on CD-ROM instead of keeping hardcopies. Documents can be easily scanned and saved to a CD-ROM.

If you work in the area of judgment collections, you will find the use of electronic systems to be invaluable. Spreadsheets and word processing software programs can be

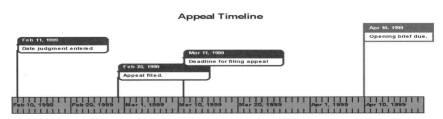

Figure 14.7. TimeMap Timeline

timesavers for the paralegal working in this area. **Spreadsheets** are files consisting of cells that allow for the performance of multiple numerical calculations. Through mail merges you can simply send out hundreds of letters and print envelopes with the touch of a button or two. **Mail merge** is an application that allows for mass mailing of form letters to numerous individuals. The paralegal can also develop form complaints where he or she simply needs to insert the appropriate information specific to the complaint such as names, amounts, and so on.

KEY TERMS

Appeal	Motion for new trial	Writ of certiorari
Appellant	Motion for reconsideration	Writ of execution
Appellee	Motion to amend findings	Writ of garnishment
Brief	and judgment	
En banc	Motion to set aside the	
Motion for directed verdict	judgment	
Motion for judgment N.O.V.	Notice of appeal	
	Oral argument	

Technology Terms

CD-ROM	Spreadsheets
Mail merge	TimeMap

USEFUL WEB SITES

http://www.findlaw.com Links to courts and court decisions
http://www.law.emory.edu/1circuit First Circuit Court of Appeal
   (other circuits available by changing circuit number)
http://www.law.emory.edu/fedcircuit Federal circuit opinions
http://www.ll.georgetown.edu:80/Fed-Ct/cadc.html DC circuit opinions

Appendix:

Paralegal Rules of Ethics

NATIONAL ASSOCIATION OF LEGAL ASSISTANTS (NALA)[1]

Canon 1.

A legal assistant must not perform any of the duties that attorneys only may perform nor take any actions that attorneys may not take.

Canon 2.

A legal assistant may perform any task which is properly delegated and supervised by an attorney, as long as the attorney is ultimately responsible to the client, maintains a direct relationship with the client, and assumes professional responsibility for the work product.

Canon 3.

A legal assistant must not: (a) engage in, encourage, or contribute to any act which could constitute the unauthorized practice of law; and (b) establish attorney-client relationships, set fees, give legal opinions or advice or represent a client before a court or agency unless so authorized by that court or agency; and (c) engage in conduct or take any action which would assist or involve the attorney in a violation of professional ethics or give the appearance of professional impropriety.

Canon 4.

A legal assistant must use discretion and professional judgment commensurate with knowledge and experience but must not render independent legal judgment in place of an attorney. The services of an attorney are essential in the public interest whenever such legal judgment is required.

1. For more information, see the NALA Web site at *http://www.nala.org.*

Canon 5.

A legal assistant must disclose his or her status as a legal assistant at the outset of any professional relationship with a client, attorney, a court or administrative agency or personnel thereof, or a member of the general public. A legal assistant must act prudently in determining the extent to which a client may be assisted without the presence of an attorney.

Canon 6.

A legal assistant must strive to maintain integrity and a high degree of competency through education and training with respect to professional responsibility, local rules and practice, and through continuing education in substantive areas of law to better assist the legal profession in fulfilling its duty to provide legal service.

Canon 7.

A legal assistant must protect the confidences of a client and must not violate any rule or statute now in effect or hereafter enacted controlling the doctrine of privileged communications between a client and an attorney.

Canon 8.

A legal assistant must do all other things incidental, necessary, or expedient for the attainment of the ethics and responsibilities as defined by statute or rule of court.

Canon 9.

A legal assistant's conduct is guided by bar associations' codes of professional responsibility and rules of professional conduct.

NALA MODEL STANDARDS AND GUIDELINES FOR UTILIZATION OF LEGAL ASSISTANTS

Guideline 1

Legal assistants should:

1. Disclose their status as legal assistants at the outset of any professional relationship with a client, other attorneys, a court or administrative agency or personnel thereof, or members of the general public;

2. Preserve the confidences and secrets of all clients; and
3. Understand the attorney's Code of Professional Responsibility and these guidelines in order to avoid any action which would involve the attorney in a violation of that Code, or give the appearance of professional impropriety.

Guideline 2

Legal assistants should not:

1. Establish attorney-client relationships; set legal fees, give legal opinions or advice; or represent a client before a court; nor
2. Engage in, encourage, or contribute to any act which could constitute the unauthorized practice of law.

Guideline 3

Legal assistants may perform services for an attorney in the representation of a client, provided:

1. The services performed by the legal assistant do not require the exercise of independent professional legal judgment;
2. The attorney maintains a direct relationship with the client and maintains control of all client matters;
3. The attorney supervises the legal assistant;
4. The attorney remains professionally responsible for all work on behalf of the client, including any actions taken or not taken by the legal assistant in connection therewith; and
5. The services performed supplement, merge with and become the attorney's work product.

Guideline 4

In the supervision of a legal assistant, consideration should be given to:

1. Designating work assignments that correspond to the legal assistant's abilities, knowledge, training and experience.
2. Education and training the legal assistant with respect to professional responsibility, local rules and practices, and firm policies;
3. Monitoring the work and professional conduct of the legal assistant to ensure that the work is substantively correct and timely performed;
4. Providing continuing education for the legal assistant in substantive matters through courses, institutes, workshops, seminars and in-house training, and

5. Encouraging and supporting membership and active participation in professional organizations.

Guideline 5

Except as otherwise provided by statute, court rule or decision, administrative rule or regulation, or the attorney's Code of Professional Responsibility; and within the preceding parameters and proscriptions, a legal assistant may perform any function delegated by an attorney, including but not limited to the following:

1. Conduct client interviews and maintain general contact with the client after the establishment of the attorney-client relationship, so long as the client is aware of the status and function of the legal assistant, and the client contact is under the supervision of the attorney.
2. Locate and interview witnesses, so long as the witnesses are aware of the status and function of the legal assistant.
3. Conduct investigations and statistical and documentary research for review by the attorney.
4. Conduct legal research for review by the attorney.
5. Draft legal documents for review by the attorney.
6. Draft correspondence and pleadings for review by and signature of the attorney.
7. Summarize depositions, interrogatories, and testimony for review by the attorney.
8. Attend executions of wills, real estate closings, depositions, court or administrative hearings and trials with the attorney.
9. Author and sign letters provided the legal assistant's status is clearly indicated and the correspondence does not contain independent legal opinions or legal advice.

NATIONAL FEDERATION OF PARALEGAL ASSOCIATIONS (NFPA) MODEL CODE OF ETHICS AND PROFESSIONAL RESPONSIBILITY[2]

PREAMBLE

The National Federation of Paralegal Associations, Inc. ("NFPA") is a professional organization comprised of paralegal associations and individual paralegals throughout the United States and Canada. Members of NFPA have varying backgrounds, experiences, education and job responsibilities that reflect the diversity of the paralegal profession. NFPA promotes the growth, development and recognition of the paralegal profession as an integral partner in the delivery of legal services.

2. For more information see the NFLA Web site at *http://www.paralegals.org.*

In May 1993 NFPA adopted its Model Code of Ethics and Professional Responsibility ("Model Code") to delineate the principles for ethics and conduct to which every paralegal should aspire.

Many paralegal associations throughout the United States have endorsed the concept and content of NFPA's Model Code through the adoption of their own ethical codes. In doing so, paralegals have confirmed the profession's commitment to increase the quality and efficiency of legal services, as well as recognized its responsibilities to the public, the legal community, and colleagues.

Paralegals have recognized, and will continue to recognize, that the profession must continue to evolve to enhance their roles in the delivery of legal services. With increased levels of responsibility comes the need to define and enforce mandatory rules of professional conduct. Enforcement of codes of paralegal conduct is a logical and necessary step to enhance and ensure the confidence of the legal community and the public in the integrity and professional responsibility of paralegals.

In April 1997 NFPA adopted the Model Disciplinary Rules ("Model Rules") to make possible the enforcement of the Canons and Ethical Considerations contained in the NFPA Model Code. A concurrent determination was made that the Model Code of Ethics and Professional Responsibility, formerly aspirational in nature, should be recognized as setting forth the enforceable obligations of all paralegals.

The Model Code and Model Rules offer a framework for professional discipline, either voluntarily or through formal regulatory programs.

§1. NFPA MODEL DISCIPLINARY RULES AND ETHICAL CONSIDERATIONS

1.1 A PARALEGAL SHALL ACHIEVE AND MAINTAIN A HIGH LEVEL OF COMPETENCE.

Ethical Considerations

EC-1.1(a) A paralegal shall achieve competency through education, training, and work experience.

EC-1.1(b) A paralegal shall aspire to participate in continuing education in order to keep informed of current legal, technical and general developments.

EC-1.1(c) A paralegal shall perform all assignments promptly and efficiently.

1.2 A PARALEGAL SHALL MAINTAIN A HIGH LEVEL OF PERSONAL AND PROFESSIONAL INTEGRITY.

Ethical Considerations

EC-1.2(a) A paralegal shall not engage in any ex parte communications involving the courts or any other adjudicatory body in an attempt to exert undue influence or to obtain advantage or the benefit of only one party.

EC-1.2(b) A paralegal shall not communicate, or cause another to communicate, with a party the paralegal knows to be represented by a lawyer in a pending matter without the prior consent of the lawyer representing such other party.

EC-1.2(c) A paralegal shall ensure that all timekeeping and billing records prepared by the paralegal are thorough, accurate, honest, and complete.

EC-1.2(d) A paralegal shall not knowingly engage in fraudulent billing practices. Such practices may include, but are not limited to: inflation of hours billed to a client or employer; misrepresentation of the nature of tasks performed; and/or submission of fraudulent expense and disbursement documentation.

EC-1.2(e) A paralegal shall be scrupulous, thorough and honest in the identification and maintenance of all funds, securities, and other assets of a client and shall provide accurate accounting as appropriate.

EC-1.2(f) A paralegal shall advise the proper authority of nonconfidential knowledge of any dishonest or fraudulent acts by any person pertaining to the handling of the funds, securities or other assets of a client. The authority to whom the report is made shall depend on the nature and circumstances of the possible misconduct, (e.g., ethics committees of law firms, corporations and/or paralegal associations, local or state bar associations, local prosecutors, administrative agencies, etc.). Failure to report such knowledge is in itself misconduct and shall be treated as such under these rules.

1.3 A PARALEGAL SHALL MAINTAIN A HIGH STANDARD OF PROFESSIONAL CONDUCT.

Ethical Considerations

EC-1.3(a) A paralegal shall refrain from engaging in any conduct that offends the dignity and decorum of proceedings before a court or other adjudicatory body and shall be respectful of all rules and procedures.

EC-1.3(b) A paralegal shall avoid impropriety and the appearance of impropriety and shall not engage in any conduct that would adversely affect his/her fitness to practice. Such conduct may include, but is not limited to: violence, dishonesty, interference with the administration of justice, and/or abuse of a professional position or public office.

EC-1.3(c) Should a paralegal's fitness to practice be compromised by physical or mental illness, causing that paralegal to commit an act that is in direct violation of the Model Code/Model Rules and/or the rules and/or laws governing the jurisdiction in which the paralegal practices, that paralegal may be protected from sanction upon review of the nature and circumstances of that illness.

EC-1.3(d) A paralegal shall advise the proper authority of nonconfidential knowledge of any action of another legal professional that clearly demonstrates fraud, deceit, dishonesty, or misrepresentation. The authority to whom the report is made shall depend on the nature and circumstances of the possible misconduct, (e.g., ethics committees of law firms, corporations and/or paralegal associations, local or state bar associations, local prosecutors, administrative agencies, etc.). Failure to report such knowledge is in itself misconduct and shall be treated as such under these rules.

EC-1.3(e)   A paralegal shall not knowingly assist any individual with the commission of an act that is in direct violation of the Model Code/Model Rules and/or the rules and/or laws governing the jurisdiction in which the paralegal practices.

EC-1.3(f)   If a paralegal possesses knowledge of future criminal activity, that knowledge must be reported to the appropriate authority immediately.

1.4 A PARALEGAL SHALL SERVE THE PUBLIC INTEREST BY CONTRIBUTING TO THE IMPROVEMENT OF THE LEGAL SYSTEM AND DELIVERY OF QUALITY LEGAL SERVICES, INCLUDING PRO BONO PUBLICO SERVICES.

Ethical Considerations

EC-1.4(a)   A paralegal shall be sensitive to the legal needs of the public and shall promote the development and implementation of programs that address those needs.

EC-1.4(b)   A paralegal shall support efforts to improve the legal system and access thereto and shall assist in making changes.

EC-1.4(c)   A paralegal shall support and participate in the delivery of Pro Bono Publico services directed toward implementing and improving access to justice, the law, the legal system or the paralegal and legal professions.

EC-1.4(d)   A paralegal should aspire annually to contribute twenty-four (24) hours of Pro Bono Publico services under the supervision of an attorney or as authorized by administrative, statutory or court authority to:

  1. persons of limited means; or
  2. charitable, religious, civic, community, governmental and educational organizations in matters that are designed primarily to address the legal needs of persons with limited means; or
  3. individuals, groups or organizations seeking to secure or protect civil rights, civil liberties or public rights.

1.5 A PARALEGAL SHALL PRESERVE ALL CONFIDENTIAL INFORMATION PROVIDED BY THE CLIENT OR ACQUIRED FROM OTHER SOURCES BEFORE, DURING, AND AFTER THE COURSE OF THE PROFESSIONAL RELATIONSHIP.

Ethical Considerations

EC-1.5(a)   A paralegal shall be aware of and abide by all legal authority governing confidential information in the jurisdiction in which the paralegal practices.

EC-1.5(b)   A paralegal shall not use confidential information to the disadvantage of the client.

EC-1.5(c) A paralegal shall not use confidential information to the advantage of the paralegal or of a third person.

EC-1.5(d) A paralegal may reveal confidential information only after full disclosure and with the client's written consent; or, when required by law or court order; or, when necessary to prevent the client from committing an act that could result in death or serious bodily harm.

EC-1.5(e) A paralegal shall keep those individuals responsible for the legal representation of a client fully informed of any confidential information the paralegal may have pertaining to that client.

EC-1.5(f) A paralegal shall not engage in any indiscreet communications concerning clients.

1.6 A PARALEGAL SHALL AVOID CONFLICTS OF INTEREST AND SHALL DISCLOSE ANY POSSIBLE CONFLICT TO THE EMPLOYER OR CLIENT, AS WELL AS TO THE PROSPECTIVE EMPLOYERS OR CLIENTS.

Ethical Considerations

EC-1.6(a) A paralegal shall act within the bounds of the law, solely for the benefit of the client, and shall be free of compromising influences and loyalties. Neither the paralegal's personal or business interest, nor those of other clients or third persons, should compromise the paralegal's professional judgment and loyalty to the client.

EC-1.6(b) A paralegal shall avoid conflicts of interest that may arise from previous assignments, whether for a present or past employer or client.

EC-1.6(c) A paralegal shall avoid conflicts of interest that may arise from family relationships and from personal and business interests.

EC-1.6(d) In order to be able to determine whether an actual or potential conflict of interest exists a paralegal shall create and maintain an effective recordkeeping system that identifies clients, matters, and parties with which the paralegal has worked.

EC-1.6(e) A paralegal shall reveal sufficient nonconfidential information about a client or former client to reasonably ascertain if an actual or potential conflict of interest exists.

EC-1.6(f) A paralegal shall not participate in or conduct work on any matter where a conflict of interest has been identified.

EC-1.6(g) In matters where a conflict of interest has been identified and the client consents to continued representation, a paralegal shall comply fully with the implementation and maintenance of an Ethical Wall.

1.7 A PARALEGAL'S TITLE SHALL BE FULLY DISCLOSED.

Ethical Considerations

EC-1.7(a) A paralegal's title shall clearly indicate the individual's status and shall be disclosed in all business and professional communications to avoid misunderstandings and misconceptions about the paralegal's role and responsibilities.

EC-1.7(b)   A paralegal's title shall be included if the paralegal's name appears on business cards, letterhead, brochures, directories, and advertisements.

EC-1.7(c)   A paralegal shall not use letterhead, business cards or other promotional materials to create a fraudulent impression of his/her status or ability to practice in the jurisdiction in which the paralegal practices.

EC-1.7(d)   A paralegal shall not practice under color of any record, diploma, or certificate that has been illegally or fraudulently obtained or issued or which is misrepresentative in any way.

EC-1.7(e)   A paralegal shall not participate in the creation, issuance, or dissemination of fraudulent records, diplomas, or certificates.

1.8 A PARALEGAL SHALL NOT ENGAGE IN THE UNAUTHORIZED PRACTICE OF LAW.

Ethical Considerations

EC-1.8(a)   A paralegal shall comply with the applicable legal authority governing the unauthorized practice of law in the jurisdiction in which the paralegal practices.

§2. NFPA GUIDELINES FOR THE ENFORCEMENT OF THE MODEL CODE OF ETHICS AND PROFESSIONAL RESPONSIBILITY

2.1 BASIS FOR DISCIPLINE

2.1(a)   Disciplinary investigations and proceedings brought under authority of the Rules shall be conducted in accord with obligations imposed on the paralegal professional by the Model Code of Ethics and Professional Responsibility.

2.2 STRUCTURE OF DISCIPLINARY COMMITTEE

2.2(a)   The Disciplinary Committee ("Committee") shall be made up of nine (9) members including the Chair.

2.2(b)   Each member of the Committee, including any temporary replacement members, shall have demonstrated working knowledge of ethics/professional responsibility-related issues and activities.

2.2(c)   The Committee shall represent a cross-section of practice areas and work experience. The following recommendations are made regarding the members of the Committee.

1. At least one paralegal with one to three years of law-related work experience.

2. At least one paralegal with five to seven years of law related work experience.
3. At least one paralegal with over ten years of law related work experience.
4. One paralegal educator with five to seven years of work experience; preferably in the area of ethics/professional responsibility.
5. One paralegal manager.
6. One lawyer with five to seven years of law-related work experience.
7. One lay member.

2.2(d) The Chair of the Committee shall be appointed within thirty (30) days of its members' induction. The Chair shall have no fewer than ten (10) years of law-related work experience.

2.2(e) The terms of all members of the Committee shall be staggered. Of those members initially appointed, a simple majority plus one shall be appointed to a term of one year, and the remaining members shall be appointed to a term of two years. Thereafter, all members of the Committee shall be appointed to terms of two years.

2.2(f) If for any reason the terms of a majority of the Committee will expire at the same time, members may be appointed to terms of one year to maintain continuity of the Committee.

2.2(g) The Committee shall organize from its members a three-tiered structure to investigate, prosecute and/or adjudicate charges of misconduct. The members shall be rotated among the tiers.

2.3 OPERATION OF COMMITTEE

2.3(a) The Committee shall meet on an as-needed basis to discuss, investigate, and/or adjudicate alleged violations of the Model Code/Model Rules.

2.3(b) A majority of the members of the Committee present at a meeting shall constitute a quorum.

2.3(c) A Recording Secretary shall be designated to maintain complete and accurate minutes of all Committee meetings. All such minutes shall be kept confidential until a decision has been made that the matter will be set for hearing as set forth in Section 6.1 below.

2.3(d) If any member of the Committee has a conflict of interest with the Charging Party, the Responding Party, or the allegations of misconduct, that member shall not take part in any hearing or deliberations concerning those allegations. If the absence of that member creates a lack of a quorum for the Committee, then a temporary replacement for the member shall be appointed.

2.3(e) Either the Charging Party or the Responding Party may request that, for good cause shown, any member of the Committee not participate in a hearing or deliberation. All such requests shall be honored. If the absence of a Committee member under those circumstances creates a lack of a quorum for the Committee, then a temporary replacement for that member shall be appointed.

2.3(f) All discussions and correspondence of the Committee shall be kept confidential until a decision has been made that the matter will be set for hearing as set forth in Section 6.1 below.

2.3(g) All correspondence from the Committee to the Responding Party regarding any charge of misconduct and any decisions made regarding the charge shall be mailed certified mail, return receipt requested, to the Responding Party's last known address and shall be clearly marked with a "Confidential" designation.

2.4 PROCEDURE FOR THE REPORTING OF ALLEGED VIOLATIONS OF THE MODEL CODE/DISCIPLINARY RULES

2.4(a) An individual or entity in possession of nonconfidential knowledge or information concerning possible instances of misconduct shall make a confidential written report to the Committee within thirty (30) days of obtaining same. This report shall include all details of the alleged misconduct.

2.4(b) The Committee so notified shall inform the Responding Party of the allegation(s) of misconduct no later than ten (10) business days after receiving the confidential written report from the Charging Party.

2.4(c) Notification to the Responding Party shall include the identity of the Charging Party, unless, for good cause shown, the Charging Party requests anonymity.

2.4(d) The Responding Party shall reply to the allegations within ten (10) business days of notification.

2.5 PROCEDURE FOR THE INVESTIGATION OF A CHARGE OF MISCONDUCT

2.5(a) Upon receipt of a Charge of Misconduct ("Charge"), or on its own initiative, the Committee shall initiate an investigation.

2.5(b) If, upon initial or preliminary review, the Committee makes a determination that the charges are either without basis in fact or, if proven, would not constitute professional misconduct, the Committee shall dismiss the allegations of misconduct. If such determination of dismissal cannot be made, a formal investigation shall be initiated.

2.5(c) Upon the decision to conduct a formal investigation, the Committee shall:

1. mail to the Charging and Responding Parties within three (3) business days of that decision notice of the commencement of a formal investigation. That notification shall be in writing and shall contain a complete explanation of all Charge(s), as well as the reasons for a formal investigation and shall cite the applicable codes and rules;
2. allow the Responding Party thirty (30) days to prepare and submit a confidential response to the Committee, which response shall address each charge specifically and shall be in writing; and
3. upon receipt of the response to the notification, have thirty (30) days

to investigate the Charge(s). If an extension of time is deemed necessary, that extension shall not exceed ninety (90) days.

2.5(d) Upon conclusion of the investigation, the Committee may:
1. dismiss the Charge upon the finding that it has no basis in fact;
2. dismiss the Charge upon the finding that, if proven, the Charge would not constitute Misconduct;
3. refer the matter for hearing by the Tribunal; or
4. in the case of criminal activity, refer the Charge(s) and all investigation results to the appropriate authority.

2.6 PROCEDURE FOR A MISCONDUCT HEARING BEFORE A TRIBUNAL

2.6(a) Upon the decision by the Committee that a matter should be heard, all parties shall be notified and a hearing date shall be set. The hearing shall take place no more than thirty (30) days from the conclusion of the formal investigation.

2.6(b) The Responding Party shall have the right to counsel. The parties and the Tribunal shall have the right to call any witnesses and introduce any documentation that they believe will lead to the fair and reasonable resolution of the matter.

2.6(c) Upon completion of the hearing, the Tribunal shall deliberate and present a written decision to the parties in accordance with procedures as set forth by the Tribunal.

2.6(d) Notice of the decision of the Tribunal shall be appropriately published.

2.7 SANCTIONS

2.7(a) Upon a finding of the Tribunal that misconduct has occurred, any of the following sanctions, or others as may be deemed appropriate, may be imposed upon the Responding Party, either singularly or in combination:
1. letter of reprimand to the Responding Party; counseling;
2. attendance at an ethics course approved by the Tribunal; probation;
3. suspension of license/authority to practice; revocation of license/authority to practice;
4. imposition of a fine; assessment of costs; or
5. in the instance of criminal activity, referral to the appropriate authority.

2.7(b) Upon the expiration of any period of probation, suspension, or revocation, the Responding Party may make application for reinstatement. With the application for reinstatement, the Responding Party must show proof of having complied with all aspects of the sanctions imposed by the Tribunal.

2.8 APPELLATE PROCEDURES

2.8(a) The parties shall have the right to appeal the decision of the Tribunal in accordance with the procedure as set forth by the Tribunal.

Definitions

"**Appellate Body**" means a body established to adjudicate an appeal to any decision made by a Tribunal or other decision-making body with respect to formally-heard Charges of Misconduct.

"**Charge of Misconduct**" means a written submission by any individual or entity to an ethics committee, paralegal association, bar association, law enforcement agency, judicial body, government agency, or other appropriate body or entity, that sets forth nonconfidential information regarding any instance of alleged misconduct by an individual paralegal or paralegal entity.

"**Charging Party**" means any individual or entity who submits a Charge of Misconduct against an individual paralegal or paralegal entity.

"**Competency**" means the demonstration of: diligence, education, skill, and mental, emotional, and physical fitness reasonably necessary for the performance of paralegal services.

"**Confidential Information**" means information relating to a client, whatever its source, that is not public knowledge nor available to the public. ("Non-Confidential Information" would generally include the name of the client and the identity of the matter for which the paralegal provided services.)

"**Disciplinary Hearing**" means the confidential proceeding conducted by a committee or other designated body or entity concerning any instance of alleged misconduct by an individual paralegal or paralegal entity.

"**Disciplinary Committee**" means any committee that has been established by an entity such as a paralegal association, bar association, judicial body, or government agency to: (a) identify, define and investigate general ethical considerations and concerns with respect to paralegal practice; (b) administer and enforce the Model Code and Model Rules and; (c) discipline any individual paralegal or paralegal entity found to be in violation of same.

"**Disclose**" means communication of information reasonably sufficient to permit identification of the significance of the matter in question.

"**Ethical Wall**" means the screening method implemented in order to protect a client from a conflict of interest. An Ethical Wall generally includes, but is not limited to, the following elements: (1) prohibit the paralegal from having any connection with the matter; (2) ban discussions with or the transfer of documents to or from the paralegal; (3) restrict access to files; and (4) educate all members of the firm, corporation, or entity as to the separation of the paralegal (both organizationally and physically) from the pending matter. For more information regarding the Ethical Wall, see the NFPA publication entitled "The Ethical Wall - Its Application to Paralegals."

"**Ex parte**" means actions or communications conducted at the instance and for the benefit of one party only, and without notice to, or contestation by, any person adversely interested.

"**Investigation**" means the investigation of any charge(s) of misconduct filed against an individual paralegal or paralegal entity by a Committee.

"**Letter of Reprimand**" means a written notice of formal censure or severe reproof administered to an individual paralegal or paralegal entity for unethical or improper conduct.

"Misconduct" means the knowing or unknowing commission of an act that is in direct violation of those Canons and Ethical Considerations of any and all applicable codes and/or rules of conduct.

"Paralegal" is synonymous with "Legal Assistant" and is defined as a person qualified through education, training, or work experience to perform substantive legal work that requires knowledge of legal concepts and is customarily, but not exclusively performed by a lawyer. This person may be retained or employed by a lawyer, law office, governmental agency, or other entity or may be authorized by administrative, statutory, or court authority to perform this work.

"Pro Bono Publico" means providing or assisting to provide quality legal services in order to enhance access to justice for persons of limited means; charitable, religious, civic, community, governmental and educational organizations in matters that are designed primarily to address the legal needs of persons with limited means; or individuals, groups or organizations seeking to secure or protect civil rights, civil liberties or public rights.

"Proper Authority" means the local paralegal association, the local or state bar association, Committee(s) of the local paralegal or bar association(s), local prosecutor, administrative agency, or other tribunal empowered to investigate or act upon an instance of alleged misconduct.

"Responding Party" means an individual paralegal or paralegal entity against whom a Charge of Misconduct has been submitted.

"Revocation" means the recision of the license, certificate or other authority to practice of an individual paralegal or paralegal entity found in violation of those Canons and Ethical Considerations of any and all applicable codes and/or rules of conduct.

"Suspension" means the suspension of the license, certificate or other authority to practice of an individual paralegal or paralegal entity found in violation of those Canons and Ethical Considerations of any and all applicable codes and/or rules of conduct.

"Tribunal" means the body designated to adjudicate allegations of misconduct.

Glossary

Key Terms

Affirmative defense. Response to the plaintiff's claim that disputes plaintiff's legal right to bring the claim.

Alternative dispute resolution. A means of settling disputes outside of the courtroom.

Answer. A pleading that responds to plaintiff's complaint.

Anticipation of litigation. Any notes, papers, memoranda, or writings prepared in anticipation of litigation.

Appeal. A request made after a trial by a party who has lost on one or more issues that a higher court review the trial court's decision to determine if it was correct.

Appellant. Litigant who files an appeal.

Appellee. The party defending against the appeal.

Arbitration. The process of dispute resolution where a neutral third party renders a binding decision after a hearing where both parties presented their case.

Assumption of risk. When a person is not allowed to recover for an injury because he or she voluntarily exposed him- or herself to a known danger.

Attorney-client privilege. Evidentiary privilege provided to a client allowing him or her to refuse to disclose and to prevent any other person from disclosing confidential communications between him or her and the attorney.

Best evidence rule. Rule requiring the original document be submitted to the court for admission.

Breach of duty. Unreasonable conduct.

Brief. Formal argument citing reasons why a trial court decision was or was not in error.

Burden of proof. The duty of proving a fact in dispute regarding an issue between the parties.

Case in chief. Part of trial in which the party with the burden of proof presents his or her evidence.

Case law. Law developed through cases that have been adjudicated.

Case strategy. The formulation of a strategy to execute a case.

Certified copies. Copies of documents that have been deemed to be true and correct copies of the originals on file in the appropriate public office.

Character evidence. Evidence describing a person's character.

Choice of forum. Process of choosing the suitable court for resolution of a legal matter.

Clergy-parishioner privilege. The right of a parishioner to refuse to divulge or have divulged by his or her clergy, the communications between him- or herself and the clergy.

Circumstantial evidence. Evidence that does not provide for personal knowledge.

Class action lawsuits. Actions involving a group of persons, things, or activities.

Client documents. Documentation provided by an individual who has retained an attorney for legal representation.

Closed questions. Inquiries asked in a form requiring only a yes or no response.

Closing arguments. The final statements to the jury or court that summarize the evidence established and the evidence the other side has failed to establish.

Commercial arbitration. The process of dispute resolution involving a dispute between two commercial enterprises.

Common law. Judge-made law.

Comparative negligence doctrine. Measures negligence in percentages and allows for a reduction in damages regarding the amount of damages assessed to the plaintiff.

Compensatory damages. Damages that consist of both special and general damages.

Competent evidence. Evidence said in the court by a competent witness.

Complaint. Pleading that commences an action and sets forth a claim for relief.

Compromise evidence. Evidence pertaining to offers of compromise.

Compulsory counterclaims. Any claims against an opposing party.

Confidentiality agreement. A contract entered between parties that protects private information.

Conflict of interest. A conflict between public and private interests in which a person's duty could lead to the disregard of another person's duty.

Consequential damages. Damages that do not flow directly from the act of the party, but only from the consequences or results of the act.

Consumer arbitration. The process of dispute resolution involving the resolution of disputes between a consumer and a supplier of goods or services.

Contract. A legally enforceable agreement between two or more parties.

Contributory negligence. Conduct by the plaintiff that is below the standard required and contributes to the negligence action that caused the plaintiff's harm.

Counterclaims. Any opposing claims presented by the defendant against plaintiff's claims.

Counts. Individual claims made by plaintiff against the defendant.

Cross-claims. Any coparty claims generated from the transaction or occurrence pertaining to the original action or a counterclaim.

Damages. Compensation that can be recovered in a court by a person who has suffered loss or injury.

Default judgment. Judgment entered against a party who has failed to defend against a claim that has been brought by another party.

Defense. An allegation made by the defendant that provides a reason why the plaintiff should not receive what he or she is claiming.

Demonstrative evidence. Evidence directed to the senses without testimony.

Denial defense. A statement of denial provided as a reason in law or fact why the plaintiff should not recover or establish what he or she seeks.

Depositions. Testimony of a witness taken on written interrogatories or oral questions.

Deposition summary. A digest or synopsis of the testimony provided by a deponent.

Deposition upon written questions. Sworn testimony of a witness in response to questions posed by the court reporter.

Direct evidence. Testimonial evidence from a witness who saw, heard, or touched the subject of questioning; evidence that establishes or proves a fact.

Discovery. The disclosure of something previously unknown or hidden.

Doctrine of avoidable consequences. Doctrine that imposes a duty on the person injured to minimize his or her damages.

Document identifiers. Numerical and/or alphabetical characters generated to identify documentation.

Document management system. An organizational system generated to maintain document integrity and assist in document access.

Documentary evidence. Evidence through documents, notes, writings, instructions, or any other similar type of object.

Domain names. Identifies the server and the file name.

Domestic arbitration. The process of dispute resolution involving the settlements of disputes where the disputing parties all come from the same legal jurisdiction.

Duty. An obligation to use reasonable care to avoid injuring the person or damaging the property of others.

Empathy. Being aware of and sensitive to the feelings, thoughts, and experiences of another without having the feelings, thoughts, and experiences fully expressed.

En banc. The full bench.

Estoppel. A principle barring an individual from denying or alleging a certain fact because of previous conduct, allegation, or denial.

Evidence. Any item or fact that can be used to prove or disprove a case.

Exemplary damages. Damages given as an enhancement of compensatory damages because of wanton reckless, maliciousness, or the oppressive character of acts complained of.

Exhibits. Evidence presented at trial.

Exhibit list. A document attached to the final pretrial memorandum and order that contains all relevant information regarding exhibits.

Ex parte. Contact outside the presence of a representing attorney.

Expert witness. An individual hired by one of the parties to provide an opinion regarding his or her specialized knowledge.

Fact witness. Individuals who describe an event they personally observed.

Final pretrial memorandum and order. Legal pleading drafted by both parties separately for the court setting forth their cases before trial.

Focus groups. A group of individuals used by attorneys to gain feedback on a case.

Freedom of Information Act (FOIA) request. A request for information that falls under the Freedom of Information Act.

Foundation. The identification of evidence sought to be admitted and connecting this evidence with case issues.

Fraud. Intentional misrepresentation of a fact to induce someone to do something.

Friendly witness. An individual with case information who generally is open and willing to help and answer questions.

General damages. Damages that generally result from the kind of wrong that the defendant has committed.

General subject matter jurisdiction. The court's power to hear and determine cases of the proceeding's general category.

Hearsay rule. Rule making most hearsay evidence inadmissible.

Hostile witness. An individual with case information who generally is not open and not willing to help and answer questions.

Husband-wife or martial privilege. The right of a spouse to refuse to divulge or have divulged by his or her spouse confidential communications made by a spouse during a legally valid marriage.

Impeachment. Questioning the integrity and/or credibility of a witness, based on prior inconsistent statements, bias, character, or contradicting facts.

In personam jurisdiction. The court's power to bind the parties to the court's judgment.

In rem jurisdiction. The court's power to adjudicate rights regarding property located within the state in which the court sits.

Independent medical examination (IME). Physical or mental examination by an appropriate provider that can be ordered by the court when controversy exists regarding plaintiff's physical or mental condition.

International arbitration. The process of dispute resolution involving the resolution of disputes between parties of different legal jurisdictions and involving international law issues.

Interrogatories. Written discovery questions prepared and sent to the opposing party before trial.

Interview. A process of questioning someone to obtain facts and information.

Investigation. A process of obtaining and observing facts and other information through questioning, observing, and tracking needed information.

Jurisdiction. The power of the court to hear a particular cause and to render a decision as to the cause before it.

Jury decision. The final decision made by a jury regarding a case.

Jury deliberations. The discussions held by jurors after the trial presentation in order to render a decision.

Jury instructions. Directions given by the judge to the jury pertaining to the laws of the case.

Labor arbitration. The process of dispute resolution involving the resolution of employment-related disputes.

Last clear chance doctrine. A doctrine that allows the plaintiff to recover in a negligence action despite his or her own negligence.

Lead-taking interview. A discussion controlled by the person asking questions of a witness.

Leading questions. Inquiries asked in a format that encourages a specific response.

Litigation. A dispute in a court of law for purposes of enforcing a right or requesting a remedy.

Loss of consortium. The loss of services in a marriage, including such things as guidance, companionship, and sexual relations.

Mandatory disclosure rules. Procedural rules that require parties who have information regarding the lawsuit to turn it over to the opposing party without being asked.

Material evidence. Evidence that tends to make a specific fact either more or less probable.

Mediation. An informal dispute resolution process in which a neutral third party helps the disputing parties to reach an agreement.

Minitrials. Nonbinding trials wherein counsel present a summary of the issues and evidence to the jury.

Misrepresentation. An intentionally false statement that is unjustifiably relied on by another.

Motion. Application made for purpose of obtaining a ruling or order requesting an action be completed in favor of the moving party.

Motion to amend findings and judgment. A request made after trial and entry of judgment asking the court to amend findings and judgment.

Motion for Directed Verdict. A request to the judge for a verdict based upon the fact that the defendant has not presented any credible evidence to rebut any elements of plaintiff's cause of action.

Motion for judgment N.O.V.. A request to have judgment entered in a party's favor notwithstanding the jury's verdict against the party.

Motion for new trial. A request that the judge order a new trial based on the fact that the trial was improper or unfair due to specified prejudicial errors that occurred or because of newly discovered evidence.

Motion for protective order. A request to the court for an order or decree protecting a person from further harassment, abusive service, or discovery.

Motion for reconsideration. A request filed by a party who is not satisfied with the results of a judicial finding.

Motion for summary judgment. A legal document used to dispose of a case when no issues of material fact exist.

Motion in limine. Motion drafted by each trial attorney to exclude evidence at trial.

Motion to compel discovery. A request to the court for an order or decree requiring answer or supplement of discovery.

Motion to set aside the judgment. A request that the judge order judgment set aside based on mistake, fraud, or newly discovered evidence.

Motion to Terminate or Limit Deposition Examination. A request made to the court to limit a deposition testimony or to terminate it.

Multiple party lawsuits. Actions involving multiple plaintiffs or defendants.

Negligence. Not doing something, that a reasonable man, under ordinary circumstances, would do, or doing something that a reasonable man would not do.

Negotiation. The process of submitting and considering offers until an acceptable offer is proposed and agreed to.

Neutral third-party witness. An individual with case information but no interest in the lawsuit who is generally open and willing to help and answer questions.

Nominal damages. Minimal damages awarded to the plaintiff when the defendant has committed a tort but when no actual loss is shown.

Nonbinding arbitration. A process of dispute resolution where a neutral third party renders a nonbinding decision after a hearing where both parties have presented their case.

Notice of appeal. Legal document initiating the appeal process in federal court.

Objections. Adverse reason or argument.

Official witness. An individual with case information usually as a result of his or her official capacity.

Open-ended questions. Inquiries asked in a format that requires more than a yes or no answer.

Opening statements. Outline or summary of the case and of anticipated evidence to be presented by the attorney to the jury.

Oral argument. Structured discussion between the appellate lawyers and the panel of judges focusing on the legal principles in dispute.

Order. Document from the court or judge that is not included in a judgment.

Original jurisdiction. Power of the court to try a case.

Paraphrase. Restatement in fewer words of a statement previously made.

Parol evidence rule. Prohibits admission of evidence to vary the terms of a written agreement.

Pattern jury instructions. Forms that provide the judge with directions to the jury pertaining to the laws of the case.

Permissive counterclaims. An opposing party claim generated outside of the transaction or occurrence that is the subject matter of the opposing party's claim.

Personal jurisdiction. The power a court has to make a party appear before it.

Physician-patient privilege. The right of a patient to refuse to divulge or have divulged by the physician the communications between the patient and his or her physician.

Praecipe. Legal document that provides instructions to the process server regarding the proper service of documents.

Preponderance of the evidence. A standard of proof in civil cases where the evidence demonstrates the facts sought to be proven are more probable than not.

Prima facie case. A case in which each element of the plaintiff's case can be proven.

Private source. A private entity where information is found, taken, or derived.

Privilege. A particular benefit or advantage enjoyed by a person, company, or class.

Privilege log. Document pertaining to information protected from production.

Privileged documents. Documentation withheld from production.

Produced documents. Documentation submitted in response to discovery requests.

Protective order. A decree from the court generated to protect a person from further harassment or abusive service of process or discovery.

Proximate cause. Produces injury without which the result of the act would not have occurred.

Public source. A public entity where information is found, taken, or derived.

Punitive damages. Damages to punish the defendant and deter similar conduct by others.

Real evidence. Evidence meeting certain requirements or reliability.

Releases. Documents that formalize the agreement between the parties to resolve the dispute.

Relevant evidence. Evidence that tends to make the existence of any fact more or less probable than it would be without the evidence.

Requests for Admission of facts. Written discovery asking what facts the opposing party does and does not admit to.

Requests for physical and mental examination of persons. A request that a party who has put his or her mental or physical condition at issue be required to submit to an independent medical examination to determine the extent of the injury or the physical or mental condition of that party.

Requests to produce documents or things. Written discovery used to obtain relevant documentation regarding the case from the opposing party.

Self-executing. The parties implement discovery procedures on their own, with little court intervention.

Service of process. The process that involves leaving documents with the appropriate party.

Settlement. An agreed outcome between disputing parties regarding their dispute.

Settlement brochures. An outline of the case given to opposing counsel and the insurance company in an effort to settle the case.

Settlement conferences. Simple evaluative meetings where a neutral third party reviews the case with the parties, enters into discussion of the issues, and suggests a settlement number or range.

Shepardize. A process whereby case law is checked for validity.

Skip tracing. A process used to locate individuals through third-party contacts.

Special damages. Damages peculiar to that particular plaintiff.

Specialty witness. An individual with case information usually as a result of his or her specialized knowledge.

Statement of claims. Written declaration of the claims made against another party.

Statutes. Written enactments of a legislative body.

Statute of limitations. The time period legislatively allowed for bringing an action against another party.

Stipulation for dismissal with prejudice. Legal document filed with the clerk of court dismissing the case and barring the plaintiff from refiling the claim later.

Strict liability. The failure to use care that a reasonably prudent and careful person would use under similar circumstances.

Structured settlements. A settlement wherein the plaintiff is given structured payments instead of a lump sum.

Subject matter jurisdiction. Power of the court to hear particular matters.

Subpoena. Document commanding an individual's appearance at a certain time and place to give testimony on a certain matter.

Subpoena duces tecum. Document commanding production of certain specific documents.

Summarization. The process of reviewing and condensing information obtained during an interview.

Summons. A pleading used to commence a civil action; a process directed to a person named that an action has been commenced against him or her.

Tangible or physical evidence. Physical evidence that can be touched or seen.

Testimonial evidence. Evidence obtained from a witness.

Theories of recovery. Basis of recovery against the opposing party.

Third-party/other source documents. Documentation provided by an entity not named in the lawsuit.

Third-party claims. Claims that are made against a third party not named in the lawsuit that involve the issues of that lawsuit.

Time management. A strategy formulated to efficiently complete a task.

Trial brief. Legal pleading drafted by both parties separately for the court setting forth their case before trial.

Trial notebook. A binder created for the attorney, containing all relevant trial information in some type of organized fashion.

U.S. district courts. Trial courts of the federal court system.

Venue. The proper place for the trial of the particular action.

Voir dire. "To speak the truth." The preliminary examination made by the court and attorneys of prospective jurors to determine their qualifications and suitability as jurors.

Witnesses. Individuals who testify to what they have seen, heard, or observed.

Witness list. A document attached to the final pretrial memorandum and order that contains all relevant information regarding witnesses.

Work product document privilege. Evidentiary privilege provided by any documentation prepared in the anticipation of litigation.

Work room. A room created to house all of the case documents.

Workers' compensation records. Documents generated by federal, state, or local law enforcement agencies.

Writ of certiorari. Document asking the U.S. Supreme Court to review the case.

Writ of execution. A document that asks the sheriff to take the judgment debtor's property into custody.

Writ of garnishment. A document that attaches an individual's wages.

Wrongful death. Lawsuit brought on behalf of the deceased by his or her survivors alleging that his or her death is attributable to the willful or negligent act of another.

Technology Terms

Active data. Information readily available and accessible to users.

Animation order box. Text box used to determine the sequence of each slide.

Ascending order. Sorting order from earliest event to most recent event.

Backup data. Information copied to removable media to provide users with access to data in the event of a system failure.

Bar codes. Electronic symbols attached to an image file that are searchable.

Bar code labels. Labels that have printed bar codes on them for digital exhibit retrieval.

Bar code wands. Hardware created to read bar codes.

Bitmap. Type of image file.

Case management software. Programs that organize the litigation practice by tracking information central to the case.

Cells. Text boxes within a spreadsheet containing pertinent data or information.

CD burning. The process that involves saving information onto a CD-ROM.

CD-ROM. Device for recording digital information on computer disc.

CD writers. Hardware developed to electronically place information onto a CD-ROM.

Charts. A graphic that illustrates a point using lines, bars, or pies.

Columns. The vertical section of a table.

Computer animations. Computer generated video illustrations of an activity or an event.

Computerized conflicts database. A database created to confirm whether conflicts of interest exist.

Custom animations. Unique setting available in PowerPoint, allowing the user to determine the type of animation.

Databases. A software application that includes fields, forms, queries, and reports.

Database queries. A database application that allows for combined or single field searching.

Database reports. Documents generated from a database sorting and/or search.

Database sorting. A software application available to arrange database fields in chronological, numerical, or alphabetical order.

Document mamagement software. Programs that track documents produced in disparate formats.

Deposition database. A group of fields created to organize and search deposition testimony based on a summary of this testimony.

Deposition summary tables. A group of columns and rows created to organize and search deposition testimony based on a summary of this testimony.

Digital evidence. Evidence presented in digital form.

Digital exhibits. Exhibits that are scanned into electronic image file formats.

Digital video transcript (DVT). A digital transcript placed in digital format.

Dii load file. File created specifically to link Summation database entries with their related image files.

Directory. Collections of links to Web sites compiled by people, not software.

Document database. A group of fields created to organize and search for documents based on document summaries or abstracts.

Domain name. The part of a Web address (URL) that identifies the server and file name.

E-mail. Electronic mail.

Favorites folders. Items created within your Internet browser allowing you to organize your preferred Web sites.

Fields. A primary database component including data pertaining to a specific topic or issue.

Forms. A primary database component that allows for the collection of specific information through the use of fields.

Full Boolean searches. Database searches that allow for multiple information and field searching in a database simultaneously.

Full-text search capability. Searching a database for complete text.

GIF. Type of image file.

Graphics. Electronically animated pictures.

Hyperlink. A software application that allows for the connection of several files through hypertext links.

Image file. Electronic file consisting of a photocopy of the original document scanned.

Images. Files generated from the scanning of documents.

Imaging software. Software that allows you to convert paper documents to electronic images.

Internet. Group of computers that are connected to one another and share a common computer language.

JPEG. Type of image file.

Litigation support software. Programs that emphasize the storage and management of the large quantity of documents produced in litigation.

Macros and lookup tables. A database application developed to shorten a computer application process for the user.

Mail merge. An application that allows for mass mailing of form letters to numerous individuals.

OCR. Optical character recognition.

Personal Digital Assistant (PDA). A handheld, satellite-accessible device used to access e-mail, office calendar or tickling systems, phone numbers, and addresses while away from the office.

PowerPoint. Software program that allows the user to create graphic presentations.

Presentation mode. An option in PowerPoint used when giving slide presentations.

Presentation software. Programs designed to present electronic image files.

Rapid fire digesting. Simultaneous copying of highlighted testimony into a note while it is being created.

Real-time transcript reporting. A method of court reporting that involves receipt of the transcript immediately, as the testimony is being given.

Replicant data. File clones.

Reports. A primary database component generated as a result of a database search and/or sort.

Residual data. Information that appears to be gone, but is still recoverable from the computer system.

Rows. The horizontal section of a table.

Scanner. A machine developed to take electronic photocopies of documents and photographs.

Search engine. Full-text indexes of Web pages compiled by software, not people.

Slides. Documents created in PowerPoint that can be added into a presentation.

Spreadsheets. Software-generated documents consisting of columns and rows that allow for mathematical calculations.

Summation notes. Electronic sticky notes attached to a transcript that allow for searching and issues establishment, as well as attachment of image and audio files.

Surfing. The process that involves searching for information on the Internet.

Synchronizing video deposition. Video transcripts that have been electronically synchronized to track with the written transcript.

Tape backup. A device for recording digital information on tape.

Templates. Preformatted forms generated to assist in the creating of documents.

Text boxes. Graphic boxes that allow for the entry of text.

Thumbnails. Miniature graphics of image files containing descriptive text and bar codes identifying the files.

Tickler system. A system created to manage deadlines.

TIF. Type of image file.

Timeline. A graphic that depicts facts in chronological order.

TimeMap. Software program designed to generate timelines.

Universal Resource Locator (URL). An address for a resource on the Internet.

Videoconferencing. A method for facilitating conferences via satellite or land lines.

Web site. The address location of a Web page.

Word comments. Electronic notes attached to Microsoft Word text indicating the author and the thought.

Word processing tables. Software-generated documents containing text and consisting of tables and rows.

World Wide Web. Network of different documents connected to each other through hypertext embedded in the documents.

Index

Alphabetization is letter-by-letter (e.g., "Courtrooms" precedes "Court systems").